S0-AFP-590

Congratulations

You have just purchased a book that was developed by hospitality industry experts.

Keep this book — you will use it throughout your career.

PRINCIPLES
of
FOOD AND BEVERAGE
OPERATIONS

Educational Institute Books

PRINCIPLES
of
FOOD AND BEVERAGE
OPERATIONS

Jack D. Ninemeier, Ph.D., CHA

the EDUCATIONAL INSTITUTE
OF THE AMERICAN HOTEL & MOTEL ASSOCIATION

Disclaimer

The author, Jack D. Ninemeier, is solely responsible for the contents of this publication. All views expressed herein are solely those of the author and do not necessarily reflect the views of the Educational Institute of the American Hotel & Motel Association (the Institute) or the American Hotel & Motel Association (AH&MA). Nothing contained in this publication shall constitute an endorsement by the Institute or AH&MA of any information, opinion, procedure, or product mentioned, and the Institute and AH&MA disclaim any liability with respect to the use of any such information, procedure, or product, or reliance thereon.

Neither AH&MA nor the Institute make or recommend industry standards. Nothing in this publication shall be construed as a recommendation by the Institute or AH&MA to be adopted by, or binding upon, any member of the hospitality industry.

Accredited by the Accrediting
Commission of the National
Home Study Council

Library of Congress Cataloging in Publication Data

Ninemeier, Jack D.
    Principles of food and beverage operations.
    Includes index.
    1. Food service management. 2. Restaurant management.
3. Bartending. I. American Hotel & Motel Association.
Educational Institute. II. Title.

TX911.3.M27N563   1984   647'.95'068   84-18766

ISBN 0-86612-017-3

Editor: Timothy J. Eaton

Contents

4 Challenges of Food Service Management 63

Part II
Customer Expectations

5 Food Service Marketing 83

6 The Menu Sets the Pace 103

7 Standard Recipes Provide Consistency 131

Part III
Satisfying Customer Expectations

Part IV
Planning Food and Beverage Operations

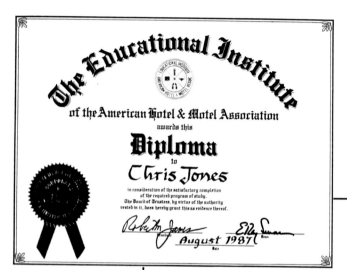

This text, used in conjunction with the corresponding student manual, is one in a series of courses available through the Educational Institute of the American Hotel & Motel Association leading to completion of a certification program. To date, nearly half a million individuals have benefited from Educational Institute programs, distinguishing the Institute as the world's largest educational center for the hospitality industry. For information regarding the available programs, please contact:

> The Educational Institute of AH&MA
> 1407 South Harrison Road
> P.O. Box 1240
> East Lansing, Michigan 48826
> (517) 353-5500

Preface

Principles of Food and Beverage Operations has been written to provide an introduction to the exciting world of food service. However, unlike other introductory texts, this book takes a unique approach to discuss topics of relevance to the food and beverage manager. Simply stated, today's food and beverage operation must have an increasing emphasis on the customer. In recognizing this vital concern, a marketing approach has been taken in the development and writing of this reference. If marketing is the "business from the perspective of the customer," then a focus on the customer must be given the highest priority as all details of the food and beverage operation are planned, implemented, and evaluated.

The best way to describe the objective of this book may be to state, first, what the book will *not* enable the student to do: it is doubtful that anyone will know how to manage a food and beverage operation as a result of reading and studying this book. Indeed, the topic is so complex that most professionals literally spend a lifetime learning and perfecting their management and technical skills.

What, then, is the purpose of the book? There are three primary goals which I had in mind as I wrote this text: (1) to provide a basic introduction for those who are considering careers in the food service industry, (2) to provide some technical information for those who are aspiring to management positions in food and beverage operations, (3) to provide a source of information for food and beverage training programs.

It has been a challenge and a pleasure to research, write, rewrite, and review the subject matter in this text. It can truly be said that this book has been written by the industry for the industry. I wish to acknowledge food and beverage professionals who have brought their many years of knowledge and experience to the task of providing input to the writing of this reference. The review committee members deserve special mention for their efforts: Richard A. Bruner, The University Club, Lansing, Michigan; John D. Correll, Pizzuti's, Canton, Michigan; Michael E. Hurst, 15th Street Fisheries, Fort Lauderdale, Florida; Angie Vlahakis, School of Hotel, Restaurant and Institutional Management, Michigan State University; and Ferdinand Wieland, Hotel du Pont, Wilmington, Delaware.

Additionally, many unnamed professionals with whom I have come in contact during years of study, writing, research, teaching, consulting and reading also deserve a special—but anonymous—mention.

I also wish to thank George R. Conrade, Director of Educational Programs at the Educational Institute of the American Hotel & Motel Association, Marj Harless, Managing Editor/Assistant to Director of Educational Programs, and Karen Newton and Tim Eaton, staff editors at the Educational Institute, for their commitment to excellence (and their quest of keeping the author on the track of meeting deadlines).

Finally, this book is dedicated to E. Ray Swan, Executive Director, Educational Institute of the American Hotel & Motel Association. Ray has been a personal and constant source of inspiration to this writer and has been responsible for bringing the Educational Institute to the forefront of hospitality education in both the United States and, literally, the world. "Hats off" to this fine professional, role model and friend.

Jack D. Ninemeier
East Lansing, Michigan

PART I

Overview of the Food Service Industry

The food service industry is very broad and complex. We will begin our study of the industry by looking at the reason food service exists: to serve the customer. The phrase "managing for the customer" not only serves as the title to Chapter 1, it also sets the scene for the entire book. We will examine the "people" aspect of the food service operation by focusing on the people within the business (owners, managers, and employees) as well as suppliers, the community, and government regulatory agencies which impact upon it. Our study would not be complete without also looking at the relationship between the food and beverage department and other departments within the operation.

Once we have emphasized the need to serve the customer, we will take a close look at the food service industry itself. In spite of its diversity, you will notice similarities in food service organizational structures, operating procedures, goals, and strategies.

Next, we will examine what you need to prepare for a job in the food service industry. You must know how to get along with people and be aware of career development activities which, when properly planned, will affect you for a lifetime.

There are basic challenges of management. We will explore these within the context of activities which you, as a manager, must perform. The customer must never be forgotten as management decisions are made. Each management activity directly relates to one or more segments of the market being served. Part of your job is to constantly look at the operation from the customer's perspective.

1

Managing Food Service for the Customer

Management Challenges

As a result of studying this chapter you will:

1. be aware of the need to develop, both within yourself *and* your employees, a consistent attitude of hospitality which recognizes the overriding importance of the customer to the success of your food service operation.

2. understand the concept of "wants and needs" and know about the importance of assessing what each public desires in its relationship with your food service operation.

When we use the term "food service" throughout this book, we are referring to a segment of the hospitality industry which is involved with feeding people when they are away from home. What do we mean by the hospitality industry? The hospitality industry has three different components: food service, lodging, and travel. Since food service is often a part of lodging accommodations (consider restaurants and other food outlets in many hotels, motels, motor hotels, etc.), and since there are many other food service operations that cater to the traveling public, you can see that food service is an integral part of the entire hospitality industry.

When you think of hospitality, what comes to mind? A dictionary definition may refer to the generous, cordial, and pleasant reception of guests. This concept of hospitality began with travelers who were welcomed into an innkeeper's home with a handshake and an offer to share whatever was available. It extends to the present day in many operations when the guest is welcomed at the front door by the host/hostess and, sometimes, by the owner or manager.

You can see that the special focus on the customer is an essential ingredient in each segment of the hospitality industry and in every component of the food service industry as well.

It should be obvious that the customer is very important to the success of the food service operation in a restaurant or hotel. These are commercial operations which exist primarily to offer and to make a profit from food and beverage sales. However, not all food that is served away from home is provided at hotels and restaurants. There is a wide variety of institutional food service operations which offer food along with other services; for example, the military, schools, colleges, nursing homes, and hospitals.

You now have learned one important point: all segments of the hospitality industry should focus on the customer and each type of food service operation, regardless of where it "fits" into the hospitality industry, must also share this concern.

Since the customer is so crucial to the success of the food service operation, it is important that all employees develop and practice an attitude of hospitality which reflects the customer's importance. This concept may be easy to imagine, but it is frequently difficult to practice. Problems caused by lack of concern for the customer are evident in too many food service operations. Therefore, you must continually look at your operation from the customer's perspective.

The Customer and Other Publics

The public is the sum of all the different people with whom your food service operation must relate. An obvious public is the customer of your food service operation. This person may be referred to as a guest (in a hotel or restaurant operation), as a patient (in a hospital), as a resident (in a nursing home), as a student (in a school or college), or by any other name. No matter what primary public is served by your food service operation, that public must be given careful attention in all phases of the operation.

In addition to the customers, there are other publics about whom your food service operation must be concerned. These include departments in the organization, suppliers, the community, government regulatory agencies, and even the employees of the food service operation itself. Food service is a people business. People are served by the operation, people serve the operation, people make things work, and people contribute to problems which cause the operation to fail.

If you are beginning to think that a food service manager must virtually be a psychologist, you are absolutely correct! The food service manager who is skilled only in managing food and beverage products, facilities, equipment, energy, money, time, and procedures will not be successful. As a food service manager, you must also be knowledgeable about and be able to influence the behavior of a variety of people (customers, employees, etc.).

Role of the Food Service Manager

From a marketing perspective, your role as manager is to build a customer base and manage other aspects of the operation. You cannot attain organizational objectives unless "people" concerns are effectively addressed. With the exception of some institutional food service operations where a guaranteed base of customers exists (a prison or a mess hall on a ship), customers usually are not captive—at least not for long time periods. It is true that hospital patients consume meals while staying in the hospital and residents must eat while staying in nursing homes. However, both the hospital and the nursing home are affected by poor public images about food service and declining patient/resident counts can occur.

In most food service operations, there is a high correlation between customer participation and the success of the operation. That is why your role in building a good customer base and in retaining it by constant attention to the customer's concerns is so very important to the success of the organization.

Managing for Your Customers

You must manage the operation for your customers. Since a manager is a customer builder as well as an administrator, you must focus on both the customer and the "bottom line." If you make decisions which reflect the wants and needs of your customers, fewer problems are likely to occur. Managing for your customers increases the probability that the right decisions will be made. Managing only for profit may lead to trouble.

Perhaps some examples will help you understand how important the customer is in almost any operating decision. Consider the management decision you must make when food costs increase. What should you do? Food costs can be lowered by reducing the portion size or by purchasing a lower quality product. Is this a good idea? How about increasing the selling price to compensate for increased food costs? If you choose any of these alternatives without considering the impact upon your customers, problems can occur. Customers who purchase the product because of its size, quality, or price/value will immediately be dissatisfied. At the very least, sales of this menu item will decrease. The worst that can happen is that customer count and your operation's economic objectives will suffer.

What are better alternatives? How about considering the customers:

- Offer two portion sizes—one at the same price, but a smaller portion—or another at a higher price, but with the same size portion. This plan will give customers a choice and, depending upon their concern about prices, questions about value may not occur.

- Recognize the fact that it is always easy to raise prices and that this can result in problems. You may want to institute an aggressive program of operating control to confirm that all incurred costs are reasonable. Often, an intensive self-analysis will uncover many areas in which costs can be reduced. This approach will benefit the customers as well as your operation.

Let's look at another example. What if your operation hires a server to pass bread and coffee to customers seated at the table? All this server must do is generate sales equal to wage, benefit, and related expenses. If this can be done, the atmosphere and reputation of your operation will be enhanced. You may, however, decide to eliminate this function in order to cut costs. Then suppose that costs do decrease, but so does customer satisfaction. What price should you pay to ensure that your customers are satisfied and that they receive the attention they deserve as being critical to the continued existence of the operation? Only the food service manager who "knows" the customer can answer this question.

The Importance of Hospitality

You know that you must recognize how important your customer is to the success of the operation. You also know that the customer must be considered when operating decisions are made. Now think about the customer in another way: you, as the manager, must set the pace for a friendly experience within the operation. All too often, employees look at customers as "problems." Have you ever heard someone say, "This would be a good place to work—if only we didn't have customers?" Of course, this is silly, but all too often many employees are serious when these views are expressed. They seem bothered by the need to serve the customers. Perhaps this is due, in part, to a feeling of servitude or inferiority when one person must serve another person. If this is the case, effective employee recruitment and selection procedures can eliminate people with these attitudes before they are even hired. You can instill an attitude of hospitality which permeates your operation by the effective use of selection procedures, training, supervision, and personal example.

Let's look at what can happen when an attitude of hospitality does not exist. Have you ever watched a television commercial that shows a smiling attendant at a fast food operation inviting you to visit the property? How about the friendly smile pictured in newspaper and magazine advertisements? The employees in the actual food service operation often do not resemble the friendly, smiling, courteous employees pictured in the advertisements. Is this a disappointment? Of course, even if it is only on a subconscious level. Contrast this example with a property where friendly people seem genuinely happy that you have chosen to spend your money there.

Recognizing the Individual Customer

Is the difference between these employees only a matter of personality? The ability to relate to people *can* be influenced by personality. However, it is very likely that the friendly employee has a manager who is also friendly and who has instilled an attitude of hospitality in the employees because of concern for the customer. You must set the pace so your customer has a friendly experience. Fortunately, procedures to practice hospitality are not difficult or complex. However, if you do not like people, if you cannot show a genuine concern for others, and if you are not able to relate to people, perhaps a management job in the hospitality industry is not in your best interests. As an employee, you must relate to your boss and your peers; as a manager, you must interact with employees and customers. The food service industry is truly a "people business." Your job is not to open the door and wait for the cash register to ring. You must first develop an experience which the customers will like, then train and supervise your employees to provide this experience, and, finally, promote the experience to the customers so it will generate business. The customer's visit to the food service operation, whether it is a commercial or an institutional operation, should be a pleasant experience and a break from daily routine. You and your staff contribute to the customer's experience and help determine whether the food service operation will be successful.

You need to be concerned about the customer as an individual—not as part of a large, faceless mass of people who can be satisfied by mass production, mass communication, mass feeding, or mass service. People want to be recognized as individuals—don't you? Customize your food service operation (both the products and the service components within it) to better recognize the individual wants and needs of the customers. The special touches that some managers use to distinguish their property from others in the customers' minds are important.

Wise managers will identify regular customers by name, will remember the table which they prefer, will offer special items, will prepare other items in certain ways, and will pay special attention to the individual customer. If this sounds difficult—after all, the manager has a million things to do—you are right. The food service manager's job is complex and not everyone can do it!

Who Has Concerns about the Food Service Operation?

We have emphasized the need for you to be aware of and to be concerned about the many publics with which you interact. Let's look more closely at each of these publics. The word "publics" is used to mean a group of people with common interests and common characteristics. Your job, as manager, is easier when you identify the publics and define their common interests. You can then attempt to meet their interests by developing and implementing special management strategies. Figure 1.1 is very important to this book and will be used as a focus of discussion throughout. Let's examine what it is saying and then we will review what it really means.

The organization comprises the food service operation and, perhaps, other departments. In a restaurant, the organization may be synonymous with the food service operation; they are the same. In a hotel, however, there are several departments (only one of which is the food service operation) that constitute the entire hotel organization. Likewise, hospitals, schools, nursing homes, etc., are organizations that have many departments besides the food service operation.

One public—ownership—has an overall concern for the entire organization. In a corporation, ownership might be represented by the stockholders; in a partnership, the owners are two or more people with investment interests; and in the case of a single entrepreneur, the owner is frequently the manager, too.

The manager and the employees within the food service operation are additional publics. You must relate with peers in other departments to help ensure that the goals of the total organization, along with those of the food service operation, are attained.

The internal publics of the food service operation can be defined as follows:

1. ownership

2. management staff

3. employees

4. personnel in other departments of the organization (if applicable)

You may think that the food service operation is the building, the atmosphere, or the food being served. In reality, the food service operation is people. Their role in the success of the operation will be discussed later in the chapter and throughout the book.

The customer is the primary public which will contribute to an organization's long-term success. Other publics include the suppliers to the organization, the community, and government regulatory agencies. This mix of internal and external publics and the effectiveness of the re-

Figure 1.1 The Food Service Publics

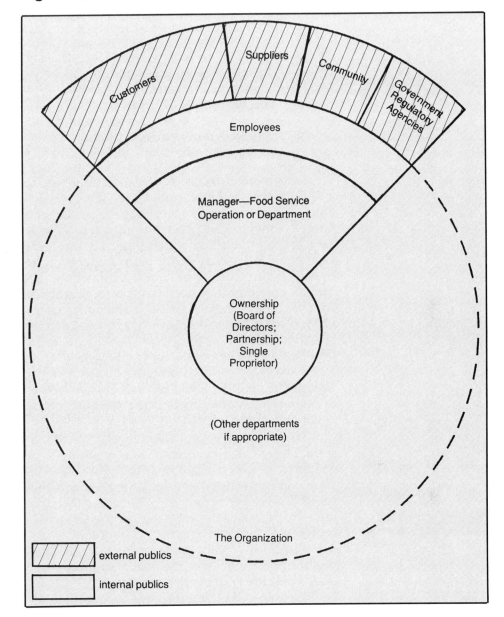

lationships that are established between them will also influence the long-term success of the organization.

Let's take a closer look at these publics to find out what each desires in its relationship with the food service operation.

Customers   Basically, customers are interested in satisfying their wants and needs to the maximum extent possible. They visit the food service operation in order to do this. The wants and needs of customers are influenced by factors such as:

•   the object of the visit (a quick meal or a dining experience)

- the concept of value (price relative to quality)

- absolute price (the price that the customer will not go beyond even if the purchase is deemed to be of value)

- social/economic factors

- demographic concerns such as age, sex, marital status, etc.

- ethnic or religious concerns

Let's expand upon the customer's desire to satisfy basic wants and needs (of which the customer may not even be conscious). What are examples of wants and needs that the customer may desire to have met? Some customers may desire a quick meal. They want to finish as fast as possible in order to do something else which is more important to them. Other customers may be there for a special occasion or they may want to reward themselves by having a terrific dining experience. Still other customers may be interested in impressing someone (a client or a personal friend). Others may be seeking adventure or an escape from the routine of their daily lives. Whatever the reason or incentive, the customer has specific needs or wants which he/she is attempting to meet by visiting the dining establishment. As you will see in Chapter 5, you must attempt to identify why people come to your property and decide what types of customers are most likely to visit your property. Then you should develop marketing strategies to bring the customers to your property and to keep them coming back.

The discussion about wants and needs has focused upon the concerns of the customer who makes a dining decision about a commercial property. However, as noted throughout this chapter, you must expand your concept of food service to encompass the customer in the institutional food service operation. Perhaps this can best be done by determining why the customer is present at the facility. In the case of a school, the individual's primary goal might be to obtain an education; in a hospital, it might be for health care; and in a nursing home, the primary goal might be personal care. The role of food service must be discovered within this parameter of need satisfaction.

What does the institutional customer want and how can it best be provided within the limitations imposed by operating costs, nutrition, and related concerns? The answer to this question will enable you to plan and provide a food service operation which meets the secondary needs of your customers. Menu choices, "around the world trips," ethnic selections, and participation in the menu planning process are examples of techniques which you can use to make a physiological need—the need for food—interesting for the customer. A personal and professional concern to do this is part of the definition of a professional food service manager and is often incentive enough to undertake these actions. The need to eliminate problems such as negative feedback, reduced participation, and related spinoff effects provides important additional reasons why you should consider the customer as institutional food service menus are planned. In order for you to make useful decisions, the customers' wants and needs must be specifically identified and then addressed as operating decisions are made.

Ownership

What are the objectives of the owner of the food service operation? In economic terms, an objective would be to maximize profits in commercial operations or to minimize expenses in institutional food service operations. However, this objective is broad and probably ambiguous. First of all, the owner must satisfy customers in order to protect the economic and time investments that have been made in the operation.

The owner also has personal wants and needs which must be met by the food service operation. These may be merely economic. However, many times, economic rewards are only an intermediate step in purchasing things that are satisfying to the owner. Frequently, they may involve other factors such as ego, the need for accomplishment, or striving to attain personal goals.

The owner is at the focal point of the relationship between the internal and external publics of the food service operation. The manager who is between the owner and the customer must frequently interpret and analyze the customers' needs and wants to help ensure that the operation does, in fact, meet them.

Management Staff

The concerns of the management staff in the food service operation can be summarized as involving efforts to satisfy performance requirements imposed by the owner (in order to retain one's job!) and to also fulfill personal wants and needs. The customer plays a vital role in providing a place of continuing employment for the manager so it is in the manager's—as well as the food service operation's—best interests to do what is necessary to satisfy the customer.

Many times, the owner and the manager are the same person. Then protecting investments, meeting other performance requirements, and fulfilling personal wants and needs are combined. When this occurs, the priority attached to pleasing the customer should become even greater since the risk of losing business is likely to have more dramatic and long-reaching effects.

Employees

What are the concerns of the employees in the relationship between the customer and the food service operation? They are the same as management's concerns: performance standards must be met in order for employees to retain their jobs and, of course, personal wants and needs must also be met.

Many theories of motivation, human relations, and leadership address the need to mesh organizational goals with those of the employees. The customer is critical to the success of the food service operation. If the employee wants the job, either as an end in itself or because of wants and needs which can be met as a result of employment, the goal of pleasing the customer will be important. However, if the relationship between satisfied customers and continued success is not known, emphasis may be placed on something else. As already noted, the staff members who make recruitment and selection decisions can help reduce potential problems by considering the personalities of applicants who will be required to meet and serve the customers.

Other Departments

Staff members in other departments of the organization are also involved with the food service operation even if only indirectly. Therefore, they are involved in the relationship between the customer and the food service operation. Consider, for example, the school or college where food service is de-emphasized. When this occurs, inadequate resources to support food service may cause serious problems. Policies about meal serving times, costs to be allocated to food service, and the objectives which have been established for the food service operation itself will all be influenced by the attitude of other internal organizational staff members toward food service.

Suppliers

Companies that supply products and services to the food service operation are an external public with special concerns about this relationship. As a business operation, suppliers have concerns that their investment and other performance requirements will be met, so you must guard against having an "I win—you lose" attitude in negotiations with suppliers. This approach is, at best, short-sighted. Rather, you should recognize that a relationship stressing fairness and mutual satisfaction must be established with all suppliers.

Suppliers and their employees may be prospective customers of your food service operation. As residents of the community, supplier representatives have an opportunity to discuss good and bad aspects of your operation with various people.

The Community and Government Regulatory Agencies

The community within which the food service operation is located has definite concerns and is involved in an ongoing relationship with the property. In many instances, entire sections of communities may be revitalized or may deteriorate due to the status of hospitality-related operations. Food service operations employ citizens in the community who may be professional members of civic and related groups; these employees can have very creative input in the design of the community's future.

Government regulatory agencies ensure that applicable laws and regulations are followed and collect taxes and other fees as required. These agencies have a vested interest in the success of the food service operation and represent an important public with which the operation must relate.

In summary, each food service public has special concerns, wants, and needs which must be addressed and met in the relationship that is developed with the operation. You should be aware of this and find ways for the publics to satisfy their concerns in relationships with your operation.

What Do You Think?

We have presented a good case for management concern about the many publics—especially the customer—with whom the food service operation must be involved. Management concerns of all types are an important focus of this text. Throughout the rest of the book we will speak to you, the reader, as if you were already a manager. We encourage you to imagine yourself in such a position. In this way, we hope to help you see through management's eyes the issues and materials presented and prepare yourself for a rewarding career in the hospitality business.

2

A Close Look at the Food Service Industry

Management Challenges

As a result of studying this chapter you will:

1. have an appreciation for the history of the food service industry and how it impacts upon the industry today.

2. gain an understanding of the role that management companies have in the food service industry.

3. know about the role of and differences between multi-unit and single-unit food service operations.

4. see how franchising has contributed to rapid growth in the industry and understand both its advantages and disadvantages.

5. know about the many different types of operations that comprise the food service segment of the hospitality industry.

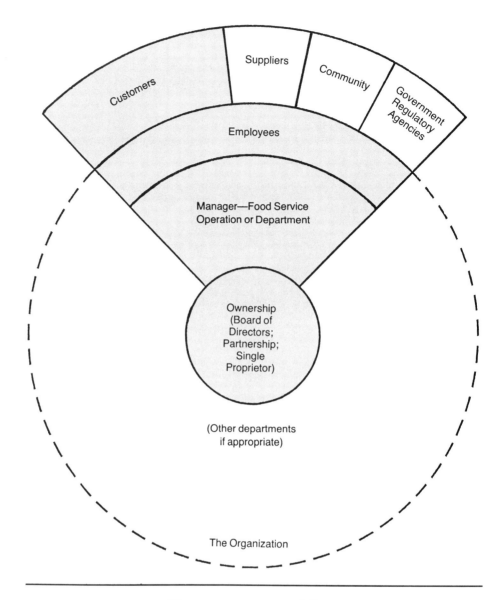

Focus on the
Food Service Publics

Chapter 2 provides background information about and an overview of the food service industry. As such, it focuses attention on the owner, manager, and employees of the food service operation. Their relationships are (or can be) influenced by the type of organizational structure which has evolved over a 5,000-year history of serving people. Activities which have proven successful in the past will be continued; those which cannot withstand the test of time will be discarded.

Employees at all organizational levels of the food service operation will benefit from reviewing the reasons for and sources of our special concerns about the customer. The need to show genuine concern about the customer is present in every type of food service operation—single- or multi-unit, franchised or company owned, self- or management company operated. Therefore, even while we focus our attention on the industry itself, the customer being served should always be the first priority.

What do you think of when you hear the term "food service"? Do you picture a dining room with starched white tablecloths in an expensive restaurant . . . a coffee shop in a hotel with a multi-storied atrium . . . a truck stop on a busy interstate . . . a fast-food outlet in the suburbs . . . a low-priced steak house or other type of "family food" operation . . . feeding workers on an oil rig in the North Atlantic . . . or a concession operation in a professional sports arena? Do you think about dietary services in schools, colleges, hospitals, nursing homes, and related institutions? Or do you think primarily of military operations or exclusive country clubs? With just these few examples, you can see that the food service industry is vast; it encompasses every type of food service operation used to serve people away from their homes.

The purpose of this chapter is to provide an overview of a complex, large industry. We will look at some of the most important elements in the organization and management of food service operations of all types. But remember, whereas we spend a chapter on these topics, entire books can be written about them. Therefore, we are presenting an overview, painted with a broad brush, of a very large industry. If you are thinking about a career in food service, this information may be of great interest as you make a vocational decision that will affect the rest of your life. If you are already working in food service, the information will provide a good background that you will need to plan and develop a career in this fascinating industry.

An overview of the food service industry should start at its beginning. Let's see how the food service industry got to where it is today.

Evolution of Lodging Food Services

Early Inns   Service operations as we know them today in hotels and motels actually evolved from early inns and other rest shelters. In fact, our concept of hospitality is embodied in the innkeeper who welcomed guests with an extended hand—often into his/her own home for a meal and lodging. Travelers in ancient times needed "bed and board." While the inn was a necessity, many properties also provided eating, drinking, and entertainment for their guests along with sleeping accommodations. The innkeeper had to prepare food with the produce that was available.

There was usually plenty of wine and often beer, plus cheeses, various vegetables, and all types of cakes and buns. Meat, if available, included goat, pork, and lamb; sausages and fish were consumed, too. By the time of the Roman Empire (established in 27 B.C.), inns and taverns were commonplace.

The Church

The church, generally the only recognized institution from one country to the next, maintained hospices (a type of inn), monasteries, and other religious houses which were havens for travelers. One religious order, The Knights of Saint John of Jerusalem which was founded in 1048, established many cathedrals and monasteries to protect pilgrims traveling to and from Jerusalem.[1] In effect, the church operated the first hotel chain!

English Inns

In England, there were a few inns (ale houses) that rented rooms as early as 1400. As would be expected, inns were located in large towns, at major crossroads, and at ferry landings. Some inns were actually private homes with one or several bedrooms. Others were large and contained as many as 20 or 30 rooms. English inns were also located along routes that people traveled. Whether it was by foot, horseback, stagecoach, or along water channels, travelers had to rest and eat. Inns provided necessary services for weary travelers. Later, the railroad not only speeded travel, but also eliminated the need for many countryside inns. However, with the advent of automobiles in the early 1900s, there was a resurgence in the need for lodging and food service operations along routes between major cities.

Taverns

The evolution of inns and taverns in the United States was not significantly different from that just described for England. While the food was often simple, it was plentiful; beer and rum were also usually served.[2] A tavern known as Cole's Ordinary was opened in 1634 by Samual Cole. ("Ordinary" is an English term which refers to a mid-day meal or supper consisting of a dish which is the specialty of the host.) It was the first tavern in Boston and probably the first in the American colonies. In the United States, as elsewhere, lodging and food service accommodations followed travel patterns.

In modern times, the hospitality industry has both grown with, and mirrored, the changes in disposable income and the cost and convenience of travel. As improvements in transportation occurred, travel became possible for greater numbers of people, and lodging accommodations located in convenient areas for travelers grew and flourished.

The Development of Restaurants

"Eating Out"

We have already noted that it is difficult, if not impossible, to separate discussions about food service in lodging properties from discussions about separate establishments offering only food and drink. "Eating out" was often mixed with the need to travel; however, taverns, snack bars of all types, bakeries, and cook houses offered opportunities to purchase food at sites not affiliated with lodging operations. For example, Herculaneum, an ancient city at the foot of Mt. Vesuvius in southern Italy, was buried in a volcanic eruption (A.D.79). The ruins show that there were a number of nearly identical snack bars, suggesting that they might have been part of a chain under a single ownership.[3] In England, coffee houses appeared in the mid-1600s and by the early 18th century there were approximately 3,000 coffee houses in London.

Early Restaurants

Restaurants, as we know them today, began in 1765 in Paris, France. There is an interesting story about the proprietor of, perhaps, the first public restaurant. Before 1765, public food services were only offered in inns and catering operations ("traiteurs" prepared and catered meals for parties and private homes). A guild (union) of traiteurs was formed with limited membership. When a soup vendor invented a dish of sheep's feet and white wine sauce, he was brought to court by the guild because of alleged competition. However, the court ruled that this specialty dish did not compete with the guild and the vendor was allowed to continue. The soup vendor merchandised the soups as "restaurants"—restorers of energy. Because of his publicity, the soup kitchen became famous and even the king of France wanted to taste the specialty which created the public commotion.[4]

After the French Revolution (1789-1799) many restaurants were opened in Paris. Chefs were unemployed since they had lost their jobs with the wealthy who had left the country and there was a vast reservoir of talent available to work in the kitchens. There were restaurants—good and bad—which catered to all segments of the market (similar to the restaurant industry today).

First U.S. Restaurant

In the United States, credit for the first restaurant is generally given to Delmonico's which was established in New York City in 1827. The Delmonico family operated nine restaurants until 1923. The restaurants are remembered for lavish banquets and extensive menus (371 separate dishes could be ordered). In general, the name "Delmonico's" stood for exemplary French-American dining. Relatively few cities—or people—could support and frequent restaurants like Delmonico's which offered high cuisine and high prices. Then, as now, the vast majority of American eating places offered more simple, less expensive food items for their customers.

Drive-In Restaurants

By the 1920s, there were enough automobiles in the United States to support a new market for food service: the drive-in restaurant. People could eat in their cars due to curb service and the car hop. In the 1960s, this innovation was replaced with indoor fast-food restaurants and nothing has impacted more on the food service industry. Since then, sandwiches—primarily hamburgers—have ruled the food service industry in many ways. (Hamburgers can be traced back to medieval times, but they were first served on a bun at the St. Louis World's Fair in 1903.) Today there is chicken, fish, and salad bars, but the hamburger is still "king."

Hotel Restaurants: Are They Any Good?

In "the old days" hotel restaurants enjoyed reputations for high quality food and excellent service which were unmatched and deserved. During the past twenty years, however, they have lost their first-place position to free-standing competitors who have done an excellent job of keeping up with the marketplace and its changing desires.

In their search over the years for a larger share of the market, free-standing restaurant operators began to feature fun and excitement in dining packages composed of unique food, beverage, service, and ambience. Meanwhile, chefs still ran hotel kitchens and were not attuned to dining alternatives available to the general public. Hotels still had quality food and service, but they catered to the diner who was seeking convenience—not an experience.

Other factors also affected the hotel restaurants' business: motorists had problems with parking in downtown hotel locations, and hotels did not recruit new talent (young people were lured into the less bureaucratic restaurant business). The major factor was, however, *a failure to respond to the marketplace.*

Finally, in response to the challenge, hotels began to develop and feature creative restaurant concepts that appealed to the guest and to the local market as well. Stereotyped restaurants that were identical throughout a multi-unit chain were replaced with concepts designed for a specific location and the market it served. Today, local food preferences and dining habits are seriously studied as are the local competitors. Facilities designed to appeal to the local market are built into hotels as they are constructed or are remodeled as part of an integral, expensive design program.

Today, although hotel restaurants have not regained their early dominance, the food and beverage operation in many hotels is a renewed host to many customers who want to go to "the best place in town" and who select the lodging property as the winner of their entertainment dollar.

You have learned just some of the fascinating aspects in the history of the food service industry. However, the industry is not standing still today—it is rapidly expanding and changing. Perhaps you can refer to these pages in 10 or 15 years and add your own lines about what has happened to the industry since you entered it.

Objectives of Quantity Food Service Operations

Food service operations obviously exist for a reason. Their objectives should be defined and stated so that everyone understands what is trying to be accomplished.

Generally, the food service industry can be divided into two different segments based upon economic objectives. The first segment, commercial operations, wishes to maximize or at least generate a satisfactory level of profit. The commercial food service operation exists in order to make money (for example, restaurants and hotels). The second segment, institutional operations, has a different economic objective: to minimize expenses from food services while maintaining quality requirements. The institutional operation exists in facilities whose main function is not to generate income or profits (for example, hospitals, nursing homes, the military, and schools). Each of these examples exists for reasons other than to offer food service—hospitals must care for the ill, nursing homes must care for the aged, the military must defend the country, schools must educate, etc. However, in the course of their main function, these facilities must offer food service to patients, military personnel, students, and others.

Economic Objectives

Actually, the task of separating operations into "for-profit" and "not-for-profit" categories is not as simple as it sounds. There are many for-profit management companies which operate food services in institutions. In these cases, while the facility itself does not wish to make a profit from the sale of food items, the company managing their food service program certainly does.

The matter can be complicated even further when a management company owns or operates a hospital or nursing home and then subcontracts dietary services to another for-profit company. Additional information about different segments of the food service industry will be presented later. However, in this discussion about the objectives of food service, it is important to note that the economic motive—profit maximization or cost minimization—is of primary concern to any food service operation.

Besides economic objectives, many food service operations have other goals which can include the following:

The goal of remaining strong in uncertain times. Many food service operations do not want to just maintain the status quo—they want to grow. This is a challenge during times when costs are increasing, employees are becoming more vocal and demanding, and when markets are changing, requiring greater value for money spent on food service.

The goal of maintaining and conveying a proper image to the public. The food and beverage operation in a hotel, for example, must be compatible with the primary function of the property. Likewise, a single unit in a multi-unit chain operation must strive for consistency as it meets minimum requirements established by the organization. In an institutional dietary services operation, the program must be compatible with activities of the parent institution. Even a free-standing restaurant has marketing and related concerns about the "statement" it is making to the public.

The goal of good human relations. Food service managers in both commercial and institutional operations can benefit from considering goals which focus on the way they interact with their employees. The term "employees" includes not only subordinate staff members, but personnel at all management levels. Considering ways to retain employees and make maximum use of the contributions they can provide makes good business sense.

The goal of relating to society.   Food service operations can, by the way they conduct their affairs, help meet broad societal concerns such as nutrition, energy conservation, providing jobs for handicapped people, etc. Institutional operations can also focus their attention on community outreach efforts, emergency feeding plans, etc. Any food service operation which exists only to "take" and not "give back" to the community will not be successful in the long run.

The goal of professional concern.   Managers in some properties may contribute to their profession by donating time, money, and other resources to advance the food service industry.

The purpose of this discussion is not to set goals for all food service operations. It merely outlines the broad range of concerns which can be addressed as goals for individual food service operations are developed. Unfortunately, many operations do not have defined goals; in fact, some properties may never have addressed these concerns. Goals should not be established "because the book says so"; food service managers need to have statements of purpose to serve as a benchmark for decision-making. If you know what you want to do (expressed in goals), it becomes possible to decide whether alternate methods will better accomplish these goals and then you can evaluate the success of management efforts.

The Food Service Industry Today

You now know that the scope of the food service industry is vast. The industry offers a great many opportunities for people to consume food away from home, so convenient definitions about commercial and institutional food service operations do not always work. For example, earlier we defined commercial food services as operations which exist to make a profit from the sale of food items. Is this true for the retail or leisure market, bars and taverns, etc.? They may—or may not—wish to make a profit from food sales. They primarily exist for reasons other than to provide food service. How should they be classified?

Likewise, when we consider institutional food services, especially those operated for profit management companies, they need to be reclassified. Some institutional food service operations do exist primarily to provide food service (examples may include business and industry food service, programs for the elderly, and sports feeding programs). The food service industry does not lend itself to a simple organizational picture; there are food service operations in many more places than just restaurants or hotels.

Let's look more closely at some of the categories of the food service industry.

Separate Eating and Drinking Places

Separate eating and drinking places can be single-unit properties (one property owned by a person, partnership, or corporation) or multi-unit properties (a chain of two or more properties owned by a person, partnership, or corporation).

Separate eating and drinking places are frequently classified into the following categories:

Limited Menu Restaurants – These operations have a limited variety of menu items. Typically, the customer walks to the service counter (or drives up to a service window) and orders food. Then the customer carries the food to a table if there is inside seating or consumes the food in a car. Some limited menu properties may, of course, offer table service.

Full Menu Restaurants and Lunchrooms – These operations offer a wider variety of menu items and offer table service. They may be open for only one meal period or for 24 hours daily. Some offer a "California style" menu where items that are usually served for breakfast, lunch, and dinner are offered at all times. Full menu restaurants and lunchrooms generally have indoor seating and may or may not serve alcoholic beverages.

Social Caterers – They prepare meals for large or small banquets and may provide food service in off-site locations.

Public Cafeterias – These operations are often similar to full menu restaurants and lunchrooms because they offer a wide variety of menu items, but table service may be limited. Their markets include families and, as the check average increases, business people and adults without children.

Ice Cream, Frozen Custard Stands – These operations offer primarily frozen dairy and related products.

Bars and Taverns – These operations serve alcoholic beverages and only limited food services are offered.

Retail Market Food Service

This segment of the food service industry consists of four distinct categories which are part of the retail sales market:

Department Stores – Today's modern department stores sell products of all types, from clothing to appliances, and frequently have employee and public dining facilities.

Variety and General Merchandise Stores – These smaller stores sell more specialized items and they, too, frequently have food service operations for employees—even if only vended services are provided.

Drug and Proprietary Stores – These stores may have public dining outlets and often vended services for employees.

Other Specialized Retail Stores – Grocery stores, convenience food stores, gasoline stations, and a variety of other properties also sell food items for on- or off-premises consumption.

Food service in these operations may range from simple "lunch counter" or cafeteria service to formal, high-check average table service.

Business and Industry Food Service

Business and industry food services are offered in the following categories:

Contract Feeding – cafeterias and business offices

Internal Feeding – plants and business

Water-borne Employees – ships, oil rigs, etc.

Mobile On-street Catering – "meals on wheels" programs which involve canteen operations that visit construction sites and factories, and street vendors who sell a variety of products

Food Vending Machines – snacks to complete meals offered for customers and/or employees

Programs in business and industry operations encompass vending services in a manufacturing plant assembly line and gourmet dining facilities in executive dining rooms in large banks and insurance companies. Often, these programs are subsidized by the employers in order to offer a unique "fringe benefit" to employees. Feeding programs for employees can exist in almost any type of work situation—from white collar, to blue collar, to "no collar" jobs. Naturally, people must eat and the business and industry segment of food service provides feeding opportunities.

Leisure Market Food Service

Food service in theme parks and for sporting events in arenas, stadiums, and racing tracks is a large and very exciting segment of the industry. Also included in this segment are food service operations in drive-in movie theaters, bowling lanes, summer camps, and hunting facilities. These programs may be self-operated (managed by the facility itself) or operated by contract management companies. An increase in the public's leisure time will yield an increase in sales to this market segment.

Student Market Food Service

Categories of food service in the student market include:

Self-operated Programs – in public and parochial elementary and secondary schools

Management Company Operated Programs – public and parochial elementary and secondary schools

Self-operated Programs – in colleges and universities

Management Company Operated Programs – colleges and universities

Elementary and secondary schools may participate in the federally subsidized National School Lunch Program and related Child Nutrition Program. Some programs, such as those in large cities, may serve hundreds of thousands of meals daily. School food service programs may include—in addition to traditional lunches—breakfast, milk, supplemental feedings, community operations, and senior citizen meals. It is certainly a big and complex industry.

The college and university food service market is tremendous. There are more than 3,000 accredited post-secondary schools in the United States. There are another 3,000 or more trade schools which, while they may have vending machines and/or snack bars, do not offer room and board or extensive food service operations. Perhaps 1,500 of these post-secondary schools have food service of some type under a contracted arrangement with a for-profit management company. Of the remaining 1,500 schools, an estimated 500 offer only vending machines or manual buffet food services; 1,000 schools are large enough to have extensive food service programs for boarding students and others attending classes.[5]

Hotel/Motel Market Food Service

In 1981, food and beverage sales approximated 23.8% and 9%, respectively, of total sales dollars generated by the United States lodging industry.[6] This suggests that the food and beverage departments are much more than casual operations offered for the convenience of guests. In fact, many hoteliers and management personnel realize that food and beverage operations generally cannot generate required profits on the basis of only in-house sales; extensive patronage by the community is necessary for food and beverage operations to realize their economic goals.

Health Care Market Food Service

Hospitals and nursing homes of all types make up a primary segment of the health care food service market. Some of these facilities are privately owned; others are run by the government. Besides traditional acute care hospitals and nursing homes that provide permanent residence for their patients, there are also care homes for the blind, for orphans, and for mentally and physically handicapped people. Programs which are self-operated and managed by for-profit companies are included in this category.

As is true with many types of institutional food service operations, there is an emphasis on nutrition. In many operations, the patients and residents receive 100% of their daily food intake at the sites; concern about nutrition becomes important in order to protect the health and well-being of the patients, residents, and guests. In other facilities, nutrition is important because of its recuperative effects. Trained specialists called dietitians are often retained on a full-time or consulting basis and, in some cases, the dietitians might actually manage the food service operation. In other cases, they provide only specialized assistance to managers in areas involving clinical and therapeutic dietetics.

Transportation Market Food Service

Food services offered to air and rail passengers while in transit, terminals, interstate highways, and passenger and cargo lines are included in this segment. These services may be provided by a for-profit management company or they may be operated by the transportation company itself. Services can range from vending operations to sandwich and "short order" preparation to extravagant, expensive food service. The American public is traveling more; a corresponding increase in this market segment is expected.

Other Food Service Markets

There are many other food service operations. Consider, for example, programs operated by correctional (penal) institutions, religious seminaries and convents, and government-sponsored programs.

Cities may have athletic facilities, library or reading rooms, and city clubs (there are approximately 2,000 city clubs in the United States) that cater to the social needs of urban areas.[7] There are also about 4,900 private country clubs that offer sports such as golf, swimming, and tennis.

Recap: The Food Service Industry

Figure 2.1 recaps sales, purchase, and growth information for the total food service market. Note that, in 1982, total market sales approximated $133 billion! The commercial market, including for-profit contract companies in institutional operations, accounted for approximately 85% or $112 billion of these sales. The remaining 15% of sales was generated by self-operated food service institutions in health care, education, business and industry, and the military.

Food Service Industry Giants

You now have some idea about the many different types of food service operations which make up the industry. Another way to get an idea of its scope is to review basic information about the giants of the industry—those companies that are at the top in sales. Figure 2.2 shows the 20 largest companies in 1982.

Maybe there are some surprises on the list. Have you heard of all the largest companies? (Institutional contract feeders like ARA Services, Canteen Corporation, and Saga Corporation are not as widely known as others.) Did you know that the Food and Nutrition Service program of the U.S Department of Agriculture is the nation's fourth largest food service program? (Compared to McDonald's Corporation it is fourth in sales; however, there are many more school units than McDonald's outlets—90,500 compared to 7,259.) Did you know that Pillsbury, Marriott, Holiday Inns, General Mills, and the military are also in the food service business?

Are you interested in restaurant operations—the industry segment that most people associate with the food service industry? Figure 2.3 lists basic information about the 50 largest properties in 1982. It's hard to imagine a restaurant grossing about $30 million annually, but Atlantic City's Bally's Park Place Casino Hotel did! Look at the food and labor cost percentages. They range all across the board. Can you see why one cannot pick out any magic cost percents that will guarantee high sales or big profits?

Figure 2.1 Food Service Industry Summary

	1981 Sales ($000,000)	1981 Purchases* ($000,000)	1981 vs 1980 % Growth	1982 Sales ($000,000)	1982 Purchases* ($000,000)	1982 vs 1981 % Growth	1987 Projected Sales ($000,000)	% Compound Annual Growth Nominal	Real
Total Market	125,155	55,886	9.1	133,300	58,700	6.5	198,663	8.3	3.0
Commercial/Contract	105,814	41,907	9.5	112,833	44,378	6.6	172,250	8.8	3.5
Institutional/Internal	18,677	11,978	6.9	19,755	12,254	5.8	25,431	5.2	0.4
Military**	664	2,001	8.5	713	2,068	7.2	982	6.6	1.4
MAJOR MARKET SEGMENTS									
Eating/Drinking Places	82,209	29,725	10.0	88,377	31,871	7.5	136,798	9.1	3.7
Eating Places	73,888	26,710	10.4	79,640	28,706	7.8	125,826	9.6	4.2
Full Menu Restaurants & Lunchrooms	38,538	14,318	9.2	41,183	15,233	6.9	62,681	8.8	3.4
Limited Menu Restaurants	30,809	10,775	12.3	33,705	11,787	9.4	56,456	10.9	5.4
Hotel/Motel Market	7,133	2,381	8.1	7,369	2,446	3.3	10,731	7.8	2.5
Transportation Market	1,966	860	4.5	2,131	929	8.4	3,305	9.2	3.8
Leisure Market	2,618	967	6.3	2,806	1,025	7.2	4,290	8.9	3.5
Retail Market	3,622	1,320	7.9	3,790	1,372	4.6	5,661	8.4	3.0
Business/Industrial Market	7,961	8,575	8.2	7,843	8,676	−1.5	10,961	6.9	1.7
Student Market	6,828	4,969	7.0	7,347	4,847	7.6	8,279	2.4	−2.1
Health Care Market	10,634	5,213	7.2	11,339	5,554		15,402	6.3	1.6

Source: "16th Annual Restaurant Growth Index," Restaurant Business, *September 1983, p. 84.*

*Purchases include all food, nonalcoholic, and alcoholic beverages (does not include equipment or supplies).
**Sales data based on post exchanges and clubs; purchase data based on post exchanges, clubs & troop feeding.

Figure 2.2 The Food Service Giants

(1)
McDonald's Corp.
Oak Brook, Ill.
Franchisor (fast food/hamburgers)
1982 sales: 7,809
1981 sales: 7,129
Units (1/1/83): 7,259
Units (1/1/82): 6,739
'82 will go down as the year of the attack on Big Mac, with comparative commercials, Playmobile recall and mystery illness all clouding the picture for industry's No. 1. Still, sales were up nearly 10%, unit count grew by 520, and all other figures were typically impressive. Co. "just got slapped around" a bit, says Pres. Mike Quinlan. Look for Golden Arches over Yugoslavia in the coming year.

(2)
The Pillsbury Co. Restaurant Group
Dallas, Texas
Franchisor (diverse restaurants)
1982 sales: 2,982.1[B]*
1981 sales: 2,775.6**
Units (1/1/83): 3,698
Units (1/1/82): 3,449
At Burger King, they try harder: 3,361-unit chain, hungry for increased market share, runs 2 comparative ad campaigns, inks minority-trade pact, names Jeff Campbell pres. Results? $2,520MM systemwide sales, 10% real AUV growth. On tap: salad bars, set to be nationwide by 7/15. At S&A Corp.: Bennigan's happy with $165MM in 92 units; Steak & Ale chalks up $233MM in reduced 183-unit size. Co. sold 69 Poppin Fresh units (est. $62.1MM sales). Figures for calender '82.

(3)
Marriott Corp.
Washington, D.C.
Diverse foodservice/lodging
1982 sales: 2,667.5*
1981 sales: 2,090.5*
Units (1/1/83): 2,052
Units (1/1/82): 2,049**
The more, the merrier: Host Intl. and Gino's boosts specialty restaurant, air travel and Roy Rogers businesses. 101 Gino's became RR in '82; 74 will in '83. Hotel rooms increased 22%. Added here to co. restaurant and contracting revenues ($1,367.2MM) are estimated sales of Gino's/Rustler's (being capitalized by corp.); est. hotel, theme park, cruise ship F&B; sales of franchised Big Boys and Roy Rogers. (Excludes est. 392 Big Boys paying Marriott no fees.)

Source: "R & I '400': Balance of Power," Restaurants and Institutions, *July 1983, pp. 87, 90, 92, 94, 98.*

*R & I estimate; **company estimate or projection; †commercial equivalent; (A) former data included non-foodservice sales;
(B) adjusted method in reporting figures; (C) franchisees sales estimate

(4)
U.S. Dept. of Agriculture Food and Nutrition Service
Washington, D.C.
Government institutions
1982 sales: 2,470.7†
1981 sales: 2,798.9†
Units (1/1/83): 90,500
Units (1/1/82): 91,225
Nutrition program advocates fighting strongly for funding restoration, while Reagan administration seeks more cuts. Schools, students still dropping from meal programs. (Units shown here are schools in lunch program, 10/82.) USDA purchases of commodities shown for school lunches, summer meals, child care, elderly meals, summer camps, charitable institutions. Fy end 9/82.

(5)
KFC Corp.
Louisville, Ky.
Franchisor (fast food/chicken)
1982 sales: 2,426*
1981 sales: 2,349.3*
Units (1/1/83): 6,550**
Units (1/1/82): 5,958
Gotta face it: KFC does it right. New made-from-scratch biscuits now in 2,000 domestic stores, where they account for 8.5% of sales. Co.-owned stores averaged $468M for the year, franchises $355. Co. experienced real growth for the 4th consecutive year. Plans call for addition of up to 120 stores this year. Parent co. Heublein acquired by R.J. Reynolds in '82. Figures include 93 H. Salt, 56 Zantigo, 7 Galley units. Fy end 6/83.

(6)
PepsiCo Foodservice Division
Purchase, N.Y.
Franchisor (diverse restaurants)
1982 sales: 1,985
1981 sales: 1,601.7*
Units (1/1/83): 5,593
Units (1/1/82): 5,398
All they want to talk about is Personal Pan Pizza; the new menu item, introduced in spring of '83, has potential to double Pizza Hut's lunch sales. Chainwide, Pizza Hut (with est. sales of $1,330MM in est. 4,009 units) is implementing new decor packages, automated dough-handling equipment (to ensure consistency). Sibling Taco Bell (est. sales $655MM in est. 1,584 units) experienced 12% unit growth; introduced Taco BellGrande, Taco Light; installing drive-throughs.

(7)
Holiday Inns, Inc.
Memphis, Tenn.
Diverse foodservice/lodging
1982 sales: 1,868.2
1981 sales: 1,861.8
Units (1/1/83): 3,229*
Units (1/1/82): 3,265*
Holiday Inns' new image is a strong one. Co. eliminating older properties, refurbishing viable ones and rolling out a new, improved product. The "No Excuses" Room Guarantee has been extended with continued confidence. Co. plans on rolling out 2 new concepts: an all-suite concept; and Crowne Plaza, a subchain of upscale properties (9 are now under construction). Perkins' sales of $170MM in 311 units included here.

(8)
ARA Services, Inc.
Philadelphia, Pa.
Foodservice management
1982 sales: 1,640.8†ᴮ
1981 sales: 1,600
Units (1/1/83): 2,800
Units (1/1/82): 3,000
Giant international caterer is in training for 1984 Summer Olympics in L.A. Meanwhile, fs. organization restructured from geographic to service market hierarchy. Battered by layoffs and plant closings among heavy-industry clients, ARA seeks to build business in light manufacturing and service workplaces. Leisure, air travel-related businesses are coming out of recession with good growth momentum. Fy end 10/82.

(9)
Wendy's International, Inc.
Dublin, Ohio
Franchisor (fast food/hamburgers)
1982 sales: 1,632.4
1981 sales: 1,424
Units (1/1/83): 2,430
Units (1/1/82): 2,229
Wendy's clearly has little trouble attracting its Kind of People to its restaurants. Sales up a comfortable 15% over '81 figure. AUV now $702M. Year was marked by hugely successful rollouts of Taco Salad and Bacon Cheeseburger. Meanwhile, co. decided to take its Sisters Chicken & Biscuits concept nationwide. 25 Sisters now in operation report AUV of $850M. New, hard-hitting ads intended to counter Burger King's marketing drive.

(10)
Imasco USA
Rocky Mount, N.C.
Franchisor (fast food/hamburgers)
1982 sales: 1,308ᴮ
1981 sales: 1,108
Units (1/1/83): 2,165
Units (1/1/82): 1,408
New names, new faces: After Hardee's acquired Burger Chef in early '82, co. was reorganized as holding co. Imasco USA by its Canadian parent. Under Imasco USA: Hardee's Food Systems ('82 sales of $1.1 billion); and Burger Chef Systems ('82 sales of $300MM). Customer counts, unit sales up in both, with heavy dealing, promotions, new menu items. Figures for calender '82. PC: Imasco Ltd.

(11)
International Dairy Queen, Inc.
Minneapolis, Minn.
Franchisor (diverse restaurants)
1982 sales: 1,233
1981 sales: 1,125
Units (1/1/83): 4,902
Units (1/1/82): 4,805
The royal family is shrinking — and growing. Golden Skillet's 148 family restaurants, $35MM sales included for first time. But American DQ, 4,754-unit subsidiary, continues to upgrade system by closing unprofitable stores. Finally gave nod to "Queen's Choice" hard ice cream; it's now being added chainwide, along with ¼-lb. chili dog, 168-unit intl. division will grow by another 22 in '83; new markets include Cypress, Thailand. Systemwide AUV rose to $252M. Fy end 11/82.

(12)
Denny's Inc.
La Mirada, Calif.
Franchisor (diverse restaurants)
1982 sales: 1,094.2
1981 sales: 1,015
Units (1/1/83): 1,967
Units (1/1/82): 1,882
What's next for Denny's? Acquisition (bought 22 Alphy's, 26 Vip's, 48 Sambo's units in '81-'82)? New concepts (opened, in a converted Winchell's Donut House, Uncle Jeb's Ribs)? Upscaling (added china and glassware in Denny's, where employees don vests in evening)? Current count: 1,109 Denny's (sales of $933.7MM), 858 Winchell's (sales of $160.5MM). Corporate after-tax profits increased 18% in '82. Denny's AUV rose to $922M, Winchell's to $191.3M.

(13)
Saga Corp.
Menlo Park, Calif.
Diverse foodservice/management
1982 sales: 933.7
1981 sales: 864
Units (1/1/83): 1,176
Units (1/1/82): 1,145
The saga continues. B&I accounts down by 14, but colleges/universities and schools up 3; hospitals/retirement homes up 16. Saga as franchisor: Sales up 5% in Stuart Anderson's Black Angus Cattle Co.; 15% in Straw Hat Pizza; steady in Velvet Turtle. Chairman/CEO Lynch comments on '83: "We are enthusiastic . . . but remain cautious . . . because of the continuing recession." Co. "continues to invest in discretionary programs designed to benefit future periods."

(14)
General Mills Restaurant Group, Inc.
Orlando, Fla.
Diverse restaurants
1982 sales: 933.4*
1981 sales: 839.4
Units (1/1/83): 546*
Units (1/1/82): 480
R&I forced to estimate sales, units this year; co. crawled back into shell. Red Lobster (est. $691MM sales, 346 units) moving ahead with regional menu items, new lighter decor. York Steak Houses (est. $158.4MM sales, 144 units) located primarily in shopping malls across northern half of U.S. Other concepts include The Good Earth, Darryl's, The Olive Garden, Casa Gallardo. Plans to have 950 units open by '87; projects '87 sales of $2 billion. PC: General Mills, Inc. Fy end 5/83.

(15)
Canteen Corp.
Chicago, Ill.
Diverse foodservice/management
1982 sales: 915
1981 sales: 894
Units (1/1/83): 950
Units (1/1/82): 850
Aggressive marketing in all divisions. Major thrust into school lunch programs. Promoting park operations for business meetings and conventions during off- and fringe-seasons. Testing game-cup promotions in both vending and manual employee-feeding units. Almost 80% of new business is in non-cyclical, white-collar or growth industries. Opened 15 Gulliver's units in '82; 15 more planned for '83. PC: Trans World Corp.

(16)
The Sheraton Corp.
Boston, Mass.
Lodging
1982 sales: 900
1981 sales: 840
Units (1/1/83): 1,251
Units (1/1/82): 1,138
Sheraton's success due to policy of 3-way diversification by geographic location, function, type of ownership. A total of 37 Sheratons opened in 13 countries in '82. Co. set new records in total sales, profits, product growth; occupancy rates averaged 70%. More than 100 hotels are under construction or in final planning, extending system into 68 countries. Sheraton "Style" ad campaign will continue worldwide. Guest Bonus coupons among '83 promotions. PC: ITT Corp.

(17)
U.S. Navy Food Service
Systems Office
Washington, D.C.
Military
1982 sales: 823.2†
1981 sales: 795.2†
Units (1/1/83): 660
Units (1/1/82): 653
Riding the wave of the future: Navy fs. prepares to go electronic. At NAS Alameda, Calif., Navy soon will test a fully automated fs. accounting and internal control system, including ID card scan at electronic cash register. Meanwhile, item pricing — tied to electronic registers — to be systemwide in U.S. by '86. Equipment, training are toughest challenges. Fy end 9/82.

(18)
U.S. Army
Fort Lee, Va.
Military
1982 sales: 748†
1981 sales: 755.3†
Units (1/1/83): 1,108
Units (1/1/82): 1,100
A leaner Army: Fs. management has orders to trim labor requirements, administrative counts — and calorie counts! Labor-intensive recipes being weeded out; convenience products on the rise. New administrative controls cut costs. Low-fat preparation of entrees, lower-calorie desserts and breakfast foods stressed. Big push on nutrition education. Fewer personnel authorized subsistence. (Precise data substituted for '81 sales est.) Fy end 9/82.

(19)
Hilton Hotels Corp.
Beverly Hills, Calif.
Lodging
1982 sales: 640.8^C
1981 sales: 563.7*
Units (1/1/83): 944*
Units (1/1/82): 944*
Conrad Hilton began establishing his empire with his first hotel in 1919. Today 426 Hiltons, offering 129,692 guest rooms, span the nation. Conrad should be proud: despite poor economy and a 5% decrease in occupancy rates for co.-managed properties, sales are up. Future growth for co. seems targeted toward multi-destinational sites, with many airport properties open or in the works. Co. currently expanding into intl. market under Conrad Intl. banner.

(20)
W. R. Grace Restaurant Group
Costa Mesa, Calif.
Diverse restaurants
1982 sales: 634
1981 sales: 598
Units (1/1/83): 607
Units (1/1/82): 622
On the fast track: Grace brought former Burger King Pres. Lou Neeb over to head up concentrated expansion of new fast-food division. That already includes 137 Del Taco units ($52MM in sales) plus concepts under development. Other Grace performers — stars Gilbert/Robinson (68 dinner houses) and El Torito (90 dinner houses) — together turned in strong '82 sales of $394MM. Coffee-shop division — reportedly being reorganized — took in $188MM in 256 jojo's, Coco's units.

Figure 2.3 Nation's Highest Volume Independent Restaurants

	Total Sales ($000)	Alcohol Sales (% of Total)	Cost of Sales (%)	Labor Cost (%)	Employees (#)	Seats (#)	Avg. Dinner Check ($)
1. Bally's Park Place Casino Hotel, Atlantic City, NJ	29115	35.3	30.9	46.6	951	1625	—
2. Windows on the World, New York, NY	21042	28.9	26.7	34.7	485	585	36.75
3. Tavern On The Green, New York, NY	19000	30.0	—		420	514	—
4. Anthony's Pier 4, Boston, MA	12400	27.8	35.2	27.0	330	900	24.00
5. The "21" Club, New York, NY	12000	33.3	32.7	27.0	275	300	67.50
6. Spenger's Fish Grotto, Berkley, CA	11236	18.6	—	—	240	330	7.00
7. Kahala Hilton Hotel, Honolulu, HI	10990	24.2	27.5	42.9	517	550	19.96
8. The Dining Room, Chicago, IL	10757	31.8	33.1	—	225	210	35.00
9. Market Square, New York, NY	9233	18.8	33.9	·34.9	215	740	4.00
10. The Rainbow Room & Rainbow Grill, New York, NY	8839	24.9	23.2	32.5	215	660	32.00
11. Zehnder's Restaurant, Frankenmuth, MI	8583	10.1	24.9	32.3	350	1390	6.76
12. Mai-Kai, Ft. Lauderdale, FL	8000	41.3	36.1	39.0	200	650	23.50
13. Frankenmuth Bavarian Inn, Frankenmuth, MI	7757	9.3	17.4	34.2	420	1320	8.50
14. Rascal House Restaurant, Miami Beach, FL	7257	0.9	38.6	33.6	248	440	5.75
15. The Gateway Restaurant, Laie, HI	6643	-0-	22.5	11.0	84	985	13.00
16. The Kahler Hotel, Rochester, MN	6618	14.6	30.5	40.4	280	800	9.25
17. Maxi's Dining Room, Portland, OR	6351	26.9	30.9	25.0	267	505	15.00
18. Daphne's, Miami, FL	6350	34.7	32.2	34.6	232	420	16.50
19. Maxwell's Plum, New York, NY	6100	29.5	—	—	225	230	—
20. Clyde's of Tysons Corner, Vienna, VA	5908	39.9	28.6	24.1	213	395	25.00
21. Tangier Restaurant, Akron, OH	5700	30.7	32.5	30.0	210	900	15.00
22. Ralph & Kacoo's Restaurant, Baton Rouge, LA	5685	10.5	40.1	45.0	130	545	14.50
23. Lily Langtry's, King of Prussia, PA	5335	37.8	25.1	21.5	158	592	26.90
24. Clifton's Brookdale Cafeteria, Los Angeles, CA	5201	-0-	33.1	24.4	159	834	2.96
25. Pea Soup Andersen's, Buellton, CA	5200	7.7	23.2	23.0	148	650	3.75
26. Ormsby House Hotel/Casino, Carson City, NV	5092	23.7	43.6	36.2	230	—	—
27. Sportsmen's Lodge Restaurant, Studio City, CA	5030	22.9	27.9	44.3	169	320	14.70
28. Daphne's, Elizabeth, NJ	4896	34.3	33.4	32.3	150	226	17.00
29. *Gibby's Steaks & Seafood, Fort Lauderdale, FL	4800	12.5	42.0	30.0	160	650	18.54
29. *The Rusty Pelican, Key Biscayne, FL	4800	29.2	26.0	25.0	128	430	20.00
31. The Park Room, New York, NY	4754	24.3	30.8	—	100	195	35.00
32. Twin Oaks, Cranston, RI	4540	25.0	50.0	—	120	440	—
33. *Red Lion Ontario, Ontario, CA	4500	22.2	33.2	11.5	270	250	18.00
33. *Pea Soup Andersen's, Carlsbad, CA	4500	13.0	23.7	25.0	136	1000	4.25
35. Bishop's Restaurant, Lawrence, MA	4450	25.8	47.2	22.0	185	725	16.00
36. Pea Soup Andersen's, Santa Nella, CA	4400	13.1	23.1	22.0	115	650	3.75
37. Nick's Fishmarket, Chicago, IL	4315	27.0	35.9	30.0	90	160	40.00
38. Nick's Fishmarket, Houston, TX	4223	32.4	33.8	27.0	90	345	42.00
39. Clifton's Century City Cafeteria, Los Angeles, CA	4042	-0-	31.9	23.9	115	486	3.42
40. Sea Watch Restaurant, Fort Lauderdale, FL	4029	24.3	41.9	24.3	115	270	15.70
41. Willow Valley Farms Restaurant, Lancaster, PA	4008	-0-	39.8	22.8	126	600	6.75
42. *Jimmie Walker, Kemah, TX	4000	49.5	28.1	21.7	102	500	16.00
42. *Pals Cabin, West Orange, NJ	4000	18.0	35.3	27.0	85	355	9.30
44. The Warehouse Restaurant, Marina del Rey, CA	3974	24.3	34.4	20.5	78	420	15.25
45. New River Storehouse, Fort Lauderdale, FL	3910	47.1	32.2	26.0	215	425	20.25
46. Stouffers Denver Inn, Denver, CO	3901	24.8	29.1	—	200	575	10.05
47. Tommy Lancaster, New Albany, IN	3900	9.0	35.6	31.0	293	290	—
48. Applewoods, Oklahoma City, OK	3873	14.8	36.3	32.0	130	250	14.50
49. Newport Restaurant and Pub, Miami Beach, FL	3840	10.2	33.8	25.6	163	670	11.50
50. The Pirates' House, Savannah, GA	3786	17.2	30.6	38.1	213	350	15.75

Source: Courtesy of Restaurant Hospitality, Cleveland, Ohio, June 1983, p. 104.
*Denotes tie.

While some of the properties are large (26 properties have 500 or more restaurant seats), others are small (seven properties have 250 or fewer restaurant seats).

Now look at check average (sales volume divided by number of people served). Nine properties have check averages in excess of $25 for dinner. By contrast, 12 properties have check averages of less than $10.

What does Figure 2.3 tell you? It obviously points out the great diversity in the nation's largest restaurants, which is a reflection of the entire industry.

The Management Company Controversy

We have already noted that for-profit management companies often manage food service operations in institutional food service facilities. While there is a trend toward increased use of this alternative, it is fairly controversial. Institutional operations have traditionally focused on nutrition and other factors which de-emphasized economic concerns. Today, as pressures for cost containment accompany reduced income, there is a need to manage food service operations as professional businesses. When this can be done on a self-operated basis, problems may not occur. However, when economic goals of cost minimization cannot be met, the management company alternative is realistic.

Advantages of Management Companies

Those in favor of management companies cite the following advantages:

- Organizational resources of large nationwide companies can focus on solving specific problems in the individual units with expertise, automation, and savings brought about by effective negotiations with food suppliers.

- Contract management companies can often operate dietary programs at a lower cost than their self-operated counterparts.

- Reduced internal direction by staff administrators is another plus. Facility administrators, trained in areas other than food service operations, can delegate responsibilities for much decision-making to professional food service managers.

Disadvantages of Management Companies

Opponents of management companies cite the following disadvantages:

- Loss of internal control means that management companies may have too much discretion in matters that affect the public image, long-range operating plans, and other important issues.

- Questions justifying involvement of a profit-making business in the operation of a health care, educational, or other institutional food service program are often raised.

- Miscellaneous operational problems include concerns that the company will decrease quality, increase costs, or take other contractual shortcuts.

- The institutional operation may depend too much on the management company. What will it do if the management company wants to discontinue the contract? How long will it take the operation to implement their own program or find another management company?

- Higher operating costs are also possible when management companies are used. How is it possible to use a management company to *reduce* costs when now we are suggesting that operating costs might *increase*? The answer is, of course, that it all depends upon the specific management company and on the food service operation. The issue of minimizing costs while at the same time retaining quality is at the heart of the food management company controversy.

During your career you will certainly have opportunities to consider the management company alternative. There are excellent jobs and opportunities with companies which are, in effect, a "chain" of institutional food service accounts. Students, currently employed staff members, and institutional administrators should consider both the advantages and disadvantages of using management companies—just as they would review other alternatives available to them.

Multi-Unit and Single-Unit Food Service Operations

The fast-food segment of the restaurant industry is dominated by chains. Familiar names can also be seen in Figure 2.2.

The first big chain operator was Fred Harvey; by 1912, his company operated a dozen large hotels, 65 railway restaurants, and 60 dining cars. John R. Thompson was another early chain operator. By 1926, he controlled 126 self-service restaurants in the Midwest and the South.[8] Today, among other properties, the company operates Henrici's table service restaurants.

Food Service Chains

Perhaps other food service chains are more familiar to you. Stouffers, Marriott, and Howard Johnson all started their operations during the 1920s. Today, of course, fast-food chains such as McDonald's, Wendy's, Burger King, Kentucky Fried Chicken, Denny's, and Red Lobster are familiar to almost everybody. Specialty operations like Houlihan's and Bennigan's plus cafeteria chains—Furr's in the Southwest and Bishop's in the Midwest—are also generally known.

How Chains Grow

How do chains grow? There are several ways:

1. An entrepreneur may build a successful business and expand it as capital and circumstances permit.

2. Some chains want nothing but "company stores." Other food service operations "package" their operating procedures, systems, name, logo, etc., and sell the rights to operate units. This concept, called franchising, is very significant in the food service industry and helps account for the rapid growth of this segment of the market. We will look more closely at franchising later in this chapter.

3. Some companies operate "company stores" and sell franchise opportunities to investors.

4. Sometimes, chains buy other chains. For example, Marriott purchased both Host International and Roy Rogers, and Hardee's purchased Burger Chef. For-profit management companies also operate chains within the commercial sector of the industry. Saga Corporation operates Straw Hat Pizza, the Velvet Turtle, and Stuart's Black Angus restaurant chains.

Advantages of Chains

What are the advantages of restaurant chains? Large chains can more readily gain access to cash and credit and generate long-term leases on land and buildings. This is not as feasible for many single-unit properties. The multi-unit chain also can afford to make more than one mistake. The independent operator who makes mistakes is out of business. Related to this is the ability of a multi-unit company to experiment with different menus, themes, designs, operating procedures, etc. As it discovers the correct "mix," the multi-unit company can develop a consistent package for use by all its properties. The independent single-unit operator has limited opportunities to undertake extensive experiments.

Multi-unit companies can afford staff specialists who are experts in finance, construction, operations, recipe development, etc. Single-unit operators must be well-rounded and undertake most, if not all, of these responsibilities as a routine, ongoing part of their jobs.

Chains have another advantage from a control perspective. They are able to generate internal financial information which can be used as a base of comparison between properties. An independent operator usually knows how well he/she is doing, but is unaware of what performance standards should be. A multi-unit company operating many properties within a certain geographic area should be able to more easily generate standard cost control information which can be used to identify problems in specific properties.

**Disadvantages
of Chains**

However, there are problems that confront multi-unit companies. It might be difficult for these companies to keep up with changing markets, economic conditions, etc. As chains grow, a bureaucracy involving a large amount of paperwork, rules, and procedures can slow them down. Top management may lose the motivation to keep up and what is best for the company might not always receive the highest priority.

You already know that multi-unit companies are big and will be getting bigger, dominating an even greater share of the total food service market. Is there a place for the single-unit operator? The answer is yes. The individual entrepreneur who can spot a market whose wants and needs are not currently being met may be able to capture it. By continually providing good prices and value to customers, the independent operator may be able to compete successfully with the multi-unit chains.

**Single-Unit
Operations**

Statistics work against the single-unit operation. A large number of all restaurants which open are not in business five years later; many operators are lured into the business because of the fact that people must always eat and "why shouldn't they eat at my place?" The restaurant industry is one where relatively little capital is required for entry. Consider, for example, that land, facilities, and equipment can be leased. The minimal amount of inventory which is necessary to open can often be purchased on several weeks' credit.

Theoretically, then, one can generate sales and use the proceeds to pay for inventory costs. Of course, in the "real world" things do not happen like this. Profit, if any, is not directly converted into cash. Income from charge customers and travel and entertainment credit card purchases may not be available immediately. Likewise, some expenses may need to be prepaid. (We will discuss financial management of food and beverage operations in more detail in Chapter 16.) At this point, you should realize that, while the possible rewards of restaurant ownership are great, so are the potential risks. Management of food and beverage operations—instead of ownership—is an alternative being selected by increasing numbers of people in the industry.

Advantages and Disadvantages of Franchising

How can a commercial food service operation be managed? There are several ways:

- The owner can operate/manage a property.

- An investor can hire professional management to run the business.

- An owner can purchase a franchise and operate a property under his/her own management.

- An owner can purchase a franchise and hire professional management.

- An investor can purchase a franchise and have a franchise company operate it.

What Is Franchising?

You can see that there are several alternatives for operation of a restaurant. The franchise has been of particular interest to the restaurant industry; it is a primary reason why multi-unit chains have expanded as rapidly as they have.

Franchising in the fast-food business dates to at least the early 1920s and 1930s when A&W Root Beer and Howard Johnson's franchised some of their units.[9] The franchisor (the company selling the franchise) can expand the business by signing up a franchisee. The latter is often a local business person with investment funds. However, large companies seeking investment options may also purchase a franchise. The franchisee is usually responsible for generating funds necessary to start the business. In addition to initial franchise fees, the franchisee may be required to pay:

- royalty fees assessed on the basis of a specified percentage of sales or other factors.

- advertising costs, sign rental fees, and other costs such as stationery and food products (it may be against the law to stipulate, as part of the franchise agreement, that the franchisee must buy products of any kind from the franchisor).

Advantages of Franchises

The franchisee usually benefits from the relationship (that is certainly the objective). Benefits often include:

- higher sales because of national advertising.

- national contributions toward local advertising campaigns.

- higher sales because of name recognition with the company (the customer knows what to expect because of the consistency of most chain properties).

- group buying opportunities to lower food purchase prices.

- tested operating procedures which specify how things should be done as part of the package which the franchisee purchases with the initial franchise fees.

- start-up assistance, company sponsored training programs for management staff, training resource materials for other employees in the property, etc.

There is no doubt that many food service franchisors and franchisees have been tremendously successful. When franchisors are successful, they can command high fees and there can be long waiting lists to buy a franchise. Often, the franchisees are screened, and there may be little choice in the areas (territories) that are available for purchase.

Disadvantages of Franchises

You should be aware that there are also some possible disadvantages to franchised food and beverage operations. The contract is generally very restrictive; the franchisee has little choice about the style of operation, the products served, services offered and, perhaps, even methods of operation. The menu might be set, along with the decor, required furnishings, and production equipment. Since the franchise agreement is drawn up by the franchisor (the franchisee can accept or reject it), the document generally favors the franchisor. The agreement may be fixed; there may be little left to negotiate. This causes problems if there are disagreements between the two parties.

As with any hospitality operation, ownership and/or management of a franchise operation is not easy. There are long hours of very hard work involved. Problems are constant and many are in need of immediate attention. Usually, you cannot walk away from a franchise operation without significant financial loss.

Your Future in the Food Service Industry

There are some additional things that you should know about the food service industry. The number of commercial and institutional operations offering food services is going to increase. This growth, in turn, will yield more jobs of all types and levels of responsibility. If you want to get involved in this thriving industry—read on and remember that there will be a place in it for you.

Working in the Food Service Industry

You should realize that the public has many impressions (and misconceptions) about what work in the food service industry is like. Let's try to clarify some points. No matter what organizational level you are dealing with, the work is hard. At lower organizational levels, it might be hard in a physical sense. The industry is labor intensive and no one has found a way to replace people with equipment. At higher organizational levels the work is still difficult—there are important decisions with great ramifications that must be made. As is true in any business, the amount of pressure and frustration which this can create is of real concern. Other problems include the fact that work hours can be long and that, at least in the commercial sector, most food service people work when other people play. Food service employees must be available during the times when customers want to dine so this means working evenings, weekends, and holidays.

Interestingly enough, institutional food service operations—which are often underrated by people aspiring to food service positions—often count among their benefits the fact that they have more traditional work hours (at least for management staff). Weekends, holidays, and vacation times are also more likely to be free of responsibilities.

The Concept of Service

Some people may feel that, by definition, "service" positions are unattractive. There is no question that the food service industry involves serving guests, patients, residents, and others. If you think there is a social or status stigma attached to the concept of service, then a position in the food service industry may not be for you. On the other hand, the spirit of hospitality and the desire to help others is a drawing card for many people. In institutional food service operations, there are many people whose high point of the day is the food they are provided.

Salaries and Benefits

Wage and salary compensation and related benefits, at least at starting levels, are not high. In 1983, starting salaries for entrance positions were around minimum wage. Entrance positions for college and university graduates were approximately $15,500. However, as is true with any career decision, the question should not be, "What is the starting pay?" but rather, "Where will I be in compensation and benefits five years from now?" When this question is asked, the food service industry is in a very competitive position with other vocational and professional alternatives. College graduates with five years of experience or less can be running multi-million dollar restaurant operations, earning a salary in excess of $30,000, and receiving "a piece of the action." Staff members starting in entrance position "fast track" operations (fast-food establishments and other rapidly expanding companies) can easily be department heads earning very attractive salaries—perhaps with incentive and bonus plans to provide additional compensation.

Since food service operations are everywhere, geographic preference is generally an easier objective to attain in the food service industry. Where do you want to live? Wherever it is, there are likely to be opportunities in the food service industry.

Challenges of Food Service

Regardless of what segment of the industry you enter, the sheer challenge of the job is a tremendous incentive. Do you want an opportunity to make decisions that will affect many people and many dollars over a long period of time? The example of a young person managing a multi-million dollar business has already been given. The responsibilities of dealing with large numbers of employees and customers can also be cited.

How do you get involved in food service work? You might already be employed in a food service position. You should—if you haven't already—talk with your supervisor about professional development opportunities within the operation. Maybe you are already convinced that food service is for you and are trying to get basic information about the subject. You should talk to your school faculty and placement officers and with management staff in existing properties about opportunities that are available. Many students work in the food service industry while they are studying it. This gives them experience, a chance to see what the industry is like "from the inside," and an opportunity to consider career possibilities with the employer (the student may be considered for possible positions after school is finished).

Opportunities in Food Service

Perhaps you are not a student or currently employed in the industry. If you are interested in the food service industry, you should contact a school or college in your area which offers a hospitality education program. You may be able to take courses or obtain placement advice from them. For example, the Educational Institute of the American Hotel & Motel Association offers home study courses that cover all major areas of hotel, motel, and food service operations. Designed so you can study at your own convenience, Educational Institute courses offer you a planned, career-long program of professional growth and development. You should also check with local hospitality operations about employment opportunities. Your primary objective should be to get your foot in the door. When this occurs, there will be many possibilities for you to consider as career decisions are made.

We have presented an overview of the vast and complex food service industry. Next, we will focus on what you should do to get ready for a position in the food service industry. What kinds of skills and attitudes will be helpful? What kind of experiences will help you advance "up the organizational ladder"? How do you effectively plan a career path in the industry? What must you do to get along with customers, fellow employees, and your superiors in a very "people intensive" industry? These and related topics will be discussed to give you a competitive edge in obtaining a fulfilling and responsible professional position in the food service industry.

NOTES

1. Donald E. Lundberg, *The Hotel and Restaurant Business,* 3rd ed. (Boston, Mass.: CBI, 1979), p. 15.

2. Lundberg, p. 21.

3. Lundberg, pp. 203 - 210.

4. H. Berberoglu, *The World of the Restaurateur* (Dubuque, Iowa: Kendall/ Hunt, 1981), p. 29.

5. These statistics were supplied by: National Association of College and University Food Service, East Lansing, Mich., Michigan State University, 1982.

6. Pannell Kerr Forster, *Trends in the Hotel Industry*, U.S. ed. (New York, 1982), p. 14.

7. Club Managers Association of America, *Club Management Operations,* 2nd ed. (Dubuque, Iowa: Kendall/Hunt, 1983), pp. 3-4.

8. Lundberg, p. 203.

9. Lundberg, p. 297.

3

Getting Ready for the Industry

Management Challenges

As a result of studying this chapter you will:

1. be able to practice basic principles helpful in strengthening your relationship with customers, fellow employees, and your supervisor.

2. be able to develop a potential career path in the hospitality industry.

3. understand many of the functions which food servers perform and recognize how they relate to the customer and to the success of the operation.

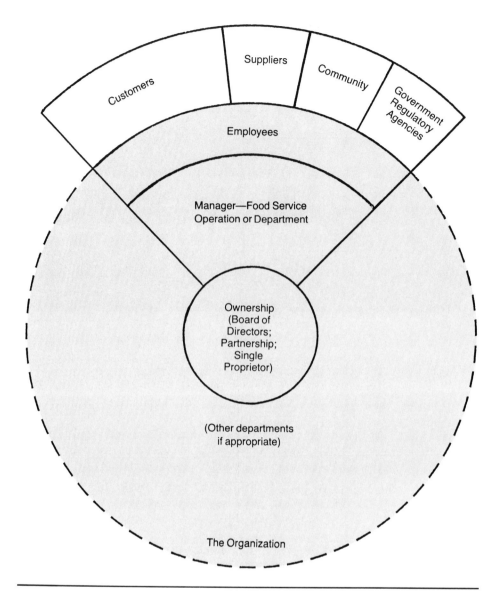

The Organization

Focus on the Food Service Publics

Chapter 3 focuses attention on the actual work (functions) performed by personnel in the food service industry. As such, it examines the relationship between three internal food service publics—the owner, the manager, and the employees. It also discusses common career progression paths and reviews basic principles of getting along with people. Both subjects are important in the relationship between the internal publics of the food service operation. Since some food service personnel perform work which impacts upon the entire organization, the relationships with another public (other departments within the organization) are also affected by information presented in this chapter.

In Chapter 2, you learned that the world of food service is vast and yet, in many ways, procedures used to manage the differing types of food service operations are very similar. This chapter will focus on the basic organizational structure of food service operations. Similarities between all segments of the industry will be emphasized and differences will be pointed out where appropriate.

As noted in Chapter 2, it is difficult to discuss many aspects of food service operations without at least considering the objectives that have been developed for them. For what purpose are food service operations organized? The answer is, of course, to attain organizational objectives. It is obvious that the objectives of the food service operation must be known as organizing attempts evolve. Perhaps a practical example will illustrate the relationship between developing objectives and "organizing for action."

We have noted that all food service operations have an economic objective. (Institutional operations want to minimize expenses; commercial properties want to maximize profits.) The way that the organizational structure is developed affects the ability to attain either of these goals. However, you should consider that the process of organizing affects work efficiency, communication ability, effective delegation of authority and responsibility, and similar concerns. Don't all these factors affect bottom-line profit or cost? The bottom line is the last line in an income statement for a commercial property or an operating statement for an institutional facility. Since economic goals focus on profit or cost levels, the bottom line is often a good indication of management's effectiveness.

Let's look at another example. Suppose that a commercial property has a goal concerning human relations. Perhaps it wishes to recognize individual differences, seek employee input during the decision-making process, design work to meet each person's needs, etc. The way that the organizational structure is developed affects the property's ability to do this. If, for example, one supervisor must direct the work of many employees, there is less likelihood that he/she can provide the individual attention necessary to foster human relations concerns. Consider also the case of the institutional food service operation which wants to ensure that nutrition requirements are met in all meals, that proper nutrition education is given to all patients and residents who need it, and that community outreach efforts in areas dealing with dietetic services are also provided. It is obviously necessary that the organization provide personnel for these responsibilities. Professional people who are competent in these areas must be hired and time allocated for them to perform the required duties.

All the objectives of the food service operation, then, must be considered as the organization is developed. The first question to ask is, "What are we going to do?" The answer is, "Attain specified objectives." The second question to ask is, "How can we best do it?" The answer requires that you consider alternative organizational plans and select the most useful one for your food service operation.

We will review alternative organizational plans for various types of food service operations later in this chapter. Before we do, however, let's take a close look at some food service functions. What types of jobs are there in food service? What do people who perform these functions do?

Required Positions in Food Service

The food service industry is labor intensive. This means that a large number of people are required to do the work necessary to attain food service objectives. Technology has not "caught up" with the needs of the industry; science has not found a way to replace people with equipment. Robotics (using automated equipment in industry) has not proven useful in food service—at least not to any significant extent. There was some experimentation with computerized kitchens as early as the 1960s. While this effort yielded some automated and specialized equipment (see Chapter 17), much of the work, at least in the kitchen area, has not changed in decades.

Top Management Functions

What are top management functions in food service? What do people who are responsible for these functions do? The best answers to these questions can be given when different types of operations are discussed individually. In large, multi-unit chain operations, top management may begin with a board of directors. This group is responsible for the long-range strategic planning of the company and for high-level evaluation and decision-making activities which affect current operations.

A chairman of the board may be elected/appointed to coordinate the work of this group. Many operations also retain a chief executive officer (CEO) who serves as an intermediary between the board of directors and operating managers. Very large conglomerates which have several food service operations and, perhaps, business interests in nonfood service areas may have a series of presidents and vice presidents to assume responsibility for specific companies. An example of an organizational structure of top management in large companies is shown in Figure 3.1. Although it is oversimplified, Figure 3.1 does show the chain of command from the board of directors to unit managers. In this example, the company's board of directors, which is elected by stockholders, appoints a chairman of the board and a chief executive officer. These people may or may not be the same individual. The chief executive officer directs the president of each company (the three companies are controlled by the board of directors). Each president, such as the president of Company B, has regional vice presidents who supervise regional or area directors. These staff members direct the work of unit managers who control specific operations in individual properties.

Even though it is contrary to the impressions of employees in specific food service operations, it is common to refer to unit managers (general managers of hotels or restaurants) in large companies as "middle management," not "top management." Figure 3.1 shows why this is so;

Figure 3.1 Organizational Structure of Top Management in Large Companies

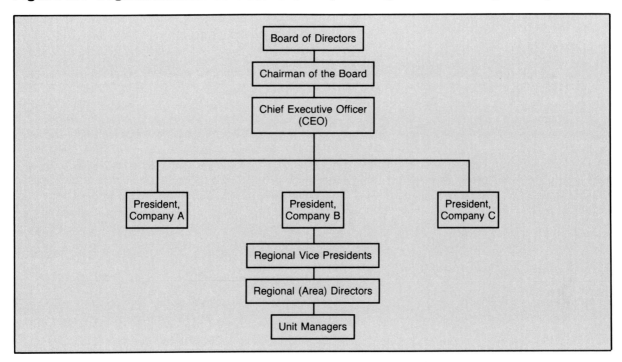

Figure 3.2 Organizational Structure of Top Management in a Hotel

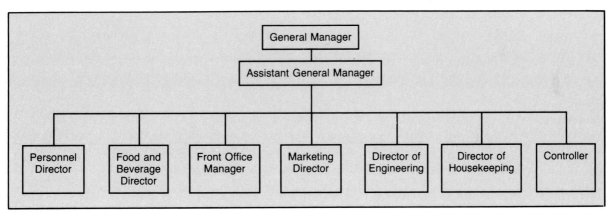

individuals with unit responsibilities are relatively far down on the company's organization chart.

With obvious modifications, the organizational structure for food management companies would be similar. However, these companies generally have divisions dealing with schools and colleges, health care, vending operations, etc.

Now let's look at the concept of top management in a specific property. Figure 3.2 shows what many hotels refer to as the "executive council." This group is made up of top management staff in the property and

Responsibilities of Managers

Everyone has a boss—including the food and beverage manager. Let's look at the functions that are peformed by the general manager and the food and beverage manager in a hotel:

GENERAL MANAGER

Directs overall marketing, sales, and merchandising programs aimed at developing maximum profitable business volume for rooms, food and beverage, and other sales. Identifies market opportunities. Establishes sales goals and long-range plans consistent with hotel and corporate objectives. Directs internal and external advertising and approves copy and media expenditures within established budget. Maintains favorable media relations to develop and maintain goodwill and favorable attention for the hotel from all publics, including stockholders. Identifies the needs and wants of publics in order to maintain a total service mix that is consistent with the hotel's key markets and maintains the hotel in a leading competitive position. Attends and takes an active part in various functions, meetings, associations, and activities outside the hotel.

FOOD AND BEVERAGE MANAGER
(Manager—Catering, Manager—Dining Rooms)

Supervises and directs banquet sales and customer contact programs aimed at maximizing facilities used for social functions. Plans and develops profitable/innovative a la carte and banquet menus and merchandising programs that meet the needs of customers in every profit center in regard to price and type of service with the objective of optimizing sales and earnings. Conducts an effective inside selling program by maintaining a guest-oriented staff that conveys a total service image, promotes guest awareness, and satisfies all needs and wants of guests. Implements and supervises a reservation system that maximizes seat turnover while providing an atmosphere conducive to fine dining.

consists of at least the general manager, assistant general manager (there are also resident managers in some large properties), and various department heads. Note that in Figure 3.2 there are seven department heads. The food and beverage director is responsible for food service activities in the property. He/she is, however, on the same organizational level as the department heads who are responsible for other functions of the property. Again, if this hotel is part of a large nationwide chain, staff members in Figure 3.2 might technically be referred to as "middle management" rather than as "top management."

Figure 3.3 views top management in a free-standing restaurant. The controller deals with financial aspects of the property while the general

Figure 3.3 Organizational Structure of Top Management in a Restaurant

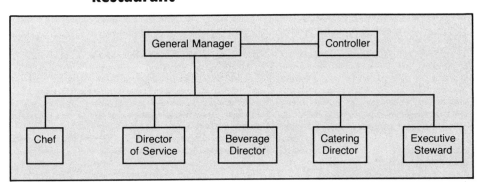

manager has, in effect, five department heads. The chef is concerned about food production and the director of service has front of house responsibilities. ("Front of house" is a food service term that refers to the areas of the property with which guests come in contact, e.g., dining room, lobby, lounge, public restrooms, etc.) The beverage director assumes responsibility for the beverage operation, the catering director manages tasks relating to banquets and other special functions, and the executive steward deals with purchasing and sanitation.

As a final example of top management structure, consider Figure 3.4. You may be surprised to see that, while the names are different, the actual reporting relationships between positions are similar. Traditionally, top level staff in institutional operations are referred to as administrators—not managers—as in most commercial operations. Administrators practice the art of "administration" instead of "management," although the terms mean essentially the same thing.

Intermediate Management Functions

Intermediate managers are those who are in the direct chain of command. They are in key positions through which communication flows up and down the organization, and they are responsible for supervising other staff members. Examples of intermediate managers include assistant department heads and supervisors at various organizational levels.

Supervisory staff are frequently referred to as "linking pins." This means that they link higher management to lower levels of employees and vice versa. They must represent top management to employees and, at the same time, transfer the wishes and concerns of their employees to higher management. Frequently, the supervisory position is the first level of management. Employees who exhibit superior knowledge and skills and who desire promotion to positions with more responsibility often become supervisors. As Figure 3.5 indicates, the role of a supervisor is critical to the success of any food service organization. It is a complex job—certainly not for everyone—but an interesting position to which a competent employee can aspire.

Description of Management Functions

The preceding discussion has focused on intermediate management functions. Now we will turn our attention to personnel who are responsible for management functions.

Figure 3.4 Organizational Structure of Top Management in a Hospital

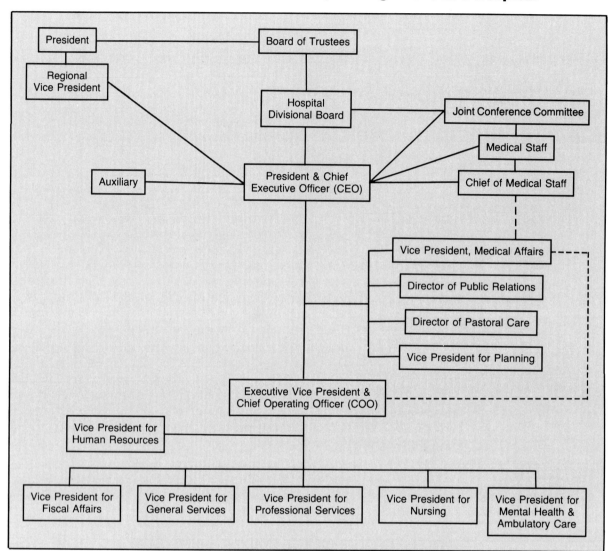

Figure 3.5 Responsibilities of a Supervisor

- Directs the work of employees
- Assists in staff recruitment and selection procedures
- Utilizes principles of work simplification
- Is involved with staff orientation, training, and performance review
- Motivates and communicates well with groups
- Implements necessary work changes
- Disciplines employees effectively
- Manages conflict within the organization
- Generates employee interest and participation in the work which must be done
- Works with unions
- Controls labor costs
- Helps develop and administer wage and salary compensation programs

Figure 3.6 Job Description: Restaurant Manager

I.   Basic Responsibilities

Responsible for meeting all budget goals; for ensuring that quality standards for food and beverage production and service to guests is constantly maintained; for meeting with clients and booking special catered events; for supervising, scheduling, and training the food and beverage controller and assistant manager; for delegating general management tasks to assistant manager; for verifying through analysis of source documents that all income due is collected from food and beverage sales; for designing/improving existing cash security and recordkeeping/accounting systems; supervises department heads in absence of Assistant Restaurant Manager.

II.   Specific Duties

A. Develops, with department head assistance, operating budgets.

B. Monitors budget to control expenses.

C. Serves as restaurant contact for all advertising/marketing activities.

D. Supervises, schedules, and trains Food and Beverage Controller and Assistant Restaurant Manager.

E. Provides required information needed by the controller for payroll, tax, and financial statement purposes.

F. Reviews all operating reports with department heads; conducts regular and ad hoc meetings to correct operating problems.

G. Meets with clients; plans and prices special catered events.

H. Designs and improves restaurant cash security and cash disbursements systems.

I.   Conducts cost reduction/minimization studies.

J. Audits source documents to ensure that all monies due have been collected.

K. Delegates miscellaneous administrative tasks to assistant managers.

L. Serves as restaurant's contact with insurance agent, attorney, banker, and accountant.

M. Works on special problems as assigned by owner.

N. Reviews department reports; makes recommendations and follows up to ensure that all problems have been corrected.

O. Available to provide assistance as needed during periods of busy, peak service business.

III.   Reports to

Owners.

IV.   Supervises

Assistant Restaurant Manager, Food and Beverage Controller; responsible for department heads in absence of the Assistant Restaurant Manager.

V.   Equipment Used

Must be able to operate all equipment in restaurant.

VI.   Working Conditions

Works in all areas of restaurant; long hours, standing and walking are routine components in the job.

VII.   Other

Must know how to operate and do minor maintenance and repair work on all food production and service equipment and building heating, ventilating, air conditioning, plumbing, and electrical systems. Must be tactful and courteous in dealing with the public.

Figures 3.6 and 3.7 show, respectively, job descriptions for a restaurant manager and for a director of dietetic services. They are representative of the tasks which managers must perform and also indicate many of their responsibilities. Taken collectively, they answer the question, "What do managers do?" As the person in charge of operations for the property (whether it be a self-contained restaurant, food and beverage operation in a property, or institutional food service operation), the gen-

Figure 3.7 Job Description: Director of Dietetic Services

I. General Functions

The Director of Dietetic Services designated by Administration will be responsible for managing the total department. He or she will be responsible for maintaining functional relationships between Administration, Nursing Services, other departments and departmental staff of Dietetic Services. He or she will be responsible for implementing and maintaining a system of quality assurance. He or she will be responsible for developing and administering a policy and procedure manual for all Dietetic Services activities. Prepares necessary financial and operational reports as required.

II. Specific Responsibilities

A. Develops departmental regulations in conformance with administrative policies and procedures and sets standards for the organization and supervision of Dietetic Services.

B. Meets at least weekly with Assistant Directors of Dietetic Services to determine standardization and management effectiveness.

C. Develops and administers a training program for management and supervisory personnel.

D. Develops policies and procedures governing the handling and storage of food supplies and equipment.

E. Maintains financial records as required by Administration (monthly cost report).

F. Meets with staff to review progress and make future plans for Dietetic Services.

G. Monitors daily operations to ensure quality food service to patients, employees, and visitors.

H. Maintains safety and sanitation standards to ensure compliance with all regulatory agencies.

I. Prepares realistic budgets for each cost center. Monitors the budget for conformance. Takes necessary action when there is a deviation from the budget.

J. Reviews and evaluates the performance of supervisory staff.

K. Administers the preparation of job descriptions, scheduling manuals, and guide books covering all phases of the Dietetic Services operations.

L. Attends professional meetings and conferences to keep informed of current ideas and trends in the field of hospital food services.

M. Performs other related duties as requested by the Vice President of General Services.

III. Education

Director of Dietetic Services must have a minimum of a Bachelor of Science degree in Food Service Management, Nutrition, or Business Administration. A Masters degree is preferred.

IV. Experience

Director of Dietetic Services must have at least a minimum of five years experience in all phases of hospital food service preparation and administration.

Courtesy of St. Lawrence Hospital, Lansing, Michigan.

eral manager is basically responsible to a higher level manager or to the board of directors for all aspects of the operation of the food service program. Much of this work involves planning exactly how to attain organizational goals, developing procedures to implement the plans, and then evaluating the extent to which goals have been attained. Various properties, of course, delegate differing levels of responsibility to general managers. However, the ultimate success or failure of the property rests with the abilities of top level management and management staff. Management staff functions refer to personnel who serve in an advisory or special assistance capacity to intermediate line managers. Common examples of staff management functions in food service operations include:

Purchasing. This department helps the food service operation by working with line (user) departments to develop food purchase specifications and purchasing procedures. It also selects suppliers and otherwise ensures that the best product is purchased at the right time, in the right quantity, and at the right price.

Personnel. Large food service operations often have a department where staff specialists recruit applicants for vacant positions, conduct preliminary employee selection activities, and make recommendations to user department staff. The final selection decision rests with the line (user) department—not with the personnel department.

Accounting. The controller and his/her staff of accountants are frequently responsible to the unit manager, but sometimes to area or regional managers above the level of the general manager. They develop and help interpret financial statements so that top line management staff can make effective decisions. In many lodging operations, the accounting department is responsible for food and beverage receiving and storage activities. Large commercial properties frequently have a food and beverage controller working under the direction of the property's controller. These staff specialists help design precosting systems, determine menu selling prices, audit guest checks and data machine sales register tapes and, in general, develop specialized records and reports for use by top management.

Other Staff Specialists. While not at the unit level, large chains frequently have staffs of attorneys, real estate specialists, construction experts, etc., to assist in their continuous expansion efforts. As already noted, many institutional food service operations have staff dietitians and/or nutritionists who help design menus to ensure that nutritional requirements are met. For-profit management companies have chefs, data processing specialists, and other trained personnel who provide specialized assistance to individual units called "accounts" or "clients."

From the discussion so far in this chapter, it is obvious that it takes a great deal of skill and knowledge—along with a very positive attitude—to effectively manage a food service operation. Organizational goals cannot be achieved without the assistance of other personnel within the food and beverage operation.

Back of House Positions

Let's take a look at some of these positions by reviewing the functions and activities which may be performed by employees.

Kitchen-Related Positions. Common positions include (a) chef, (b) cook, (c) assistant cook, (d) kitchen assistant, and (e) pantry-service assistant.

Chef. In addition to performing managerial duties, the chef plans menus with the restaurant manager; is responsible for recipe standardization and overall food quality; assists in development of food purchase specifications; prepares daily entrees; conducts studies resulting in "make or buy" and other decisions; oversees planning for and conduct of special events; develops procedures for food production; and performs miscellaneous production tasks.

Cook. Under the direction of chef in charge, the cook prepares and cooks soups, sauces, and all food items to be sauteed, baked, poached, steamed, braised, roasted, grilled, broiled, or fried; carves and cuts meats; and prepares cold meat and seafood salad plates, cold sandwiches, hors d'oeuvres, and canapes; and opens oysters and clams.

Assistant cook. The assistant cook helps cooks or chef in the preparation of foods for cooking; trims, peels, cleans, grinds, shapes, mixes, or portions foods preparatory to cooking; may do simple cooking under instruction or guidance of cooks or chefs.

Kitchen assistant. Under the direction of kitchen supervision, this person prepares all raw vegetables, salads, sandwiches, appetizers, desserts, and dressings; steams, broils, fries, sautes, and bakes raw vegetables; prepares soups.

Pantry-service assistant. Under the direction of kitchen supervision, the pantry-service assistant supplies dining room and banquet pantries, soda shop, and cafeteria with necessary items, such as food, utensils, china, glassware, silver, and related operating supplies; prepares beverages and assists in serving food when required.

Steward Positions. These sanitation-based positions include (a) chief steward, (b) service operator—specialist, (c) service operator—general, and (d) service operator.

Chief steward. Under the guidance of kitchen supervision, the chief steward directs the activities of a shift of service crew employees.

Service operator—specialist. This person performs nonroutine and special cleaning in hotel food areas in order to maintain a high level of cleanliness and sanitation.

Service operator—general. Under the direction of kitchen supervision, this person scrapes, washes, and stores pots, pans, and steam kettles; performs janitorial and special cleaning tasks in food and beverage areas.

Service operator. Under the direction of kitchen supervision, the service operator cleans and stores china, glass, silver, and related equipment according to hotel sanitation policies.

Storeroom Positions. Common positions include (a) hotel stores helper and (b) stores and receiving clerk.

Hotel stores helper. This person assists in storing, checking, and dispensing food and related items in the storeroom.

Stores and receiving clerk. Under the direction of supervisor-stores, this staff member verifies that the quality, size, and quantity meet specifications and that the price reflects the items ordered and billed.

Bake Shop Positions. Common positions include (a) senior baker, (b) baker, and (c) baker's assistant.

Senior baker. Under the guidance of chef in charge, the senior baker specializes in all phases of bakery preparation and must be able to bake any variety of bakery products following recipes.

Baker. Under the guidance of chef in charge, the baker prepares less complex bakery products such as bread, rolls, pies, and plain cakes; may be called upon to produce more complex bakery products.

Baker's assistant. Under the direction of chef in charge, the assistant helps in the preparation of bakery products such as bread, rolls, pies, and cakes.

Front of House Positions

Functions and activities performed by personnel in front of house positions can be separated by dining room and cafeteria operations.

Dining room captain. The dining room captain reports on duty a half-hour earlier than food servers; is informed by the manager or assistant manager of special activities and business expectations; checks all phases of table preparation, side stands, supplies, wine buckets, trolleys (flaming, Caesar), linen, etc.; completes *mise en place* (a French term meaning to put everything in place); discusses all pertinent information, special features, special visitors, expected business load, soup of the day, what to sell, wines, etc., with assigned staff.

In addition, this person greets and helps seat guests; may present menus and take orders; dispatches orders taken through food servers either to the bar or kitchen; serves wines, prepares for and does tableside preparation, checks and constantly surveys table supplies; helps serve the main course; prepares flaming desserts, offers after-dinner drinks, coffee, espresso; upon request, presents check, tells guests goodbye and asks them to return.

Food server. Under the direction of dining area supervision, this person serves food and beverages to guests at tables.

Assistant food server. Under the direction of food server and dining area supervision, this person sets up tables with proper appointments, removes dirty dishes and waste from tables, and transports them to cleaning areas.

Bartender. Under the direction of dining area supervision, the bartender mixes and serves drinks to guests at bar or tables and issues mixed drinks and wine upon food server's request.

Service bartender. Under the direction of dining area supervision, this person mixes drinks and issues wine for service to the guest upon food server's request.

Beverage server. Under the direction of dining area supervisor, this employee serves beverage and food items to guests in lounge areas.

Cafeteria assistant. Under the direction of related area supervision, the assistant prepares and supplies food for cafeteria stations, and participates in food service when needed; transports dirty dishes from tables to cleaning area; maintains cleanliness of work station, and reports unsafe equipment to supervision.

Cashier/checker. Under the direction of related area supervision, this person checks and totals the price of food on customer's tray and receives payment for it.

Sample Organization Charts

As you learned earlier in this chapter, an organization chart shows relationships between various positions in an operation. This chapter concludes with a review of sample organization charts for typical food service operations in both commercial and institutional settings. They will help you:

- understand where each position fits into the overall organization of different types of operations.

- note the similarity between various types of operations.

Obviously, as a food service operation becomes larger, more employees are needed. It is also necessary to make the work more specialized so additional job positions are needed. When this occurs, it is more difficult (and vital) to ensure that the many activities of management are carried out.

Organization of Small Restaurant

Figure 3.8 shows how simple the organization of a small food service operation can be. Let's suppose that the restaurant manager is the owner. The cook, bartender, and host/hostess (or cashier) may report directly to this official. Then a third level of the organization is formed; it consists of assistant cooks and dishwashers (supervised by the cook), beverage servers (supervised by the bartender), and food servers (supervised by the host/hostess or cashier). Of course, every operation is different. The restaurant manager could prefer a "flat" organization; perhaps every person—regardless of what position he/she occupies—is supervised directly by the restaurant manager. On the other hand, a small property may have a fourth organizational level (food servers supervise bus persons or assistant cooks supervise preparation assistants). You will want to remember this simple organization when details of management principles are reviewed in Chapter 4.

Figure 3.8 Organization Chart for a Small Restaurant

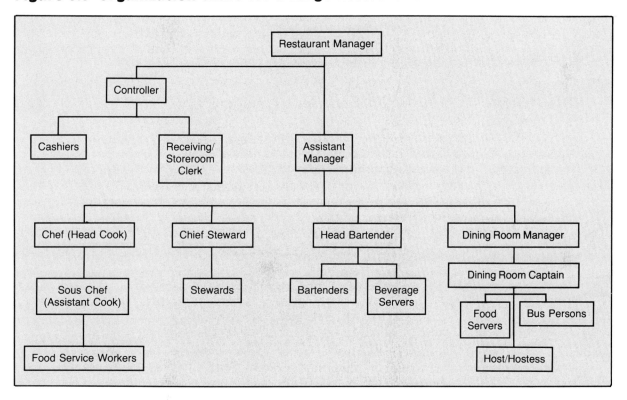

Figure 3.9 Organization Chart for a Large Restaurant

**Organization
of Large
Restaurant**

Figure 3.9 shows a possible organization chart for a large food service operation. In this example, the restaurant manager immediately
supervises two positions: the controller (who is responsible for cashiers
and a clerk) and the assistant manager (who is responsible for four department heads).

The department head positions involve food production (chef/head
cook), purchasing and sanitation (chief steward), beverage production
(head bartender), and front of house (dining room manager). Each of
these department heads also supervises employees and, in some cases,
fourth-level personnel (sous chef/assistant cook) supervise food service

workers. In contrast to Figure 3.8, a greater amount of direction and communication are necessary in the large operation. The same needs—to produce food and beverages, to serve products, and to purchase and clean up—are necessary in both operations. It is only the degree of specialization which falls within each position that makes the difference between the organizational structures of the small and large properties.

Organization of Food and Beverage Department in a Small Hotel

Figure 3.10 shows the relationship between each department in a small hotel and the relationship between positions within the food and beverage department.

Note that the boss of the food and beverage director is the general manager and that he/she supervises an assistant food and beverage director who, in turn, directs the work of a bar supervisor (beverage), kitchen supervisor (food), and a dining room supervisor (service). The other department heads (executive housekeeper, maintenance chief, front office supervisor, and sales director) are on an equal organizational level with the food and beverage director. (The department heads, along with the general manager, comprise the executive council of top-level managers within the property.)

Organization of Food and Beverage Department in a Large Hotel

Figure 3.11 shows the organization of a food and beverage department in a large hotel. While it appears complex, note that banquets, beverage operations, dining room outlets (restaurants), sanitation (steward), and food production are just as necessary to a large operation as they are to a small operation. A major difference is that, as the operation becomes larger, personnel with specialized skills are needed. Also, the large property probably has a purchasing department; this task is not the chief steward's responsibility.

Organization of Food and Beverage Department for a Country Club

As illustrated in Figure 3.12, major organizational differences occur at the top; the members "run" the club. They elect a board of directors, who appoint an executive committee; this commitee hires and supervises the club's general manager. The assistant manager of the food and beverage department directly supervises the manager of any specialty food and beverage outlet (such as a "19th hole" snack bar/lounge), the executive chef, executive steward, dining room manager, reservations (banquet) manager, and the bar manager. Within the food and beverage department itself, the positions and reporting relationships do not differ greatly from the food and beverage department in a large hotel or restaurant.

Organization of University/ College Food Services

Figure 3.13 focuses attention upon the food service operation in one residence hall of a university/college. In this operation, the unit (residence hall) manager is the food service manager's boss. The latter official directly supervises personnel with responsibilities for production, service, and student employees. The coordinator of food services for the university is in a staff (advisory) relationship to the area manager. By contrast, in many university food service organizations, the unit manager is directly responsible to the coordinator of food services. There are

Figure 3.10 Organization Chart for a 200-Room Hotel

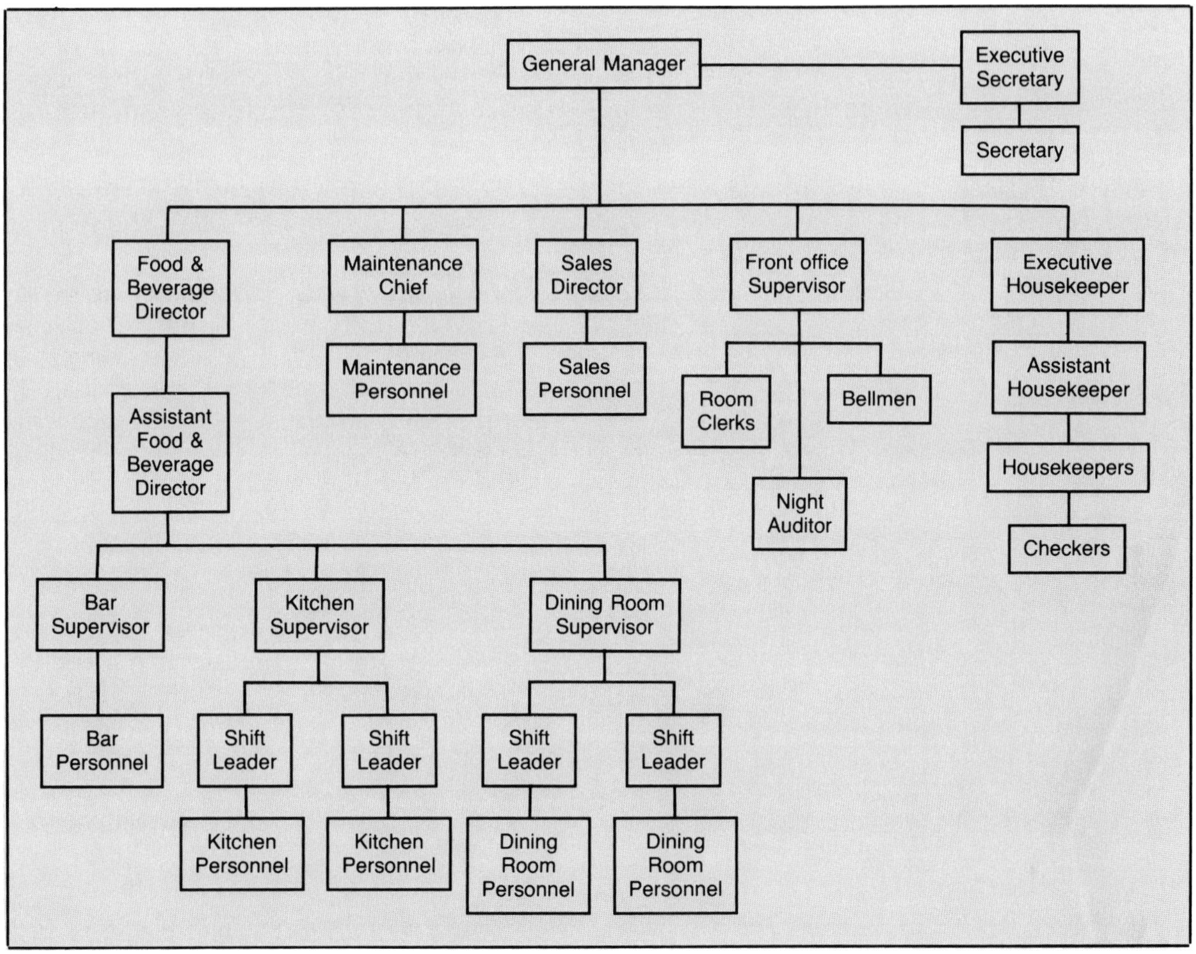

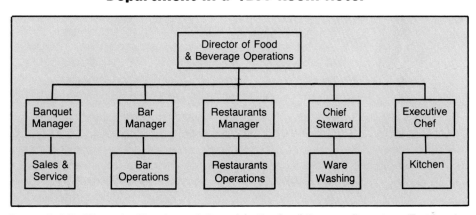

Courtesy of Mississippi Management, Inc., Jackson, Mississippi.

**Figure 3.11 Organization Chart of Food and Beverage
Department in a 1200-Room Hotel**

Source: Jack D. Ninemeier, Planning and Control for Food and Beverage Operations *(East Lansing, Mich.: Educational Institute of the American Hotel & Motel Association, 1982), p. 8.*

Figure 3.12 Organization Chart for a Country Club

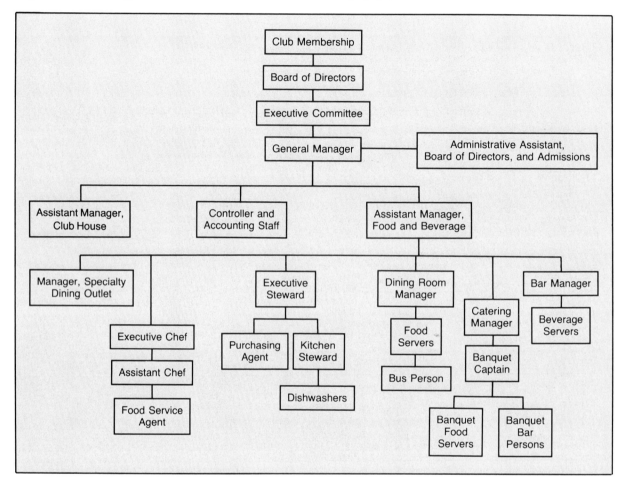

many units; each is supported by an area manager and central university administrative personnel as well. A smaller college structure might combine activities such as menu planning, purchasing, and coordinating efforts with other departments into the position of unit manager. He/she might be concerned with these planning and external responsibilities as well as with the day-to-day operation of food services within the residence hall.

Organization of Hospital Dietary Services

Figure 3.14 shows the organization of a typical hospital dietetic services department. Note that one assistant director essentially coordinates back of house production and related staff and supervises personnel working on the cafeteria line. A second assistant director is involved with the service of food to patients (assembling patient trays, reconstituting food in galleys, and transporting food to patients) and also coordinates the therapeutic work performed by dietitians. In some health care facilities, the service of food to patients is done by nursing staff or by personnel responsible to nursing staff (not dietary services).

Figure 3.13 Organization Chart for University/College Food Services

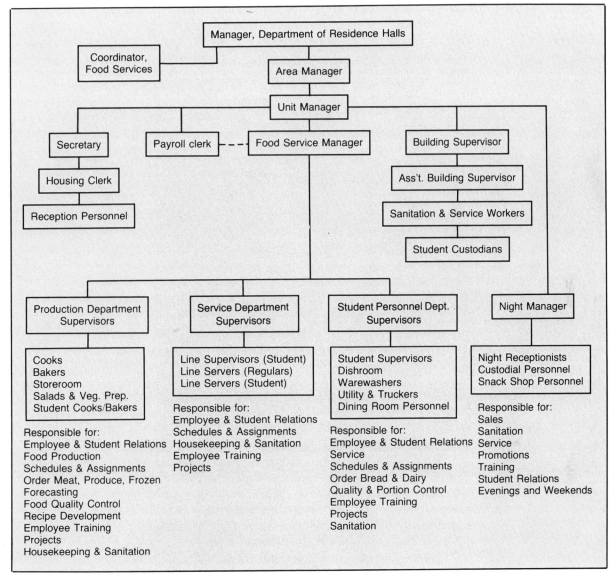

Courtesy of Michigan State University, East Lansing, Michigan.

Career Paths in Food Service

Where do you begin and how do you advance within the food service industry? There are many possible career paths. Everyone has different interests, knowledge, and abilities and, therefore, differing aspirations and opportunities to advance "up the organizational ladder."

Still, some idea about "Where do I go next?" can serve as a base for planning and decision-making. You can trace a career of increasing responsibility by reviewing an organization chart; job requirements be-

Figure 3.14 Organization Chart for Hospital Dietary Services

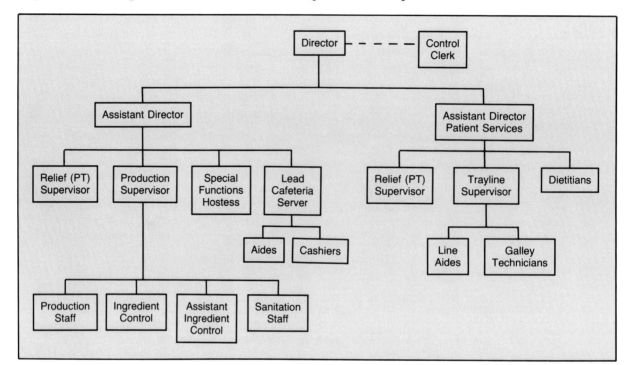

come greater, work tasks are more difficult and challenging, pay and benefits increase, etc., as positions at higher organizational levels are attained. If you are currently employed, look at your operation's organization chart for long- and short-run advancement opportunities.

It is also possible to view career progression from an industry-wide rather than an organizational perspective. While there is no established, industry-approved advancement route, a typical career progression is shown in Figure 3.15. Where you actually go depends upon (1) what you want to do, (2) where you are now, (3) opportunities which evolve, and (4) your skills, abilities, attitudes, and interests.

As you advance beyond entry-level positions, the need for interpersonal skills—the ability to get along with people—becomes more important. This is discussed at length elsewhere in the chapter. However, you should know that in the "people" business of food services, the ability to work with and through others will get you to the top much more quickly than concentrating on performing technical skills.

One suggestion is to obtain experience in the industry while you are a student. Not only will you learn things which can be useful later, but also:

● you will be able to bring experiences to class that will help put facts in perspective.

● you will make contacts with people who can help you with employment after graduation.

Figure 3.15 Typical Career Progression in the Food Service Industry

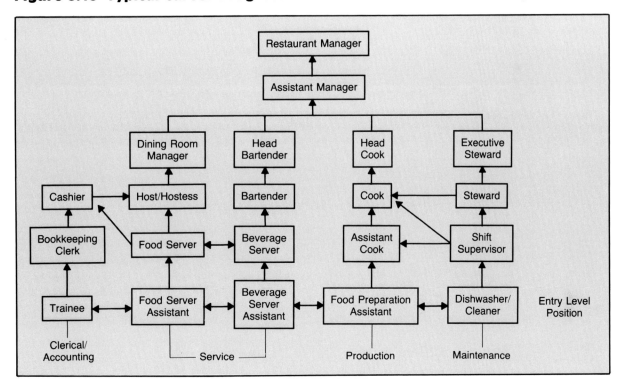

- you will be showing that you are interested in the food service industry.

Developing and Maintaining Relationships with People

You have learned that food service is a people business and that you must know how to get along with each of the publics influencing the food service operation: the owner, manager, personnel in other departments within the organization, and external publics including the customer, suppliers, the community, and, often, government regulatory agencies.

In some ways, recognizing the need to relate to others is just common sense. The ability to effectively interact with people is part of the art of managing a food service operation. You have heard the phrase "born leaders" and this suggests that some people are just naturally able to get along with others. Knowing the basic techniques of relating to others will help you develop and maintain good relationships with people. Let's look at some of these techniques.

Getting Along with Others

Most people want to get along with others; few people want to be disliked. Therefore, when you begin a new relationship with a customer, supervisor, fellow employee, etc., you can be pretty confident that both you and the other party want the relationship to evolve into a pleasant one.

You should also be aware that dealing with people—not lack of technical skills—is the biggest problem most people face. In other words, you are not the only one who can benefit from developing better skills in interacting with people. All of us can. Requirements to do this include the need for a pleasant personality—one that does not offend—and, of course, the ability to communicate.

It is true that many aspects of our personality are established early in life. Let's take a look, however, at some techniques which, over time and with practice, can be built into our personality.

One of the most basic rules which you should learn deals with the problems caused by criticism. People do not categorize themselves as being bad or think that they have a bad attitude and do bad things (recall our discussion in Chapter 1 that people act at any time to help satisfy their basic wants and needs). The words which were spoken or the actions which were taken by someone whom you later wish to criticize were, at the time, best for the person who has offended you. Think about your reactions when someone criticizes you; you become defensive, resentful, and have a need to justify your words and actions. Rather than criticizing another person, a more effective approach is to try to understand why the person has done or said a certain thing. You can do this by looking at the situation from their perspective, recalling that they will react in a way which they think is best (coming close to meeting their wants and needs) for them. A basic rule of getting along with people is to be careful with negative criticism, it seldom does any good!

Satisfying Wants and Needs

Let's look further at what we, as humans, want since we realize that people attempt to satisfy these wants and needs through their words and actions. A list of what most normal people want would include the following:[1]

1. health and preservation of life

2. food

3. sleep

4. money and things that it will buy

5. eternal life

6. sexual gratification

7. the well-being of our children

8. a feeling of importance

Think about yourself for a moment. Are these among the things that you want? Aren't your concerns about these things pretty much the same as those of other people? Wouldn't you address these concerns in your words and actions?

Of the items in the above list, we will focus on a person's need to be and feel important. Attending to the customer, showing genuine concern for the customer, being courteous to your boss and to your peers, etc., are examples of ways that you can recognize the importance and human dignity of individuals, show appreciation for what they do for you, and, above all, be interested in them. Consider the customer that has just spilled a beverage in the dining room. What is the difference between the food server who walks up and says "Here's a towel" and another food server who rushes up and makes a genuine attempt to help the customer because he/she wants to minimize the negative effect that the event will have on the customer's dining experience?

You can tell when another person is sincere and when he/she is being superficial. Consider the person who says "How are you?" with no genuine feeling; it is almost the same as "Hello" when you compare it to the next person who really is asking the question out of concern.

Increasing Interpersonal Skills

Let's look at some more techniques which you can use to increase your interpersonal skills. First of all, do things and talk about things that the other person desires—not what you desire. What is your reaction to a person who consistently talks about himself/herself and wants others to do only what he/she wants to do? Your reaction probably is to avoid the person and this can happen to you if you use this approach.

Another technique that will be very useful in your relationship with customers is to look at things from the other person's point of view. In Chapter 1, we noted a variety of reasons why a customer may visit your food service operation. Try to consider the experience from the customer's perspective. What would you like and how would you like to be treated if you were in the situation? The answer to that question can be helpful in formulating your reactions to the customer. Remember that people tend to do things because they—not others—want to do them. The secret here is to make the other person want something. The food server who tells a customer how *really* good something is and the food service employee who shows genuine concern for the customer will, respectively, encourage the customer to want to order the menu item and to return to the property.

Many techniques for getting along with people are built into the definition of hospitality. You must want to help people, to greet them in a friendly manner, and to smile and be friendly. People love to hear their name, so use it! The ability to listen and to encourage others to talk about themselves can be used in both the front and the back of the house. When you do speak, consider talking in terms of the other person's interests: do things to make the other person feel important.

A few final techniques can help you begin the task of improving your interpersonal skills:

- avoid arguments

- respect the other person

- don't tell the other person that he/she is wrong too bluntly; find something good in the argument being made

- admit when you are wrong

- when new ideas are being developed, let the other person think that the idea is his/her own

- don't talk too much

- look at things from the other person's perspective

- respect the other person's opinion

- use praise generously; use criticism sparingly

Of all the techniques noted in this section, those concerning the need to look at the situation from the other person's perspective and of having a genuine concern and respect for the other person are among the most important. These concepts can form the structure for a new approach which you can use in interacting with people. Give it a try; practice and evaluate the situation so that you can continually modify your approach in dealing with people. You will be surprised at how much you can accomplish, how easy it will be, and how much better you will feel as a result.

NOTES

1. Dale Carnegie, *How to Win Friends and Influence People* (New York: Pocket Books, 1964).

4

Challenges of Food Service Management

Management Challenges

As a result of studying this chapter you will:

1. know what kinds of resources are available for the food service manager to attain objectives.

2. understand that the management process is complex and made up of several distinct subsystems which are applicable to all food service operations.

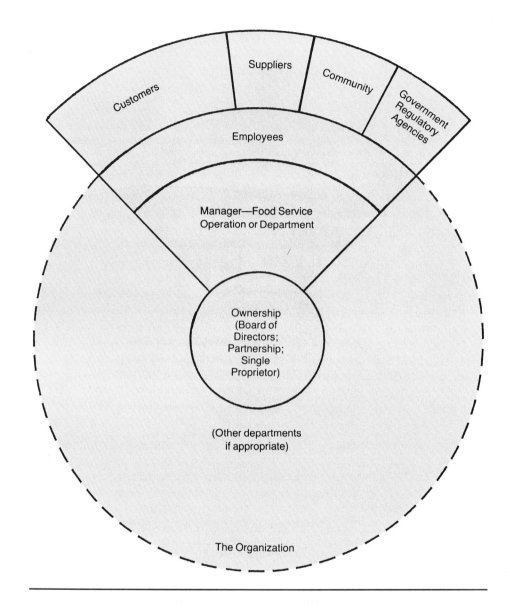

Customers

Suppliers

Community

Government Regulatory Agencies

Employees

Manager—Food Service Operation or Department

Ownership (Board of Directors; Partnership; Single Proprietor)

(Other departments if appropriate)

The Organization

Focus on the Food Service Publics

Chapter 4 analyzes the broad, complex system of management. The process can be modified as necessary to fit the needs of a specific operation. However, it is critical to the success of the entire food service operation, and the relationship between each of the publics is also affected by the topic of this chapter. Stated simply, the job of management is to first assess the customers' wants and needs, and then to plan, organize, coordinate, staff, direct, control, and evaluate to ensure that the customers' desires are met within the framework of organizational limitations and goals. In so doing, the management staff makes decisions which affect all of the operation's internal and external publics. Information in this chapter is crucial to the success of a food service operation.

You may have been surprised to learn in previous chapters that there are really more similarities than differences in the way that commercial and institutional food service operations are organized. In this chapter, you will learn that the same thing applies to the way that food service operations are managed at their most basic level. Regardless of whether the food service operation is trying to make a profit or to keep within measured expense levels while attaining dietary goals, the basic procedures for managing the operation are similar. The general principles of management are the same whether you are concerned about managing a commercial or institutional food service program, retail clothing store, barber shop, gasoline station, or any other type of business enterprise. There are some obvious differences; for example, the products which are managed in the above examples (food and beverages, clothing, gasoline). Still, given the context in which we will discuss management in this chapter, you will see that the similarities outweigh the differences.

What Is Management?

You are learning how a food service operation is managed. What, then, is management? Simply stated, the management process that you are studying really involves using what you've got, to do what you want to do. What you have as you manage a food service (or any other) operation are resources; what you want to do is attain organizational objectives.

There are seven basic types of resources that are available to a food service manager as he/she attempts to achieve organizational objectives.

1. People

2. Money

3. Time

4. Procedures

5. Energy

6. Materials

7. Equipment

All resources are in limited supply; you will never have enough material (food and beverage products), money, time, etc., to do everything that you would like. Your job, as manager of a food service operation, is to determine how best to use the limited resources that are available to achieve organizational goals.

How do you do this? You do it by making decisions—the food service manager is a decision-maker! In this context, a "good" food service manager is one who can make the right decision when solving important problems (those which are most critical to attaining the goals of the food service operation). A "bad" food service manager is one who is unable to make the correct decision about the most important problems facing the organization.

You will note that we have referred to food service goals/objectives several times. Goals are important: they need to be considered, agreed upon, written down, and used as a base or foundation when management decisions are made and when systems and procedures are determined, implemented, and evaluated. As you read this book, you will find many more times when food service goals must be considered as an integral part of the management process.

The Management Process

The process by which food service operations are managed can often best be discussed by separating the entire process or system into individual components. These can be viewed as subsystems, tasks, activities, and/or functions. You must be involved in several different types of activities when you manage the food service operation. It is the purpose of this chapter to discuss, in some detail, each of these activities.

Figure 4.1 illustrates each of the basic management tasks and shows how they relate to each other. As you will see, the management process begins with planning; it is necessary to develop long- and short-range strategies to meet goals. Organizing and coordinating must be carried out to develop channels of delegation and communication so that all parts of the organization work together. Staffing activities include selecting, training, and maintaining the best possible people for the job. You must direct and supervise employees and, at the same time, know when and how to take any necessary corrective action to "keep on the course" of attaining organizational goals. Finally, you should evaluate the extent to which organizational goals have been met. To the extent they have not been met, revisions and plans are necessary; if initial goals have been met, others can be established. The management process then becomes cyclical and is repeated as the organization grows and evolves. Don't be concerned if the process just described seems complicated. Part of the difficulty occurs when you attempt to understand the management process without considering in more detail each of the activities just described. The following sections of this chapter will focus on each activity. At the end of the chapter we will "put it all together" to show how food and beverage managers can use basic management principles in their operations.

Figure 4.1 Overview of Management Process

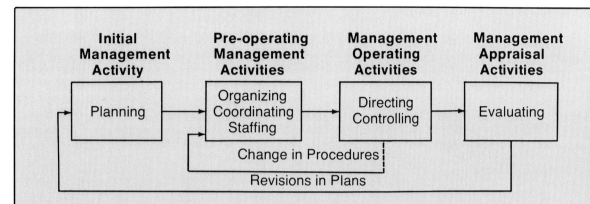

1. The desire to attain objectives leads to organizing, coordinating, and staffing activities.

2. Once personnel are selected, management can implement directing activities and develop control systems. Putting these responsibilities into action during ongoing operations is crucial. The manager finds out if plans and pre-operating activities succeeded or failed.

3. Management must evaluate the effectiveness of action taken to bring actual operating results within tolerable limits of standard plans. Appraisal may lead to changes in organizing, coordinating, and staffing.

4. The evaluation of the entire planning and management process may show that revisions are required in broad plans which, of course, affects the planning task.

Source: Jack D. Ninemeier, Planning and Control for Food and Beverage Operations *(East Lansing, Mich.: Educational Institute of the American Hotel & Motel Association, 1982), p. 16.*

Planning

Planning must occur at every management level in the food service operation. For example, at the highest levels in the organization, strategic planning is undertaken to develop long-range plans in order to attain long-range goals. At intermediate management levels, operational plans are developed to attain short-range goals. At lower management levels, routine planning is undertaken in the day-to-day process of managing the operation.

Let's look at an example of a multi-unit (chain) company. At top management levels, the board of directors, chairman of the board, and chief executive officer are attempting to establish goals which will not be attained for several—perhaps five or more—years. Where does the organization want to be at that time? What will be the requirements of the investors? What will be the state of the economy? What markets will the company be attempting to reach and how will it reach them?

These and related concerns are being addressed by top level management while intermediate levels of management (for example, the unit general manager) focus on meeting this year's budget and on economic planning for the coming year. The department heads are looking at their specific responsibilities in terms of current and future budgets as well as working with lower levels of management to solve operating problems. At lower levels of management, supervisors might be planning next week's labor schedule, costing tomorrow's banquet, making routine decisions about short-range problems, or setting goals which they think can be met within a short time period.

Planning is important because it not only establishes where you want to go, it also tells you how to get there. Every manager—regardless of his/her position or type of company—must plan.

Normally, planning is a formal process. You should not plan just "when you get around to it." Time should be set aside for personnel at each organizational level to establish goals, discuss how to attain them, and to revise goals if necessary. As we have already noted, objectives must be established before plans can be developed. Objectives indicate what you want to do; plans tell how you propose to attain objectives.

Plan First. As noted in Figure 4.1, planning is necessary before other management tasks can be performed. This principle applies at all levels within the organization. Often, you may get into a routine and feel comfortable doing things in certain ways. As this occurs, you believe that there is less time available for long-range planning. Lack of planning can lead to emergencies and, in effect, you become a "fire fighter." You are too busy resolving unexpected problems (which could have been avoided through effective planning) to have time to plan.

Past and Future. Obviously, you must have some idea about the future as you make plans. What has happened in the past can often serve as a predictor for the future. For example, when you develop operating budgets, you use the numbers from previous years as a base. Likewise, when you establish goals, you must look into the future to ensure that objectives—and plans to attain them—are reasonable.

Communication. You must, of course, have access to complete information. If you do not, it is likely that the plans which are developed will be inadequate. This emphasizes the need for all levels of management to communicate with each other. While this is easily said, there is a tendency for individual departments to consider their own concerns and goals rather than those of the entire operation.

Managers must contribute to plans which affect their employees' work. If, for example, the food and beverage director in a hotel is developing an operating budget for his/her areas of responsibility, it would be wise to get information from the chef and beverage manager before plans are finalized. Staff members are more likely to help attain plans when they have been able to formulate them. This makes them "our plans," not "their plans."

Flexibility. Planning should be flexible since no one knows exactly what the future will bring. Some food service managers take a reasonable amount of time to develop plans and then, because of the time invested, become unwilling to make changes even though conditions warrant it. One obvious example is the operating budget. What if the budget is developed with a specified level of sales income, and actual income is less? What do managers do about this? How do they attempt to control costs and generate increased business at the same time? The ability to be flexible when plans are developed and implemented is critical to your success as a food service manager.

Planning from the Top. Planning for food service operations must start at the top of the organization. Imagine the difficulties which would occur if the unit manager let his/her department heads decide what they are going to do entirely on their own. Or what about the chief executive officer who delegates all of the planning authority to presidents of autonomous companies? When planning begins at the top of the organization, for example, a board of directors formulates long-range plans and lower levels of management contribute ideas about how they fit into these plans. While a participative approach is developed, the initial focus of planning—and certainly the ultimate decisions about courses of action—must rest with top management. As a result of establishing a definite course of action, staff members at all organizational levels know what they are going to do and are assured that their short-range plans adequately fit into the long-range plans that have been developed.

Limitations. Plans must consider limiting factors. External factors which limit the planning process would be a closed room due to remodeling, street improvement projects which deny access, high unemployment rates in a community, etc. These factors must be considered as plans are developed.

Implementation. Obviously, plans must be implemented, but there are food service managers who violate this principle. Plans may be neatly laid out on paper and staff meetings held; however, for whatever reason, the plans are not implemented. Not only is this a waste of limited organizational resources, but it is very frustrating for affected staff members who have provided input and anticipate organizational changes.

Importance of Planning. The above discussion has illustrated some of the basic management principles which are important in planning. You may work in or know about operations where the planning process is inadequate or even faulty. In these cases, it is unlikely that goals will be met. Even worse is the food service facility that ceases operation because of poor planning (this can happen to institutional food services as well as those in the commercial segment of the industry).

You should now realize the importance of planning and understand that managers at all organizational levels must plan as an important part of their job. Many failures to attain organizational goals can be traced to a lack of effective planning. As noted above, this applies to food service operations as well as to other businesses.

Organizing   You learned how a food service operation is organized in Chapter 3. As suggested, you must ask and answer the question, "How can we best assemble and make use of our limited resources as we strive to attain goals?" The answer to that question depends on how your operation is organized. It is absolutely critical, of course, that each part of the food service operation contributes to objectives. While this is easily stated, it is often more difficult to accomplish. For example, when ineffective recordkeeping and accounting systems are in use, it may not be obvious that the food operation, room service, or some other activity is actually losing money. Even if this is acceptable, the point is that it should be known. Once problems are identified, you can attempt to control them. There is no manager that would purposely make a decision which hinders the attainment of goals; you must know what is going on to ensure that this doesn't happen inadvertently.

When the organizational structure is developed, it is important to consider the number of employees that one supervisor manages. Normally, it is not possible for one person to directly supervise 20 or 30 staff members. As the size and complexity of the operation increases, so must the number of positions and organizational levels.

Authority and power should flow in an unbroken line from the top to the bottom of the organization. Since the organization has been developed to most effectively attain goals, the power to make decisions about how to use resources must be available at all levels. For example, it is very bad for a supervisor to have responsibility for something, but not have the power to do what is necessary to get it done. The supervisor should not need to go to higher management levels to get approval for things that he/she must do as part of the ongoing job.

Each employee should have only one supervisor. If an employee has two bosses, what should he/she do when both give different instructions at the same time? The activities to be performed should be considered when departments are structured within the food service operation. For example, in the organization charts shown in Chapter 3, food production responsibilities are grouped into a food department, beverage responsibilities are listed together, and catering (special functions) duties are classified in a unit.

When departments are organized, it is generally not a good idea to have each one be responsible for policing itself. For example, the food and beverage controller (part of the accounting department)—not the food and beverage director—should be responsible for assessing the extent to which the department has met its economic goals.

You should recognize the difference between line (decision-making) and staff (advisory) positions; the relationship between these two concepts must be understood as organization charts are developed. You should also realize that relationships between departments in the organization are important. What happens, for example, when the dining room manager wants clean table linens by a specified time and this causes problems with the laundry (housekeeping) department? Or what happens in a restaurant when there are free appetizers during cocktail hour in the lounge? (Do food preparation personnel have time to prepare these items in addition to their other work?)

A final principle that should be stressed is that the structure of an organization evolves throughout the life of a business. There are many food service operations today which have organization charts buried in an employee handbook that do not reflect current operating procedures at all. For example, an organization chart can indicate that the cook's supervisor is a chef when, in fact, the food and beverage director has assumed the responsibility for directing this employee's work.

By now, you should realize that the management activity of organizing is much more than developing an organization chart and then forgetting about it. An organization chart must give an accurate and current picture of how the resources of the organization are brought together to attain objectives.

Coordinating

In order to consider the management activity of coordinating, you must understand how the process of delegation works. Delegation, itself, means that power can be "passed down" the organization. However, responsibility—having to account for the use of power—cannot be delegated. Perhaps a simple example will clarify this. The food and beverage department head may be responsible to the property's general manager for all aspects of the food and beverage operating budget. The department head may delegate the authority to make decisions about how the beverage operation should work to the beverage manager, but he/she is still responsible to the general manager for meeting budget goals. Authority can—and should—be passed down the organization to the lowest point possible; however, the responsibility still rests with the individual identified in the organizational plan.

Somebody must be responsible for every action that is taken. Contrast this principle with the common activity of "passing the buck" and "getting the runaround" when a decision must be made.

In many ways, the management activity of coordinating is the same as the process of communication. There must be effective channels of communication to transmit messages up and down the organizational structure. It is also necessary that peers (those at the same organizational level) effectively communicate with each other. Department heads need to interact with each other as much as supervisors in the same or different departments. You have probably heard the phrase "interdepartmental cooperation." This refers to the need for activities to be coordinated between all affected segments of the organization. Each department should help the organization meet its goals; however, frequently decision-makers put their departments first.

In a labor intensive operation such as food services, there are bound to be informal employee groups who formulate common goals and who meet because of common interests which may or may not be in harmony with those of the organization. Instead of ignoring these groups, you should first recognize that they exist and then use them to help further the goals of the organization. While this is easy to say, it is more difficult to do. We will discuss this further when principles of directing (supervising) are reviewed later.

At this point in the management process, you should know:

- objectives to be met.

- plans and strategies to attain objectives.

- how limited resources can best be put together to attain goals.

- how power and responsibility are spread throughout the organization.

- how communication should flow through formal organizational channels.

Now we will focus on personnel aspects of the food service operation.

Staffing

The process of staffing involves recruiting applicants and making selection decisions. The goal of staffing is to bring the very best qualified employees into the food service operation. In order to do this, jobs must be defined in terms of the tasks to be performed. In Chapter 3, we advocated the use of a job description to list required tasks in a job. Therefore, if you have a vacancy for a cook, the job description indicates exactly what tasks an employee in that position would perform. This makes it much easier to recruit. If you were looking for a job, wouldn't you want to know exactly what the job involves? The job description spells it out.

A second staffing tool which lists the personal qualities necessary to perform the job effectively is a job specification. We all bring different amounts of knowledge, experience, and common sense to any job for which we apply. A job specification indicates the amounts of these attributes which are judged necessary for successful performance.

All possible sources of job applicants should be considered. Personnel departments in large properties, depending upon the position, recruit from within the organization. You can also ask currently employed staff members for suggestions, work with state employment services, advertise, and otherwise ensure that all possible channels have been utilized.

In some operations, the opposite approach is used. Some managers think that the more people they recruit, the more work it will cause them, so they try to limit the number of job applicants. From the perspective of the total organization, this is usually a very poor strategy.

Use of application forms to aid in the decision-making process, selection tests, and other screening devices (such as checking references) should be an important part of the recruitment/selection process. Often, however, very little planning is done. When somebody quits, the next person who walks through the door is hired. No wonder there are so many labor-related problems in the hospitality industry!

An employee's early experiences on the job affect his/her relationship with the organization. Therefore, a well-planned employee orientation program is necessary to properly introduce the new employee to his/her supervisor, co-workers, and the organization in general.

When staffing plans are made, you should recognize the importance of matching the vacancy with the person rather than hiring an employee and then asking what he/she can do. Employees who perform well at one organizational level may not necessarily perform adequately at a higher level. For example, a good cook who is able to effectively do all the physical tasks involved with cooking may not be a good head cook. The skills—essentially dealing with people—are often quite different than the work done at a lower organizational level.

Directing

For the purpose of our discussion, directing means the same thing as supervising. It deals with all the ways in which you must relate to your subordinate employees when work is being done. Examples of specific tasks within the directing activity include training, performance reviews, and procedures to discipline employees, as well as the ongoing supervision task itself.

Human relations is a big part of a manager's job. Therefore, ways to mesh organizational goals with those of food service employees become important. Employees should have input into decisions that affect them; employees can be motivated when you address their personal needs on the job.

When directing food service employees, you should know how to gain cooperation, give orders, and use leadership styles which bring out the best in employees. In addition, an effective manager knows how to change attitudes and how to implement changes.

Scheduling labor to meet economic goals and to satisfy personnel requirements is a very important part of your job. You must know exactly how much labor is needed, work within these parameters, and treat all employees fairly. (The management activity of control is discussed next and reviews the subject of labor in detail.)

The many activities that deal with managing people are complex and sometimes difficult. People talk back—unlike other resources that must be managed. Also, employees are individuals and, while this can be fascinating and challenging, it is a difficult thing for many managers to understand. In many supervisory situations, it is useful to think about how you would like to be treated. Chances are that your employees may share many of the same concerns that you have.[1]

Controlling

Since the personnel-related activities of staffing and directing have been discussed, we can now turn to resource control. There is no assurance, of course, that goals will be attained just because effective plans have been developed, resources organized, and staff selected. For this reason, you must develop and implement control systems.

When you think of control, do you think of physical tasks such as locking the storeroom door, checking standard recipes, or weighing incoming products on a scale? If you do, you are only partially correct. The process of control actually begins with the establishment of performance standards which indicate what you can expect if nothing goes wrong.

You may develop an operating budget which indicates your expected sales and cost levels. Alternatively, you may look at recent financial statements (especially income statements) or use national and other averages as a source of what you hope your sales and expense levels will be. Once performance standards are established, you must measure the extent to which the goals are met.

Costs and Sales Levels. The entire system of managerial accounting has evolved for just this purpose. In addition to generating data needed for income tax records or statements to governing boards, you can use financial information to determine what costs and sales levels actually were. Then you can compare the variance between standard and actual costs after standard (expected) income levels and costs are known, and after actual results of the operation have been assessed. If the variance is excessive, corrective action can be taken to reduce it. (The corrective action phase of control deals with physical activities such as those noted above.) You can then evaluate whether corrective action has reduced the variance between standard and actual costs.

Spinoff Effects. Another purpose of control is to see whether there have been any spinoff effects on other areas of the operation. For example, if food costs are too high, they might be reduced by purchasing lower quality foods and/or serving smaller portions. However, these procedures can cause a decrease in sales because of obvious marketing problems. The wise food service manager not only looks at whether or not food costs are reduced as a result of the corrective action, but also judges whether it impacts the total food service operation.[2]

Quality and Quantity Levels. In addition to understanding the process of control described above, you should be aware of several basic principles. For example, the performance standards which are established must define and incorporate desired quality and quantity levels. In food service operations, it is always critical that quality requirements be established first and that these serve as minimum basic parameters within which you must solve problems. You should also develop control systems which will indicate problems on a timely basis; to know several months later that a control problem exists is obviously of little help. For this reason, food service managers often develop daily or weekly assessment procedures to supplement the monthly information which is provided by their accountants/bookkeepers.

You should also be aware that controls must be worth more than they cost. For example, to use a system that costs $50 weekly in labor to save $35 is not a good idea. On the other hand, spending $500 for a piece of equipment that will save $50 a week is very reasonable; the payback time in this example is only ten weeks.

We have already noted the importance that operating budgets play in control systems. You should now realize that accurately developed and consistently used operating budgets are a necessity in your endeavor to attain organizational goals.

Rational Procedures. You must use rational procedures to determine how priorities for control should be set. Consider, for example, that variances for sales, food, and beverages are all excessive. What should you do first? It is important to spend time on areas of greatest concern—problems that are keeping your property from obtaining its goals. Without accurate numbers that tell you what standards should be and what costs actually are, this process cannot be implemented.

Preventive Control. Finally, you should realize that preventive control procedures are more effective than imposing controls on the food service operation *after* things go wrong. The detailed description of the control process described earlier in this chapter is preventive because it attempts to establish standards and then to measure actual performance. This is much better than "putting out fires" after problems have occurred.

Evaluating   Just as the first management activity—planning—is often overlooked, so is the last management activity of evaluation. It is common for food service managers to believe that they always do a good job and that evaluation is unnecessary. Other managers may believe that they are doing the best possible job and cannot do any better, so it is useless to evaluate the effectiveness of their actions.

Both of these approaches to evaluation are, of course, incorrect. You must evaluate how well organizational goals are being attained. Then, if you are on target, you can move on to accomplish new goals. If goals are not being met, you must develop alternate strategies to accomplish them.

You must, as an ongoing part of your job, evaluate more than just goal attainment. Employees must be formally evaluated through a performance review process and the effectiveness of training programs which are implemented must be evaluated. Evaluation is a routine, ongoing activity that should be practiced by all managers who supervise employees.

It is hoped that this emphasis on evaluation will ensure its priority when you manage your food and beverage operation. The task is simply too important to be done "whenever there is time." Evaluation helps measure goal attainment, establishes new and revised organizational objectives, and assigns (or reassigns) organizational resources.

As with control, evaluation must be timely. It should be performed within time limitations so that alternate plans can be developed and implemented and before goals are judged to be unattainable. When possible, evaluation techniques must present an objective (not a subjective) appraisal of your food service operation.

Some food service managers develop psychological resistance to evaluation. Examples of this have already been noted. Also, many managers fall into a routine of always doing things a certain way. If evaluation is not part of this routine, it is less likely to be undertaken. As precedent is established and the status quo is maintained, changes in procedures stemming from the evaluation process are difficult to implement.

Food service managers, in any type of operation, must occasionally ask, "How well are we doing?" The answer to this question refers to the organizational goals which have been developed. If these goals have been realistically stated and are not being met, the evaluation process will have served its purpose: it will have identified a problem.

Awareness of a problem is the first step toward resolving it. While trained, experienced managers might be able to undertake the evaluation process subconsciously, a formalized system of evaluation is more effective for most people.

Although the concept of "management by objectives" presents concerns to some food service managers who have used it, it is briefly discussed below in order to recap the evaluation process and because it can be used in almost every food service operation.

Suppose that a food service manager at any organizational level has regularly scheduled performance reviews with his/her supervisor. At the time of the reviews, measurable objectives for the manager's performance and his/her department can be established for the forthcoming period. Until the next review, the manager follows mutually developed procedures to achieve the established goals. The supervisor provides help as needed to minimize problems that the manager encounters in attaining the goals. At the next performance review, the supervisor and the manager discuss the extent to which goals have been met and establish future goals.

This example of management by objectives, while brief and simplified, illustrates several points about the evaluation process. First of all, goals must be established. Second, staff members must be helped as necessary in order to attain them. Third, the extent to which goals have been met should be reviewed. Differences between actual performance and expectations (goals) suggest areas for future improvement. This process can be used with modifications by personnel at all organizational levels— from the manager being evaluated by his/her supervisor to the entry-level employee being evaluated by his/her boss.

How Should You Evaluate?

First: Make sure that someone is responsible for the evaluation; if "everyone" does it, "no one" does it.

Second: Establish the standards used to measure and define satisfactory performance.

Third: Inform the personnel who are involved in the activities being evaluated about what they are supposed to do and give them all necessary resources to do their job.

Fourth: Assess the actual results or the present conditions.

Fifth: Compare "what should be" (the standard) and "what is" (the present condition).

Putting the Management Process Together

You have now had a chance to read about each of the activities which make up the overall process called "management." While it is probably helpful to discuss each task in sequence, you should realize that managers at all organizational levels apply principles of each management task at the same time. For example, the manager of a food production department might simultaneously:

1. Provide input to next year's operating budget (planning).

2. Deal with problems caused by improper delegation (organizing).

3. Work with a colleague in another department on a job-related matter that concerns both departments (coordinating).

4. Develop new job descriptions and job specifications (staffing).

5. Carry on routine supervisory activities (directing).

6. Establish standard food and labor costs (controlling).

7. Conduct employee performance reviews (evaluating).

By now you should realize that a wise, experienced manager is one who can apply management principles across a wide spectrum of concerns. He/she should be able to move rapidly from a specific situation—calling for specialized knowledge, experience, and common sense—to several unrelated problems.

Figure 4.2 illustrates the process of management and shows how management activities relate to both the resources that must be managed and financial and control systems which must be used in their management. Note that the management activities just discussed (planning, organizing, coordinating, staffing, directing, controlling, and evaluating) serve as an umbrella over the entire food service operation.

Strategies **Marketing.** Plans and strategies for marketing (see Chapter 5) are equally important for commercial and institutional food services. Menus set the pace for both the planning and management of the rest of the food service operation. For example, the menu determines what resources are needed and how they will be utilized, the type of equipment and layout required for product preparation, and the skill levels and number of employees that are necessary. The menu also has obvious implications for time, procedures, and finances.

Importance of Products. There is a great emphasis on products in food service operations. Therefore, operating procedures for purchasing, receiving, storing, issuing, producing, and serving are necessary (these

Figure 4.2 Overview of Management System for Food and Beverage Operations

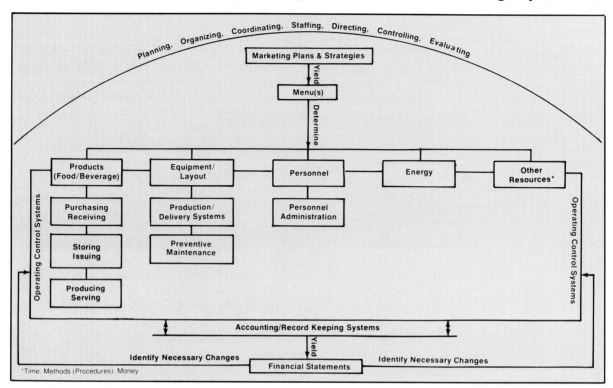

Source: Ninemeier, Planning and Control, *p. 11.*

topics are discussed in Chapters 11-15). Equipment and layout concerns make it necessary to have operating procedures for production and delivery systems and for preventive maintenance. Personnel needs—recruiting and selecting—lead to the entire process of personnel administration; many of the techniques for managing people have been noted in this chapter.

Financial Information. Figure 4.2 also indicates the role of accounting and recordkeeping systems in the management process. These systems yield financial information that summarizes how well resources have been used to meet organizational goals.

By now, the components of the management system which is used to operate food services should be more familiar to you. You will, of course, better understand the basic principles of management as you read this book. You will find that, as you advance up the organizational ladder of food service operations, the knowledge you gain plus the experience you accrue will make you a better manager. You will be able to apply management principles to a variety of problems; when you understand the management process which must be used, it will be easier to decide what must be done.

What Is Success?

What do we mean when we say that a food service operation is "successful"? Some people may define success as "making money" or "not having any customer complaints." Actually, the components of success in food service operations relate to both of these factors:

- There must be a growing customer base.

- There must be a satisfactory "bottom line."

Without customers, bottom-line goals cannot possibly be met; concern about the customer is critical. However, the operation cannot be successful if operating procedures to consistently present desired products and services to the customers are not available, or if inadequate management systems mishandle the property's limited resources.

The successful food service manager must be an expert in both marketing (customer-based) and operating control decisions.

NOTES

1. The Educational Institute of AH&MA has developed an entire course in supervisory development. For additional information contact the Educational Institute of AH&MA, 1407 South Harrison Rd., East Lansing, Mich. 48823.

2. For further information about the control process see Jack D. Ninemeier, *Planning and Control for Food and Beverage Operations* (East Lansing, Mich.: Educational Institute of the American Hotel & Motel Association, 1982).

PART II

Customer Expectations

Marketing is the concept of looking at your operation from the customer's perspective. We will spend a chapter focusing our attention on (1) market research, which is used to get to know what the customers want and need; (2) advertising, which tells potential customers that you have what they want and need; and (3) procedures to build repeat business.

The menu is the single most important tool that you will use to implement your plans. We will focus our attention on the menu and, along with a discussion of standard recipes, will explain how important it is for food quality requirements to be established and consistently implemented by a food service operation.

An increasing number of customers are becoming concerned about nutrition. This topic, plus practical procedures to help ensure that meals served meet nutritional requirements, will be discussed. You must also be concerned about sanitation and safety. After all, you have a professional *and* personal obligation to protect both customers and employees from harm. Many sanitation and safety rules are common sense. Many of us already know what they are. Therefore, emphasizing their importance is really all that is necessary. You must implement and consistently practice these safeguards to protect employees and customers.

5

Food Service Marketing

Management Challenges

As a result of studying this chapter you will:

1. know about ways to define the wants and needs of the customer.

2. understand procedures useful in building a growing base of repeat customers.

3. know how to analyze different advertising media in order to assess those which are "best" for a specific food service operation.

4. know objectives of public relations programs and examples of activities which might be of public interest.

5. learn about the marketing techniques of internal selling, promotion, and personal selling.

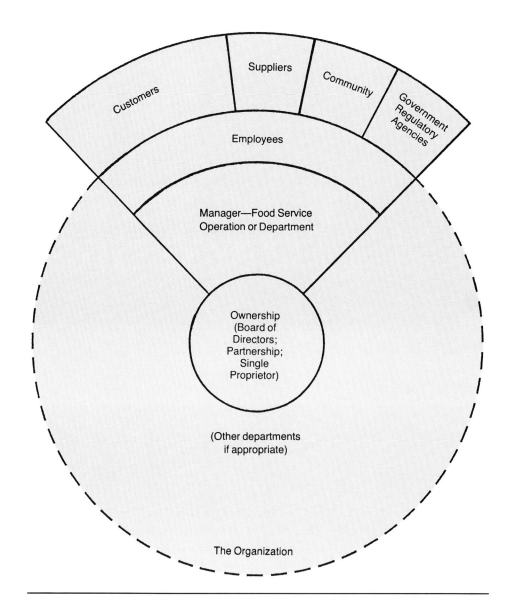

Customers

Suppliers

Community

Government Regulatory Agencies

Employees

Manager—Food Service Operation or Department

Ownership (Board of Directors; Partnership; Single Proprietor)

(Other departments if appropriate)

The Organization

Focus on the Food Service Publics

Chapter 5 focuses on procedures to enhance the relationship between the food service operation and all its many publics. Since marketing is "the business from the customer's perspective," procedures to assess the customers' needs, to influence their participation in the operation, and to keep them coming back are at the heart of this chapter's message. The relationship with the customer is of paramount concern in this chapter. Likewise, since the same marketing principles are useful in working with all the food service publics, other departments within the organization and the external publics are affected by procedures stressed in this chapter. Finally, since the owner, manager, and employees of the food service operation are also among its publics, relationships between them can also be improved by application of marketing principles presented in this chapter.

Marketing is essential to the success of food service operations. It encompasses a broad range of activities that are performed by food service employees to provide the consumer with food, beverages, and service. Marketing is often mistakenly equated with selling or advertising and public relations. While it does include these activities, marketing also deals with a great many other functions.

Besides selling, advertising, and public relations, other marketing activities include marketing research, needs assessment, product development, pricing, and promotion. In a food service operation, each of these activities is done in varying degrees to accomplish two main marketing functions: (1) to discover what food, beverages, and services the customers need and want, and (2) to provide these items to the customers at convenient locations and times, and at prices that they are able and willing to pay.

All of the marketing activities listed above are used to attract new customers to your food service facility and persuade current and past customers to patronize it repeatedly in the future. Personal selling, advertising, and publicity can be especially useful to inform the public about your facility and to attract new customers. Other marketing activities such as public relations (which includes customer relations), customer feedback, solicitations, prizes, and promotions can be very helpful in persuading customers to return to your facility many times in the future.

Repeat Customers

Repeat or regular customers are the backbone of most successful food service operations. Few food service operations can be profitable in the long run without a high percentage of repeat customers. Getting customers to try a food service facility is relatively easy; people like to try a restaurant for the first time for novelty, variety, adventure, and many other reasons. However, persuading customers to patronize a restaurant on a regular basis is generally much more difficult.

In order for a food service operation to have a high percentage of repeat customers and long-run success, it must properly utilize many marketing activities as well as good management techniques discussed throughout this text. Marketing activities are not enough for success unless they are combined with an efficient operation that includes careful employee recruitment and selection, proper orientation of new employees, adequate employee training, high employee motivation and morale, complete written policies and procedures, proper staffing, and financial cost controls. A well-managed, efficient operation leads to high food quality, cleanliness, and proper service, which are the main contributing factors in the long-term success of any food service operation.

This chapter was written and contributed by Marc Gordon, Lecturer, School of Hotel, Restaurant and Institutional Management, Michigan State University.

There are many marketing activities which can help encourage repeat customers and contribute to the future success of your food service operation. Several of these activities such as advertising, public relations, publicity, selling, and promotions will be discussed in detail later in this chapter. Other marketing activities that encourage repeat business include creating the proper atmosphere, offering good price/value to customers, and providing personal service with many extras. Examples of personal service extras are addressing repeat customers by name when they arrive and seating repeat customers at tables supplied with matchbooks engraved with their name.

All of the above marketing activities, along with a well-managed food service operation, will in turn create another strong marketing tool: the repeat customer. A loyal, satisfied repeat customer will provide your food service facility with a great deal of positive "word of mouth" advertising and goodwill. "Word of mouth" advertising can be much more powerful than other forms of advertising and is often the main reason why a food service facility maintains a great reputation and remains profitable for many years.

The Marketing Emphasis

Until the 1930s, companies in the United States marketed goods and services from a production standpoint. These companies produced goods and services in mass quantities that they believed consumers wanted and needed. Mass production allowed the companies to make many products that were affordable to the average consumer. Consumers purchased these products prior to the 1930s as fast as companies could produce them. The job of marketing was to sell those goods and services that the companies decided to produce.

During the Depression of the 1930s, the marketing emphasis began to change from a production emphasis to a consumer-oriented emphasis. Consumers could no longer buy all the goods and services that companies were producing so companies faced the severe problem of disposing of the mass-produced products. Instead of being concerned with how to make more products, manufacturers focused on producing goods that consumers really wanted. After World War II, the consumer-oriented marketing emphasis was resumed by manufacturers and has continued to expand.

The consumer-oriented emphasis has evolved into the marketing concept used by most producers of goods and services in the United States today. The job of marketing is to determine what consumers want and then to inform production so that goods and services will be produced to meet those wants. After the company is producing goods and services wanted by consumers, marketing is responsible for informing consumers that the goods and services are available. Selling, advertising, and promotion are methods that marketing typically uses to inform consumers about product availability and to urge them to buy.

Marketing Research

Determining what goods and services consumers want and need is usually accomplished by marketing research and various needs assessment activities. Marketing research should be done prior to the construction of a food service facility and continued periodically during its operating life cycle.

Feasibility Study   Marketing research done prior to the opening of a food service facility is usually in the form of a feasibility study. The feasibility study analyzes a proposed site for the facility to determine what type would be popular with the people located near the proposed site. Once it is determined what type of food service facility would be most popular at a particular site, then a financial analysis is made to determine the potential for the financial success of the facility. If the proposed facility has a reasonable chance of success at a particular location, the investors would then proceed and build the facility.

Location. This is considered the most important element in the success of any food service facility. A restaurant, for example, that has great food and service, beautiful decor, a wonderful atmosphere, and low prices will typically fail if it is in a poor location. Conversely, a poor quality restaurant can succeed in the *short run* if it is in a great location. Some of the factors that are used to determine whether or not a proposed site is in a good location for a food service facility include the number of people in the surrounding metropolitan area, the number of people living or working within walking distance, the number of people within easy driving distance, the availability and convenience of parking, traffic flow patterns, the distance from exits off main highways, and other nearby outlets that draw customers such as stores, banks, movie theaters, and competitors.

Customer Demographics. Once a proposed site is considered to be in a good location (easy accessibility to a sufficient number of potential customers), then these potential customers should be analyzed in terms of demographics and customer preferences. Customer demographics include factors such as average age, sex, marital status, average number of children, average family income, white collar workers versus blue collar workers, and urban customers versus rural customers. You can discover customer preferences by surveying a representative sample of potential customers. Surveying can be accomplished through personal interviews, telephone interviews, or direct mail questionnaires. Potential customers are asked about food preferences; how often they dine out; how far they are willing to travel to dine out; how much time they have to spend on breakfast, lunch, and dinner; and how much money they are willing to spend at a food service facility for each meal period. You can also obtain demographic information from these customer surveys.

After demographic information and food service preferences are obtained from potential customers, you should decide what kind of menu, level of personal service, price range, type of beverage service, decor, and hours of operation would best match the needs and wants of your operation's potential customers. With a good location and a thorough knowledge of what type of food service operation would best suit the needs and wants of potential customers, you must analyze your competition and the financial feasibility of a proposed facility before making the final decision of whether or not to go ahead with the project.

Analyzing the Competition. In analyzing your competition for a food service facility at a proposed site, you should determine how well existing food service facilities are meeting the needs and wants of the customers and how financially successful they are. When conducting this analysis of the competition, you should try to ascertain the strengths and weaknesses of each competitor, how long each competitor has operated at his/her current location, how busy each competitor is at various meal periods on different days of the week, and how current customers feel about each competitor.

After analyzing the competition, you will be in a good position to estimate the number of customers that the new food service facility should expect to attract at a proposed location. This reasonable estimate would come from a combination of potential customers in the areas that are not currently being satisfied by existing facilities or potential customers that would patronize the new food service facility instead of existing facilities. Once you have estimated the number of expected customers for your new food service facility, then this estimate becomes the basis for the financial feasibility analysis of the project.

Financial Analysis. The final step in the feasibility study of a proposed food service facility is the financial analysis. Unless a proposed food service facility is financially feasible, it should not be constructed, no matter how much you want the facility to be built. A good feasibility study should give you reliable data from which to make reasonable decisions concerning various aspects of the proposed food service operation and accurate estimates of the number of expected customers. Once these decisions and estimates have been made, you can then conservatively estimate projected revenues and expenses to ascertain whether the proposed facility will provide sufficient return on investment to make the project feasible. The feasibility study, therefore, is an essential tool used by investors to evaluate a proposed project, and it ultimately determines whether or not a proposed food service facility will be constructed.

Needs Assessment Activities After a food service facility is in operation, marketing research is often done to determine what customers like and dislike. Various types of needs assessment activities are typically done, such as customer surveys and customer comment forms. Customer surveys are questionnaires given to individuals and groups after they have eaten meals or attended banquet functions to find out how they liked the food, service, cleanliness, price, and atmosphere. Customers are also asked about their likes, dislikes, and suggestions for improvement.

Customer comment cards are very similar to customer surveys. Customer comment cards are tent-shaped cards usually located on each table that ask the customer specific questions in rating various aspects of the food service facility. Sometimes, the back of customer checks can also be used for customer comments. Customer comment cards and customer surveys allow you to better understand what your customers want and need. This understanding will allow your operation to continually meet and satisfy its customers' needs and be financially successful over a long period of time.

Advertising

One of the major elements of marketing is advertising. You can use advertising to inform the public about your food service facility and to persuade the public to patronize it. Advertising comes in many forms and utilizes many different media including newspapers, magazines, radio, television, billboards, and direct mail. Each medium has its advantages and disadvantages which you must evaluate to determine how to best use advertising dollars.

When evaluating how to best use advertising dollars, you must try to determine which medium has a target audience that most closely matches your food service operation's target market. Your operation's target market is generally obtained from the marketing research activities which have defined who your customer is and where he/she is located. Once your target market customers are known, as well as where they are located, then the medium that best reaches these customers at the lowest cost should be used for advertising. For example, a radio station that has a rock 'n' roll format would probably be an effective medium for reaching a teenage target market.

Newspapers

Newspapers are used extensively by food service operations to advertise their messages. Advertising in newspapers has many advantages including a well-defined circulation, a broad demographic reach, intensive coverage of its local market, targeted readership, immediacy, and flexibility. Newspapers are located in every significant market and almost every family in the country can be reached by this medium. For many families, the local newspaper is the only print medium that is purchased and read.

Newspapers have a well-defined circulation so you can estimate fairly accurately how many people will purchase the newspaper daily and where these people live. Newspaper advertising rates are determined by average daily circulation, and the cost per unit of circulation is low compared to other media. Newspapers have a broad demographic reach in which they appeal to many diversified groups. People of all ages, races, nationalities, occupations, classes, and income levels read the local newspaper. Food service operations that have a broad appeal and a broad target market, such as family restaurants and fast-food facilities, can benefit greatly from newspaper advertising.

Advantage: Intensive Coverage. A significant advantage of newspaper advertising is the intensive coverage of the local area. This coverage is so thorough and complete that often it is referred to as saturation coverage. An independent food service facility, such as a non-chain family restaurant, can reach almost all families in the area by an advertisement in the local newspaper. Chain restaurants with several outlets throughout the local area can get very effective coverage by advertising a common message and listing the address of each outlet. For example, a fast-food chain can advertise a weekly special and list the location of all participating chain outlets.

Advantage: Target Readership. Another advantage of local newspaper advertising is target readership. Even though newspapers have a broad target market, they do offer methods to target readership within the overall broad market. One method is flexible positioning. Newspapers are normally divided into several sections which appeal to various market segments. Many restaurants advertise in the entertainment section along with other forms of entertainment. Hotels with packages including rooms as well as food and beverages often advertise in travel and entertainment sections. Food service facilities that have a target market of business patrons on expense accounts often advertise in the business section of the newspaper. Also, facilities that offer special bar promotions related to sporting events on television may advertise these promotions in the sports section of the local newspaper.

Advantage: Geographic Editions. Another method to target readership within the broad market of local newspapers is to utilize geographic editions. The local newspaper of a large, metropolitan area such as New York or Chicago will have several geographic editions within its total circulation, such as northside, southside, northwest, suburban, and statewide. A small restaurant on the north side of the city, for example, would find it much more cost effective to advertise in the northside edition of the city's newspaper than to advertise in the entire circulation of the newspaper. The northside edition would have a higher cost per unit of circulation, but a much lower total cost and much less wasted circulation. The residents reached by the northside edition of the newspaper would be included in the target market of the small restaurant because of their close proximity and convenient access to the restaurant.

Advantage: Immediacy and Flexibility. Newspapers have the advantage of immediacy and flexibility. If you decide that an advertisement is desirable, you can place it in the local newspaper very quickly. Unlike other media, the lead time for placing an advertisement in the newspapers is very short. Magazines, billboards, and television advertisements may take weeks or months to prepare, produce, and place in their respective media. Newspaper advertisements can be placed with one day's lead time in many instances. Newspapers allow for a great deal of frequency and flexibility. Advertisements can be run several days in a row or on several consecutive Sundays for greater impact. Also, late closing dates and deadline hours give you great flexibility in cancelling or repeating an advertisement. You therefore have the ability to gauge how effective an advertisement is and adjust quickly to the results.

Disadvantage: Short Life. Newspapers have several disadvantages that you should consider. One disadvantage of the newspaper medium is its short life and limited "pass-on" potential. Readers of newspapers typically skim through pages fairly rapidly and spend a short period of time reading the newspaper in total. Often, advertisements are merely glanced at or skipped entirely. Newspapers also become obsolete very fast. Once they are read initially, they are rarely used for future reference and almost always are thrown away quickly. Nothing is more dull to readers than yesterday's news. Because of their short life, newspapers are most often read only once and are never passed on to anyone else in the future.

Disadvantage: Poor Reproductive Quality. The quality of the paper and the high speed of printing make for less than outstanding duplication. Food service managers that want to display sumptuous food dishes, elegant table settings, or beautiful decor are severely limited by the detail and display potential of the newspaper medium. Newspapers have the advantage of visual impact, but this impact is limited in comparison to magazines. In order to make newspaper advertisements effective, you should limit the visual display to eye-catching attractive formats that do not require high quality reproduction.

Disadvantage: Limited Opportunity of Market Segmentation. Food service managers that want to target their advertisements to a specific market are severely limited. Even though placement in various sections of the newspaper allows for some target marketing, there still remains a tremendous amount of waste involved if you want to reach a specific target market. For example, a luxury hotel that wishes to advertise its very expensive food service outlets in the local newspaper will reach thousands of local residents who could never afford to patronize these outlets. The target market for the hotel may be persons between the ages of 35 and 65 who earn $50,000 or more annually. Only a small portion of the circulation of the local newspaper would fit this target market. The rest of the circulation would be wasted.

An exception to limited market segmentation would be some national newspapers such as the *Wall Street Journal*. The *Wall Street Journal* reaches a small target market made up of business managers, executives, and professional people that earn a high annual salary. The *Wall Street Journal* segments the market even further by offering geographic editions such as the East Coast Edition and the Midwest Edition. Expensive restaurants located in major cities such as New York or Chicago that cater to the high income business market may find it much more cost effective to advertise in the regional edition of the *Wall Street Journal* than to advertise in the local newspaper. The cost of the advertisement in the *Wall Street Journal* would be higher per unit of circulation, but the waste factor would be much lower. Therefore, the food service manager would make better use of advertising dollars by utilizing the *Wall Street Journal* in this example.

Magazines   Another advertising medium that you can use is magazines. Magazines have many advantages including high quality reproduction, color availability, prestige, credibility, audience selectivity, and a long life span. Customers are favorably impressed by the high quality of paper and the excellent reproduction that magazines offer. Also, true-to-life colors can be used in magazine advertisements. You can take advantage of this high quality reproduction by showing off your operation's appetizing food items and beautiful food service facilities.

Advantage: Prestige and Credibility. Food service operations that advertise in national magazines such as *Time* and *Newsweek* gain a great deal of prestige and credibility. Only large food service operations can afford to advertise in national magazines because of the very high cost involved. Local food service operations, however, can advertise in several prestigious local magazines, especially in large metropolitan areas. These local magazines often include restaurant review sections and periodic reviews of local food and beverage establishments. Local food service managers often like to advertise in these magazines since many subscribers use them as sources for determining where to eat and drink in their respective communities.

Advantage: Audience Selectivity. Unlike newspapers which reach broad markets, magazines have a much more select group of readers. There is a magazine designed for whatever target market the food service manager is trying to reach. Whether the key factor is age, sex, income, vocation, geographic location, or interests, there is a magazine which is heavily read by people possessing each key factor. For example, *Business Week* and *Fortune* appeal to the business executive of high income. Travel and host magazines that are given out by hotels, convention bureaus, and chambers of commerce appeal to tourists and visitors from out of town. Restaurants like to advertise in these magazines to reach visitors, especially if the restaurants have a good reputation that out-of-towners may have heard of previously. Airline magazines also cater to visitors coming into a big city. Here again, restaurant managers like to utilize the prestige and credibility of major airline magazines to attract visitors to their establishments during their stay in the city.

Advantage: Long Life Span. Unlike a newspaper advertisement that becomes obsolete in one day, a magazine advertisement can last a week, a month, or even longer. Magazines often get passed on from one reader to another many times during their long life spans. Magazines that are delivered to home subscribers will normally stay in a visible location until the next edition arrives. During this period of a week or a month, the magazines may be read by several family members as well as visitors to the home. Magazines can also be kept around doctors' offices, barber and beauty shops, airlines, trains, and hundreds of other locations where people read to pass long periods of waiting. As a result of this long life span and the strong possibility that the magazine will be passed on from one reader to another, one advertisement in a magazine may end up being read by five times the number of people in its circulation. Consequently, an advertisement in a magazine with a circulation of 100,000 subscribers may reach 500,000 people or more.

Disadvantage: Time Constraints. One serious limitation of the magazine medium is its time constraints. A full-color magazine advertisement can be difficult to make and may require many weeks or months to produce. Artwork, engraving the color plates, designing the layout, and writing the advertising copy can each take a great deal of time. Unlike newspapers that offer immediacy, magazines require much more time. They have deadlines well in advance of their distribution in order to complete and produce thousands of copies. In addition, distribution and mailing take several days. You will not have the opportunity to make last minute changes or cancellations like you can with newspapers. This lack of flexibility can hurt you if you are advertising a special discount on a particular food or beverage item, and the cost of the item suddenly rises after the advertisement has been produced and submitted to the publisher. Also, you cannot react quickly to meet your competition with magazine advertisements because of these time constraints.

Disadvantages: High Costs, Waste Circulation, and Reduced Ability to Repeat Advertisement. Magazine advertisements generally have much higher production costs and higher costs per unit of circulation than newspaper advertisements do. Even though magazines offer less waste circulation than newspapers because of targeting markets, there still remains some waste circulation. Many magazine readers are not conveniently located near the food service facility or do not fit into its clientele for various reasons. Also, because of the long lead time involved with magazine advertising, you can only communicate with customers infrequently compared to other media. Growing food service operations may feel limited with magazine advertising if they want to convey their messages to the public frequently.

Radio   The radio medium offers some advantages such as saturation, geographic and demographic selectivity, immediacy, strong frequency, and relatively low cost. Almost 99% of all households in the United States have at least one radio. Radio advertisements can potentially saturate an entire local area. If you want to reach people within a convenient driving range of your property, they can be reached via the local radio station. In addition to this geographic selectivity, you can reach specific target markets by matching the radio station's format and the time of day for broadcasting their commercials to the target market of your property. For example, if your operation features jazz entertainment in its lounge, you would be able to reach your target market by advertising on the local radio station featuring a jazz format. If business people were a target market, you could advertise on an "easy listening" station during early morning or late afternoon rush-hour time periods.

Advantage: Immediacy. Radio commercials can be produced very quickly and put on the air almost immediately. If you want to get a message out quickly to beat your competitors, you will find radio advertising advantageous. Also, the radio medium allows for high frequency of message distribution. If you want to saturate the public with a message, you can have your commercial repeated many times during the day on several different radio stations. Fast-food chains with new promotions often use radio stations to repeat their message continuously over a several-day period. A final advantage of radio advertising is its relatively low cost. Radio commercials generally cost little to produce and the cost per unit of circulation is also low in comparison to other methods.

Disadvantage: Uses Only Audio. You cannot show delicious food or pleasant atmosphere using a radio so you are severely limited in what type of message you can convey with this medium. Lack of visual presentation also means that listeners do not usually pay as close attention to the radio as they do to television. Often, radio commercials are partly or even completely ignored by radio listeners. In addition, radio commercials have an extremely short life span. Once the commercial is aired, it is gone forever unless it is repeated. Unlike magazine advertisements that can be read several months later, radio commercials have no long-term value. Therefore, you can only use radio commercials for short-term messages such as an upcoming Mother's Day brunch. In spite of audience selectivity, radio also has the problem of some wasted coverage.

Television Television has some similarities to radio, but also several differences. Television has the main advantage of combining sight with sound. No other medium can combine sight and sound with motion to make such a highly appealing presentation to the senses of its audience. You can show off your operation's food, beverages, atmosphere, decor, and other highlights by using television. Television commercials can show chefs preparing magnificent food items while food servers can be shown giving friendly service and preparing specialty items at tableside. Unlike radio, television has the advantage of maintaining a high attention level in its audience so viewers retain many advertising messages.

Advantages: Saturation, Frequency, and Audience Selectivity. Like radio commercials, television commercials can saturate the local viewing area (over 95% of the households in the United States have at least one television). You can run your commercials several times a day on several different television stations to achieve high frequency and reinforcement for your advertising messages. Also, you can reach specific audiences by choosing television shows and time periods that appeal to an audience that closely matches your target market. If you manage a fast-food or family restaurant, for example, you might want to run your television commercials on Saturday mornings during cartoon shows to reach the children's market.

Disadvantages: Cost and Lead Time. In contrast to radio, television has the disadvantages of high costs and long lead times in getting commercials on the air. Television commercials can be very expensive to produce and air time can be extremely costly. A large industry food service operation could spend as much as $100,000 or more to produce one television commercial. A one-minute commercial aired during prime time on national television can cost $250,000 or more. Even on local television, commercial time can cost thousands of dollars for one minute or less. In addition, producing and airing a television commercial can require months of lead time. If you need to get your advertising message quickly to the public, television would not be a practical medium to use. Like radio, television also has the disadvantages of a very short advertising message life span and a significant degree of waste coverage in spite of efforts to selectively target audiences.

Outdoor   Outdoor advertising is a medium that is widely used by the food service industry. The two types of outdoor advertising that are used extensively by the food service industry are billboards and exterior signs located on a property. Billboards along highways are extremely vital to roadside food and beverage establishments. Billboards are also used all around large metropolitan areas to promote local food and beverage facilities. Exterior signs are used by almost all food service managers to attract customers and to briefly inform them of the establishment's name and what food it has to offer. Outdoor advertising is basically a "reminder" medium that tries to grab the attention of potential customers who pass by the billboards or signs. Outdoor advertising must be eye-catching, bold, dynamic, and graphic to effectively accomplish its purpose.

Advantages: Broad Reach, Huge Circulation, and Low Cost. Outdoor advertising is indeed a mass medium that tries to communicate with everyone. Billboard and sign messages reach hundreds or thousands of people each day as they pass by. Outdoor advertising also has high repeat exposure which helps to reinforce its messages. The cost per unit of circulation is very low compared to other media. Billboards and signs can be fairly expensive to produce, but once they have been produced, their rental or upkeep costs are relatively low. Outdoor advertising can have a long life span of between 30 days and several years. Even though the transmission of the message generally lasts only a few seconds as people pass by quickly, outdoor advertising has a long life because it repeats the message over and over again.

Disadvantage: Limited Message Length. Unlike other media which can elaborate on the advertising message by using lengthy copy or dialogue, billboards and signs must be extremely brief. Because copy is so severely limited, you will only be able to use outdoor advertising to make a few brief points. When people drive by a billboard or sign at 55 miles per hour, they do not have time to read long copy and detailed information. Therefore, you should not use outdoor advertising for introducing new packages or specials that require explanation. Outdoor advertising also has the disadvantage of no audience selectivity because you do not have control over who passes by and reads the message. A great deal of waste circulation is inherent in outdoor advertising and, in addition, it has the disadvantage of limited creativity. There is only so much creativity that can be used on a poster or sign compared to a television commercial.

Direct Mail   A final advertising medium that you can use is direct mail. Direct mail advertising is simply sending out the advertising message through the mail. The advertising message can be in the form of brochures, coupons, or various announcements. Direct mail advertising is used by many food service managers, especially by managers of clubs and other establishments with private memberships. The main advantage of direct mail advertising is audience selectivity and specific target marketing. Only those people who fit the food service operation's target market are placed on the mailing list to receive advertising material.

The best illustration of direct mail advertising is when it is used by a private club. In this example, the club's membership represents its total market since nonmembers cannot patronize the club. The club manager, therefore, has perfect audience selectivity when promotional information is mailed to all club members. Sometimes, restaurant managers collect the business cards of all patrons at the cashier station when the patrons are leaving and paying their checks. These business cards are then compiled into a mailing list for announcing future special promotions. Restaurants that are located in business districts often mail coupons to all companies located nearby for discounts on food or free drinks. Another example of using direct mail advertising to target a specific market is when food service managers with banquet rooms send wedding package information to couples who announce their engagements in the local newspaper.

Advantages: Personalization, Flexibility, and Measurability. With direct mail, you can personalize your advertising message to the customer; the customer receives very impersonal messages from other media. Direct mail advertising also offers great flexibility. Advertisement mailings can be started or stopped at your discretion without regard for lead time and cancellation deadlines. Direct mailings have the advantage of measuring how well an advertisement has succeeded. If you send out 1,000 discount dinner coupons, the number of coupons that are eventually redeemed will indicate the success of the promotion. If the promotion was successful, you can use it again in the future. The effect of advertisements in other media often cannot be measured.

Disadvantage: Cost. Producing a high quality professional brochure or information packet is very expensive. Other costs include envelopes, postage, and the labor involved in compiling the mailing list and getting the advertisements into the mail. The overall cost per unit of circulation for direct mail advertising is generally greater than for any other medium. The cost is greater because of the high degree of audience selectivity and the low amount of waste circulation. Another major disadvantage is the "junk mail" image that is associated with any direct mail advertising. Overcoming this image can be a difficult problem for you to resolve if you utilize this form of advertising.

Publicity

Publicity is similar to advertising because it involves mentioning your food service operation in the media. The media can publicize your food service operation by discussing such items as its food, beverages, service, atmosphere, table settings, prices, personnel, or physical surroundings. Only the four major media—newspapers, magazines, radio, or television—publicize food service establishments. Unlike advertising, publicity appears in the editorial section of the medium (advertising is commercial communication while publicity is noncommercial). The media charge for advertising space or commercial time, but publicity is free. You control the content and placement of advertisements in the media, but you cannot control publicity about your food service operation. Even though you cannot control editorial comments in the media about your food service operation, you can try to generate as much positive publicity as possible. You can plan most of the publicity by anticipating upcoming newsworthy events and informing the media in hopes that they will cover these events and create favorable publicity. Newsworthy events that could involve publicity include the grand opening of your food service operation, the opening of a new wing or remodeled section, the opening of the facility under new ownership or new management, or the celebration of a significant anniversary of the food service facility. You could inform the media about these events and invite them to attend. Often, food service managers have a party in conjunction with these events to celebrate and to please members of the media.

Another example of planned publicity is informing the media about significant accomplishments of food service employees. For example, the media might be very interested in covering a story about an employee who saved a customer from choking to death. Such a story would focus a lot of favorable attention on the employee and on the food service establishment. The media might also be interested in featuring human interest activities involving food service employees. For example, a relay race from one end of town to the other end of town between teams of food servers could be planned to raise money for charity. Each team member would carry trays of food or beverages down city streets and pass the trays to their teammates until each team completed the race. The team finishing first without spilling its food or beverages would win a prize and each team would have sponsors donating money to charity on its behalf.

Some publicity is unplanned and unexpected. The most typical example of unplanned publicity in the food service industry is when the media sends someone, unannounced, to evaluate the food service operation. Afterwards, the evaluator publishes or broadcasts a story about the food service establishment in which various aspects of the operation and the entire facility are rated. This type of unplanned publicity can be favorable or unfavorable. Of course, food service managers always strive for favorable publicity, but sometimes unplanned events such as fires or accidents occur which result in unfavorable publicity beyond their control.

Public Relations

Public relations, as the term indicates, consists of the relationship between your food service operation and the public. You should maintain good relations with the media, your competitors, the Chamber of Commerce, the Convention Bureau, the Trade and Visitor's Bureau, business groups, trade associations, government groups, employees, and especially current and future customers. Public relations is very broad and encompasses many activities including advertising and publicity. You will probably spend the majority of your time on various public relations activities.

A typical public relations activity that many food service operations engage in is charity work. Many large and small food service operations support and help raise money for major charitable organizations. Food service operations help charities by collecting donations from employee paychecks, sponsoring fund raising activities, helping to support telethons, and directly contributing company funds. Other examples of public relations activities that are done by food service operations are sponsoring little league teams, bowling teams, Boy Scouts and Girl Scouts, and supporting local community organizations.

The many public relations activities that you and your employees should perform include maintaining good customer relations. The purpose and benefit of good public relations is satisfying and pleasing the public in order to increase the business and long-run profits of your food service operation. Satisfying customers and properly handling their problems and complaints is a major contribution to good public relations and to the success of your operation. Even handling emergency situations such as fires and accidents in the best possible way can create a favorable impression of your operation in the eyes of the public and will increase its opportunity for long-term survival and success.

Internal Selling

Internal selling is another marketing technique for increasing sales and profits. Internal selling occurs when servers use suggestive selling techniques to sell additional amounts of such high-profit items as orange juice, appetizers, cocktails, glasses of wine, and desserts. Servers who aggressively promote the selling of these high-profit items can have a significant effect on the success of your food service operation.

Internal selling also refers to in-house signs and displays that promote the sale of food and beverages. Examples are signs in the entrance area suggesting daily specials, menu clip-on cards promoting daily specials and specialties of the house, table tent cards with various promotional messages, and special displays. For example, many food service operations use a dessert cart to display mouth-watering desserts. The power of visual suggestion can be overwhelming when the server rolls the cart directly to the table in front of the customers. Special displays such as dessert carts can definitely increase the sale of profitable food and beverage items and become a key marketing tool for food service operations.

Special Promotions

Special promotions are widely used in almost all food service operations; they are limited only by your imagination. Special promotions include such techniques as couponing, product sampling, contests, packages, premiums, gift certificates, rebates, discounting, and bonus offers. You can use these techniques for several purposes including increasing the public's awareness of your operation, attracting new customers, keeping regular customers happy, speeding up slow periods, and spotlighting special events.

Couponing. Couponing is very common with food service operations. Quite often, coupons are printed with some special offer to entice potential customers (for example, a coupon that entitles a customer to two drinks for the price of one). Coupons can be given out personally, included in direct mail advertising, or printed in newspapers and magazines. Coupons are generally combined with one of the other special promotion techniques such as bonus offers or discounting to increase food and beverage sales, especially during slack periods.

Product Sampling. You can use product sampling to acquaint customers with new food items to determine if they like the items and to suggest that they order them. For example, you may pass around samples of a particularly tasty appetizer to customers after they are seated to interest them in ordering the appetizer from the menu.

Contests. You can also organize contests to increase sales. A contest should prove cost-justifiable for your operation by increasing sales to offset the cost of prizes given to the contest winners. Dance contests and best costume contests are two types of contests that beverage outlets use to increase sales. Each of these contests could offer a cash prize or a dinner for two in the restaurant to the winners. Fast-food chains frequently have game contests with large grand prizes in hopes of attracting thousands of additional customers into their establishments on a national scale.

Packages. These can be used to combine several items at a discount price to attract new customers and to increase total revenue. One example is a wedding package for food service operations that have banquet space capable of handling wedding receptions. Here the hors d'oeuvres, entrees, wine with dinner, and dessert table could be combined into a special per person package price. The package price would be considerably less than buying each item individually at the regular price. Other examples could be dinner/theater packages combining dinner for two with two theater tickets, and hotel weekend packages combining food and beverages with hotel rooms.

Premiums. These are gifts that you can give to customers who pay the regular price for food and beverages. You could give free movie tickets to each adult eating dinner on Wednesday night, the slowest night of the week for most restaurants. Fast-food chains generally use premiums more than any other type of food service operation. Fast-food chains like to give away gifts, especially to children on the assumption that the children will ask their parents to take them to the fast-food outlet to receive their gifts. Premium items that are frequently given away by many fast-food chains are large soft drink glasses with popular children's characters on them. Typically, if a large soft drink is purchased at the regular price, then the child can keep the glass at no extra charge.

Gift Certificates. Used most often by chain restaurants or exclusive restaurants to help generate increased sales, food service gift certificates are handled the same way as gift certificates that are sold in retail stores. Fast-food chains like to sell gift certificates in small denominations, especially around Christmas. These small denomination certificates allow children who are on limited budgets to buy gifts for their parents and relatives. Fast-food chains benefit from these sales and the promotion that results when children ask their parents to take them to the fast-food outlets for a meal.

Refunds and Rebates. Refund offers or rebates are not used extensively by food service managers as promotional techniques. Refunds or rebates are used more frequently by manufacturers of various products such as appliances and automobiles. If your operation caters to business people on expense accounts, you could successfully use a rebate offer. You could send out rebate coupons to all businesses in your local area, allowing for a $5 rebate on each guest check involving four or more full-priced meals. Business people would be attracted by such an offer because it allows them to put the entire amount of the guest check on their expense accounts while receiving $5 in cash. Your operation could significantly increase its business as a result of this rebate program, more than enough to offset the cash rebates given out.

Discounting. This is a promotional technique that is used extensively by many food service managers. It is simply a discount price on food and beverage items to attract more customers and increase total sales. There are a variety of ways to use discounting: you can offer $1 off any large pizza, price all regular drinks at $1.25 until 7 p.m., have pitchers of beer for $2 on Monday nights, or reduce any chicken dinner on the menu by 50%. If you combine discounting with redeemable coupons, you can gauge how customers are utilizing these discount offers.

Bonus Offer. This is another promotional technique that is widely used in the food service industry (it is very similar to discounting). An example of a bonus offer is when the customer buys a food or beverage item at the regular price and then receives a bonus, while discounting involves the customer paying a reduced price for the initial food or beverage item. For example, you can offer customers three dinners at the regular price and a fourth dinner free, two drinks for the price on one on Thursday nights, or one large pizza at the regular price and a second pizza at 50% off the regular price. You can also use bonus offers with redeemable coupons; they can be very effective in attracting new customers and increasing your food and beverage revenue.

Personal Selling

Personal selling (outside selling) is a marketing technique that is not often used in the food service industry. Personal selling involves hiring salespeople to generate sales for your food service operation. Manufacturers, wholesalers, and retailers of products use salespeople very extensively. Only food service operations that have large banquet or hotel food service facilities would have any need for salespeople and personal selling. Sales efforts are required in order to book these banquet facilities so the revenue that these facilities can produce will be maximized.

Banquet salespeople send out brochures, banquet menus, or packages to prospective groups and follow up these mailings with personal sales calls. They also handle all group inquiries and personally discuss the details involved with putting on their banquets or meetings. Banquet salespeople work with the chef and other management people in designing banquet menus and packages (such as wedding packages). Then they go out and sell these menus and packages to help increase the total revenue of the entire food service operation. The difference between personal selling and internal selling is that personal selling uses salespeople to sell groups on large food and beverage functions, while internal selling uses service employees to suggestively sell items on the menu to individual customers.

You now have read of several activities related to marketing—selling, advertising, public relations, marketing research, needs assessment, product development, pricing, and promotion. Marketing is clearly very important to the success of a food service operation. When it is working, it not only brings new customers in, it keeps them coming back.

6

The Menu Sets the Pace

Management Challenges

As a result of studying this chapter you will:

1. know how important a menu is; it communicates with the customers and provides a structure for the operation of the food service program.

2. understand how the menu impacts upon all aspects of the food service operation.

3. know the differences between each type of menu and understand when each type should be used.

4. be able to plan a menu that incorporates the operation's and the customer's basic concerns.

5. realize the importance of incorporating basic menu planning concerns into the development of buffet and banquet menus.

6. recognize the large number of constraints which must be considered as the menu is planned.

7. learn basic principles that are important in menu design and how they can effectively sell desired products to the customer.

8. understand popular methods to establish menu selling prices.

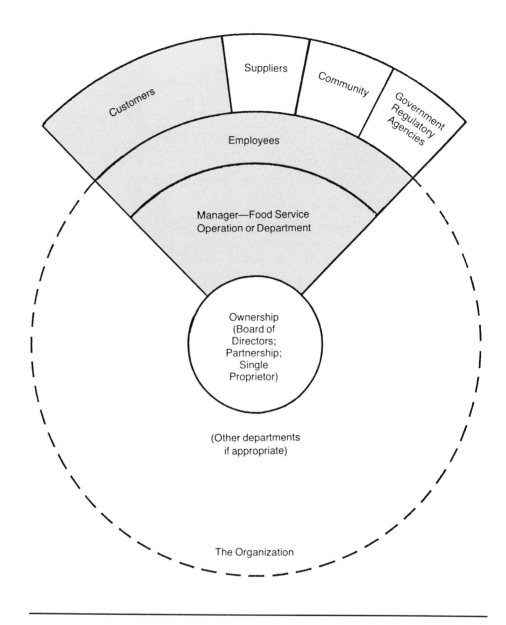

Customers

Suppliers

Community

Government Regulatory Agencies

Employees

Manager—Food Service Operation or Department

Ownership (Board of Directors; Partnership; Single Proprietor)

(Other departments if appropriate)

The Organization

Focus on the Food Service Publics

Chapter 6 focuses on the menu. It is the primary marketing tool used to communicate with the customer. The products it offers or does not offer are a primary influence on the potential customer's desire to patronize the food service operation. Likewise, the way in which the menu presents the products and services will influence which ones will be ordered by the customers. The menu also "dictates" food service operating procedures and specifies the type and amount of work which must be done.

What do you think of when you hear the word *menu*? Do you think of a marquee above the counter in a fast-food restaurant which lists available items and selling prices? Do you think of a bright, glossy, multi-colored menu that you are handed when you go out to a family-style sit-down property? Or do you think of a padded, velour-covered "book" that you might be given in an elaborate, expensive property? Regardless of what you think a menu is, a food service operation uses it to tell diners about food items which are available.

Given this broad definition it is, of course, possible to have a "verbal" menu (early restaurants and coffee houses did not use printed menus). You may be aware of properties today where food servers recite from memory items that are available. Many properties—even those with printed menus—may have "house specials" or "daily specials" that are not included on a printed menu, but are mentioned by food servers at the time of ordering.

Perhaps you have seen menu boards. Some properties use a sign posted at the entrance to the restaurant or, depending upon the dining room layout, a public notice of available items that can be viewed by all customers. The marquee behind the walk-up counter in a fast-food operation is an example of a popular type of menu board.

The Menu as a Marketing Tool

The menu is a very powerful in-house marketing tool. This is important not only in a commercial property, but also in an institutional operation such as a hospital or nursing home. When you consider that the menu planner in a health care facility must be concerned about providing many types of special diets—low salt, high protein, etc., plus the regular patients'/residents'/ meals—then the task of providing variety in a large number of different menus can become very challenging.

Figures 6.1 and 6.2 show, respectively, a menu for a hospital and a menu used in the executive dining room of a large metropolitan bank. As an interesting sidenote, the bank's food service program is operated under contract with a for-profit management company. The bank employs a food service professional to serve as a liaison between itself and the management company. These menus indicate how operations tell their "customers" what is available, and they also confirm that noncommercial food services can offer dining experiences which are just as exciting as those available in commercial properties.

Two other menu examples are shown in Figures 6.3 and 6.4. The former is a dinner menu used by a U.S. Air Force Officers' Club. The latter is a luncheon menu from a private social club. Both of these menus illustrate some excellent principles of menu design which will be discussed in this chapter.

Figure 6.1 Hospital Breakfast Menu

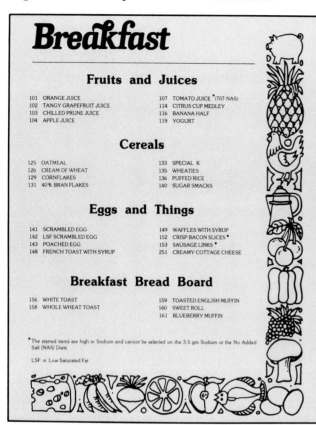

Breakfast

Fruits and Juices

101	ORANGE JUICE	107	TOMATO JUICE *(707-NAS)
102	TANGY GRAPEFRUIT JUICE	114	CITRUS CUP MEDLEY
103	CHILLED PRUNE JUICE	116	BANANA HALF
104	APPLE JUICE	119	YOGURT

Cereals

125	OATMEAL	133	SPECIAL K
126	CREAM OF WHEAT	135	WHEATIES
129	CORNFLAKES	136	PUFFED RICE
131	40% BRAN FLAKES	140	SUGAR SMACKS

Eggs and Things

141	SCRAMBLED EGG	149	WAFFLES WITH SYRUP
142	LSF SCRAMBLED EGG	152	CRISP BACON SLICES *
143	POACHED EGG	153	SAUSAGE LINKS *
148	FRENCH TOAST WITH SYRUP	251	CREAMY COTTAGE CHEESE

Breakfast Bread Board

156	WHITE TOAST	159	TOASTED ENGLISH MUFFIN
158	WHOLE WHEAT TOAST	160	SWEET ROLL
		161	BLUEBERRY MUFFIN

*The starred items are high in Sodium and cannot be selected on the 3-5 gm Sodium or the No Added Salt (NAS) Diets.

LSF = Low Saturated Fat

Courtesy of St. Lawrence Hospital, Food and Nutrition Services Department, Lansing, Michigan.

Figure 6.2 Menu Used in Executive Dining Room of a Major Corporation

CLASSIC CUISINE
Medallions de Boeuf Banquiere
Sirloin of Beef Flavored with Madeira Sauce,
Served with Braised Celery, Carrots, and Roast Potato

Saumon Grenobloise
Salmon Filet with a Lemon Caper Butter,
Garnished with Potato Nature and Green Timbale

Paupiettes de Veau Champignon
Loin of Veal Enhanced with a Mixed Mushroom Sauce,
Served with Rice Pilaf and Brussels Sprouts

TRADITIONAL SELECTIONS
Beef Stew
Garnished with Garden Vegetables

Broiled Lake Trout
Served with Braised Celery

DESSERTS
Sauteed Bananas with Apricot
Served with Lady Fingers and Whipped Cream

Assorted Pastries
Fruit Yogurts
Ice Cream Sundaes

Entrees may be served without sauce if desired.
We would be happy to substitute a vegetable selection.

Courtesy of the First National Bank of Chicago, Chicago, Illinois.

Figure 6.3 Portion of Dinner Menu Used by U.S. Air Force Officers' Club

The Flambe House Specialties

Chateaubriand King Henry VIII 8.25 per person
A gourmet's delight that we are proud of. Served with Mushroom Caps, Bouquetiere of Vegetables, and Sauce Bearnaise. Flamed and carved at your table. (For two or more)

Filet au Poivre Flambe au Brandy 8.50
Pepper Steak flamed, served with our special sauce, mild or hot

Filet a la Top Four 8.95
A tender and juicy Prime Filet Steak, prepared in a sauce of Garlic, Butter, Brandy, Mushrooms and Burgundy Wine. Flamed at your table

Filet Tradewinds Flambe 8.95
Charcoal-broiled Filet Mignon topped with Asparagus Tips, Crab Morsels, and Sauce Bearnaise

The Pride of the Club

Veal Oscar 8.50
Filet of Veal sauteed, topped with Crabmeat Morsels and Asparagus Tips with Sauce Bearnaise

Shish Kabob 7.75
Tender cuts of Beef broiled on a skewer with Onions, Mushrooms, Tomatoes and Peppers

Prime Rib of Beef au Jus 7.95
A thick juicy cut of Beef in its own natural juices, carved at your table

Chicken Cordon Bleu 7.25
A traditional favorite. Ham and Swiss Cheese between Breasts of Chicken and topped with a savory Wine Cheese Sauce

The Charbroiler Delights

T-Bone Steak 8.95
A beefeater's delight, this juicy T-Bone is broiled to fit your taste

Filet Mignon 8.25
The King of Beef—a tender lean cut of Prime Beef, broiled to perfection. A palate tantalizer.

Choice Cut New York Steak 7.75

Courtesy of Tradewinds Non-Commissioned Officers' Club, Hickman Air Force Base, Hawaii.

Figure 6.4 Portion of Luncheon Menu from Private Social Club

LUNCHEON BUFFET
Create your lunch from a wide variety of hot and cold food selections.
Beverage included.

SOUP, SALAD AND SANDWICH BUFFET 5.75	SOUP, SALADS AND HOT BUFFET SELECTIONS 7.75

EGGS

THREE EGG OMELETTES Choice of Ham, Cheddar Cheese, Fresh Mushrooms. 3.95	EGGS BENEDICT Poached eggs on Canadian bacon and toasted English muffin. Hollandaise sauce. 4.95

QUICHE du JOUR
Our chef prepares a different quiche daily.
5.75

SANDWICHES

REUBEN Corned Beef, Sauerkraut and Swiss, grilled on rye. Homemade thousand island dressing 5.25	DELMONICO STEAK On toast. Served with onion rings 8.95
BURGERS Sirloin, 8 ounces 3.95 with Cheddar 4.25 with Bacon and Cheddar 4.50	SAUTÉED BREAST OF CHICKEN On a Kaiser roll. Melted Monterey Jack cheese. 4.95 STACKED HAM AND TURKEY Broiled with Swiss cheese on light rye. Open-faced. 4.85
HOT CORNED BEEF AND SWISS On a Kaiser roll. Onion ring garnish. 4.95	
OPEN-FACED TUNA SALAD Broiled on dark rye with tomato and Monterey Jack cheese. 4.65	*The* UNIVERSITY CLUB Three layers. Sliced turkey, bacon, lettuce, and tomato, on toast. 4.95
SNOW CRAB MELT Monterey Jack cheese over Snow crab salad, on a toasted English muffin. 6.95	TUNA OR CHICKEN SALAD White, Wheat or Rye Bread. 4.50

CHEESE SPECIALTIES

WELSH RAREBIT Hot cheese and ale sauce on toast points, strips of bacon. En Casserole. 4.25	CRÊPES a la GRECQUE Lightly seasoned spinach, eggs and Feta cheese in two delicate crepes. Mornay sauce. 4.95

SIDE ORDERS

HOME STYLE FRENCH FRIES 1.50	SAUTÉED MUSHROOMS 2.25
ONION RINGS 1.75	

Courtesy of the University Club of Michigan State University, East Lansing, Michigan.

Samples of breakfast, lunch, dinner, and banquet menus from the Hotel du Pont in Wilmington, Delaware, are illustrated in Figures 6.5-6.8. They show the wide range of exciting techniques that you can use to communicate with the public.

Figure 6.9 shows a menu for a high school participating in the USDA National School Lunch Program.

Menu Functions

The menu also performs two other basic functions. First of all, it establishes the operating needs for your food service organization; it dictates what must be done and how it must be done. Second, the menu is the primary coordinating tool that you will use to implement each of the management functions noted in Chapter 4. Consider the following examples:

The menu stipulates what food items must be purchased. For example, if ground beef or green beans are needed to prepare items required by the menu, these food products must be purchased.

The menu dictates the nutritional content of meals being served. This is obviously important in institutional services where 100% of the residents' dietary intake is often supplied by the food service operation (the military, correctional facilities, nursing homes, etc.). Likewise, when hospital patients are recuperating from illness, nutritional concerns become critical.

Traditionally, commercial food services have not been concerned about nutrition. However, today the typical American consumes 40% or more of his/her meals away from home (and this rate continues to increase), so the responsibility which all food service operations must assume for providing nutritious meals must be re-examined. Many observers say that commercial food service operations should have, at least, the components of a well-balanced meal for the customer who desires to select them.

Personnel staffing needs depend on the menu. People must be available to prepare required food items. While convenience foods impact on the amount and type of production labor needed, it is still true that food service personnel must be available to produce, reconstitute, and/or serve all menu items being offered. The menu also determines the skill which food service personnel must have. Contrast the personnel needs of a sandwich shop with those of a gourmet dining facility. Food service operations must employ the right number of personnel, with the proper skills, to do what the menu requires.

The menu influences equipment needs. Equipment must be available to produce, reconstitute, and serve items required by the menu. As you will see, the menu is a primary consideration when equipment concerns are addressed. Equipment needs are far different when the menu requires only grilled sandwiches and deep-fried potatoes versus a full-range menu requiring equipment for baking, steaming, broiling, and frying types of food products.

The menu dictates facility layout and space requirements. There are basic principles of layout and design which are important (see Chapter 17). The amount of space needed for equipment and how the equipment

Figure 6.5 Portion of Hotel Breakfast Menu Figure 6.6 Portion of Hotel Luncheon Menu

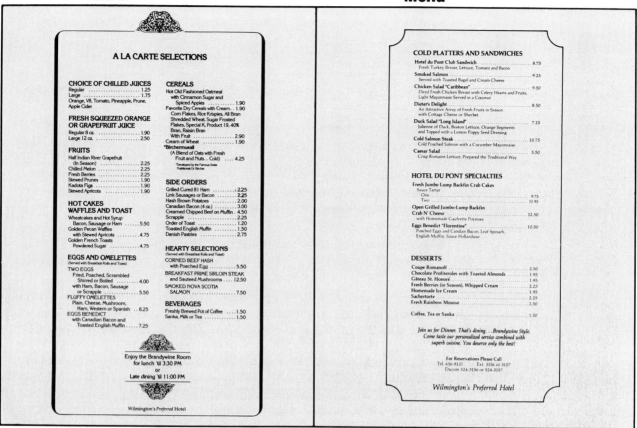

Figure 6.7 Portion of Hotel Dinner Menu Figure 6.8 Hotel Banquet Menu

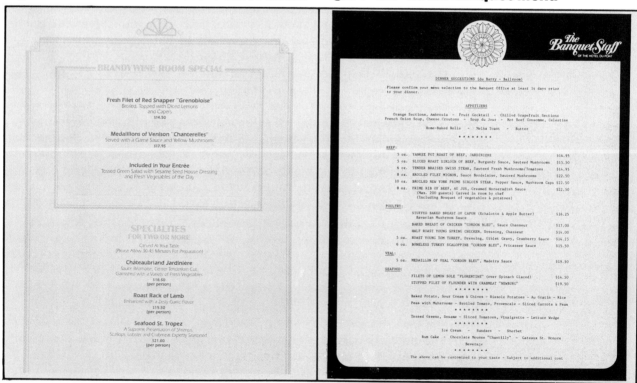

Hotel, breakfast, luncheon, dinner, and banquet menus courtesy of Hotel du Pont, Wilmington, Delaware.

Figure 6.9 Alternative-Choice Menu Used in a High School

BITE RIGHT MAY 1983

HIGH SCHOOL MENUS
FAIRFAX COUNTY PUBLIC SCHOOLS
OFFICE OF FOOD SERVICES

MONDAY	TUESDAY	WEDNESDAY	THURSDAY	FRIDAY
See Cafeteria Menu Board for Special Menus	**Regular Hot Lunch Menus**	Students $ .85; Adults $1.30		May 31 through June 3 -- Manager Planned Menus
Meat Ball Sub or Pork Barbecue¯(2, 16) or Porkette¯on Bun (9, 23) --CHOICE OF TWO-- French Fries Vegetable of the Day Assorted Fruits Assorted Salads Milk	MEXICAN OFFERINGS Burritos w/Melted Cheese+ or Nachos w/Chili & Cheese+ Sauce (5/3, 17) Tacos¯w/Meat/Cheese+ (10, 24) Hot Roll/Butter (All Tuesdays) --CHOICE OF TWO-- Vegetable of the Day Assorted Salads and Fruits Peach Cobbler, (5/3) Peach Shortcake (5/10) Cherry Shortcake (5/24) Milk	Oven Fried Chicken (5/4, 25) Hot Turkey Sandwich or Turkey/Beef Pot Pie (5/11) Golden Turkey Nuggets (5/18) Glazed Cinnamon Roll (5/4, 18, 25) --CHOICE OF TWO-- French Fries (5,4, 18, 25) Whipped Potatoes (5/11) Green Veg. of the Day (4, 25) Vegetable of Day (5/11, 18) Assorted Salads and Fruits Fruit Juice (4, 18, 25) Milk	Spaghetti w/Meat Sauce + (5,19) French Bread - - - - Little Smokie Beef Sausages +- (12, 26) or Batter Fried Fish with Macaroni & Cheese+ Hot Roll & Butter - - - - See Menu Board for CHOICE OF TWO Selections Special Menu on May 19, Optional	Choice of: Cheese Pizza or Meat¯/Cheese Pizza or Pepperoni Pizza+ --CHOICE OF TWO-- Vegetable of the Day Soup of the Day Tossed Salad Assorted Fruits Milk
	Hot Sandwich Menus	Students $ .85; Adults $1.30		
Hamburger or Fishcheeseburger+ or Sliced Turkey Sandwich --CHOICE OF TWO-- Soup of the Day French Fries Assorted Salads Assorted Fruits Milk	Hamburger;Cheeseburger;+ or Peanut Butter & Jelly Sand. w/Cheddar Cheese+ Wedge --CHOICE OF TWO-- Soup of the Day French Fries Assorted Salads Assorted Fruits Milk	Hamburger or Grilled Cheese+ or Deli Sandwich+ --CHOICE OF TWO-- French Fries Assorted Salads Fruit Juice Milk	Hot Ham and Cheese+ Sandwich or Hot Dog or Turkey Sandwich --CHOICE OF TWO-- Potato Rounds Assorted Salads and Fruits Fruit Juice Milk	Cheeseburger+ or Pork¯Barbecue or Egg Salad Sandwich --CHOICE OF TWO-- Soup of the Day French Fries Assorted Salads Assorted Fruits Milk
	Super Sack Menus	Students $ .85; Adults $1.30		
Peanut Butter and Jelly Sandwich Fresh Fruit/Cheese+ Fruit Juice Milk	Deli Sandwich+ Potato Chips Salad Fruitsicle Milk	Ham and Cheese+ Sandwich Vegetable Sticks Corn Chips Fruit Milk	Chicken/Egg Salad Sandwich Potato Chips Fruit Juice Fruit Milk	Sliced Turkey Sandwich Munch 'n Crunch (dried fruit, nuts, granola) Fruit Milk
	Big Bite Menus	Students $1.25; Adults $1.50		
Barbecued Big Pork Rib¯on Steak Roll or Double Bite (Hamburger, Ham and Cheese)+ on Sesame Roll --CHOICE OF THREE-- French Fries Mixed Vegetables Assorted Salads Assorted Fruits Milk	Roast Beef on Sesame Seed Roll with Horseradish Sauce or Double Burrito w/Cheese+ (Tomato Sauce Optional) --CHOICE OF THREE-- Ranch Fries Corn on Cob Assorted Salads and Fruits Fruit Juice Milk	All Beef Quarter Pounder on Roll or Reuben on Rye (Corned Beef, Cheese+ and Sauerkraut) --CHOICE OF THREE-- French Fries Green Beans Assorted Salads and Fruits Fruit Juice Milk	Steak Sub or Steak & Cheese+ Sub or-Large Deli Sub+ --CHOICE OF THREE-- Potato Rounds Three Bean Salad Lettuce and Tomato with Pickle or Onion Assorted Fruit Milk	Twin Burger (2 hamburger patties, 1 slice cheese)+ or Chicken Fillet on Roll --CHOICE OF THREE-- French Fries Corn on Cob Soup of the Day Assorted Salads Assorted Fruits Milk
Salad Bar Daily	Assorted vegetables, fruit, cheese, meat, bread & milk		Students $ .85; Adults $1.30	

+Foods may contain artificial flavors, artificial colors, MSG, BHA, or BHT ¯Foods containing some pork meat Menus subject to change due to late deliveries
Sodium Bisulfite, a preservative, is NOT used in the preparation of any school lunches.

Courtesy of Dorothy Van Egmond-Pannell, Director of Food Services, Fairfax County Public Schools, Virginia.

is placed differ in an establishment with a simple sandwich menu and one with a full range of menu items.

The menu determines front of house service requirements. Contrast a self-service sandwich operation with an establishment offering tableside flambe (flaming) service. In the first instance, no dining space is needed and/or the amount of square feet needed per guest is relatively small. In the second instance, seating space must be available with wide aisles between tables for moving and operating flambe equipment. When the menu requires tableside preparation of items, service will be slower, table turnover will be reduced, and fewer guests will be served. Table turnover refers to the number of times that dining room seats are occupied during the meal shift. For example, if 300 guests are served during a dinner period and the dining room has 122 seats, the seat turnover is 2.5 (300 guests $\div$ 122 seats $=$ 2.5 turns). The implication of this statistic is very important. In any given property, an increase in the number of guests correlates with higher revenue. In effect, the food service operation is "renting chairs." The amount of revenue generated is a factor of the number of guests served and the amount of money spent by each guest during a meal.

The menu determines front of house decor and design. Few properties would feature simple sandwiches in an exquisite dining room with white tablecloths and strolling musicians.

The menu establishes cost control procedures. The food service manager must control costs. Three primary costs—food and beverage products, labor, and capital (equipment and facility)—have already been noted. Procedures for controlling costs begin with determining standard costs (allowable or expected) which will be incurred when there are no operating problems. While techniques to establish these costs are beyond the scope of this book, the process begins with an analysis of the menu.[1] When the menu requires expensive food items, extensive labor, capital, and other needs, these costs will be reflected in the standard costs which are developed as part of the control system.

It is usually harder to control costs when many items are being prepared by a large number of food service employees. Also, control of sales income in the front of the house becomes more difficult.

The menu dictates production requirements. The menu tells you what items must be produced and how they must be produced, but there are other production implications of a menu which you must review.

- Preparation time of each item

- "Batch" cooking (preparing small quantities as close to the point of serving time as needed)

- The need for and length of pre-processing time

- Creative use of leftovers

The menu dictates serving requirements. You have learned that the type of menu impacts upon how food is served to customers, but it also affects how it is made ready for service. In commercial restaurants, procedures for timing orders and communicating between service and production personnel must be established. Often, when many menu items are being prepared, a large number of service staff are needed. An expediter—a member of management who serves as a coordinator between production and service—is sometimes used. Space to put large food serving trays and to make up plates with a variety of food items should be available. Ways to confirm that "what was ordered is what is served" are necessary. The point at which the food is plated and provided to food servers often creates operating problems.

In an institutional operation, the point of production/service is also critical. Tray assembly lines or cafeteria serving lines may be needed with all the attendant product placement, labor staffing, and guest flow concerns. Likewise, mobile equipment may be needed to transport food from production areas to service areas. Selection of disposable or reusable items also becomes a concern at point of service.

By now you should realize exactly how important the menu is. Almost everything that goes on within a food service operation is related to the menu.

So far, we have viewed the menu from the perspective of the guest in the front of the house and the manager's perspective in the back of the house. There is one additional function of the menu: it is the tool which implements your property's marketing plan. The menu is an important element in the feasibility study which pinpoints whom your operation is to serve, where it should be located, and if it can meet its economic objectives.

There is a truism in the food service industry which states, "Everything starts with the menu." The menu dictates much about how your operation is to be organized and managed, the extent to which it will meet its goals, and even how the building itself—and certainly the interior—should be designed and constructed.

While many managers recognize the importance of the menu, there are some who don't. A commercial property, for example, might be designed around an idea of the owner's about decor or a "catchy" name. Success for these operations is unlikely unless significant thought is also given to the food that will be offered. Since the menu implements the property's marketing plan, it becomes necessary to first identify exactly what the target market wants and, second, to build a menu around these items. Once this is done, the menu itself sets the pace for the entire food service operation.

Much of the above discussion about implementation of the marketing plan has focused specifically on the commercial food service operation. Does it also apply to the institutional food service operation? The answer is yes. What do you think are the major complaints of patients in hospitals or residents in nursing homes? Do you recall what you thought about the food which was offered when you were in school? Where do riots in correctional facilities often begin?

The institutional food service manager must consider marketing—looking at foods that are offered from the perspective of the guest—just as much as his/her counterpart in the commercial sector does.

Unfortunately, some institutional food service managers have menus available because "they've always offered them" or they feature/omit certain foods according to their own personal preferences. Some menu planners think that their personal preferences will carry over to those of the guests, patients, and other people being served. This is certainly not correct. When menus are planned, the preferences of the customers—not the menu planner—must be paramount.

Basic Types of Menus

Even though there are many different types of menus, there are basically two ways to classify them: (1) from the perspective of how food items are offered and priced or (2) by how much they change. Let's look at these types of menus so that you will have a good understanding of the many possibilities.

Menus With Grouped and Individual Offerings

One basic type of menu is the a la carte menu. Each item on the menu is made available—and generally priced— individually. For example, the diner may have a choice of salads, entrees, vegetables, desserts, beverages, etc., and each item must be ordered separately. By contrast, a table d'hote menu is one in which all the courses of a meal are grouped together and offered at one price. The diner really has little or no choice about what to order; this is especially true when there are few, if any, substitutions from which to select.

It is common in many food service operations in the United States to use a combination of a la carte and table d'hote menus. For example, a diner may have a choice of several entrees—each listed at a different price. Along with the entree selections, there may be several meal accompaniments (salad, dressing, vegetables, etc.) which may or may not be offered as choices. Often, desserts and beverages are offered separately and priced individually. In an effort to combat costs, many steak houses today charge an additional price for a potato which is often available as an integral part of the meal in other properties.

Fixed and Cycle Menus

A second way to classify menus is to look at whether they are fixed or cyclical. A fixed menu is one which does not change from day to day. Many restaurants and hotels design a menu that will be used for several months before it is changed. Daily specials may also be offered, but there is still a basic, set menu which forms the core of the property's menu offering. In contrast, a cycle menu changes daily. Institutional food service operations that serve the same guests each day are an example. Public cafeterias—especially those that cater to the same patrons (such as workers on their lunch hours)—may offer changing menus to reduce boredom and retain or increase business.

With a cycle menu, a basic menu is carefully planned for a specified number of days. For example, managers may plan a 24- or 29-day cycle menu (the same menu will be offered every 24th or 29th day). However, the length of time between identical menus is long enough so that boredom will not result. Some menu planners even incorporate item choices into their cycle menu, thus reducing still further the likelihood that their customers will grow tired of the menu. Advantages of a cycle menu (and, for that matter, a fixed menu) over a menu that changes randomly include the following:

1. After you plan a basic cycle (or fixed) menu, you don't need to spend as much time on it in the future.

2. When the same menu items are prepared at the same time, it becomes easy for you to standardize food preparation procedures.

3. It is possible to "match up" employee and equipment workloads dictated by the menu.

4. You can make more effective use of available equipment.

5. The purchasing task can be simplified.

6. Food inventories are easier to control.

When cycle menus are used, there is the possibility of repetition which may cause customer complaints. You must address these concerns when cycle menus are planned. You may want to develop seasonal cycle menus in order to take advantage of products which are more readily available, and therefore less expensive, during certain months. Of course, cycle menus should be modified when special holidays or other occasions occur within the cycle.

The basic types of menus which have been discussed (menus with grouped and individual offerings and fixed and cycle menus) can be combined. For example, a restaurant may have a fixed a la carte menu while an institutional property may offer a cycle table d'hote menu. Given the importance which the menu plays in the success of a food service operation, it is good that you will have a wide variety of options available as this critical management tool is developed.

Objectives for Proper Menu Planning

Obviously, you must plan a menu which is "good" from both the customer's perspective and that of your food service operation. What is "good"? Characteristics of an effective menu which you can incorporate into the menu planning task include the following:

The menu must attain marketing objectives. Marketing is, simply, looking at your food service operation from the customer's perspective. What does your customer want or need and how can it be provided in the menu? Your answer to that question becomes a listing of food and other available items which is referred to as the menu.

Marketing was discussed in detail in Chapter 5. Remember that you must consider your market when you plan the menu. For example, if your customers are teenagers, young singles, or married people with families, this will affect the type of menu that you plan. In this context, then, the question really becomes, "What do my customers want?" In an institutional food service operation, you must ask still another question: "What do my customers need?" You have already learned that nutritional concerns are important in these operations since, in some cases, the food provides the patient's entire dietary intake. In other cases, a patient's recovery may focus on the type of food provided.

At any rate, in a commercial food service operation, the menu implements the marketing plan and is a deciding factor in its success or failure. In an institutional operation, an inadequate menu can cause innumerable complaints and, even more seriously, dramatically affect the health and well-being of the consumer. You *must* plan the menu from the consumer's perspective; this marketing objective is critical.

The menu must be cost effective. Commercial and institutional food service operations both should plan menus which recognize financial restraints. Generally, commercial propeties cannot attain profit objectives unless product costs— dictated by the menu—fall within a specific range. Cost minimization goals in the institutional food service operation are the menu planner's responsibility (this topic is discussed in more detail in Chapter 16). In any case, whether you plan a menu for a commercial or institutional operation, you must correlate the menu with the budget and its estimate of allowable food expenses. A poorly planned menu which does not incorporate economic requirements of your operation simply cannot help—and may be a detriment—in attaining profit or minimal cost goals.

The menu affects quality objectives. A menu is what you use to implement the quality objectives of your property as they relate to food products that are prepared and served. Quality concerns are closely related to marketing concerns. It is important that you clearly understand all quality requirements and develop menus which incorporate these standards in food items. Consider the following example:

In order to be of the highest possible quality, a particular food item must be prepared immediately before service. However, the manager is planning a menu for a cafeteria line (buffet or special table service banquet) and wishes to include the food item. It would simply not be practical in this type of situation.

Think about the restaurant menu planner who wants to place a number of "prepare to order" types of items on the menu. What are the implications of the need for work space and how many production employees will be needed to prepare a large volume of these items during times of high guest counts?

Quality is an elusive concept which relates to the inherent excellence and superiority of the product from the consumer's perspective. Quality is often overlooked when menus are planned. The goals of Cesar Ritz (whose name is associated with first-class hotelkeeping throughout the world), Georges Auguste Escoffier (renowned chef and writer on cooking), and others who were not satisfied until the very best product or service were offered set very high examples of quality. Examine your property's own quality standards when you plan the menu. When discussing quality, we are talking about the difference between "something to eat" and an elegant dining experience. Again, look at the menu from the consumers' perspective. What do they want? How can you provide it? You must not be satisfied until the total aesthetic needs of your market are met.

Closely aligned with quality objectives are nutritional concerns. We have already noted that the institutional food service operation generally must—and the commercial property should—be concerned that the components of a well-balanced meal are available from among the menu items.

Quality also relates to the presentation of menu items which must be considered when the menu is initially planned; i.e., color, flair, texture, palatability, consistency, and customer appeal. For example, consider the menu planner who plans hot dogs, string beans, and french fries for a school lunch program. This menu does not incorporate quality concerns.

Truth-In-Menu Concerns

You are responsible for "telling the truth" as menus are designed. Indicating "fresh gulf shrimp" when the product is actually frozen Pacific Ocean shrimp violates truth-in-menu concerns. Avoid using misleading menu descriptions. Some states have, or are considering, laws to regulate these types of concerns. You should not need the dictate of a law to recognize the obligation you have to honestly inform the customers about items which are available.

Figure 6.10 Priority Concerns of Menu Planner

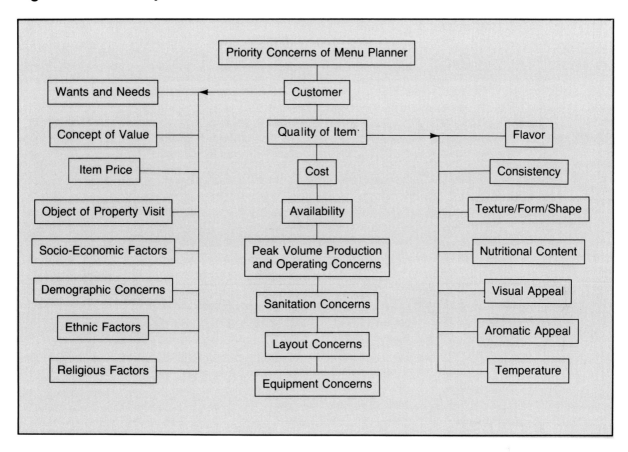

Menu Planning Procedures

How exactly should you plan a menu? We have consistently expressed concern that the customer to be served must be given the highest priority in the process of menu planning. Figure 6.10 reviews the menu planning process with a special focus on the customer. At the same time, it defines many of the factors which determine the wants and needs that will motivate the customers. As you can see, they are the end product of a special mix of many factors which are unique to the customers. This further emphasizes the importance of using basic marketing principles to carefully define *who* the customer is and *what* he/she desires from the food service operation being considered. Certainly in the commercial sector—and as often as possible within the institutional environment—the question, "What does the customer want?" should become the starting point for menu planning. The process from this point on actually becomes one of elimination. That is, of all the items you think your customers want, some must be eliminated because of:

- Cost

- Image

- Unavailability of ingredients

- Inadequate equipment and/or space

- Inadequate personnel and/or skills

- Difficulty in developing or retaining adequate quality as products are produced

Proper menu planning takes time. You should not do it because the printer needs the menu next week. Adequate time and priority must be given to menu planning; it is probably the single most important tool you can develop to attain all of your property's objectives.

Helpful aids for planning a menu include the following (each should be readily available for you to use):

1. Copies of old menus including the menu currently used by your property

2. Standard recipes (see Chapter 7)

3. Inventory information and listings of seasonal foods, best buys, etc.

4. Cost per portion or similar information

5. Sales history

6. Production records

Since the task of menu planning is fairly complex, you should find a workplace which is free from interruptions. Menus must, of course, be planned on a by-meal basis (breakfast, lunch, and dinner). You may want to first classify categories of food items by respective meal periods. For example, eggs, pancakes, and french toast would be classified as breakfast items; sandwiches and casseroles would be considered lunch dishes; and salads, meats, and fish would be planned for dinner.

After classification by meal period is completed, it is often helpful to develop a sample meal pattern (see Figure 6.11).

After the meal patterns are established, you can "slot" appropriate menu items into each pattern. Procedures to do this differ, depending upon whether you use a cycle menu (with or without choices) or a fixed menu.

Planning the Cycle Menu

When a cycle menu is used (see Figure 6.12), you should develop complete menus for every day in the cycle. Usually, entrees are planned first and are slotted into each meal period for each day in the menu cycle. The need for variety, recognition of customer preferences, use of specialty dishes, etc., become important considerations. Likewise, access to

Figure 6.11 Sample Meal Patterns for Breakfast, Lunch, and Dinner

Breakfast Pattern	Lunch Pattern	Dinner Pattern
1. Fruit or Juice	1. Appetizer	1. Appetizer
2. Cereal (cooked or assorted whole)	2. High Starch Food	2. High Starch Food
3. Entree	3. Entree	3. Vegetable
4. Bread and Butter Items	4. Vegetable	4. Entree
5. Beverage	5. Salad	5. Dessert
	6. Dessert	6. Salad
	7. Bread and Butter Items	7. Bread and Butter Items
	8. Beverage	8. Beverage

Note: Items that meet requirements without changing (e.g., bread, butter, beverage) are commonly listed last in a pattern.

equipment, personnel, time constraints, food availability, and cost also must be considered as entree items are initially planned.

Next, you should choose a high starch food for each menu. For example, if the menu pattern (see Figure 6.11) requires a high starch item, it could be part of the entree (such as a meat dish served over rice or a casserole dish containing potatoes). If a high starch item is not part of the entree, it would, of course, need to be added.

Now you should plan the fruits and/or vegetables which are necessary to accompany each entree. You have many options; the wide variety of fruits and vegetables that are commonly available will enable you to accent the entree and starch items with side dishes which will be attractive and, therefore, complement the presentation being planned. It is at this point that color, texture, and shape become important. In many operations, the three items just mentioned—entree, high starch, fruits and/or vegetables—will constitute the main dish; however, it is important for you to consider any necessary garnishes at this time.

The next step may involve selecting lunch and dinner salads, desserts, and soups, followed by breads and cereals for breakfast. Finally, plan any appetizers (if necessary) and breakfast fruits or juices. Frequently, beverages remain the same for each meal; if not, they must also be selected.

After you have developed a tentative menu for each day, you should carefully confirm that costs and nutritional requirements are met. Then compare days to review repetition and related concerns.

When cycle menus are offered, the menu planning process becomes more complicated; you must consider the combinations of items most likely to be consumed so that necessary nutrients are included. Concerns about equipment (can all entrees be prepared in available ovens?) and labor (can the present staff prepare several entree items from scratch?) should also be addressed.

Figure 6.12 Sample Cycle Menu

WEEK I	MONDAY	TUESDAY	WEDNESDAY	THURSDAY	FRIDAY
ENTREES Choose 1	Hamburger with bun Chili	Submarine Sandwich Ground Beef and gravy	Pizza Cheese Sand-wich Bologna	Spaghetti with meat sauce Tunafish Sand-wich	Tacos Sloppy Joes with bun
FRUITS AND VEGETABLES Choose 2	French Fries Celery Sticks Applesau	Mashed Pota-toes Cabbage Apple-	Buttered Green Beans Carrot sticks	Tossed Salad Buttered Spinach	"Roundabout" potatoes Orange Juice
BREAD OR SUBSTITUTE	Saltines (with				
BONUS!					
MILK Whole or 2%	Milk				

WEEK II	MONDAY	TUESDAY	WEDNESDAY	THURSDAY	FRIDAY
ENTREES Choose 1	Toasted Cheese Sandwich Meatloaf with gravy	Pizza Turkey-Ham Sandwich	Fish in bun Chicken or Turkey Supreme	Hamburger and bun Macaroni and Cheese	Lasagna Hot dog and bun
FRUITS AND VEGETABLES Choose 2	Mashed Pota-toes Vegetable Soup Slice Pea	Buttered Corn Tossed Green	French Fries Confetti Cole Slaw	Tater Tots Beets in Orange Sauce	Buttered Green Beans Finger reli-
BREAD OR SUBSTITUTE	Hot r (wi loa butt mar				
BONUS!					

WEEK III	MONDAY	TUESDAY	WEDNESDAY	THURSDAY	FRIDAY
ENTREES Choose 1	Tacos Egg Salad Sandwich	Hot Dog and bun Meat Turnover with gravy	Spaghetti and meat sauce Turkey Sand-wich	Pizza Tunafish Sand-wich	Hamburger and bun Ravioli
FRUITS		resh Green Salad azed Carrots ange Smiles		Carrot sticks Mexicorn Applesauce	Hashbrown potatoes Cabbage-pine-apple salad Vanilla pud-ding w/fruit
		t roll and			Garlic bread and butter or marga-rine

WEEK IV	MONDAY	TUESDAY	WEDNESDAY	THURSDAY	FRIDAY
ENTREES Choose 1	Sloppy Joes with bun Beef Stew	Baked Fish Beefaroni	Hamburger and bun or cheese burger	Baked Chicken Toasted	Pizza Submarine
FRUIT AND VEGETABLE Choose 2	Celery sticks Buttered Corn Orange Slush				
BREAD OR SUBSTITUTE	Cheese Biscui with beef stew and but-ter or marga-rine				
BONUS!	School Peanut Butter Cup				
MILK Whole or 2%	Milk				

WEEK I	MONDAY	TUESDAY	WEDNESDAY	THURSDAY	FRIDAY
ENTREES Choose 1	Hamburger with bun Chili	Submarine Sandwich Ground Beef and gravy	Pizza Cheese Sand-wich Bologna	Spaghetti with meat sauce Tunafish Sand-wich	Tacos Sloppy Joes with bun
FRUITS AND VEGETABLES Choose 2	French Fries Celery Sticks Applesauce	Mashed Pota-toes Cabbage Apple-salad Fruit Cocktail	Buttered Green Beans Carrot sticks Fruit Gelatin	Tossed Salad Buttered Spinach Apple Crisp	"Roundabout" potatoes Orange Juice Banana
BREAD OR SUBSTITUTE	Saltines (with chili)	Roll (with ground beef)		Italian Bread (with spaghetti)	
BONUS!		Peanut Butter Cookie			Oatmeal Cookie
MILK Whole or 2%	Milk	Milk	Milk	Milk	Milk

Courtesy of Vera Jehnsen, Oakland Schools (Intermediate School District of Oakland County), Michigan.

Planning the Fixed Menu

The complexity of fixed menu planning in a commercial property varies by type of facility. For example, table service restaurants are different from properties offering cafeteria or buffet service. You need to consider the type of restaurant, check average (the amount spent by one person on a meal), and marketing concerns when the menu is planned. Many commercial properties have ethnic themes such as French, Italian, and Mexican or offer certain atmospheres like railroad stations, old English inns, etc. Theme and atmosphere must also be reflected by the menu which is planned.

You must know whether your business is transient (it changes every day—the menu can remain the same without relying on daily specials) or whether it is highly repetitive (business people at lunch—daily specials must be changed with great regularity).

When fixed menus are planned, you must first consider entrees. Consider not only types of entrees, but also cost, preparation method(s), and adherence to theme and atmosphere. When planning the entree base, you can develop a wide range from which to choose or a narrow set of, perhaps, only four or five entrees. You may feel that you should have something for everyone and, therefore, provide a wide range of entrees. This approach creates many problems which must be resolved in the back of the house. For example, a wider variety of items must be ordered (with more purchase specifications), received, stored, issued, and prepared. A corresponding amount of preparation equipment and number of personnel with the necessary labor skills must also be available. Production/service problems are more likely to occur, too. The reverse approach—having only a few entrees available—reduces these types of problems considerably. There is a trend in the United States today toward specialty/theme restaurants that offer relatively few entrees. In addition to focusing on a specific segment of the market (marketing techniques and associated costs are reduced), many in-house production and serving problems are also minimized.

When you plan a menu for a commercial property, items offered by your competitors (who are trying to attract the same customers) must, of course, be considered. What are customers purchasing in other properties? Why? What is their cost? What can you do to make your products special—and more attractive—to potential customers? These and related questions with marketing implications constitute a primary source of concern for menu planners in all types of commercial properties.

After entrees are selected, you must determine complementary items to fill each of the slots required by your property's menu pattern (see Figure 6.11). A common procedure is to plan appetizers and/or soups, followed by high starch items and/or vegetables (if not part of the entree), and then accompanying salads. Finally, other menu components such as desserts, breads, and beverages should be planned.

Planning Buffet Menus

A buffet, with its arrangements of large varieties of food, can be particularly attractive. Sometimes an ice carving, tallow sculpture, flowers, or other decorations enhance the presentation. The popularity of a buffet is due to the variety of items offered and to the addition of novelty foods which can provide an "adventure in eating" to diners. If buffets are featured daily, menu selections must, of course, change. However, since the number of items which can be available on a buffet is extensive, it is generally easy to maintain adequate variety.

Factors which you must consider when buffet menus are planned include the following:[2]

1. Total per portion costs

2. Production feasibility/ease

3. Popularity of alternate items

4. Need to retain quality for, perhaps, long time periods

5. Lack of portioning problems

As with other menus, you should select entrees first when the buffet menu is planned. Naturally, their selection is based upon the price charged for the buffet. Inexpensive buffets usually include various cold cuts, entree salads, and chicken, ham, etc. In contrast, buffets which offer "high ticket" items include extensive varieties of meats, seafoods, and gourmet dishes.

The popularity of buffet items obviously affects the costs. If high-cost food items are popular, they will be chosen before low-cost buffet items. You must carefully consider sales history information (the actual quantity of each menu item sold during a several-week time period) in order to assess the approximate cost of buffet food consumed. As you will see in Chapter 16, costs will impact upon the subsequent selling price of the buffet.

After entrees are selected, you should choose hot foods such as high starch items and vegetables. As with any other type of menu, these items must "fit into" the other food offerings; color, texture, cost, etc., must be considered. Select salads of all types—vegetable, fruit, gelatin-based—after other hot foods have been finalized. Then choose desserts, breads, and beverages which will complement the other available food items.

Planning Banquet Menus

Basically, procedures for planning banquet menus are similar to those used to plan other menu types. Properties doing extensive banquet business often develop pre-set banquet menus in varying price ranges that can be presented to guests for their study and selection. These properties also plan specific menus when the guests desire them. Properties with infrequent banquet business may develop menus specifically for these occasions and/or sell dinners pre-chosen off the regular menu.

Menu Planning Constraints

You know that the menu impacts upon almost all of the resources available to your food service operation. These resources, then, are constraints that you must recognize as menus are planned. Consider the following:

Facility Layout/Design and Equipment. You must have space and equipment available to produce all items required by the menu. (Alternatively, convenience foods may need to be prepared.)

Available Labor. An ample number of employees—with the required skill levels—must be hired to manage, prepare, and serve all items on the menu. If skilled labor is not available to prepare menu items, it may be necessary for you to implement training programs or to reconsider items which are being planned for the menu.

Ingredients. Before final selections are made, you should choose the standard recipe which will be used. Also, make sure that all ingredients required by each recipe are available during the time span in which the menu will be used. If certain fresh seafoods are required, but will not be available, this has an obvious implication.

Marketing Implications. Food service operations in both commercial and institutional facilities must recognize the customers' wants and needs and reflect them in the menu which is planned. While it may be "practical" to serve a menu that provides many items which, unfortunately, are not preferred by the customers, you should eliminate these items from further consideration. You probably realize that people eat for reasons other than to satisfy hunger. Dining can be an experience which meets a person's social and psychological needs as well as his/her physiological needs. As we have already noted, food is only one aspect of the experience which many customers desire as they visit commercial food service operations. Foods offered on the menu should complement the experience being offered to the customer.

Quality Levels. You must appreciate the quality requirements which are to be incorporated into food items offered on the menu and know—from the customer's perspective—the level of quality which is expected. If, for any reason, your operation cannot provide menu items to the desired degree of quality, the items should not be offered. The availability of skill, knowledge, equipment, specific ingredients, etc., all affect the degree of quality in food items. If any of these elements are missing, quality will suffer.

Cost Concerns. While Chapter 7 discusses food costs in detail, you should realize now that food items which are expensive to prepare must be priced at a level to compensate their high costs. You need to know the cost of menu items to be offered, plus possible selling price ranges. If the food costs for an item being considered are excessive, you may decide that the item cannot be offered. Economic goals which relate to a required return on investment in a commercial operation, or to minimizing expenses in an institutional operation, may limit your alternatives.

Nutrition. In institutional food service operations, especially, you must make items available that provide the daily dietary requirements necessary for the clientele being served.

Calculating Menu Selling Prices

Commercial food service operations, along with many institutional facilities, must establish selling prices for menu items which are planned. Prices determine, in large measure, whether economic goals of the operation are met. However, many managers use very subjective pricing methods which do not relate profit requirements—or even costs—to the selling price which is established. Managers may talk about the "art of pricing" and suggest that intuition and knowledge of the customer's ability to pay become the most important considerations. While these factors are important, there are additional techniques which you can use to help ensure that prices are not too high (so other food service operations will have a competitive edge) or too low (causing profit levels to suffer).[3]

Let's see how the pricing plan works in many properties. A new food item is to be offered. The manager determines that a 40% food cost is desirable. He/she may calculate the standard food cost for the item in question to be $3.00. Therefore, a selling price of $7.50 is established: $3.00 (food cost) ÷ 40% (food cost percentage) = $7.50. If the manager does not like this price, another price of $7.25, $7.85, or $6.15 can be established. When questioned, the manager may state that intuition was used to establish the 40% food cost, or that it represents the national average, or that it is based on a former food cost percentage. In reality, here is how pricing methods work.

Popular Pricing Methods

You already know that there are problems with common pricing methods in the food service industry. Let's look at some of these to learn why.

The Reasonable Price Method. When this method is used, the food service manager sets a price which he/she thinks will represent a value to the customer. The manager assumes that he/she knows—from the customer's perspective—what is fair and equitable. In other words, the manager asks, "If I were a customer, what price would I pay for the product being served?"

The Highest Price Method. When this plan is used, the manager sets the highest price that he/she thinks a customer will pay. The concept of value is stretched to the maximum and is then "backed off" to provide for a margin of error in the manager's estimate.

The Loss Leader Price Method. With this plan, an item (or items) may be set at an unusually low price with the rationale that customers will be attracted to the property for its purchase and will then select other items while they are there. For example, beverage or food prices are set low to bring the customers in, but purchases of other items are necessary to meet profit requirements.

The Intuitive Price Method. The manager takes little more than a wild guess about the selling price. Closely aligned with this plan is a trial and error price; if one price doesn't work, another price is tried.

The Profit Pricing Method

The above methods are quite common, but they are generally ineffective because they do not consider profit requirements and the product costs necessary to put the item on the table. These methods may be used because they have always been used or because the price setter does not know the product costs/profit requirements. In today's market, with increased consumer demands for value and dining, and with inflation creating higher purchase prices for products needed by the property, these plans will no longer work.

You can use information about profit requirements and product costs to help set selling prices. Once profit requirements are known (this concept is discussed in Chapter 16), they can be treated as a "cost" and factored into the price setting decision in the same way that all other costs are. For example, if your property has a separate operating budget for food and beverage products, the information can be used to establish a mark-up factor. (A mark-up factor indicates the amount that food costs must be increased to cover direct food expenses, other allowable costs, and contributions toward the property's total profit needs.)

Figures 6.13 and 6.14 show, respectively, procedures to establish base selling prices in properties with one and two profit centers. A profit center is a department within an operation which generates income and increases associated costs. Generally, food service operations without alcoholic beverages have only one profit center (food). Operations offering both food and beverages have two profit centers. (The term "beverage" refers to drinks containing alcohol.) Occasionally, large restaurants and hotels will establish a third profit center—catering—to more accurately reflect income and associated costs on a specific department basis.

Procedures such as those just discussed that incorporate profit requirements, product costs, and information from the operating budget (which must be established anyway) can help in the menu pricing task. They provide a much more practical approach to pricing menu items than the subjective ways which were noted earlier.

The Myth of the Food Cost Percent

Many food service managers attempt to establish a reasonable food cost percent to use as a basis for menu pricing. Their theory is that the lower the food cost percent, the better the operation. In other words, the lower the percentage of income needed to pay for food, the larger the percentage of income available for all other expenses and profit. While this theory sounds good, it can easily be disproved.

Menu Item	Total Cost	Menu Price	Food Cost %	Contribution Margin
Chicken	$1.50	$4.50	33%	$3.00
Steak	$3.00	$7.00	43%	$4.00

Figure 6.13 Profit Pricing: One Revenue Center

If your property offers only food or beverage, 100% of the profit must be obtained from these sales. Consider the following examples: A manager prepares an annual operating budget and estimates that (a) total food sales will be $300,000, (b) non-food expenses will be $189,000, (c) $15,000 of profit will be required, and (d) the standard food cost of a menu item will be $1.40.

Step 1: Calculate Allowable Food Cost

$300,000
(total
forecasted
food sales)
−
[$189,000
(non-food
expenses)
+
$15,000
(profit)]
=
$96,000
(allowable
food costs)

Step 2: Calculate Price Multiplier

$300,000
(budgeted
food sales)
÷
$96,000
(allowable
food costs)
=
3.13
(price
multiplier)

Step 3: Calculate Base Selling Price of Menu Item

3.13
(price
multiplier)
×
$1.40
(standard
recipe cost)
=
$4.38
(base selling
price)

In the example above, the base selling price of the menu item is $4.38. This base price must be adjusted by factors which include perceived customer value, competition, price rounding, and traditional prices charged.

As the preceding example shows, chicken has the lowest food cost percent (33% compared to a 43% cost for the steak). According to the traditional view, the sale of chicken will help the operation more than the sale of steak. However, as shown by the contribution margin, only $3.00 is left over from the sale of chicken to pay for all other costs and to make a profit contribution. In the case of steak, $4.00 remains. Which would you rather have left to pay for nonproduct costs and to contribute to profit: $3.00 or $4.00? You want $4.00, of course; the menu item with the *highest* food cost percent yields the greatest contribution margin. Your goal, then, should be to *increase* the contribution margin—not decrease the food cost percent. The old saying, "You can't bank a percent" is correct!

Competition and Pricing

One of the most important concerns in setting the selling price relates to competition (other businesses attempting to attract the same customers). Most operations have competitors that offer similar products and, perhaps, service and atmosphere to customers in the same market. You must first note who your competition is, study the menus, know what items are being purchased, and know the selling prices.

One way to reduce the problem of competition is to differentiate your product from a similar product being sold. For example, your property and another property may offer a steak item. Your competitor has entertainment; your property offers an attractive atmosphere. While the price charged for the steak is still important, there are other factors which may influence the customer to visit one—or the other—property.

Figure 6.14 Profit Pricing: Two Revenue Centers

If your property offers both food and beverages, the required profit can be generated from either food or beverage sales. (When operating budgets and menu selling prices are established for products offered by properties with two profit centers, costs must be allocated between profit centers.)* It then becomes necessary to determine what profit will be contributed by each profit center as menu selling prices are established. Consider the following example: The food and beverage operation must generate $20,000 of before-tax profit, and the annual operating budget estimates that (a) total food sales will be $150,000, (b) total beverage sales will be $50,000, (c) total food costs will be $51,000, (d) total non-product costs will be $120,000, (e) standard food costs for one portion of the menu will be $3.85, and (f) standard recipe cost for a drink will be 40¢.

Step 1: Calculate Profit From Food Sales

$$\$150,000 \text{ (food sales)} - \left[\left(\$120,000 \text{ (total non-product expenses)} \times 75\% \text{ (pro-rated share)} \right) + \$51,000 \text{ (food cost)} \right] = \$9,000 \text{ (profit from food sales)}$$

For the purpose of this example, non-product costs are allocated on the basis of sales. Total sales are $200,000 (food sales of $150,000 plus beverage sales of $50,000). Food sales represent 75% of total sales ($150,000 ÷ $200,000 = 75%). While allocation on the basis of sales is not always accurate, it is convenient to use in this example.

When profit from food sales is known, the menu pricer should confirm that the remainder of the before-tax profit ($20,000 − $9,000 = $11,000) can be generated by the beverage operation.** If this is not a reasonable expectation, adjustments in the calculations will need to be made in order for the food profit center to generate a larger percentage of profit for the property. Assume that the $9,000 profit from food sales is reasonable. The price multiplier and base selling price for food can be established as follows:

Step 2: Calculate Price Multiplier: Food

$$\$150,000 \text{ (budgeted food sales)} \div \$51,000 \text{ (budgeted food costs)} = 2.94 \text{ (price multiplier)}$$

Step 3: Calculate Base Selling Price: Food

$$2.94 \text{ (price multiplier)} \times \$3.85 \text{ (standard food costs)} = \$11.32 \text{ (base selling price)}$$

As noted in Figure 6.13, the food item's base selling price will need to be adjusted to compensate for other factors.

Once the profit to be generated by and the expenses to be incurred from operation of the food program are known, beverage program profit and base selling price calculations can be made as follows:

Step 1: Calculate Profit From Beverage Sales

$$\$20,000 \text{ (total required profit)} - \$9,000 \text{ (profit from food sales)} = \$11,000 \text{ (pre-tax profit required from beverage sales)}$$

Step 2: Determine Allowable Beverage Costs

$$\$50,000 \text{ (total beverage sales)} - \left[\left(\$120,000 \text{ (total non-product expenses)} \times 25\% \text{ (pro-rated share)} \right) + \$11,000 \text{ (profit from beverage sales)} \right] = \$9,000 \text{ (allowable beverage costs)}$$

Step 3: Calculate the Price Multiplier

$50,000 (budgeted beverage sales)	÷	$9,000 (allowable beverage costs)	=	5.56 (price multiplier)

Step 4: Calculate Base Selling Price of Drink

5.56 (price multiplier)	×	$0.40 (standard recipe cost)	=	$2.22 (base selling price of drink)

As noted above, the base selling price for the drink must be adjusted to address the factors of competition, perceived customer value, etc.

* For additional information see: Hotel Association of New York City, Inc., *Uniform System of Accounts for Hotels*, 7th rev. ed. (New York: Hotel Association of New York City, Inc., 1977).
** For additional information see: Jack Ninemeier, *Beverage Management: Business Systems for Hotels, Restaurants and Clubs* (New York: Lebhar-Friedman, 1982).

One technique which is used to lure customers from the competition is to lower the selling price so it will bring more customers into the property. It may—if the items being offered by the competition are "substitutable" in the mind of the customer. When this is the case, the customer will often select the least expensive item. However, if there are differences that are important to the customer, this technique will not work.

Conversely, you may want to raise selling prices so that fewer items will need to be sold in order to maintain the required profit level. Does this work? The problem is similar to the one just noted. Customers may or may not continue to buy the product based on their desire and/or need for it.

We are really talking about a concept called elasticity of demand. While the topic is beyond the scope of this book, it involves trying to determine how the sale of more or fewer menu items, based on increased or decreased selling prices, would affect the total revenues.[4] For example, if a reduced selling price leads to the sale of enough additional items to increase the product's total revenue, the price should generally be lowered. However, if total revenues decrease because of fewer sales at a higher selling price or fewer increased sales when prices are lowered, the plan is not effective.

Presenting the Menu

After a menu is planned, priced, reviewed, and finalized, it must be organized into a format which can be presented to the consumer. As we have already pointed out, this can be done verbally, but in most cases, a printed menu is used. Whether it is stuck on a menu board, burned into a bread cutting board, or printed on expensive parchment, basic principles of menu design should be used. Note the distinction between

Figure 6.15 Possible Menu Styles

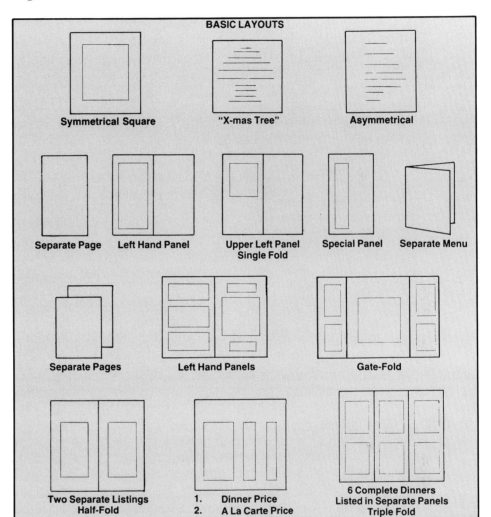

menu planning and menu design. The former refers to selecting the food items which are included on the menu. The latter is how the items chosen by the menu planner are to be presented to the customer. Techniques and procedures for designing a menu include the following:

- The menu should be clean and make effective use of space. It is the most important in-house marketing tool that is available to represent the operation.

- Attention should be given to the menu cover as well as to its interior. Remember that the menu implements the operation's theme. First impressions are always important.

- There are many different styles of menu layout. You must consider both the number of menu items to be listed on the menu and the sequence (meal pattern) which will be followed. Figure 6.15 shows examples of menu styles where differing numbers of pages/panels are used. Menus can be designed using many sizes of paper, in different shapes, and with different folds. Creativity helps make the menu memorable and can be an important way of complementing your operation's theme.

- The menu copy is important; names given to food items must be understood. Descriptions of menu items must generate both interest and sales. Any general information which is provided about the food service operation must complement the desired image.

- Carefully consider type style and/or lettering of the menu. Normally, the copy should be easy to read. Size, color, style, and background are among the factors which affect the ease with which menus can be read. In many operations, dining room lighting is much dimmer than in office work areas where menus are designed. Wise menu designers make sure that these factors are taken into consideration.

- Carefully consider the type of material on which the menu is printed. For example, inexpensive paper can be selected if menus will be used only once (such as disposable place mats with the menus printed on them). If menus will be re-used for long time periods, higher quality paper becomes very important. Treated papers that resist tears, discoloration, and soil, plus durable menu covers, can help protect menu pages.

- Some operations use menu clip-ons or inserts to advertise daily specials.

- Color gives the menu variety. Since cost increases as colors are added to the menu, many designers try to work within the restraints of two colors. Usually, a dark ink on a white or light-colored paper makes the menu easier to read.

- The menu planner (food service manager)—not the menu printer—should make the most important menu design and merchandising decisions.

- The menu should not appear crowded. Some designers like to allow approximately 50% of the menu for blank space (wide borders, space between menu listings, etc.). Common mistakes include type that is too small, lack of description about food items, and limited use of design techniques to set off items which the house wants to sell.

- If the operation sells liquor, wine, and related items, say so on the menu!

- Be sure to include information about the facility's address, telephone, and hours of operation. Some guests may want to take menus home (this is often acceptable when menus are inexpensive; when expensive menus are used, smaller "take home" versions can be made available).

- It is possible, but often not practical, to have separate menus for each meal period, beverages, children, etc. Operators must consider their specific needs. For example, you may use a permanent menu cover and insert menus for changing meal periods. Items that are offered at specific meal periods also can be combined on a single menu (the "California style" menu used in family sit-down restaurants allows guests to order eggs, steak, or dessert at any time the property is open—and this is often 24 hours a day).

- Frequently, the leading items in a list are the most popular. Once you know the items you want to sell, they can be placed at the head of a list, boxed, or otherwise set apart on the menu to increase sales. Items on the right-hand page of a two-page, side-by-side menu may be the best sellers; the middle panel in a three-panel menu may be the best location.

- It is better to replace menus than to scratch out old prices and replace them with new, higher prices. To resolve this problem, menu designers may indicate "market price" on items with fluctuating costs. A large quantity of menu stock also can be printed without prices. As prices change, old menus can be discarded and new copies of the stock used with prices neatly handwritten on the menu.

The Importance of the Menu

Throughout this chapter, the importance of proper menu planning is emphasized; it should receive high priority. You should schedule a formal time to plan the menu and establish a definite deadline for completing the task. It is often beneficial, in both institutional and commercial food service operations, to obtain ideas about the menu from employees (cooks, serving personnel, etc.) and consumers (customers, patients, etc.). After all, since these individuals must work with and/or eat the items being produced, their suggestions can be very helpful. This technique is much better than the all-too-common practice of the manager and/or chef planning the menu without outside assistance.

Your existing menu is not "cast in stone" just because an item has always—or never—been offered. Re-examine menu items as new menus are planned. After all, the food habits and preferences of consumers change. You have an obligation to keep up with these changes and, when possible, to incorporate them into the menu.

NOTES

1. Interested readers are referred to Jack D. Ninemeier, *Planning and Control for*

Food and Beverage Operations (East Lansing, Mich.: Educational Institute of the American Hotel & Motel Association, 1982).

2.   Eleanor F. Eckstein, *Menu Planning*, 2nd ed. (Westport, Conn.: AVI, 1978), pp. 162-167.

3.   The remainder of this discussion is based on Ninemeier, *Beverage Management: Business Systems for Hotels, Restaurants and Clubs* (New York: Lebhar-Friedman, 1982), pp. 97- 102.

4.   Interested readers are referred to W.H. Cunningham and Isabella C. Cunningham, *Marketing: A Managerial Approach* (Cincinnati, Ohio: Southwestern, 1981), pp. 384-387.

7

Standard Recipes Provide Consistency

Management Challenges

As a result of studying this chapter you will:

1. understand the importance of using standard recipes from the customer's and the operation's perspective.

2. know the advantages of using standard recipes.

3. know how to develop standard recipes and modify them as necessary when you need a different number of portions, or a different portion size.

4. realize the importance of carefully evaluating standard recipes.

5. know about the need to precost standard recipes after they are developed.

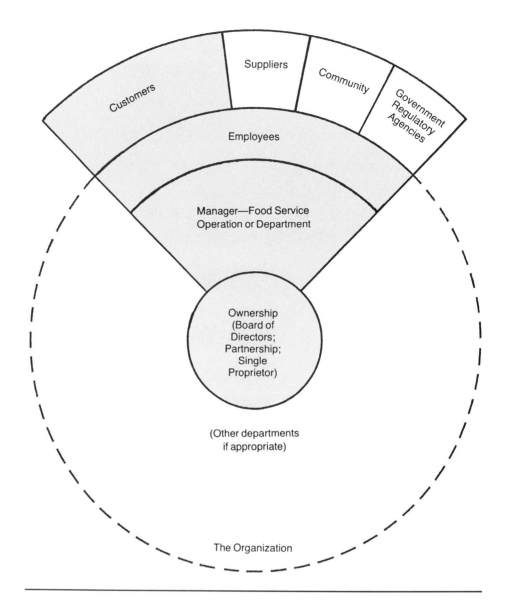

Focus on the
Food Service Publics

Chapter 7 focuses on standard recipes. They are at the heart of the relationship between the food service operation and the customer. After all, the customer's decision to participate in the food service operation is, in some measure, related to the consistent quality of menu items that are served. Since standard recipes actually "implement" the menu, they have a role to play in the relationship between the food service manager and the owner. The owner will be concerned if economic and other objectives are not met because of problems relating to the food and to the recipes used to prepare the products.

After reading Chapter 6, you now realize how important the menu is to the success of a food and beverage operation. If the menu is the "road map" to achieving an operation's goals, then standard recipes are the directions which help the operation keep on course. A standard recipe is a blueprint for production that has been developed and tested to ensure that a consistent product is produced. Standard recipes are just as important to the beverage operation as they are to the food operation since they serve the same purpose.

We will review the many advantages of a standard recipe in the next section. As an overview, however, the single most important advantage of a standard recipe is consistency:

- Consistency from the perspective of the customer—Each time a customer orders the product, it will be prepared and served in the same manner. It will also be the same size portion and will represent a consistent value (price relative to quality) for the customer.

- Consistency from the perspective of the operation—As you learned in Chapter 6, the product cost is an important factor in establishing menu selling prices. If the cost of a menu item served to a customer differed each time it was prepared (because various quantities of ingredients were used or because different portion sizes were served), there would be no base product cost available to establish the selling price.

The purpose of this chapter is to emphasize the need which any commercial or institutional food service operation has for standard recipes. They are an absolute must in the professional management and operation of modern food service programs.

Advantages and Disadvantages of Standard Recipes

Advantages of Standard Recipes

There are advantages to using standard recipes besides the consistency of appearance, cost, and taste noted above.[1]

Predictable Yield. Standard recipes provide predictable yield; you will know the number of portions which will be produced. You can then control production so that costs will not increase because of leftovers. Also, if the number of portions to be produced is accurately known, there is less likelihood of runouts which might disappoint guests.

Less Supervision. Standard recipes mean that less supervision is required. Production staff know the quantity that is needed and the preparation method to be used for each item. Guessing is eliminated; production personnel need only follow the recipes.

Efficient Production Scheduling. Standard recipes help with production scheduling. Each recipe indicates the equipment needed and helps predict the amount of time each procedure requires. Then you can more effectively schedule production personnel and necessary equipment.

Reduced Labor Costs. When standard recipes are used, employees with less skill are required (production staff do not need to be creative, they only have to follow instructions). As the amount of required skill is lessened, more people become available to fill jobs and labor costs are reduced accordingly.

Written Procedures. When standard recipes are used, management staff do not become dependent on employees. Consider, for example, the operation that employs a chef who "has the recipes in his/her head." What happens when the chef does not come to work or quits on short notice? If written procedures are available, staff members with less experience can prepare the item. Granted, inexperienced personnel may be slow and make mistakes, but it will be better than having employees who know nothing about production methods.

Standard Portions. Standard recipes yield standard portion sizes. As you will see, standard portion sizes are at the heart of the cost control system.

Standard Recipes Can Reduce Reliance on Inventory Control

Use of standard recipes can help reduce your reliance on inventory control procedures. How? Let's look at a specific example. Suppose that 20 pounds of ground beef are needed to prepare 80 portions of a casserole item; an additional 40 pounds of ground beef may be needed for preportioning into hamburger patties needed for the day's production. Therefore, 60 pounds of ground beef are withdrawn from refrigerated storage. First, you can check at the end of production to ensure that the required number of portions of casserole items and patties were produced. Second, using a cash register (actually, an electric data machine), you can run an item analysis to assess the number of portions of each item which were sold. The difference between the number of portions prepared and sold, less any adjustments for returns, burns, etc., should represent the number of products remaining. The use of standard recipes and the process just described provides a "menu balancing system" to help account for all products. As this approach is used, and you account for food products, you can make sure that any food cost problems are not traceable to storing, issuing, producing, and/or serving activities. This is a major advantage of using standard recipes.

Each of the advantages listed above applies to the use of standard food or standard beverage recipes. Standard recipes are an absolute necessity in an effectively managed operation.

There are some additional concerns which emphasize the importance of standard recipes; they have an impact on both the beginning and on the end of the food/beverage production cycle. When standard recipes are used, you can better control the quantity of food items which are needed for preparation. Therefore, standard recipes aid in product purchasing. Even if purchasing is done subjectively, you can "match" the amount of each ingredient used with the number of portions prepared and/or forecasted to be prepared. As you gain experience, the purchasing system can be fine-tuned in an effort to eliminate excess buying or stock-outs.

Evaluation is a final step in almost every management process. Standard recipes aid in this task because they provide a benchmark for judging quality. You must ensure that recipes are prepared correctly and that they yield products of desirable quality. Since this quality is established through the use of standard recipes, it is practical to evaluate the products against the standard. If the standard recipe has been tested and is correct, you can assume that more employee training and/or supervision is required if the product does not meet quality requirements.

Disadvantages of Standard Recipes

We have discussed the advantages of using standard recipes. Are there any disadvantages? There really are none. However, food production personnel who are not used to working with standard recipes may need time to locate them for use in the day's production. This would usually not be a problem in the kitchen area where, for example, a cook may need to learn to prepare relatively few menu items. In the bar area, when there is great business activity, it is impractical to require that the bartender locate each recipe before preparing a drink. This is unnecessary anyway; a standard recipe does not need to actually be in the work station area in order for it to be followed. After a cook prepares a menu item several times or a bartender mixes a drink several times, they will remember items, quantities, and procedures. Recipes must always be followed, but they do not need to be continually read. The following concerns about standard recipes are minor when compared to the advantages already noted in their favor.

Time Consuming. Modifying existing recipes and developing, testing, and implementing standard recipes takes time. You will see later in this chapter, however, that it is not necessary to discard all recipes and procedures and start over again when implementing a standard recipe plan. Instead, existing recipes can be standardized and, if this is done over a scheduled time period, it will not be an inordinately large task.

Training Required. Food and beverage employees must be trained to use the standard recipes. Training is always necessary to ensure that product and/or labor costs are not excessive.

Negative Attitudes. Personnel who have never used standard recipes can have negative attitudes about them. Cooks and bartenders may feel that they can no longer be creative or independent. They may also resent the need to "put things down on paper." You can minimize these types of perceived disadvantages by explaining why standard recipes are important and necessary. Employees should also be involved in developing and implementing standard recipes. Through positive action, management can show employees that standard recipes are critical to the operation's success and affirm that they must be consistently used.

Procedures for Developing Standard Recipes

When standard recipes are developed, you do not have to discard the operation's existing recipes and start over. These recipes can be standardized so that they are useful. It is important that standard recipes be developed for each single item listed on the menu. You should first establish that standard recipes must be used and then explain to food and beverage production staff that a process to develop them will be undertaken. Basic procedures to use in developing standard recipes include the following:

Decide on the desirable yield. If 50 portions of a menu item are prepared for slow periods and 100 items are needed for busy times, recipes should be designed to yield these servings. When applicable, recipes should be developed to use with standard modular size pans.

Decide whether to use weights or measures or both. Weighing is always more precise than measuring and it is just as possible to weigh water and other liquids as it is to measure them.

Express all quantities in usable figures. Avoid fractions and convert all measures into the largest possible units. For example, change 4/8 cup to 1/2 cup, four cups to one quart, and three teaspoons to one tablespoon. Obviously, it is essential to have all the necessary weighing/ measuring tools in order to properly follow the recipe. It does little good to specify a three-ounce quantity of an ingredient when a measuring scale is not available.

Be consistent. Use the same abbreviation in all recipes and know equivalent weights and measures. Figure 7.1 provides a good start.

List all ingredients in the order they are used. Always use correct terminology in any necessary qualifying statements. For example, what does "one cup whipping cream" mean? Does it mean one cup of cream which has been whipped or does it mean one cup of cream which must be whipped?

Give directions in detailed, concise, and exact terms. Tell how to mix (by hand or by machine) and provide the exact time plus speed if a machine is used. State the size and type of equipment needed and always list exact temperatures, cooking time, and other necessary controls. It may also be helpful to provide suggestions about recipe variations.

Provide directions for serving. Indicate the type and size of the serving dish to be used. Also indicate serving equipment—ladle or scoop—

Figure 7.1 Equivalent Weights and Measures

1 pound	=	16 ounces	3/4 cup	=	12 tablespoons
1 tablespoon	=	3 teaspoons	1 cup	=	16 tablespoons
1/4 cup	=	4 tablespoons	1 quart	=	4 cups
1/2 cup	=	8 tablespoons	1 gallon	=	4 quarts
1/3 cup	=	5-1/3 tablespoons (or 16 teaspoons)	2 pints	=	1 quart
2/3 cup	=	10-2/3 tablespoons (or 32 teaspoons)	2 cups	=	1 pint

and specify the number and yield of servings which are expected. If garnishes or sauces are needed, these should be listed.

Use pictures. If necessary, show pictures of the finished product after portioning to give additional help to production and/or service staff.

Revise and check recipes periodically once they are developed. Concerns about accuracy, improved or newer methods of equipment, and time-saving steps should always be addressed.

Now that you have some idea about techniques for properly developing a recipe, let's take a closer look at exactly how the process is undertaken. When planning a menu and selecting standard recipes, always be certain that all ingredients required by the recipes will be available for the duration of the menu. Fresh mushrooms, seafood, or certain fruits may not be available or may be very expensive if a menu is used over several months. You may wish to exclude this item from the menu or, at least, list it as a special (when available) to avoid customer disappointment.

A time period for standardizing all recipes should be established. You may decide that three recipes will be standardized at each weekly cooks' meeting, or that you will spend one hour a week with the head bartender to develop standard beverage recipes.

To develop the recipe, ask the cook or bartender to verbally recite how the item is prepared. What ingredients and how much of them are used? What are the exact procedures used to produce the item? What are the cooking/baking temperatures and times? What portioning or control tools can be used? On what plate or in what glassware is the item served? Is there a garnishment that is needed?

You can also closely observe the cook or bartender who is preparing the item and record the process. If the recipe is "talked through" first, you should still watch the item being prepared to confirm its accuracy. It is important to write everything down. Discuss the recipe with other production staff; their ideas and assistance will contribute to the preparation and accuracy of the recipe.

You may first standardize a recipe to yield a relatively small quantity. This amount can be prepared and evaluated by production staff and, perhaps, selected guests. Then the recipe can be carefully expanded to yield the appropriate number of portions as in Figure 7.2 .

It will be easier to modify and work with standard recipes if they are selected from a reliable source. Trade magazines, quantity food cookbooks, the "friendly competition," etc., are examples of good sources of

Figure 7.2 Adjusting Quantities in a Standard Recipe

Recipe sizes or the number of portions (yield) can be increased or decreased by calculating an adjustment factor. This is done by dividing the new yield by the original yield.

Example 1. The recipe yields 100 portions; you want 225 portions of the same size.

225	÷	100	=	2.25
(new yield)		(old yield)		(factor)

Multiply the quantity of each ingredient in the original recipe by 2.25 to determine the amount needed for the new, greater yield.

Example 2. The recipe yields 75 portions; you want 35 portions of the same size.

35	÷	75	=	.47
(new yield)		(old yield)		(factor)

Multiply the quantity of each ingredient in the original recipe by .47 to determine the amount needed for the new, lower yield.

Example 3. The recipe yields 75 ¾ cup servings; you want 125 ½ cup servings.

First, determine the total yield of both recipes.

Old recipe: 75 ¾ cup servings (75 x ¾) = 56.25 cups

New recipe: 125 ½ cup servings (125 x ½) = 62.50 cups

Second, divide the new yield by the old yield.

62.50	÷	56.25	=	1.11
(new yield)		(old yield)		(factor)

Multiply the quantity of each ingredient in the original recipe by 1.11 to determine the amount needed for the new recipe — and be sure to serve a ½ cup rather than ¾ cup portion.

Source: Jack D. Ninemeier, Planning and Control for Food and Beverage Operations, *(East Lansing, Mich.: Educational Institute of the American Hotel & Motel Association, 1982) p. 27.*

standard recipes which can be the basis for developing recipes in your operation.

**Sample
Standard
Recipe**

A sample standard food recipe is illustrated in Figure 7.3. Note the following:

- The recipe yields 69 portions of approximately six ounces each.

- The Amount Column in the far left margin of the recipe can be adjusted to yield a larger or smaller quantity than the number of portions (69) or portion sizes (six ounces) written on the recipe. There are several instances when this tech-

Figure 7.3 Sample Standard Food Recipe

	Fish Fillets Almondine		IX. MAIN DISHES — FISH 2
_____ Yield	69 portions		Baking Temperature: 450° F
_____ Portion size	6 oz.		Baking Time: 14-15 min.

Amount	Ingredients	Amount	Procedure
_____	Fish fillets, fresh or frozen 6 oz. portion	25-26 lb.	1. Defrost fillets if frozen fish is used. 2. Arrange defrosted or fresh fillets in single layers on greased sheet pans.

_____	Almonds, toasted, chopped or slivered	1 lb.	3. To toast almonds:
			  a. Spread on sheet pans.
			  b. Place in 350° oven until lightly toasted.
			    Approx time: 15 min.

_____ _____ _____ _____ _____	Margarine or butter, softened Lemon juice Lemon peel, grated Salt Pepper, white Weight-margarine-almond mixture	2 lb. 8 oz. ½ c 2¾ oz. 4 tbsp. 1 tbsp. 4 lb.	4. Add almonds, lemon juice, lemon peel, salt, and pepper to softened margarine or butter. 5. Mix thoroughly. 6. Spread margarine mixture on fillets as uniformly as possible. *Amt per fillet:* #60 dipper 7. Bake at 450°F for approx 15 min or until fish flakes when tested with fork. 8. Sprinkle lightly with chopped parsley or sprigs of parsley when served.

Reprinted with permission from Standardized Quantity Recipe File for Quality and Cost Control *by* Institution Management Department, Iowa State University © 1971 by The Iowa State University Press, Ames, Iowa 50010.

nique can be handy. For example, on busy weekend evenings, 150 portions may be prepared rather than the smaller number used for weekday evenings. In this case, you can make adjustments for larger quantities and include them in the far left Amount Column. This practice is more effective than permitting other employees to make adjustments with possible mistakes that can affect quality and costs. Perhaps smaller portion sizes may be desired for a luncheon buffet. Again, you can note quantities for adjusted portions or sizes directly on the recipe.

- The recipe indicates that a #60 dipper (which measures 60 level scoops or servings per quart) should be used to portion the sauce.

- The recipe clearly indicates baking time, temperature, and the exact procedures for preparing the menu items.

Evaluation of Recipes

Perhaps the most important step in modifying and implementing standard recipes is prior evaluation to ensure that all quality concerns have been addressed. Frequently, a tasting committee or panel is used.

Figure 7.4 Menu Item Rating Scale

Name of Menu Item: _____		Date: _____ Sample Number: _____			
Instructions: Check ( ) your feeling toward the characteristics specified for the menu item being evaluated.					
			Characteristics		
Your Rating:					
Like Very Much					
Like Moderately					
Like Slightly					
Neither Like/Dislike					
Dislike Slightly					
Dislike Moderately					
Dislike Very Much					
Comments					

It can include management staff, cooks, other interested employees, and even guests. Much of the menu evaluation will focus on product characteristics. For example, baked goods may be evaluated on the basis of external appearance and/or flavor. Meats might be judged according to aroma, tenderness, and juiciness, while the color, moisture content, texture, and taste of cooked vegetables may be considered. To help evaluators rate the results of standard recipes, a menu item rating scale such as the one shown in Figure 7.4 can be used. This form enables the members of the tasting panel to evaluate five product characteristics which you feel are most important (more than five characteristics can be evaluated by using a second scale). Input from sources such as the menu item rating scale can be very helpful when the quality of items prepared according to standardized recipes is evaluated.

It is also important to evaluate the standard recipe from a back of house production perspective. Do production and management staff agree that the recipe is clear, concise, accurate, and readable in regard to:

- amounts (specified in weights and/or measures)?

- types of ingredients?

- instructions?

- directions for service?

Evaluation will ensure the efficient use of time and energy and help eliminate human error as much as possible. Market suitability, available equipment, skills, and number of labor hours should also be reviewed. The menu item must lend itself to the type of service being provided by the operation and item costs must be in line with the operation's allowable costs and/or selling prices.

Recipe Precosting Procedures

After a recipe is standardized, it becomes possible to predict the cost of preparing one serving (or many servings) of the menu item. This information is extremely important in all food service operations—both commercial and institutional. Commercial operations generally base item selling prices partly on product costs. In a commercial food service operation, each menu item might be sold at a different price which can reflect a reasonable mark-up from actual food costs. By contrast, beverages are grouped into categories (such as house highball, house cocktail, call highball, call cocktail) and the same selling price is generally charged for any drink falling in a certain category even though actual product costs are different. This is usually the only practical method since it is possible to offer thousands of drinks made with various combinations of many beverage products. However, there is less of a direct relationship between product costs and subsequent selling prices in institutional operations. An awareness of food costs is still important, though, since specified budgeted amounts for product expenditures cannot be exceeded.

As you have learned, standard recipes are at the heart of systems which should be used to establish portion costs and subsequent selling prices. When standard recipes are used and closely followed, you will be able to calculate portion costs. The sum of the recipe's ingredient costs is divided by the number of portions which the standard recipe yields to determine the standard portion cost.

For example:

$75	÷	50	=	$1.50
(recipe cost)		(portions)		(standard portion cost)

The prices for ingredients listed in standard recipes can be obtained from current invoices. While the basic method for calculating standard portion costs is the same for both food and beverages, each is discussed below. Recall that you must:

- Use current product prices. Later, consider whether additional costs (or lower costs) must be used *to compensate* for ingredient costs which will be incurred during successive months.

- Estimate ingredient costs for the short term and use these adjusted costs as the basis for precosting.

Figure 7.5 Standard Portion Cost Worksheet: Menu Item

A. Name of Menu Item *Fish Fillet Almondine*
B. Portion Size *6 oz. Fish / # 60 Scoop Sauce*
C. Number of Portions *69*

Ingredient	Amount	Cost/Unit	Total Cost
1	2	3	4
Fish Fillets	*26#*	*2.89*	*75.14*
Almonds	*1#*	*3.15*	*3.15*
Butter/Margarine	*2½#*	*1.35*	*3.38*
Lemon Juice	*½ cup*	*1.90/16 oz. (2 cups)*	*.48*
Lemon Peel	*3 lemons*	*.25/each*	*.75*
Salt	*TT*	*—*	*—*
Pepper	*TT*	*—*	*—*
		Total	*82.90*

$82.90 Total Cost (col. 4)	÷	69 Number of Portions (C)	=	$1.20 Standard Portion Cost

Source: Ninemeier, Planning and Control, *p.32.*

Calculation of Standard Portion Cost: Food

To calculate the standard portion cost for a menu item, a simple worksheet can be used (see Figure 7.5).

1. Each recipe ingredient is listed in Column 1 and the amount of each ingredient is shown in Column 2. It is impractical to cost some ingredients, especially a small amount of an inexpensive item. Note that no costs are included for salt and pepper. The symbol "TT" means "to taste."

2. The cost per purchase unit is listed in Column 3. To calculate the total cost of the ingredient, multiply the amount (Column 2) by the cost (Column 3). For example, consider fish fillets:

26 lbs. (amount)	×	$2.89 (unit cost)	=	$75.14 (total cost)

3. Total ingredient cost for the recipe is shown at the bottom of Column 4. The total ingredient cost for preparing 69 portions of fish almondine, according to the recipe, is $82.90.

4. The standard portion cost of the menu item (the cost to prepare one portion of the recipe) is calculated at the bottom of the worksheet:

$82.90	÷	69	=	$1.20
(total cost)		(number of portions)		(standard portion cost)

The above process can be completed for each standard recipe. Operations which offer each menu item on an a la carte basis need go no further; by using these procedures, they have calculated the standard portion cost that can be used as the basis for monitoring program performance and for establishing menu selling prices.

Many food service operations combine menu items to form dinners or other groupings that are costed, priced, and sold together. For example, a fish fillet almondine dinner may include salad and dressing, potato, vegetable, fish entree, and bread and butter. The portion cost of each of these individual menu items must be calculated to determine the food cost for the complete dinner.

A worksheet for calculating the standard dinner cost is shown in Figure 7.6. It provides a format for determining standard food costs for all items in combination on the menu. When reviewing Figure 7.6, note the following:

1. The individual portion costs for each item are obtained from completed standard portion cost worksheets (Figure 7.5).

2. With options such as vegetable, potato, juice, and salad dressing, it would take an impractical amount of time to determine costs for all of the different combinations. The most popular choices can be costed and an average price can be used on the form. When other items are added to the dinner choice, they should fall within the cost range of the more popular items on the worksheet.

3. The cost of each menu item offered as part of the dinner should be added up to determine the dinner's total food cost. This total cost ($2.45) becomes the basis for determining standard food costs. How to use standard food cost information is discussed later in this chapter.

4. The worksheet provides five separate costing opportunities. When the cost of one ingredient increases, that recipe or item must be recosted. The revised cost is then added to the previously established cost for other dinner items in order to obtain the revised standard dinner cost.

Figure 7.6 Standard Dinner Cost Worksheet

	Item		Portion Cost				
Entree	*Fish Almondine*	*1.20*					
Veg	*Du Jour*	*.12*					
Potato	*Choice*	*.12*					
Salad/ Dressing	*Tossed Green* *choice*	*.40* *.15*					
Juice	*Tomato* *Pineapple*	*.12*					
Bread	*Loaf*	*.15*					
Butter	*Butter*	*.06*					
Other							
Garnish	*Orange/Lemon/ Parsley*	*.05*					
Condiment	*Cocktail Sauce*	*.08*					
		2.45					

Name of Dinner *Fish Almondine*

Date of Last Cost *8/1/00*

Source: Ninemeier, Planning and Control, *p. 33.*

Calculation of Standard Portion Cost: Beverage

Developing a standard portion cost for beverages is easy since there are few ingredients and each drink is individually priced and served. A standard beverage recipe is shown in Figure 7.7. Note that it also gives the type and amount of ingredients needed for each drink. The beverage recipe also provides space for ingredient costs and for calculating drink costs which can be helpful in making drink price decisions.

Note the following in Figure 7.7:

1. Ingredients are listed in Column 1.

2. The bottle size for each liquor ingredient is in Column 2.

3. The cost of the bottle of liquor is in Column 3. There are four Column 3s—an original and three price changes—to permit

Figure 7.7 Sample Standard Beverage Recipe

ITEM: Manhattan

	Date 6/19—	Date	Date	Date
A) Drink Sales Price	$2.00	$ _____	$ _____	$ _____
B) Drink Cost	$.415	$ _____	$ _____	$ _____
C) Drink Cost Percentage	20.75%	_____ %	_____ %	_____ %

INGREDIENTS	Size	Bottle Data 6/19—				Drink Data 6/19—			
		Cost	Cost	Cost	Cost	Amt.	Cost	Cost	Cost	Cost
1	2	3	3	3	3	4	5	5	5	5
Whiskey, Rye	33.8 oz/ltr	7.25				1.50 oz.	.322			
Vermouth, Sweet	25.6 oz/fifth	2.49				.75 oz.	.073			
Angostura Bitters	16 oz.	6.00				dash	.010			
Cherry						1 ea.	.010			
Water (Ice)						.75 oz.	—			
TOTALS						3 oz.	.415			

PREPARATION PROCEDURE:

Place ingredients into a mixing glass. Add ice and stir long enough
to chill. Strain into cocktail glass. Garnish with a stem
Maraschino cherry.

GLASS USED: 3½ oz. Lined Cocktail.

Adapted from Carl H. Albers, Food and Beverage Cost Planning and Control Procedures, *revised (East Lansing, Mich.: Educational Institute of the American Hotel & Motel Association, 1974), p. 126.*

the costing of the drink on four occasions before the recipe must be reproduced.

4.   The amount of each ingredient is listed in Column 4.

5.   The cost of each ingredient is listed in Column 5. The cost of the rye whiskey in the Manhattan ($7.25) is divided by the number of ounces to the liter bottle (33.8 ounces) to obtain the

cost per ounce ($.214). Since 1.5 ounces are used in the drink, the cost of the rye whiskey used per drink is $.322.

$7.25	÷	33.8	=	$.214
(bottle of rye whiskey)		(ounces in the liter bottle)		(cost per ounce)

Some beverage managers may use a reduced number of ounces in a bottle, and then increase the ounce cost, to allow for spillage, evaporation, etc.

6. Line C at the top of the recipe indicates the standard drink cost percent. The drink cost divided by the drink sales price yields the standard beverage cost percent for this item.

$.415	÷	$2.00	=	20.75%
(drink cost)		(drink sales price)		(drink cost percentage)

As noted above, the beverage cost is not as directly related to the subsequent selling price as the food cost. Rather, the type of drink (highball, cocktail, specialty) and the quality of liquor (house, call, premium) are generally assessed to establish a drink selling price.

Precosting in Institutional Food Service Operations

As already noted, the primary purpose of precosting in institutional food service operations is to aid in menu planning. Menus which are planned should, on the average, not exceed the allowable food costs that have been budgeted.

The first several procedures used to precost institutional menus involve developing and costing standard recipes according to procedures just discussed for commercial food service operations.

*   Recipes must be standardized. Usually, new menus feature a combination of menu items used previously along with new recipes (which are continuously gathered by the food service manager). Any potential recipes must be properly standardized.

*   After recipes are standardized, they must be precosted. The cost per serving information is used when the menu is precosted.

After standardization, procedures for precosting an institutional menu begin to differ from those used in a commercial food service operation. First, you should plan a tentative menu (a worksheet similar to the one shown in Figure 7.8 can be used). Notice that there are places to indi-

Figure 7.8 Worksheet for Daily Standard Food Costs

Monday / /		Tuesday / /		Wednesday / /		Thursday / /		Friday / /		Saturday / /		Sunday / /	
Item	Cost	Item	Cost	Item	Cost	Item	Cost	Item	Cost	Item	Cost	Item	Cost
Breakfast		Breakfast		Breakfast		Breakfast		Breakfast		Breakfast		Breakfast	
Lunch		Lunch		Lunch		Lunch		Lunch		Lunch		Lunch	
Dinner		Dinner		Dinner		Dinner		Dinner		Dinner		Dinner	
TOTALS													

cate breakfast, lunch, and dinner menu items to be served throughout the week. You can also calculate the per portion cost for each tentative menu item which has been selected.

Cost information can be abstracted from a cost per serving recap sheet (see Figure 7.9). Information for the recap sheet can be obtained from Figure 7.5 or from Figure 7.6. With this plan, you can keep a running list of each menu item, its portion size, and the current cost per serving. (Figure 7.9 allows for initial and precost adjustments before the form must again be reproduced.)

After the worksheet in Figure 7.8 is completed, per portion costs (the cost to serve three complete meals to one person for each day) can be totaled. Depending upon the system in use, total daily or weekly per portion costs must be equal to or less than the standard allowable daily food costs on a per person basis (the concept of allowable food cost is discussed in Chapter 6).

For example, suppose you outline tentative breakfast, lunch, and dinner menu items for each day in a week. You also list the per portion cost for each tentative menu item. The daily food costs per person for each of the seven days is as follows:

Monday $2.15
Tuesday $1.85

Figure 7.9 Cost per Serving Recap Sheet

Item	Serving Size	Cost Per Serving			

Wednesday $3.20
Thursday $2.80
Friday $2.65
Saturday $2.40
Sunday $2.20

The total weekly food cost per person is $17.25. Therefore, the average daily standard food cost is $2.46.

$17.25	÷	7	=	$2.46
(weekly food costs per person)		(days)		(average daily standard food cost)

This average daily standard food cost can be compared with a standard cost permitted by the operating budget (see Chapter 16) or any other source of standard information. If the average daily standard food cost is too high, you have two alternatives:

1. Modify the menu so that average daily standard food costs will be reduced.

2.   Produce the menu, but plan lower cost menus during the coming weeks to "even out" the average daily standard food costs.

From this brief example, you can see how standard recipes which yield standard portion costs can be used to plan institutional food service menus that meet cost guidelines.

Use of Standard Cost Information in Commercial Food Services

Earlier in this chapter, it was indicated that you should know standard food costs in order to establish base selling prices. Can you use the information any other way? The answer is yes. Basically, if you are aware of what standard costs should be, you can then assess actual costs and compare the two to determine if actual costs are higher than desired. (Both institutional and commercial food service menu planners want to ensure that menus being planned will not exceed allowable costs.)

This control activity is important. Bottom-line profit is reduced by one dollar for each dollar that food costs are higher than they need to be. One hundred percent of every cost reduction will drop to the bottom line. Therefore, development and use of standard recipes, along with precosting these recipes, will yield a standard cost useful for management and control purposes.

There are several ways to measure standard food costs. Institutional food service operations can measure standard costs on the basis of what it should cost to feed one person per day. Commercial food service managers generally measure these costs on the basis of a food cost percent. The standard food cost percent equals the standard food costs divided by standard food sales. The standard food cost is generally expressed as the planned food cost percent against which actual food costs are measured. There are several methods to calculate standard food costs. The procedure which will be discussed in this chapter is practical and reasonably accurate. It assumes that standard cost tools (standard recipes, standard portion sizes, and standard portion costs) are being used.

Determining Standard Food Costs and Food Cost Percent

In order to establish the standard food cost, you must select the time period for the study. The longer the time period, the more accurate the information. Each food item is likely to have a different food cost percent so calculating food costs involves determining a weighted average food cost. Items with a high food cost raise the average food cost percent; items with a low cost reduce it.

After the standard food cost for each item is calculated, you can observe how items with different selling frequencies at different food cost percentages affect the overall food costs. The process is actually quite simple and is illustrated in Figure 7.10.

Each menu item is listed on the left side of the form. If an item is offered for sale individually (such as soup or eggplant appetizer), it is listed

Figure 7.10 Worksheet for Determining Standard Food Costs

Item	Date Sold	Date Sold	Date Sold	Date Sold	Date Sold	Date Sold	Date Sold	Date Sold	Date Sold	Date Sold	Date Sold	Date Sold	Date Sold	Date Sold	Date Sold	Date Sold	Total Sold (A)	Sales Price (B)	Total Sales (A×B)	Food Cost (C)	Total Cost (A×C)	Food % (C÷B)
Soup	12	18	14	20	15	18	0	14	16	17	19	14	18	0	12	16	223	.90	200.70	.32	71.36	.356
Eggplant	15	21	23	16	15	18	0	17	19	26	15	14	18	0	14	21	252	1.15	289.80	.35	88.20	.304
Hamburger	35	41	38	42	30	37	0	37	39	41	41	29	37	0	33	46	526	2.35	1220.00	.95	494.00	.404
Fish	20	18	16	24	26	18	0	22	16	19	23	26	18	0	26	15	281	2.95	828.95	.85	238.85	.288
Steak	27	25	24	27	26	30	0	29	23	52	26	26	31	0	26	24	381	3.95	1504.95	1.15	458.15	.291
Stew	30	35	40	57	39	30	0	32	33	43	36	38	31	6	30	35	499	3.85	1882.65	1.16	537.90	.286
Diet Platter	11	15	17	12	15	14	0	13	13	26	11	13	14	0	10	15	193	2.95	569.35	.86	154.46	.271
Sea Platter	30	31	35	29	34	30	0	32	29	38	28	32	31	0	30	30	459	4.25	1865.75	1.35	512.65	.318
Plum Pie	12	10	18	12	11	15	0	14	8	19	11	11	16	0	12	9	178	1.95	347.10	.80	142.46	.410
C. Eclair	15	11	21	13	14	11	0	17	9	24	12	15	12	0	14	10	196	2.15	421.40	.75	147.00	.349
S. Remo	30	28	25	37	29	40	24	32	26	36	27	27	51	26	28	21	494	3.25	1605.50	.95	469.30	.292
Oysters	29	30	31	27	26	46	31	31	29	36	26	27	44	28	27	30	502	2.90	1455.80	1.20	602.40	.414
Gumbo	50	48	52	57	45	67	51	52	46	55	56	44	66	48	30	46	833	2.50	2082.50	.85	708.05	.340
S. Almondine	70	65	63	67	70	78	46	72	63	66	66	68	77	37	65	66	1033	4.95	5113.35	2.45	2530.85	.495
F. Shrimp	60	54	55	57	62	64	38	62	52	58	56	61	62	55	55	52	883	5.95	5253.85	2.01	1744.83	.338
Sea Shrimp	45	45	35	38	41	47	25	47	43	38	37	39	45	22	40	43	630	6.25	3937.50	1.85	1165.50	.296
N.Y. Strip	10	8	9	9	12	18	0	12	6	8	11	11	11	2	8	8	144	8.15	1173.61	3.45	496.80	.423
Oyster Pie	19	17	18	18	20	23	10	21	15	17	21	22	22	8	19	17	286	5.95	1701.70	2.25	643.50	.378
Pecan Pie	28	30	26	41	29	40	20	30	28	29	40	28	46	18	29	30	486	2.25	1093.50	.80	338.80	.356
Bruot	15	14	15	16	10	25	5	17	12	18	15	11	25	3	14	16	231	3.55	820.05	.90	207.90	.254

Totals: 33,368.00 | 11,862.84

Recap: $\dfrac{\$11,862.84 \text{ Total Cost}}{\$33,368 \text{ Total Sales}} = 35.6\%$ Standard Food Cost Percent

Adapted from material developed by the author and William Quain for programs sponsored by the Louisiana Restaurant Association (1979-1980).

separately on the worksheet. If it is sold as a dinner or with other items (such as seafood or a steak dinner), it is combined with the dinner.

Properties offering more than one menu—such as lunch and dinner menus—must decide whether to develop standard food cost on a by-meal or on an across-all-meals basis. If by-meal food costs are desired, each meal must be costed with a separate worksheet. There are two advantages to separate listings. First, when food cost standards are separated by meals, it is easier to compare any differences between standard and actual costs. Second, corrective action can focus specifically upon the meal period contributing higher than expected food costs so the reasons for losses can be more quickly identified and brought under control.

An accurate tally of the number of a la carte and complete meal items sold during this trial period should be kept on the worksheet. The information can be obtained from guest checks during the study period, from analyzing cash register tapes if they include these details, from a sales history record, or from any other sales records of menu items.

If a sales history record has been kept, the number of each item that has been sold can easily be transferred to the worksheet. A sample sales history record is shown in Figure 7.11. Note that the last column compiles total item sales which can be transferred to Figure 7.10.

If there is no record of past menu sales, items sold must be tallied daily during the study period. The worksheet in Figure 7.10 has space for only 16 days. Since accuracy increases as the number of days increase, two or more forms should be used to tally item sales for at least one month. Note the following on the worksheet in Figure 7.10:

1. The sales price (Column B) is the actual selling price of each menu item.

2. Total sales (Column A x Column B) represent the total income from the menu items. In the first example, 223 servings of soup were sold at $.90 each. This resulted in total sales of $200.70.

$$\underset{\text{(servings of soup)}}{223} \quad \times \quad \underset{\text{(sales price)}}{\$.90} \quad = \quad \underset{\text{(total sales)}}{\$200.70}$$

3. Food costs (Column C) represent the standard portion costs taken from either Figure 7.5 if the item is sold individually, or from Figure 7.6 if the item is a grouping of menu items.

4. Total costs (Column A x Column C) represent the total cost of all food used to produce the number of items sold. For example, soup has a standard food cost of $.32 (Column C). The total food cost, based on 223 servings of soup, is $71.36.

$$\underset{\text{(servings of soup)}}{223} \quad \times \quad \underset{\text{(standard food cost)}}{\$.32} \quad = \quad \underset{\text{(total food cost)}}{\$71.36}$$

Figure 7.11 Sales History Record

Number of Portions Served

	1	2	3	4	5	6	7	8	9	10	11	12	13	14	15	16	17	18	19	20	21	22	23	24	25	26	27	28	29	30	31	Total Sold
Date																																
Day	Su	M	Tu	W																												
Weather	Rain	Clear	Clear	Clear																												
Meals Served	386	416	330	410																												
Spec Events	-	-	-	-																												
Item																																
Soup	12	18	14	20																												
Eggplant	15	21	23	16																												
Hamburger	35	41	38	42																												
Fish	20	18	16	24																												
Steak	27	25	29	27																												
Stew	30	35	40	37																												
Diet Platter	11	15	17	12																												
Sea Platter	30	31	35	29																												
Plum Pie	12	10	18	12																												
C. Eclair	15	11	21	13																												
S. Remo	30	28	25	37																												
Oysters	29	30	31	27																												
Gumbo	50	48	52	57																												
S. Almondine	70	65	63	67																												
F. Shrimp	60	59	55	57																												
Sea Shrimp	45	45	55	38																												
NY Strip	10	8	9	9																												
Oyster Pie	19	17	18	18																												
Brulot	15	15	14	16																												
Pecan Pie	28	30	26	41																												

Source: Ninemeier, Planning and Control, p. 39.

5. The food percent (Column C÷Column B) is the standard food cost percent for each menu item. It is calculated by dividing food cost (Column C) by the sales price (Column B). In the case of soup, the food cost percent is 35.6%.

$.32	÷	$.90	=	35.6%
(standard food cost)		(sales price)		(standard food cost percent)

While the individual menu item food cost percent may be helpful, one more step is needed.

6. To calculate the standard food cost percent—against which actual food costs will be compared—the sum of the total cost column is divided by the sum of the total sales column. In Figure 7.10, standard (expected) food cost is calculated as: $11,862.84 ÷ $33,368 = 35.6%.

This standard food cost becomes the manager's goal; it defines expected food costs. If actual food costs approximate this goal, it indicates that the management team is doing a good job. However, if actual food costs are greater than standard food costs, there may be problems with the operation. The manager should check to see whether the sales mix has changed—if more items with higher food cost percents are being sold—which would increase the food cost. If this is not the case, the manager should analyze the food service operation to determine where corrective action is needed.

You should now recognize that standard recipes, per portion costs, and precosting procedures are all tools to help the management team implement a well-planned menu. The menu may be good, but without the use of standard recipes and precosting techniques, it is unlikely that economic goals in either institutional or commercial food service operations can be consistently met.

NOTES

1. This discussion is based upon Jack D. Ninemeier, *Planning and Control for Food and Beverage Operations* (East Lansing, Mich.: Educational Institute of the American Hotel & Motel Association, 1982), pp. 25-29.

8

Nutrition, Food Service, and the Customer

Management Challenges

As a result of studying this chapter you will:

1. understand why both institutional and commercial food service operations must be concerned about and incorporate procedures to maximize the nutritional content of meals being offered.

2. know why nutrition is important.

3. understand what food does for the body.

4. understand the basic function of nutrients in maintaining good health and why good nutrition is critical to your health.

5. realize that it is easy to consume adequate amounts of basic nutrients if menus are wisely planned and know how basic menu planning procedures can be modified to incorporate nutritional concerns.

6. be able to apply basic cooking principles which help prevent nutrient loss during food production.

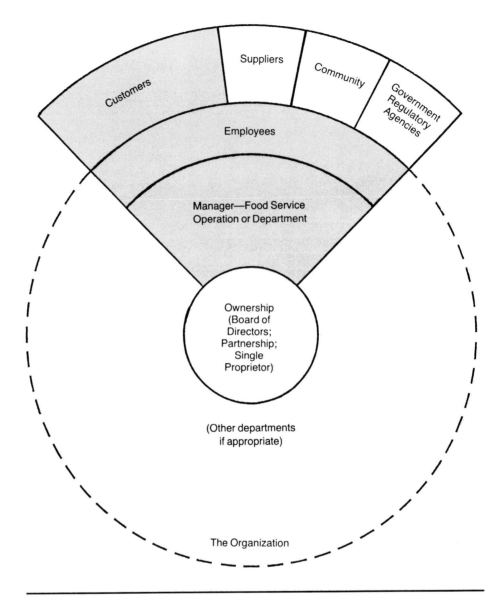

Focus on the Food Service Publics

This chapter focuses on the relationship between management (who plans the menus), employees (who prepare items required by the menus), and customers (the food service public that consumes items which are produced). We will review the importance of nutritional concerns when menus are planned and when food products are produced.

In a marketing sense, it is not your mission to educate the public about the need for nutrition; many people are already aware of and are concerned about proper nutrition. The management staff in your food service operation should recognize that this awareness is present and that it is a major factor in determining customer wants and needs. The food service operation is responsible for making nutritious food available for those customers who desire it. In institutional food service operations, this concern must be paramount: it is their professional responsibility to provide good, wholesome, nutritious meals.

Knowledge of proper nutrition and ways to "practice" it are important because you must know how to incorporate nutritional concerns into your food service operation.[1] Also, when reading and studying this chapter, you should consider how the concepts presented affect your own personal health and dietary program. It is unfortunately true that many professionals in food service, both in institutional and in commercial operations, don't seem to "practice what they preach." Many people who have studied nutrition and use the information in the management of their food service operations do not take care of their personal health. We hope you will! As you read this chapter, consider how the information can benefit you as well as the customers/patients in the food service operation you do—or will someday—manage.

Nutritional Concerns

You probably realize that one segment of the hospitality industry—institutional food service—focuses on nutrition. When an operation is responsible for all (or almost all) of the meals served to its "customers," meals which meet minimum nutritional requirements should receive top priority. Therefore, close attention to the nutritional content of the meals is important when a food service program is designed for a college dormitory, a military base, a prison, etc.

Nutrition and the Customer

What about food services operated by a commercial hotel or restaurant? Should nutrition concerns be as vital to the managers of those operations? First of all, approximately 40% of all meals consumed in the United States today are eaten away from home. It is likely that this number will increase, and it is unlikely that there will be a trend toward more at-home dining in the near future. Does the commercial food service operator have an obligation to provide nutritious food to his/her customers? While this is a question that must be answered specifically for each individual property, consider several points:

Quality. As a manager, you have a responsibility to purchase foods of the proper quality and to guard against destroying this quality (including nutritional content) because of errors in storage, processing, or service.

Wants and Needs. You must provide what your customer wants and/or needs. From a marketing perspective, your mission is generally not to educate the customer about nutrition or anything else. Therefore, one can argue that nutritional concerns about selecting foods must come from your customers and not from you.

Nutritional Availability. Assuming that the above statement is correct, you are responsible for making available items of high nutritional content within the basic four food groups. Then your customers who want these items will have an opportunity to select them.

Emphasis on Nutrition. There is a common view in the food service industry today that consumers are becoming more concerned about nutrition and health due to increased use of health foods, labeling laws, and more in-depth coverage of nutrition in elementary and secondary school health programs. If you are aware of this increasing emphasis, you can consider nutritional concerns when food service goals are set, menus are planned, and cooking procedures are evaluated.

Food and Nutrition: An Overview

This book discusses the management of food and beverage operations. In this chapter, you will learn how nutrition fits into the management process and why knowledge about nutrition is important.

Let's begin our study of nutrition by defining the term "food." As you know, food is material of either plant or animal origin which people eat. Once it is consumed, food nourishes and sustains the body and enables us to grow. Everyone needs food, of course, to live. But if we focus on the nutritional aspects, you will see that some food is better than other food.

Nutrition is the science of food. When you study nutrition, you learn about the food that you eat and how your body uses it to stay alive, to grow, to support good health, and, in general, to make you look and feel good. "Good food" is more than food that just tastes good. Good food should also be good for you from a nutritional standpoint and that's what this chapter is about.

The study of food and nutrition is very important. It is important for you—as a manager and as a person—to understand how food is used by the body to provide for energy, growth, maintenance, repair, and reproduction. You must learn how to eat proper foods in the right amounts in order to be healthy.

Food that is served but not eaten will obviously not contribute to a balanced meal or to a person's nutritional intake. For example, many institutional food service operations serve a well-balanced meal. However, if some of the components are not consumed, the nutritional content of the uneaten foods is obviously lost. Marketing—looking at the operation from the customer's perspective—is just as important in the institutional food service operation as it is in the commercial operation. What do your customers want? How can you provide it for them in a manner which they will want and accept?

Figure 8.1 Nutrients In Food

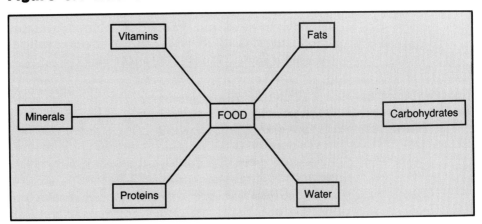

The fact that food must be consumed in order to be useful for nutritional purposes is also relevant to the commercial food service operation. We have noted that a food service manager's obligation is to make available components of a well-balanced meal for the customers' selection. The first step in consuming a nutritious meal is for the meal elements to be available. The second step requires that the components of the well-balanced meal be consumed. Making products available and acceptable from the customers' perspective is an important step in recognizing your property's responsibility to consider their nutritional well-being.

Nutrients and Food

Food is made up of chemical ingredients called nutrients, but food may contain additional ingredients which are not nutrients. There are six basic types of nutrients and each is illustrated in Figure 8.1. In order to supply energy, promote growth and repair, and regulate the body processes, nutrients must first be consumed. This occurs when food is eaten. Nutrients are then broken down into usable components in a process called digestion, absorbed into the body, and used to make up substances which the body needs for proper functioning.

It is important that the correct amount of each nutrient be provided in our diets. Everyone has a need for the same nutrients, but the amount that a person needs depends upon several factors such as age, sex, amount of activity, growth, and special life situations. Therefore, the definition of a "well-balanced diet" refers to a person who eats the right amount of each type of nutrient based upon his/her own special needs.

What Does Food Do?

You have learned that food provides the body with nutrients that are needed for good health. The main function of food is to supply energy for the body's activities and to keep the body warm. The nutrients which do this are carbohydrates and fats. Proteins can also be used as an energy source when carbohydrates and fats are not adequately supplied by our diet. This is discussed further in a later section of the chapter.

There are two other important functions of food. It provides the nutrients needed for sustaining growth and for repair of body tissue. The nutrients which are primarily responsible for these functions are protein, minerals, and water. Food must also be consumed to help control and regulate various bodily functions. Actually, all nutrients are involved in several regulation activities and a specific nutrient might be involved with more than one of these functions.

Advantages of Good Nutrition

Why is nutrition important? We have already noted that good health is impossible without good nutrition. This is important not only when you are young and growing, but for every day of your life. Nutrition affects your ability to function effectively, combat disease, and even influences how you look (nutrition affects your hair, eyes, teeth, and complexion).

Nutrition can also affect your personality. Irritability often occurs when a nutritional deficiency develops. Overweight people may show changes in their personality because of self-consciousness about their appearance. Also consider that one of your most important assets—your smile—is influenced by the appearance of your mouth, teeth, and gums. As you will see below, even your smile is affected by proper nutrition.

Your physical and mental efficiency is affected by nutrition. Many people who do not eat breakfast may not perform well late in the morning. Reaction time and work output can suffer.

Recent research indicates that children who are malnourished (do not receive proper nutrition) before birth or as infants may suffer mental retardation.[2] It is obvious that the dietary intake of the mother is critically important to the health and well-being of the child before it is born. If the mother nurses her child, the correlation between the mother's health and nutritional status and that of her child continues even after the baby is born.

Good nutrition helps your body resist infection and disease. You will learn below which nutrients are responsible for this and how they help to continually maintain the health of the human body. Let's look more closely at each of the six basic types of nutrients.

Six Basic Nutrients

Proteins

Proteins are essential elements in all living body cells. With the exception of water, they are the most plentiful substance in the body. Proteins are required to build, maintain, and repair all body tissues and they also assist with many other functions. They are necessary to maintain life and to promote growth.

Proteins are made of building blocks called amino acids. After digestion, proteins are broken down into separate amino acids which are then rearranged by the body into combinations that are needed to build required tissues.

What does protein do? Protein is necessary for body growth. Therefore, the protein requirement gets larger as the body grows since all tissues must be supplied and replenished with protein. Protein is also necessary for repair and maintenance of the body tissues. For example, the stomach lining is replaced every 24 hours and red blood cells live only four months. All tissues in the body are in a constant state of growth, maintenance, repair, and replacement. Protein can be used as an energy source, too. This occurs when the diet does not provide enough energy from carbohydrates and fats or when more protein is consumed than is needed for other activities. There are many other functions of protein. For example, it is needed to help form certain chemicals which are used to build resistance to disease. Other chemicals such as enzymes, hormones, and hemoglobin contain protein and regulate the body.

Which foods contain protein? Complete protein foods come from animal sources and include lean meat, poultry, fish, eggs, milk, and cheese. The term "complete protein" refers to foods which supply essential amino acids in amounts which closely approximate the body's requirements for making proteins. (Essential amino acids are those that cannot be manufactured by the body; they must be supplied in the diet.) Partially complete protein foods include dried peas and beans, soybeans, and peanuts. Incomplete protein foods are those that lack enough of one or more essential amino acids to adequately meet body needs. Incomplete protein foods are vegetables and other plant sources including nuts, breads, and cereals. Fruits and most other vegetables contain very little protein. A brief review of protein is shown in Figure 8.2. Note that Figure 8.2 also includes review information about other key nutrients.

Carbohydrates

Carbohydrates are nutrients that supply energy. They include starches, sugars, and cellulose. Carbohydrates come from plant sources such as fruits, vegetables, breads, and cereals. Some carbohydrates are also found in animal products; for example, milk contains lactose (milk sugar). Carbohydrates are the least expensive source of energy. They are also the second most abundant type of nutrient in American diets; only water is consumed in larger amounts.

Carbohydrates normally provide approximately one-half of the total calories consumed by most Americans. A calorie is a measure of energy which is contained in food. The body needs a certain amount of calories to work and to perform effectively. However, when more calories are consumed than are needed, they are stored by the body in the form of fat. If a person is overweight, it is often because he/she consumes more calories in the form of carbohydrates and fats than are needed.

What is the function of carbohydrates? They are the main source of fuel used for energy to conduct body processes such as digestion and respiration. Carbohydrates also help maintain proper body temperature and they eliminate the need for the body to use protein for an energy source. This is important because, as noted above, protein is needed for tissue building and other purposes. Finally, carbohydrates are necessary to form certain body compounds which are used to regulate many body activities.

Fats

Fats are another type of nutrient that provide energy. Fats (which are solid at room temperature) and oils (which are liquid at room temper-

Figure 8.2 Nutrients: Purpose and Sources

NUTRIENT	PURPOSE	PRINCIPAL SOURCES
Protein	• Builds and repairs body tissues. • Is a part of almost all body secretions (enzymes, fluids, and hormones). • Helps maintain the proper balance of body fluids. • Helps the body resist infection.	Protein of the best quality is present in eggs, lean meat, fish, poultry, cheese, and milk. Good quality protein is also found in soybeans and dried beans, peas, and nuts. Useful protein is present in cereals, breads, grains, and some vegetables; however, protein from these sources should be eaten with foods containing top-quality protein.
Carbohydrate	• Supplies energy for physical activity, bodily processes, and warmth. • Helps body use fat efficiently. • Saves protein for tissue-building and repair.	Starches: Cereals and cereal products such as bread, spaghetti, macaroni, noodles, and baked goods; rice, corn, dried beans, and potatoes; dried fruits and bananas. Sugars: Sugar, syrup, honey, jam, jellies, candy, confections, frostings, and other sweets.
Fat	• Supplies energy in concentrated form (over twice as much as an equal weight of carbohydrate). • Helps body use fat-soluble vitamins (A, D, E, and K). • Supplies elements of cell wall structure of all body tissues.	Cooking fats and oils, butter, margarine, mayonnaise, salad dressings, fatty meats, fried foods, most cheeses, whole milk, egg yolks, nuts, peanut butter, chocolate, and coconut.
Riboflavin (vitamin B_2)	• Helps body cells use oxygen to obtain energy from food. • Helps keep eyes healthy. • Helps keep skin around mouth and eyes healthy and smooth.	Milk and milk products, liver, heart, kidney, lean meats, eggs, dark green leafy vegetables, dried beans, almonds, and enriched breads and cereals. (Also present in a wide variety of foods in small amounts.)
Niacin	• Helps body cells use oxygen to obtain energy from food. • Helps maintain healthy skin, digestion, and nervous system. • Helps maintain the life of all body tissue.	Tuna, liver, lean meat, fish, poultry, peanuts, whole grain enriched or fortified breads, cereals, and peas.
Vitamin D	• Helps the body use calcium and phosphorus to build and maintain strong bones and teeth. • Promotes normal growth.	Fish liver oils, vitamin D fortified milk, irradiated evaporated milk, liver, egg yolk, salmon, tuna, sardines. (Direct sunlight also produces vitamin D.)
Vitamin B_6	• Helps body use protein to build body tissue. • Helps body use carbohydrates and fats for energy. • Helps keep skin, digestion, and nervous system healthy.	Pork, liver, heart, kidney, milk, whole grain and enriched cereals, wheat germ, beef, yellow corn, and bananas.
Folic Acid	• Helps body form red blood cells. • Aids metabolism within the cell.	Liver, lettuce, and orange juice.
Vitamin A	• Helps keep eyes healthy and increases ability to see in dim light. • Helps keep skin healthy and smooth. • Helps keep lining of mouth, nose, throat, and digestive tract healthy and resistant to infection. • Aids normal bone growth and tooth formation.	Liver, deep yellow and dark green leafy vegetables, cantaloupe, apricots, and other deep yellow fruits, butter, fortified margarine, egg yolk, whole milk, and vitamin A fortified milk.

NUTRIENT	PURPOSE	PRINCIPAL SOURCES
Vitamin C	• Helps hold body cells together. • Strengthens walls of blood vessels. • Aids normal bone and tooth formation. • Aids in healing wounds and broken bones. • Helps utilize iron. • Helps resist infection.	Citrus fruits and juices, strawberries, cantaloupe, watermelon, tomatoes, broccoli, brussel sprouts, kale, and green peppers. Useful amounts also in cauliflower, sweet potatoes, white potatoes, and raw cabbage.
Thiamine (vitamin B)	• Promotes normal appetite and digestion. • Helps body change carbohydrates in food into energy. • Helps maintain a healthy nervous system.	Lean pork, heart, kidney, dry beans and peas, whole grain, enriched breads and cereals, and some nuts.
Vitamin B_{12}	• Aids in normal function of body cells. • Helps body develop red blood cells.	Liver, kidney, milk, eggs, fish, cheese, and lean meat.
Calcium	• Helps build strong bones and teeth. • Aids in normal functioning of nerves, muscles, and heart. • Helps blood clot normally.	Milk, cheese, ice cream, sardines (including bones), and clams. Useful amounts in dark green leafy vegetables and oysters.
Iron	• Combines with protein to form hemoglobin which carries oxygen to all parts of the body. • Helps cells use oxygen. • Prevents iron deficiency anemia.	Liver, heart, shellfish, lean meat, dark leafy green vegetables, egg yolk, dried peas and beans, dried fruits, whole grain and enriched breads and cereals, dark molasses.
Iodine	• Helps thyroid gland function properly. • Helps prevent some forms of goiter.	Iodized salt, salt water fish, and seafoods.
Phosphorus	• Helps build strong bones and teeth. • Necessary part of all body cells. • Aids in normal functioning of muscles. • Helps body utilize sugar and fat.	Meat, poultry, fish, milk, eggs, milk products, nuts, and dried beans and peas.

ature) are included in this nutrient group. Some fats can be seen. They include butter, margarine, vegetable oil, and fat layers around and within meat. This type of fat, however, provides only approximately one-third of all the fat in the American diet. Fats which cannot be seen, such as fats within meat, whole milk products, ice cream, cheese, and egg yolks, provide two-thirds of the fat in the American diet.

Many doctors feel that Americans eat too much fat. A rich diet is the main cause of people being overweight. This is especially true when people do not exercise to "burn up" excess calories from diets which have too many carbohydrates and fats.

What is the function of fats? First, they serve as concentrated sources of heat and energy for the body. They provide more energy (calories) per unit than any other nutrient. Second, fat is necessary to absorb certain fat soluble vitamins (vitamins A, D, E, and K). Third, fats contribute to the flavor, aroma, and palatability of food (many foods which people like contain fats).

Vitamins   There are many different vitamins which perform various functions. Therefore, it is difficult to talk about vitamins as a nutrient type. Before discussing specific vitamins, some observations should be made:

- Vitamins are substances which are needed in very small amounts in order for the body to function properly.

- Vitamins cannot be made by the body; they must be provided by eating foods.

- In general, vitamins can be classified as nutrients which help regulate the body. Their major functions include promoting growth, aiding reproduction, digesting food, helping the body resist infection, preventing certain diseases, and maintaining mental alertness.

You can see that vitamins perform very important functions in the body. Some people are concerned that they do not get enough vitamins in the food which they eat. Synthetic vitamins produced in laboratories are often consumed in the form of vitamin pills. Synthetic vitamins are normally equal in function to and are not inferior to "natural" vitamins.

Vitamins can easily be destroyed. The way that they are handled (including cooking) affects their usefulness when they are eaten. Therefore, proper food handling techniques are important in order to preserve vitamins and all other nutrients as food is prepared.

Vitamin deficiency diseases can occur because of several conditions. Most frequently, a vitamin deficiency disease is caused by the inadequate intake of a vitamin. It can also occur when the body fails to properly absorb vitamins. Problems can also arise when too much of a specific vitamin is ingested. These concerns will be addressed as we discuss each of the important vitamins in this section.

There are two basic categories of vitamins: water soluble vitamins and fat soluble vitamins. Fat soluble vitamins are A, D, E, and K. Water soluble vitamins include the B-complex vitamins and vitamin C. Water soluble vitamins are absorbed into the bloodstream, but they are not generally stored in the body and must therefore be consumed on a regular basis. However, fat soluble vitamins are absorbed into the body along with other fat compounds. Since they are stored and can be used as needed, there is less need to consume daily amounts of fat soluble vitamins.

Let's look at the two categories of vitamins.

Fat Soluble Vitamins. As noted above, fat soluble vitamins are absorbed after digestion along with other dietary fats. They can be stored in the body rather than being excreted in urine. There are four major fat soluble vitamins: A, D, E, and K.

Vitamin A was the first vitamin ever discovered and it has many important functions. Unfortunately, it is frequently deficient in the diets of many Americans. Bones fail to grow their proper length without vitamin

A. In fact, this is one of the first symptoms to appear when vitamin A is inadequate in growing children. Vitamin A helps people see in dim light and keeps the skin soft and smooth. It also helps the linings of the mouth, nose, throat, and digestive tract remain healthy and infection resistant. Vitamin A promotes fertility because it assists in sperm production in men and helps babies come to full term within the mother. Vitamin A also plays a role in tooth development and in hormone production.

Foods rich in vitamin A include liver, egg yolk, butter, whole milk, deep yellow and leafy dark-green vegetables, cantaloupe, apricots, and deep yellow fruits.

Vitamin D is helpful in the absorption of calcium and phosphorus. Therefore, it helps form bones and teeth. If the body does not consume enough vitamin D, rickets—a disease of bones and teeth—can develop. The best source of vitamin D is the sun. When the sun strikes the skin, it changes compounds normally found in the skin into vitamin D. Unfortunately, this vitamin is not found naturally in many foods. However, fish, liver, and oils are the richest naturally occurring food sources. Milk is frequently fortified with vitamin D and in the United States this provides a very important source of the vitamin.

Vitamin E is popularly called the fertility vitamin even though it has no influence on human reproduction. Functions of vitamin E include preventing the destruction of vitamins A and C. It also helps protect body fats and fatty substances from destruction by oxidation. The best source of vitamin E is vegetable oils.

Vitamin K is called the coagulation vitamin. It assists with blood coagulation. The best source of vitamin K is dark-green, leafy vegetables. Some vitamin K is also found in fruits, potatoes, and cereals, with dairy products and meats supplying small amounts. Vitamin K is also formed in the intestine by microorganisms which live there.

Water Soluble Vitamins. As noted above, water soluble vitamins cannot be stored by the body; they are absorbed into the bloodstream. There are two basic kinds of water soluble vitamins: vitamin C and the complex of B vitamins.

Vitamin C is also called ascorbic acid and it is used to hold body cells together. It strengthens the walls of blood vessels and helps in healing wounds and resisting infections. Vitamin C produces healthy gums and helps increase the absorption of iron in the diet. The disease which results from a vitamin C deficiency is called scurvy. Insufficient quantities of vitamin C can result in sore or bleeding gums and in a tendency to bruise easily. Good sources of vitamin C include citrus fruits and juices, strawberries, cantaloupe, watermelon, tomatoes, green peppers, broccoli, cabbage, and spinach.

B-complex vitamins are mostly involved in activities which make carbohydrates and protein available for producing energy. There are several important vitamins in the B complex. While these vitamins (three of which are dicussed here) perform specific functions, their activities are essentially interrelated.

- **Thiamine** is a B vitamin which helps the body cells obtain energy from food. It also helps keep the nerves in healthy condition, and it promotes good appetite and digestion. Beriberi is a deficiency disease which results when there is an inadequate supply of thiamine in the diet. A person suffering from this disease can become irritable, nervous, and/or depressed, and may have an increased sensitivity to noise and pain. Good sources of thiamine include lean pork, heart, kidneys, liver, dry beans and peas, whole grain enriched breads, cereals, and nuts.

- **Riboflavin** is sometimes called vitamin B-2 and it helps the body cells use oxygen to release energy from food. In addition, it helps keep the skin around the mouth and nose healthy, and it affects vision. When there is a deficiency of riboflavin in the diet, there is often slow growth and general weakness. Cracks and sores appear at the corner of the mouth, and the tongue becomes slick and red. The eyes may be inflamed, hair is lost, and the ability to reproduce can be impaired. Good sources of riboflavin include milk, liver, whole grain and enriched cereals, green vegetables, fish, and eggs.

- **Niacin** is a B vitamin that helps the body cells use oxygen which is necessary to produce energy. It also promotes the health of the skin, tongue, digestive tract, and nervous system. Niacin plays a role in helping to make body proteins, fat, and some sugars. A deficiency in niacin can result in pellagra. Symptoms include extreme fatigue, skin eruptions, gastrointestinal disturbances, and sometimes mental instability. Good sources of niacin include liver, yeast, lean meat, poultry, fish, peanuts, and cereals.

Minerals   Minerals are another type of nutrient. They generally serve as building materials and as body regulators. Only 4% of normal human body weight is composed of minerals, but they are essential for building bones, teeth, and other body tissues such as muscle and hair. Minerals are important in helping to maintain the correct amount of water in each cell and they also allow certain reactions to occur within the body. Enzymes and hormones which are necessary to help carry on many bodily functions contain minerals. Likewise, other minerals are needed to send nerve messages and to allow muscle contraction. The list of minerals used by the body is long and includes calcium, phosphorus, potassium, sulfur, sodium, chlorine, magnesium, iron, manganese, copper, iodine, bromine, cobalt, and zinc.

Important minerals are outlined in Figure 8.2. Some of the minerals perform only one known essential function; others are involved in various essential and often unrelated functions. Minerals are often found in food in a water soluble form (they can be dissolved by water). Therefore, some of the same food preparation techniques discussed in this chapter to conserve water soluble vitamins are also recommended to conserve the mineral content of foods.

As you can see in Figure 8.2, many foods are sources of nutrients. You need to provide a balanced and varied diet for your customers in order to ensure that all minerals which are necessary for good health are consumed in the proper amounts.

Water   Water is a very important nutrient. There is water in every body cell, outside every cell, in the blood, and in other body fluids. In fact, about 60% of an adult's body is water and 70% of a baby's body is water. People can live longer without food than they can without water.

Water performs many important functions. For example, it serves as a solvent so that other nutrients can be used by the body. Water transports waste from the body through the lungs, gastrointestinal tract, kidneys, and skin. Water is also used as a building material for cells and it is required to make and/or use other materials in nutrients. Water regulates body temperature; it allows perspiration to occur and serves as a heat carrier as air is lost through breathing. Water is also essential as a body lubricant because fluid surrounds every joint to help it move smoothly. Saliva helps us to swallow foods, and other liquids which are made up of water help move food through the gastrointestinal tract.

Almost all foods contain water. Figure 8.3 indicates that some foods are almost 100% water while other foods contain almost no water. Cucumbers, celery, and lettuce, which physically appear quite solid, actually contain a large amount of water. Whole milk and oranges are also largely water (87%). Likewise, note the large amount of water (61%) in cooked spaghetti.

An adult should drink about six to eight glasses of water daily.[3] This closely approximates the amount of water which is lost by the body each day from respiration through the lungs, skin perspiration, and the discharge of body wastes through the kidneys and gastrointestinal tract.

You can see that water is a very important nutrient. While a small amount of water is generated as a result of chemical reactions within the body, much more water is ingested through the food that you eat. In order to be healthy, you should drink a large amount of water each day.

Food Guides for Health

After studying the above material, you should realize that there are a large number of nutrients found in a wide variety of foods which are important for health and well-being. Is there any way to develop some easy-to-remember rules which will promote good nutrition through eating habits? The answer is yes—and we will discuss them in this section. However, recall that the amount of each nutrient which is necessary for proper health varies from person to person based upon his/her own spe-

Figure 8.3 Percent of Water Content for Some Common Foods

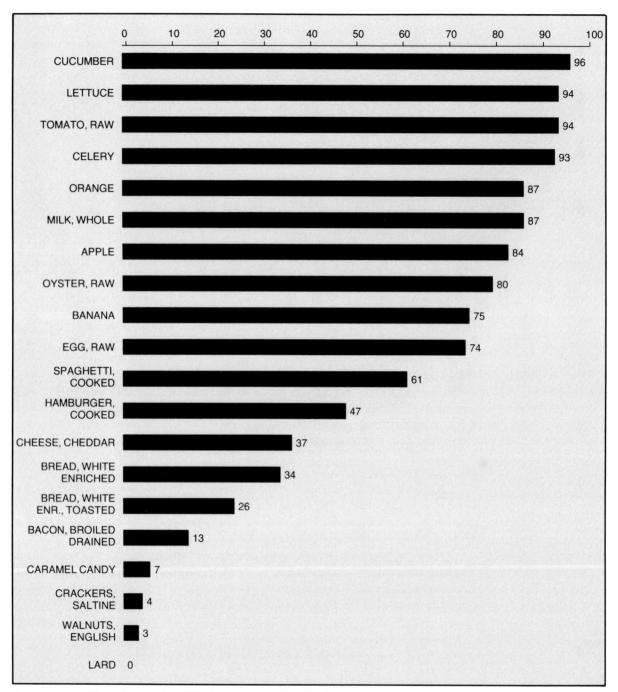

Source: Adapted from Composition of Foods, Agriculture Handbook No. 8, *U.S.D.A., 1963.*

cific needs. Therefore, while general information is presented here, it is still important to recall that it may or may not apply to a specific individual.

Figure 8.4 Information about RDAs

- RDAs provide guidelines for recommended nutritional intake for various groups within the population of the United States.
- RDAs represent average nutritional requirements only; not everyone within a specific population group needs an identical nutritional intake.
- RDAs are estimates of the nutrients that healthy people should consume.
- RDAs only provide estimates of nutritional requirements for selected nutrients — not *all* nutrients.
- RDAs should be met by consuming a variety of foods.

Recommended Dietary Allowances

Recommended dietary allowances (RDAs) have been established by the National Research Council of the National Academy of Sciences. These recommended dietary allowances provide amounts of essential nutrients that experts have judged to be adequate for the nutritional needs of most healthy people.

Knowledge about nutrition is constantly being updated so the RDAs are periodically revised. The allowances recommended for each nutrient take into consideration the variation that occurs between healthy individuals. Except for calories, each allowance is set higher than the average need. For example, the average amount of protein intake by healthy people was first determined and then, using statistical methods, this amount was increased in order to provide a recommendation which would apply to at least 95% of the population.

There are many misunderstandings about the National Research Council RDAs. Figure 8.4 attempts to clarify some of these concerns. Figure 8.4 notes that RDAs are really dietary intake guidelines for various population groups. The RDAs provide guidelines for healthy people and reflect information about only some nutrients which are required by humans. The RDAs also recommend that a person's nutritional intake be obtained from a variety of common foods—not solely from synthetic substitutes.

In addition to the RDAs established by the National Research Council, the Federal Food and Drug Administration has established a set of allowances called the U.S. Recommended Daily Allowances. These are used as a basis for voluntary nutritional labeling of food products. U.S. RDAs are based on the recommended daily dietary allowances and represent the highest level of nutrients required for any age or sex (with some exceptions). Manufacturers can use this information as a basis for determining the percent of daily allowances being provided in specified portion sizes by their products. Figure 8.5 reviews this information.

Nutrition Labeling

Perhaps you have noticed that many food products purchased in the supermarket contain information on the package label about the nutritional contents. Nutrition labeling is voluntary for processed foods except when either a nutrition claim is made for the food or when a nutrient is added to the food. In these situations, nutrition labeling is mandatory. Nutrition information on labels is being provided with increasing frequency by many manufacturers; consumers are becoming more nutrition-conscious and want this information. Food service managers in in-

Figure 8.5 U.S. Recommended Daily Allowances (RDA) for use in nutrition labeling of foods, including foods that are vitamin and mineral supplements

	Adults and Children Over 4 years		Children Under 4 years		Infants Under 13 months		Pregnant or Lactating Women	
Protein	65	g*	28	g*	25	g*	65	g*
Vitamin A	5,000	IU	2,500	IU	2,500	IU	8,000	IU
Vitamin C	60	mg	40	mg	40	mg	60	mg
Thiamine	1.5	mg	0.7	mg	0.7	mg	1.7	mg
Riboflavin	1.7	mg	0.8	mg	0.8	mg	2.0	mg
Niacin	20	mg	9.0	mg	9.0	mg	20	mg
Calcium	1.0	g	0.8	g	0.8	g	1.3	g
Iron	18	mg	10	mg	10	mg	18	mg
Vitamin D	400	IU	400	IU	400	IU	400	IU
Vitamin E	30	IU	10	IU	10	IU	30	IU
Vitamin B_6	2.0	mg	0.7	mg	0.7	mg	2.5	mg
Folacin	0.4	mg	0.2	mg	0.2	mg	0.8	mg
Vitamin B_{12}	6	mcg	3	mcg	3	mcg	8	mcg
Phosphorus	1.0	g	0.8	g	0.8	g	1.3	g
Iodine	150	mcg	70	mcg	70	mcg	150	mcg
Magnesium	400	mg	200	mg	200	mg	450	mg
Zinc	15	mg	8	mg	8	mg	15	mg
Copper	2	mg	1	mg	1	mg	2	mg
Biotin	0.3	mg	0.15	mg	0.15	mg	0.3	mg
Pantothenic acid	10	mg	5	mg	5	mg	10	mg

Source: U.S. Food and Drug Administration.

Key: g = grams; IU = international units; mg = milligrams; mcg = micrograms.

* If protein efficiency ratio of protein is equal to or better than that of casein, U.S. RDA is 45g for adults and pregnant or lactating women, 20g for children under 4 years of age, and 18g for infants.

stitutional operations, especially those dealing with various types of special diets, also require this information. While nutritional labeling information is currently of less importance to the commercial operator, many people think that this segment of the food service industry will, at some future date, also recognize the importance of becoming more nutrition-conscious. Customer demand will require that nutrition be addressed in the purchase, preparation, and service of food products which they consume.

There are many regulations which relate to nutrition labeling. Figure 8.6 shows actual information from a can of sliced stewed tomatoes. Notice that the label provides basic information about: (1) serving size, (2) servings per container, (3) calories per serving, (4) proteins per serving, (5) carbohydrates per serving, (6) fats per serving, and (7) the percentage of U.S. RDAs. The percentage refers to the amount of each nutrient in a serving based upon the total recommended amount shown in Figure 8.5.

Basic Four Food Groups

When you buy food for home use, dine out, or perform duties as a food service manager, you probably think about nutrition in terms of *food* instead of *nutrients*. However, home economists, dietitians, nutritionists, and others have worked to create a structure for developing and

Figure 8.6 Sample Label with Nutrition Information

```
                    NUTRITION INFORMATION
                        PER SERVING

       SERVING SIZE: 1 CUP ● SERVINGS PER CONTAINER: 2

CALORIES ..................... 70    CARBOHYDRATE ................ 18 g
PROTEIN ........................ 2 g   FAT .............................. 0 g


       PERCENTAGE OF U.S. RECOMMENDED DAILY ALLOWANCES (U.S. RDA)

PROTEIN ........................ 2    NIACIN .......................... 8
VITAMIN A ..................... 25    CALCIUM ........................ 8
VITAMIN C ..................... 50    IRON ............................ 6
THIAMINE ....................... 8    PHOSPHORUS .................... 4
RIBOFLAVIN ..................... 4    MAGNESIUM ..................... 8


INGREDIENTS: CUT TOMATOES, TOMATO JUICE, SUGAR, SALT, DEHYDRATED ONIONS,
DEHYDRATED CELERY, DEHYDRATED PEPPERS, FIRMING AGENTS (CALCIUM CHLORIDE
AND/OR CALCIUM SULFATE), CITRIC ACID AND NATURAL FLAVORINGS.
```

following daily meal plans. Perhaps the most common example is the basic four food plan. Figure 8.7 outlines each food group, its components, and examples of items and serving sizes within each group. The food groups and the recommended serving sizes are intended to provide a structure for a daily meal plan for most healthy individuals. However, modification of portion sizes and/or selection must be made in order to meet an individual's own specific needs for calories and nutrients. Figure 8.8 indicates the recommended number of daily servings of each food group for five consumer categories. For example, the common adult pattern is 2-2-4-4. In other words, a typical adult should consume daily two servings from the milk group, two servings from the meat group, four servings from the fruit/vegetable group, and four servings from the grain group. Other items should be consumed on an as-needed basis.

Menu Planning Implications

You have already learned that when you plan a menu in an institutional food service operation, you must be very concerned about the nutritional content of the meals. For example, in health care facilities the need to strictly follow a prescribed diet is critical to the patients' health and well-being. You can, using standard reference works, carefully calculate the number of milligrams of each nutrient which is contained in each food item offered to the patients. You can also regularly conduct nutritional audits. After a meal is served, assess the number of grams of nutrients which would have been consumed by the patient if he/she ate all the food items offered during the menu period. This process is often used by staff from government agencies who may need to assess the nutritional content of meals served to recipients or by representatives of health care facilities who have contracted with a for-profit management company to run their dietary services.

Assessing the nutritional content of food as menus are planned is not, of course, a reasonable activity for many commercial food service operations. However, as noted above, it is advantageous to understand

Figure 8.7 Basic Four Food Plan

1. **Milk Group:** These foods supply significant amounts of calcium, riboflavin, and protein.

    1 cup milk, plain yogurt, or calcium equivalent:
    - 1½ oz. cheddar cheese
    - 1 cup pudding
    - 1¾ cups ice cream
    - 2 cups cottage cheese

2. **Meat Groups:** These foods supply sigificant amounts of protein, niacin, iron, and thiamine.

    2 oz. cooked lean meat, fish, poultry, or protein equivalent:
    - 2 eggs
    - 2 oz. cheddar cheese
    - ½ cup cottage cheese
    - 1 cup cooked, dried beans or peas
    - 4 tbsp. peanut butter

3. **Fruit-Vegetable Group:** Orange or dark green leafy vegetables and fruit are recommended 3 or 4 times weekly for vitamin A. Citrus fruit is recommended daily for vitamin C.

    Example of serving sizes:
    ½ cup cooked vegetable or fruit, or juice
    1 cup raw
    Portion commonly served, such as a medium-sized apple or banana

Some good sources of vitamin A:	**Some good sources of vitamin C:**
dark green leafy and deep yellow vegetables and a few fruits:	citrus fruits
apricots	grapefruits, an orange, or orange juice
broccoli	cantaloupe
cantaloupe	strawberries
carrots	broccoli
chard, collards, cress, kale, turnip greens	brussels sprouts
pumpkin	potatoes, baked in the jacket
spinach	apples
sweet potatoes	
tomatoes	
winter squash	

4. **Grain Group (whole grain, fortified or enriched):** These foods supply significant amounts of carbohydrates, thiamine, iron, and niacin.

    Example of serving sizes:
    1 slice bread
    1 cup ready-to-eat cereal
    ½ cup cooked cereal, pasta, or grits

5. **Others:** Foods and condiments such as oils and sugars complement, but do not replace, foods from the four groups. Amounts consumed should be determined by individual caloric needs.

Source: A Guide to Good Eating — A Recommended Daily Pattern. *Courtesy of National Dairy Council.*

nutritional needs of the market being served and, when possible, to make available items which meet these needs. For example, operations that cater to teenagers should be aware of their high caloric needs and operations focusing on markets comprised of younger people should know that this group needs protein, calcium, and other nutrients. This is equally true for the commercial as well as for the institutional food service operation.

The basic four food plan illustrated in Figure 8.7 can be an excellent guide to help you plan menus. For example, you can design complete meals in such a way that one or more servings of each food group are provided in the meal. When you plan a buffet, several items from each food group can be placed on the serving line to satisfy the nutritional

Figure 8.8 Recommended Daily Pattern for Use with the Basic Four Food Groups

Food Group	Recommended Number of Servings				
	Child	Teenager	Adult	Pregnant Woman	Lactating Woman
Milk	3	4	2	4	4
Meat	2	2	2	3	2
Fruit-Vegetable	4	4	4	4	4
Grain	4	4	4	4	4
Other	Amounts should be determined by individual caloric needs				

Source: A Guide to Good Eating—A Recommended Daily Pattern. *Courtesy of National Dairy Council.*

needs of customers. A variety of food items can be available to satisfy the needs of customers who prefer a relatively light, low-calorie meal and customers who desire a heavier, high-calorie meal.

Nutrition and Your Market

Institutional food service operations have always been primarily concerned about nutrition. In many of these operations, the meals provided by the food service department are the only meals which the patients/residents see. Nutrition concerns can be easily justified if you are responsible for feeding patients in hospitals or residents in nursing homes.

What nutritional concerns should you have if you are a commercial food service manager? Historically, nutritional concerns have had a minimal impact on the management of the food service operation. However, the customer of the 1980s is more health- and nutrition-conscious. Nutrition labeling and a desire for healthy foods are two common examples. Since 40% or more of the meals in the United States are consumed away from home, you should re-examine the nutritional quality of the meals being served. Many operations offer a dieters' or weight watchers' meal and it is becoming increasingly popular to make available the components of a well-balanced meal for customers to choose if they wish.

It is true that not all customers are concerned about nutrition. Frequently, customers who desire a replacement meal for breakfast or lunch may stop at a commercial food service operation. They are more likely to have concerns about nutrition. Contrast this with the customer who is experiencing a special occasion meal at a restaurant. Nutrition concerns will probably be secondary. Therefore, you should ask yourself a simple question: "Why is the customer visiting my property?" If the answer is a replacement meal, nutritional concerns become important. If, on the other hand, the answer is a dining experience, nutrition may be of secondary importance.

Throughout this book, we have emphasized the need for you, the food service manager, to recognize the wants and needs of your customers. This concern for your customers and, at the same time, concern for the success of the food service operation, presents a challenge. You must recognize the nutritional wants and needs of your customers as well as satisfy their concerns for atmosphere, experience, and service.

Preventing Nutrient Loss in Food Service Operations

What happens if quality food is purchased, but because of mishandling during storage or preparation, the nutritional content of the food is diminished? Not only must the food service operation purchase nutritional food, but employees must practice basic principles of food preparation designed to retain nutrients.

Many of the food handling techniques discussed in Chapters 12 and 14 focus on nutritional concerns. However, several additional concerns should be addressed.

Food Handling: How Nutrients Can Be Lost

Cleaning and Trimming. When food is cleaned or trimmed more than it needs to be, many nutrients are lost. Heavy paring of vegetables is bad since a great quantity of some nutrients such as minerals are located just below the skin. If the skin and some of the underskin is removed, many of the nutrients are lost.

Oxidation. Quite a few nutrients are easily oxidized (destroyed when contact is made with oxygen). Therefore, cutting the food into small pieces, grinding it, or exposing large surfaces to air can cause a great deal of vitamin loss.

Light. Storage for an excessive amount of time can also cause oxidation. Sun rays destroy some color pigments and nutrients. Riboflavin (vitamin B-2) and pigments such as keratin (yellow) are especially susceptible to light.

Heat. Some nutrients are changed or destroyed by heat (vitamin C and thiamine). Therefore, the longer that food is cooked, the greater the chance of destroying these nutrients. Proteins can also be damaged by heat. Even when bread is toasted, some of the protein content of the cereal product is destroyed.

Water. A large number of nutrients dissolve in water, so soaking vegetables or food cut into small pieces (which exposes more surface area) is not good. Increasing the amount of time that food is in contact with liquids encourages the loss of nutrients which are water soluble. Whenever possible, foods which have been soaked in water should be cooked in the same water. After cooking, the water can be used to make soups, sauces, gravies, and related products. This helps put nutrients which have been lost in the water back in the food. If vegetables are cooked in water, the water that is left after cooking can be returned to the stockpot. If beans or other dried legumes are soaked in water, they should also be cooked in the water. This retains a maximum number of nutrients.

Food Preparation: How Nutrients Can Be Lost

There are basically two ways that nutrients are lost during food preparation:

They can be lost into a solution. Nutrients are dissolved out of food and, unless the solution into which they dissolve is reused, the nutrient value is lost. Nutrient losses can be minimized by avoiding the soaking of food, cooking food in the least amount of water, shortening cooking time, and reusing cooking liquids whenever possible.

They can be destroyed. This is the case with vitamins, but not minerals. As noted above, heat, light, and oxidation are common ways to destroy vitamins. Also, some vitamins are destroyed in an alkaline medium. For example, excess baking soda should not be used when baking products nor should it be added to green vegetables during cooking.

Some Final Concerns about Nutrition

The nutritional status of the general American public is better than in many other areas of the world. There may be a correlation between income and educational levels and nutritional status. The promotion of a basic nutritional education can do much to reduce nutrition gaps between various levels in our society.

Most institutional operations develop important operating objectives dealing with nutrition education. Perhaps some of this responsibility should also be assumed by the educational system. Likewise, what should be the parent's role in teaching children how to eat properly? Throughout the 1980s, you will see increasing concern about nutrition in all segments of the public. If you are a wise food service manager, you will have already undertaken a planned program to make nutritional menu items available to your customers/patients.

Food Habits

Unfortunately, the nutritional content of food may not affect its flavor (the "blend" of all sensory responses to food including taste, sight, smell, touch, sound, and temperature). Therefore, the incentive to practice good nutrition must come from another source. People must have an incentive or motivation to modify their eating habits in order to recognize nutritional concerns. Although food habits can last a lifetime, they do not need to.

Values can change. As we have more or less money, funds are or are not available to provide expensive foods. As we grow older, concerns about health and taste may change. Status also may become an important factor in food selection patterns. Foods which families consider necessary and/or satisfying may change. It is possible, of course, to get bored with certain foods. Through technological advances, there are more types of food that are now available. Food habits can also change because items are unavailable or available because of improved food distribution methods. When personal situations change, people have more or less time for food preparation tasks. Many people find it more convenient to dine out. The incidence of working mothers and higher levels of disposable income make these options more possible now than they ever were in the past.

Provide Well-Balanced Meals   The primary emphasis of this chapter is that nutritional concerns should be important to you as an individual and as a food service professional. There are many scientific principles of nutrition, but the bottom line is that we all need to consume well-balanced meals which meet our own individual requirements. Learning how to plan menus which consider nutritional implications and how to properly prepare foods to preserve nutrients are important steps to ensure healthful meals. You have a responsibility to provide proper nutrition for the people that frequent your food service operation.

NOTES

1.   This discussion is based upon United States Department of Agriculture, *Principles of Nutrition for Child Nutrition Programs* (Washington, D.C.: U.S. Government Printing Office, undated).

2.   Lewis J. Minor, *Nutritional Standards* (Westport, Conn.: AVI, 1983), p. 150.

3.   Henrietta Fleck, *Introduction to Nutrition*, 3rd ed. (New York: Macmillan, 1976), p. 243.

9

Sanitation: A Key Concern

Management Challenges

As a result of studying this chapter you will:

1. recognize your professional obligation to provide safe and wholesome food to the customers and employees who consume it.

2. know what conditions cause germs to grow and multiply, and how to incorporate this information into basic food handling procedures.

3. understand the importance of personal cleanliness in the protection of food.

4. practice sanitary storage conditions when holding food products.

5. be aware of sanitary practices which must be consistently followed when preparing and serving food.

6. understand basic sanitary practices which should be followed when cleaning up the facility and washing dishes, pots, and pans.

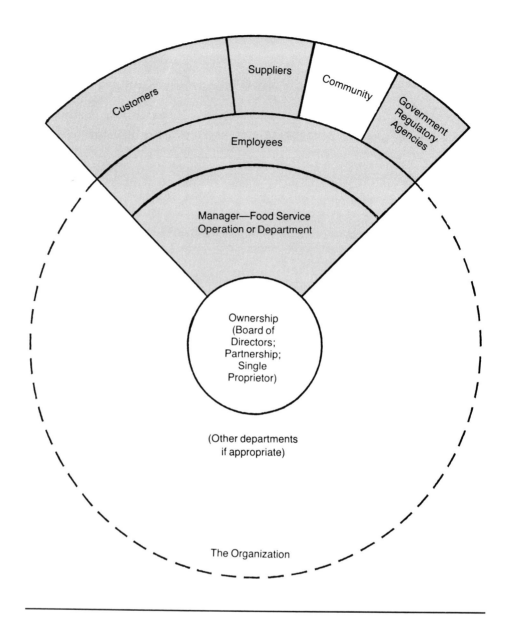

Focus on the Food Service Publics

Chapter 9 is about sanitation in food and beverage operations. Sanitation is a consistent concern which must be addressed at every stage of the food handling process. Serious illness and even death can be caused by the failure to follow simple, basic food sanitation procedures. This chapter focuses on the relationship between all members of the food service team and on the people who consume products prepared by that team. While the primary public being served is the customer, it is also true that management staff, employees, delivery personnel, and many other people come in direct contact with food produced by the operation. Sanitation concerns are much more important than just ensuring the continued success of the operation. They literally affect the health and well-being of the consuming public. Proper sanitation is vitally important to your food service operation.

An important objective of any food service operation (commercial or institutional) is to serve safe and nutritious food. In order for food to be safe, it must be clean, wholesome, unspoiled, and free of harmful germs when it is purchased.[1] In Chapter 12, you will learn that an important part of a purchasing and receiving program is, first, to purchase products from reputable suppliers (a visit to their processing/storage facilities is necessary) and, second, to carefully inspect incoming products against quality specifications to confirm that the operation's quality requirements are met.

Food products must be stored, prepared, and served under sanitary conditions. Clean equipment and sanitary work habits must be used, and employees must be healthy. As a professional food service manager, you must be assured that the food being served to customers/patients is safe and wholesome. Your concern for the consumer should translate into sanitation priorities as operating procedures are developed and as decisions are made which affect costs. It may be expensive to discard food which could otherwise generate sales income. Isn't that better, though, than risking the possibility of foodborne illness?

It is also true that sanitation concerns can be easily justified from the operation's perspective as well as from your customer's perspective. What could be more damaging to an operation than a newspaper headline which reads, "People poisoned by food at local restaurant"? When foodborne illness occurs at an institutional operation, patients can lose confidence in it. Also, strict municipal laws and inspection requirements may be imposed on the operation.

Customers, themselves, are concerned about sanitation. A nationwide survey conducted for the National Restaurant Association asked people to rank factors that they consider important in choosing or returning to a specific restaurant.[2] Cleanliness ranks number one when people want a fast-food or moderate-service restaurant. When people consider full-service restaurants, cleanliness ranks number two, second only to food quality and preparation. It is obvious that everyone—you, the employees, and the consumers—must be concerned about food safety. However, it is impossible to serve safe food unless you know what causes food to become unsafe and what must be done to ensure that food will be safe to eat. These two points will be discussed in the following sections of this chapter.

What Causes Unsafe Food?

Chemical Poisoning

There are two causes of unsafe food: chemical poisoning and harmful germs. Food can be poisoned by chemicals and pesticides. Also, some plants and animals are naturally poisonous.

Precautions. You can take many common-sense precautions to minimize the possibility of chemical poisoning. Consider the following:

Buy food from dependable sources. This may mean not purchasing food from the "back door salesperson" that offers special buys on products that were home-grown or caught in local fishing streams.

Wash all fruits and vegetables before using them. It is important for any pesticide residues or other chemical sprays used as part of the growing process to be removed.

Keep chemicals away from food. Chemicals should be stored in appropriate containers away from the areas where food is kept.

Be careful when selecting and using small equipment. Stories about chemical poisoning caused by mixing large quantities of acid-containing foods or beverages such as punch in inappropriate containers like zinc-coated garbage cans are relatively common. Likewise, the coatings on some household utensils can wear off over time, exposing food to potentially hazardous metals.

Be careful with chemicals in the food service facility. Use caution when spraying for flies, cockroaches, and other insects or when spreading chemicals for mice and rodents. Today's exotic chemicals must be handled by someone who is especially trained in their use. You probably do not have this expertise so it is best to leave the use of pesticides and related chemicals to the experts who know how to use them.

Use caution with chemical cleaners. They are used to maintain stainless steel, pots and pans, and other kitchen equipment. Chemical cleaners must be approved for use around food and should be applied according to the manufacturer's instructions.

The list of ways that chemical food poisoning can occur is lengthy, but using common sense will help you avoid them. The possibility of chemical food poisoning can be minimized by identifying problems in your operation and by training employees in the usage of proper procedures.

Harmful Germs

The second way that food can become unsafe is from harmful germs. There are actually several types of tiny living organisms which can make food unsafe. Examples of organisms found in food include bacteria, yeasts, molds, parasites, and viruses. Throughout this chapter we will use the term "germs" to refer to these and other small organisms. Since harmful germs are almost everywhere and are so difficult to control, much of this chapter will focus on what they are, how they cause food-borne illness, and, most important, what you can do to minimize illnesses associated with foods.

What Are Germs? Germs are small living organisms which are all around us. They are too small to be seen without a microscope. They vary in length, but it takes 2,500-13,000 of them, placed end to end, in order to make one inch.

Contrary to what you might think, not all germs are bad. Some germs are required to produce such foods as cheese and sauerkraut. Other germs manufacture drugs and useful chemicals. Still others are found in our intestines and help the body digest and absorb vitamin K. For example, yeast is a single-cell fungus that is used in making bread, beer, and wine.

But other germs are dangerous. They cause illness and disease if they are allowed to multiply and spread to humans through food or other contact.

Germs have different shapes. If you looked into a microscope, you would see round germs, rod-shaped germs, and spiral-shaped germs. Their shapes are not important in understanding sanitation practices, but they can help identify germs. This information is important when assessing whether germs might be responsible for an illness.

Germs Need Special Conditions to Grow. In order for germs to grow (i.e., multiply—except for certain parasites, germs do not grow in size), certain conditions must be present. Not all germs like the same conditions, but all germs need food. Unfortunately, the germs which are most harmful to people like many of the same foods that we do. These include:

- Nonacid, high-protein foods such as meat, fish, poultry, eggs, and milk

- Cream foods which contain milk, eggs, and related dairy products

- Products made from combinations of the above foods

The foods listed above are those that are most liked by germs; they can be classified as "potentially hazardous." While care in handling must be used with all foods, potentially hazardous foods must be given special attention. Any food products which are high in protein are those which are most susceptible to germ growth.

Germs need moisture to grow. Contrary to what you might think, freezing or drying foods will not necessarily kill germs. As products are dried or frozen, moisture is removed (in drying) or changed into another form (ice crystals in freezing). Germs may, however, enter a dormant stage only to continue to grow when moisture is again available; for example, when moisture is added to dry products or when frozen products are thawed.

Germs need comfortable temperatures for the environment in which they live. Scientists have determined that a "danger zone" exists between 45°-140°F. Germs will multiply rapidly if they are in foods which are at this temperature. Keeping food out of this temperature range provides a margin of safety. Food production and service personnel should do everything possible to minimize the time that foods are within this danger zone.

The acidity of the environment also affects the ability of germs to grow. Some germs can live in very acidic foods such as citrus fruits, but most germs grow best in "neutral" foods. These are foods which do not contain large amounts of acids. Unfortunately, many foods which are high in protein (meats, meat products, seafood, eggs, milk, etc.) are in the neutral acid range. This again confirms that special attention must be given to foods which are high in protein.

Oxygen is another important factor in germ growth. Many germs need oxygen to live, just as people do. However, some germs can live in either the presence or absence of oxygen, and still others grow best when there is no oxygen present.

You should now realize that many factors affect the optimal growth of germs. If you understand these factors and know how to make the environment "uncomfortable" for germs to live in, you will have the foundation for a safe, sanitary food service operation.

The Basic Rule of Sanitation

When we combine the information about potentially hazardous foods (those high in protein) with our knowledge about temperature (food should not be kept in temperatures ranging from 45°-140°F), we can develop what may be the single most important rule about food sanitation. Keep potentially hazardous foods out of the danger zone.

There are many other rules that are important, but understanding the effect of temperature on food is fundamental in fostering the safe handling of food.

Foodborne Illness

Just as there are different germs which can contaminate food, there are different illnesses that contaminated food can cause (we have used the term "foodborne illness" several times already in this chapter). There are really two basic types of foodborne illness: illness caused by poisons in the food which have been produced by germs and illness caused by the presence of harmful germs in the food. Let's look at both these types of foodborne illness.

Illness Caused by Germ-Produced Poisons

This basic type of foodborne illness (food poisoning or intoxication) occurs when germs get into the food and reproduce. When this happens, the germs produce wastes that are poisonous to people. It is the poison—not the organism itself—which produces the illness. If you can prevent these germs from entering food, the toxins will not be present. Many of the recommended food handling procedures discussed in this chapter focus on ways to prevent harmful germs from entering food.

There is one special concern about poison in the food of which you should be aware. After the food is contaminated with the poison from the germs, there is nothing that you can do to make the food safe. For example, if heat is applied to the food it will kill the germs, but it will not inactivate the poison. Once the poison is in the food, it will remain regardless of how much or how little heat is applied to it. Another problem with the poison is that it often cannot be detected by taste, odor, or color. Therefore, the common practice of "tasting the food to see if it is all right" is ineffective. At best, you will not be able to tell by taste-testing whether the food is safe. At worst, you may get sick yourself from eating foods which contain the poison caused by germs.

Types of Food Poisoning. Staphylococcal poisoning (staph) is a very common type of food poisoning. Staph germs are found on the skin and in the nose and the throat of most people. People with colds and sinus infections are likely to be carriers (people who transmit germs without having the disease or without showing any outward symptoms of the disease).

Staph germs cause problems because they produce a toxin in the food in which they grow. Foods most often involved in staph poisoning are meats, especially ham, poultry, and meat salads, and cream foods such as cream puffs, cream pies, and cakes. Illness usually occurs within four hours of eating the food. Symptoms are nausea, vomiting, abdominal pains, and diarrhea.

Another foodborne illness caused by the presence of poison in the food is botulism. Fortunately, this is rare, but it can be fatal. Botulism often results from eating improperly processed canned foods. With new methods of canning and processing, cases of botulism poisoning from commercial sources are rare. However, botulism can occur when improperly processed home-grown and canned goods are used in food service operations.

As with other food poisonings, the presence of botulism cannot be detected by taste, odor, or color. Illness generally occurs within 12-36 hours after food containing the toxin is eaten. Symptoms include dizziness; double vision; difficulty in swallowing, speaking, and breathing; weakness in the muscles; and paralysis.

Illness Caused by the Presence of Germs in Food

The second major type of foodborne illness (food infection) occurs when germs enter and then remain in the food. In this case, it is the presence of the germs themselves—not the poison they produce—which causes the foodborne illness. As noted earlier, the best thing is to prevent harmful germs from getting into or on the food in the first place.

Types of Food Infection. A food infection is the name given to foodborne illness that results from eating food in which the germ—not the toxin—is harmful to people. Salmonellosis (sam) is a common food infection. Sam germs live in the intestinal tract of animals (hogs and poultry are likely to have these germs) and people. Foods which are involved in these outbreaks frequently include meats such as ground meat, pork, and poultry; fish; eggs and egg products; and baked goods containing cream fillings.

Illness usually occurs within 12-48 hours. Symptoms include abdominal pains, diarrhea, fever, vomiting, and chills.

A second example of a food infection is gastroenteritis caused by the germ *Clostridium perfringens*. This germ is found almost everywhere: in the soil, in the intestinal tract of animals and people, and in dust. Food sources are soups, gravies, and stews that have been kept lukewarm in deep containers for long periods of time. Illness usually occurs within 8 to 12 hours after eating the food. Symptoms are abdominal pains and diarrhea.

Other Types of Foodborne Illness

There are several other types of foodborne illnesses that are caused by contaminated food. These include trichinosis, caused by eating infected or improperly cooked pork; tuberculosis and infectious hepatitis, transmitted by infected people through contaminated food or by eating utensils; and dysentery, transmitted by food or water contaminated with fecal material.

Common types of foodborne illness, information about how people become infected, a listing of foods associated with the illness, and preventive measures are shown in Figure 9.1. Recall how this information again confirms the basic rule of sanitation which you have already learned: Minimize the time that potentially hazardous foods (those high in protein) are kept in the danger zone (45°-140°F).

Service staff should know what to do when a customer complains about an alleged foodborne illness. Figure 9.2 outlines basic procedures which you can modify and adapt for your operation.

Personal Cleanliness and Health

Perhaps you have noted that many foodborne illnesses can be traced to the employees who handle foods. There are many important sanitation procedures which should be followed whenever food is handled. These procedures will be discussed throughout the rest of this chapter; however, the place to begin is really with the employee. Figure 9.3 lists basic rules of personal cleanliness that all food service employees should know and consistently practice.

Even if it is not required, a pre-employment medical examination is useful in helping to discover employees with illnesses or handicaps which may not be visible and which may affect their ability to comply with basic sanitation procedures. All food service employees should have regular physical examinations by a medical doctor. States and municipalities have different requirements for health exams. However, many jurisdictions require blood tests, chest X rays, and examinations initially upon employment and on a regular basis thereafter. Even if there are no laws that require these examinations, they are still a worthwhile investment. It is true that you can get an examination today and become ill tomorrow. It is also true that health examinations are good for you personally; they can help discover potential problems such as those relating to carriers of infectious diseases.

Figure 9.1 Overview of Foodborne Illnesses

Type of Illness	How People Become Infected	Foods Commonly Associated With This Illness	How This Illness Can Be Prevented
CHEMICAL	Eating food poisoned by chemicals from: • Insecticides. • Empty poison containers. • Food utensils containing soluble metals.	• Any food accidentally poisoned. • Especially acid food in containers or utensils.	• Carefully wash all fresh fruits and vegetables before using. • Keep all chemicals away from food. • Throw out chipped enamelware.
BACTERIAL			
1. Staph poisoning	Eating food infected by careless foodhandlers: • Germs from cuts. • Coughing or sneezing around food.	Potentially hazardous food that is high in protein content: • Custard and cream dishes. • Meat dishes (especially ham, poultry, and meat salads).	• Careful food handling habits. • School food service employees free from infections. • Thorough cooking of food followed by immediate serving or refrigeration.
2. Botulism	Eating food containing poison from the bacteria.	Canned goods which are not processed properly such as beans, corn, meat, and fish.	• Careful processing of canned foods. • School food service personnel should not use home- or school-processed canned goods.
3. Sam poisoning	Eating improperly cooked foods contaminated by: • The organism. • Contact with fecal material (often from rodents).	Foods high in protein content, especially: • Meats. • Poultry. • Eggs and egg products. • Baked products with cream fillings.	• Good personal habits of food handlers. • Thorough cooking and immediate serving or refrigeration of foods. • Good food storage practices.
4. Clostridium perfringens	Eating food contaminated by: • Food handlers. • Insects.	Foods high in protein content, especially: • Meats. • Poultry. • Sauces, soups, and gravies made with meat and poultry.	• Thorough cooking and immediate serving or refrigeration of foods. • Good food storage practices. • Good personal habits of food handlers.
5. Strep	Eating foods contaminated by: • Coughing or sneezing. • Dust, dirt from clothing, facility air.	Foods high in protein content, especially: • Milk, milk products. • Egg products. • Meats and poultry.	• Good personal habits of food handlers. • Pasteurization of milk. • Thorough cooking and immediate refrigeration of foods.
6. Trichinosis	Eating pork products which are contaminated.	Pork and pork products.	• Cook pork and pork products thoroughly (150°F or 66°C minimum in center). • Local, state, federal pork inspection.
7. Tuberculosis	Eating food infected by food handlers who carry the disease.	Foods high in milk or milk products.	• Milk pasteurization. • Proper sanitation of all eating, drinking, and cooking utensils. • Careful food handling. • Routine health exams for school food service employees.

Remember: 1. Handle foods properly:
    a. Follow good personal hygiene habits.
    b. Be careful with all foods high in protein content.

2. Keep foods at proper temperature:
    a. Minimize the time that foods are in the temperature range of 45°F (7.2°C)-140°F (60°C).
    b. Keep foods hot and keep foods cold or don't keep the food at all.

Source: United States Department of Agriculture, Food and Nutrition Services, Principles and Practices of Sanitation and Safety In Child Nutrition Programs, Washington, D.C., undated.

Figure 9.2 Procedures for Investigation of Alleged Food Poisoning

1. Obtain name, address, and phone number (home and work) of customer.

2. Inquire as to specifics of signs and symptoms.

3. Get details of food consumed: food or meal, date, hour, time customer became ill, duration of illness, medication taken for illness, known allergies, medication/inoculation taken before illness, etc.

4. Obtain name of physician consulted or hospital attended, address, and phone number (encourage customer to see physician for proper diagnosis of illness).

5. Call the company doctor (if there is one). Do not call the doctor at night unless the customer wants the doctor to come in or to speak with him/her.

6. A committee comprising the food and beverage manager, executive chef, and the area supervisor should also be notified *immediately* in order to review the production process.

7. Forward information obtained to the company physician (if there is one) for follow-up and *notify the Board of Health authorities if food poisoning has been diagnosed by a physician*.

8. Determine how many portions of same food item(s) were served. *Collect samples and specimens and send to laboratory for analysis*.

9. Determine which employee(s) prepared the suspected meal or menu item. *Send all employees involved in the production process for an examination* to detect acute or recent illness and/or the presence of illness carriers.

10. Analyze and document the entire production process to determine where and how food could have become contaminated and where there could have been an opportunity for bacterial multiplication in the food (time and temperature principle).

11. Survey and document housekeeping standards in the area where food was prepared and served. *Take a swab from the equipment and send it to a laboratory for examination*.

12. Analyze and document recent sanitation inspection results in the area where food was prepared and served.

Food service employees who are sick should not report to work. An employee with even a minor illness such as a cold, cough, open sore, or boil could easily contaminate food. An employee who has been exposed to an infectious disease should consult a doctor before returning to work.

Employee eating habits have an impact not only on productivity and costs, but also on sanitation. Establish and enforce rules about where and when employees can eat. Designate a specific area for employee use and permit eating only in those areas. Employees should be required to wash their hands after they finish eating.

Figure 9.3 Basic Rules of Personal Cleanliness

1. Bathe daily and use deodorant and antiperspirant.

2. Wear clean clothes. Many operations provide uniforms and locker areas where street clothes can be changed for clean uniforms (wear a clean uniform every day).

3. Shampoo hair as often as necessary to keep it healthy and clean. Wear it in a simple, easy-to-manage style.

4. Keep fingernails clean, well-trimmed, and free of nail polish.

5. Avoid excessive makeup and perfume.

6. Wear the proper clothes on the job.

7. Wear clean, low-heeled, properly fitting shoes with nonskid soles. The heel and toe should be completely enclosed for sanitation and safety reasons. Do not wear tennis shoes, bedroom slippers, or sandals.

8. Wear a hairnet that completely covers the hairline. Do not use hairspray as a substitute for a hairnet. Avoid hairpins and barrettes because they can slip out. Men or boys with short hair should wear caps; if hair is long, hairnets are in order.

9. Do not wear jewelry other than unadorned wedding bands. This is primarily for sanitary reasons, but also helps protect both the worker and the jewelry.

10. Do not smoke or chew gum in any food areas.

11. Do not cough or sneeze near food. It is unsanitary to carry used handkerchiefs in your pocket. If needed, disposable tissues should be used and then discarded.

12. Do not use hair spray, file nails, apply makeup, or comb hair in food service areas.

13. Wash hands with soap and warm water whenever necessary and use handwashing basins—not preparation or dishwashing sinks.

14. Use disposable towels to dry hands; hands should not be dried on dish towels, aprons, or uniforms.

15. Always wash hands before beginning work and before beginning a new food handling operation. Hands should also be washed before returning from the restroom, after touching the face or hair, and after handling soiled articles including money.

Sanitary Procedures for Safe Food Handling

Basic procedures which recognize sanitation concerns should always be followed when working around food. Let's consider some of these procedures for each step in the food control cycle.

Purchasing   All food which is purchased must be wholesome and suitable to eat. You should obtain it from legitimate commercial sources that comply

Figure 9.4 Basics of Inspection and Grading Programs

1. Generally, meats shipped in interstate commerce (products moving between states) and those shipped intrastate commerce (products moving only within the state) must be inspected for wholesomeness. A wise buyer uses only federally inspected products or ensures that state and/or local inspection programs are acceptable substitutes for federal inspection.

2. Grading of meats—or any other products—for quality is always an optional and voluntary service.

3. Inspection for wholesomeness of most seafood products is not required. However, the U.S. Public Health Service must approve shellfish beds from which these products are harvested.

4. Inspection is required for all poultry products moving in interstate commerce.

5. Eggs and egg products are generally inspected for wholesomeness.

6. The U.S. Public Health Service has issued very rigid regulations which help ensure good quality milk.

7. Inspection of cheese is voluntary. Inspection of fresh and processed fruits and vegetables is voluntary.

Source: Jack D. Ninemeier, Purchasing, Receiving and Storage: A Systems Manual for Restaurants, Hotels and Clubs *(Boston, Mass.: CBI, 1983), pp. 200-216.*

with all applicable sanitation laws. As noted previously in this chapter, avoid "back-door selling" by farmers, fishermen, and similar vendors. Likewise, prohibit the use of home-canned goods because there is a greater chance that foodborne illness will result from using them as opposed to using commercially processed foods.

When purchasing foods, be aware of the difference between inspection and grading. Inspection refers to an official examination or review of food which is made for wholesomeness. Grading refers to the quality of the food product. Figure 9.4 will help clarify inspection and grading. Figure 9.5 illustrates sample inspection stamps used by the U.S. Department of Agriculture (USDA) and other governmental agencies. These stamps certify that food products are wholesome, free of disease, and suitable for human consumption. Other stamps used as part of quality grading programs are also illustrated.

Receiving   When receiving meats and poultry, look for the USDA "Inspected and Passed" labels such as those shown in Figure 9.5. One of the most important steps in receiving is to confirm that incoming products meet your operation's quality standards, which should be stated in purchase specifications. While checking for required quality, review each food product to ensure that it is not obviously spoiled or otherwise unwholesome. Examples of specific receiving procedures follow.

- Do not accept frozen foods that feel soft, feel completely thawed, or appear to be spoiled.

Figure 9.5 Sample Inspection and Grading Stamps

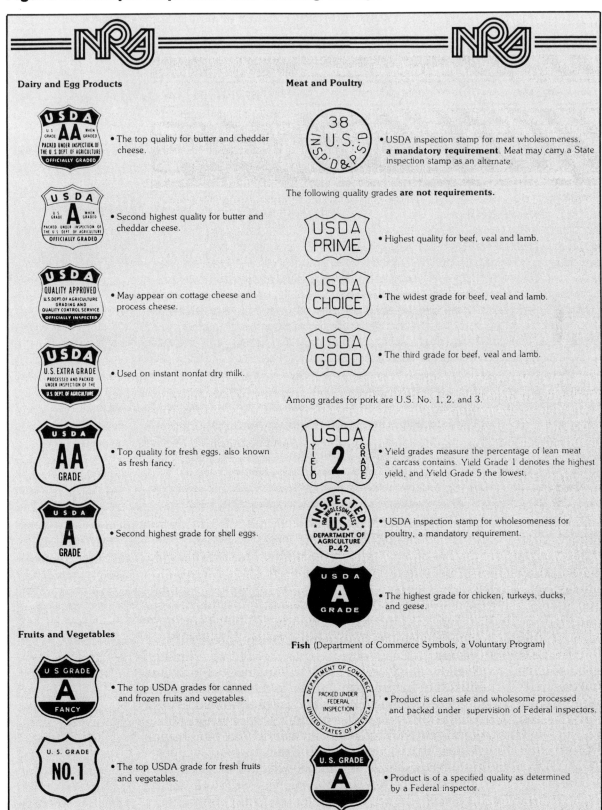

Dairy and Egg Products

- The top quality for butter and cheddar cheese.

- Second highest quality for butter and cheddar cheese.

- May appear on cottage cheese and process cheese.

- Used on instant nonfat dry milk.

- Top quality for fresh eggs, also known as fresh fancy.

- Second highest grade for shell eggs.

Fruits and Vegetables

- The top USDA grades for canned and frozen fruits and vegetables.

- The top USDA grade for fresh fruits and vegetables.

Meat and Poultry

- USDA inspection stamp for meat wholesomeness, **a mandatory requirement**. Meat may carry a State inspection stamp as an alternate.

The following quality grades **are not requirements.**

- Highest quality for beef, veal and lamb.

- The widest grade for beef, veal and lamb.

- The third grade for beef, veal and lamb.

Among grades for pork are U.S. No. 1, 2, and 3.

- Yield grades measure the percentage of lean meat a carcass contains. Yield Grade 1 denotes the highest yield, and Yield Grade 5 the lowest.

- USDA inspection stamp for wholesomeness for poultry, a mandatory requirement.

- The highest grade for chicken, turkeys, ducks, and geese.

Fish (Department of Commerce Symbols, a Voluntary Program)

- Product is clean safe and wholesome processed and packed under supervision of Federal inspectors.

- Product is of a specified quality as determined by a Federal inspector.

Source: Sanitation Operations Manual *(Chicago, Ill.: National Restaurant Association, 1979), pp. A6- A9.*

- Check all deliveries for evidence of insect and/or rodent contamination.

- Look at the condition of the delivery vehicle. If the interior looks like it has never been cleaned, maybe it hasn't! The delivery may also be contaminated if an open truck-bed rather than an enclosed truck body is used.

- Check incoming products for odor. Smells generally suggest a problem.

- Be careful about accepting any incoming products which appear damaged. If cases, bags, or other packing materials appear damaged, there is a possibility that the contents may be contaminated.

Storage   Food products that do not require refrigeration should be stored in areas that are clean, cool, and free from moisture. Dry storage areas should be well-ventilated and free from rodents and insects. Temperatures in dry storage areas should be between 50°-70°F with the relative humidity ranging from 50-60%. Use an accurate thermometer to monitor temperature ranges.

Store products on shelves that are slotted and at least two inches away from the wall. Shelves should be at least six inches off the floor in order to facilitate cleaning and air circulation. Keep all stored products away from the wall and away from dripping pipes.

Products that cannot be stored on shelves because of their size or bulk should be stored on easily movable dollies or skids. Store staples such as flour, cornmeal, and rice in rust-proof and corrosion-resistant cans with tight-fitting lids. Do not use metal food containers because they are hard to clean, sanitize, and maintain.

Use food on a first-in, first-out (FIFO) basis. In other words, products which are in storage the longest should be used first. As noted previously, do not store poisons, toxic substances, or cleaning materials in food storage or preparation areas.

Use special procedures for refrigerated and frozen storage. Keep temperatures in refrigerated storage areas between 32°-45°F with temperatures from 0° to -10°F for the freezer. Again, use an accurate thermometer to confirm and monitor these temperatures. As with shelves in dry storage areas, only slotted or wired shelves should be used in order to allow adequate air circulation. Since paper is a good insulating material, it does not allow quick cooling, so foods should not normally be stored in paper boxes. Likewise, do not line refrigerator shelves with paper or other materials. Inspect the facilities often. All shelves must be clean and products which seem spoiled or unusable should be thrown away, but be sure that you are notified first!

Place foods in proper containers before storing. All items in storage should be covered and placed in the refrigerator or freezer as soon as possible after receiving, cooking, or preparation. Store frozen foods in freezers in their original shipping containers. This is important because these packaging materials are usually moisture- and vapor-proof. When small quantities of leftovers must be frozen, process them properly and thoroughly. Mark dates on items when they are received so that it is possible to monitor stock rotation plans.

It is unwise to store products of any type directly on the floor even if they are in proper packaging containers. You can imagine the possibility for contamination when these items are lifted off the floor, placed on preparation tables, opened, and emptied. Dirt or soil on the bottom of the packages which have been stored on the floor will, of course, come in contact with preparation areas and contamination will likely occur.

The need to keep food products covered in the refrigerator is obvious. Not only does quality deteriorate when odors are absorbed by uncovered food or as food dries out, but it is also possible for items to fall into uncovered containers from storage shelves above the product.

Figures 9.6-9.8 review recommended dry, refrigerated, and frozen storage practices. You could post these practices in applicable storage areas and add any other storage rules in the empty spaces shown on the bottom of the forms.

Preparation

As you might imagine, there are a large number of basic sanitation procedures which should be followed when food is prepared. The need for frequent handwashing during food preparation has already been noted. The use of single-service, disposable gloves is also often practical. Make sure that food preparation tools and other equipment are cleaned. Contact surfaces must be especially well-cleaned between every food processing task. Examine raw, packaged, and canned products before they are used. Do not use cans that have swelling at the tops or bottoms, or those with dents along the side seams. Swelling may indicate that there is a bad seal and that germs have contaminated the product; gases given off by the germs can cause the can to swell. Dents along the side seam may suggest that the can's seals are ineffective. If canned products have strange smells, or if the contents seem foamy or milky, they should not be used.

Meats that smell strange or that have slimy surfaces should not, of course, be used. Generally, any type of food that appears moldy, cloudy, or that has a strange smell should be discarded. Remember that when foods look or smell suspicious, they should be thrown out. Do not taste foods since, as you have already learned, this type of test proves nothing and can make you ill.

Wash all raw fruits and vegetables thoroughly before preparation or serving. Also, be extremely careful when handling and preparing meat, fresh shell eggs, dry whole eggs, fish, shellfish, and any other products that are high in protein. Wash the tops of cans before opening them.

Prepare perishable foods as close to the serving time as possible. In order to kill germs, most foods should be heated without interruption to at least 140°F in the center of the food mass. Exceptions are poultry, poultry stuffings, stuffed meats, and stuffings containing meat (165°F),

Figure 9.6 Recommended Dry Storage Practices

	RECOMMENDED
NATIONAL RESTAURANT ASSOCIATION	**DRY STORAGE Practices**

✓✓ Store products off floor on clean surfaces to permit cleaning floor areas and to protect from contamination.

✓✓ Do not store products under exposed sewer or water lines or next to sweating walls.

✓✓ Store all poisonous materials, including pesticides, soaps and detergents away from food supplies.

✓✓ Store all open packages in closed and labeled containers.

Keep shelving and floor clean and dry at all times.

Schedule cleaning of storage area at regular intervals.

Date all merchandise upon receipt and rotate inventory on a "first-in—first out" basis.

Locate most frequently needed items on lower shelves and near entrance.

Store heavy packages on lower shelves.

✓✓ **DOUBLE CHECK THESE PRACTICES**

Source: Sanitation Operations Manual *, p. A19.*

pork (150°F), rare roast beef and rare beef steak (130°F). An accurate thermometer is, of course, necessary.

Thoroughly cook potentially hazardous foods. Foods that have been browned for hash or for similar dishes should be cooked immediately.

Rapid cooling is important for potentially hazardous foods. This is to minimize the time that food products are within the danger zone (45°-140°F). It is important to be concerned about the temperature in the center of the food mass—not the temperature on the surface of the food being cooled. That is why placing the food in pans with a maximum food depth of three inches or developing a cold running water bath to help the cooling process is frequently necessary. Frequent stirring, refrigeration of hot foods as soon as possible after cooking, and ensuring effective air circulation are all examples of good sanitation procedures when the food product is cooling.

Thaw frozen foods immediately before they are cooked. Freezing slows the growth of germs. When products are thawed, the surface will

Figure 9.7 Recommended Refrigerated Storage Practices

	RECOMMENDED **REFRIGERATED STORAGE Practices**
Nᴿᴬᴬ NATIONAL RESTAURANT ASSOCIATION	
✓✓	All cooked food or other products removed from original container must be enclosed in clean, sanitized, covered container and identified.
✓✓	Do not store packaged food in contact with water or undrained ice.
✓✓	Check refrigerator thermometer regularly. Recommended temperatures produce 45° F. (7° C.) or below dairy and meat 40° F. (4° C.) or below seafood 30° F. (−1° C.) or below
✓✓	Store large pieces of meat and all foods to permit free circulation of cool air on all surfaces.
✓✓	Do not store food directly on floor or base.
	Schedule cleaning of equipment and refrigerated storage rooms at regular intervals.
	Date all merchandise upon receipt and rotate inventory on a "first-in—first out" basis.
	Check fruits and vegetables daily for spoilage.
	Store dairy products separately from strong odored foods. Store fish apart from other food products.
	Establish preventive maintenance program for equipment.
✓✓	**DOUBLE CHECK THESE PRACTICES**

Source: Sanitation Operations Manual, *p. A21.*

warm first and will support germ growth. Likewise, as products are frozen, the center of the food mass will stay warm and will permit germs to grow for extended periods of time. There is, then, a continual need to properly handle frozen and thawed foods. For example, it is never safe to leave food out overnight to thaw. Potentially hazardous foods should be thawed in one of the following ways:

- In refrigerated units

- Under running water at a temperature of 70°F or below

- In a microwave oven if the product will be immediately transferred to other cooking equipment

Figure 9.8 Recommended Frozen Storage Practices

NRA NATIONAL RESTAURANT ASSOCIATION	**RECOMMENDED** **FROZEN STORAGE Practices**

✓✓	Promptly store frozen foods at a temperature of 0° F. (−18° C.) or below.
✓✓	Check freezer thermometer frequently.
✓✓	Cover all food containers.
✓✓	Wrap all food well to prevent freezer burn.
✓✓	Defrost as necessary to eliminate excessive frost build-up. If practical, defrost when the least amount of food is in storage.
	Plan your opening of the freezer. Get what you need at one time to reduce the loss of cold air.
	Remove contents to another freezer when defrosting to permit thorough cleaning and to keep contents dry.
	Date all merchandise upon receipt and rotate inventory on a "first-in—first out" basis.
	Keep shelving and floor clean at all times.
	Establish preventive maintenance program for equipment.
✓✓	**DOUBLE CHECK THESE PRACTICES**

Source: Sanitation Operations Manual, *p. A23.*

- As part of the conventional cooking process; for example, when steaks are charbroiled from their frozen state

Products that have been thawed should not be refrozen. Freezing, thawing, and then refreezing destroys the food quality (expansion and contraction of water in the form of ice damages the structure of foods).

Handle leftovers carefully. After they are removed from a production or service area, they should be quickly refrigerated or frozen and then used as soon as possible.

A common problem in many food service operations relates to the holding of hot foods until they are served. For example, casseroles, stews, gravies, and other products high in protein are often kept in a hot water bath at lukewarm temperatures for long periods of time. If germs get into these products, the time and temperature are ideal for a very serious foodborne illness. These types of foods must be kept hot (above 140°F) or cold (below 45°F) or they should not be kept at all.

Normally, do not stuff products such as turkey or meats with dressing before cooking. The meat/poultry product and the dressing should be cooked separately instead. You can imagine the potential problem when giblets, oysters, or other high-protein products are mixed into a dressing which is stuffed into a meat or poultry product being roasted. Extensive time can elapse before the internal temperature of the dressing is sufficient to kill any germs which are present. During the interim, the germs present in the dressing can be multiplying and creating a very serious sanitation problem.

Serving   The need for proper sanitary work procedures does not, of course, end when the food is prepared. Food must be safely handled when it is on a serving line, being portioned, transported, and served to guests. We have discussed the potential problems that can occur when handling protein-rich foods at any time during the food control cycle. All too often, however, hollandaise sauce (a sauce rich in egg products), meats, seafood, and sauces with ingredients from animal sources, etc., sit in the temperature danger zone in serving lines for long periods of time.

Now let's look at some proper sanitary procedures which should be followed when food is being served. These procedures apply whether food is being portioned for serving staff (who will later deliver it to guests) or whether food is being portioned for immediate service to guests, such as in cafeteria serving lines.

Cover most foods before and during service. Potential problems include contamination by dust, flies, and from sneezing and coughing. Municipal sanitation requirements often cite the need for sneeze-guards or breath protectors. These are various types of panels, often made of transparent plastic, which minimize the possibility of guests coughing, sneezing, or breathing on otherwise exposed food items in public areas.

Keep cold foods refrigerated until serving begins. Many work stations have refrigeration units which permit items to be refrigerated even during service.

Normally, hot food sections of serving counters should not be used to heat foods. Rather, these should be used to keep hot foods hot. Place foods in these units at the desired temperature. Use the equipment to maintain this temperature, not to increase it to serving temperature. To do otherwise subjects potentially hazardous foods to the danger zone for long time periods.

Know hazardous temperature zones. Keep potentially hazardous foods above 140°F or below 45°F during the time of service.

"Plate" food as needed. For food quality and sanitation reasons, "plate" food as it is needed for pickup by food service staff or customers—not before.

Use sanitary procedures to clean up spills. Make sure that spills in work station areas are promptly cleaned up with a clean, damp towel. Be especially careful when wiping spills from service plates.

Use proper tools. Tongs, scoops, or spatulas should be used for serving. Don't touch the food with your hands.

Be especially careful with eating utensils. Pick up flatware only by the handles; never touch the eating surfaces of any flatware or service-ware items.

Use a scoop for dispensing ice. It is never proper to use your hands or to use a drinking glass as a scoop. If the drinking glass breaks, slivers of glass will be scattered throughout the ice. Since you cannot distinguish between glass and ice, the entire ice bin will have to be completely cleaned.

Do not reuse food. Never reuse portions of food that have been served to customers but not consumed.

Clean portion equipment. Make sure that portion equipment is properly cleaned between each use. All too often a ladle used to portion a protein-rich casserole dish is placed on a serving counter, in a container of lukewarm (and quickly soiled) water, or otherwise mishandled between uses.

Practice sanitary personal habits. Service personnel should not cough or sneeze into their hands, smoke cigarettes, scratch their heads, touch their faces, or otherwise practice poor habits which will contaminate their hands and therefore the food that they work with.

Follow proper food handling procedures. Service personnel must follow proper food handling procedures when serving customers. These include the following:

- Do not handle serviceware and flatware by their eating surfaces.

- Carefully wipe tables with clean towels. Many customers place eating utensils, food which is being consumed, etc., on table surfaces. If these surfaces are not clean, they can easily contaminate flatware, food, or other items.

- Do not reuse food items unless they are considered "single-service with special wrapping." For example, rolls, butter, or cream in pitchers should be discarded if they are not consumed by the customer at the time of first service.

- Employees should not consume food which has been partially eaten by customers/patients.

Cleanup   The effective cleaning and sanitizing of dishes, utensils, pots and pans, etc., is one of the most important jobs in food service operations. Equipment and other small wares can be cleaned either manually or by using a machine.

Manual Cleaning. Often, local ordinances specify minimum requirements for equipment and procedures which should be used for manual dish, pot, and pan washing. Basic procedures which should be used for manual cleaning include the following:

- Remove large quantities of soiled foods from dishware with a spatula, brush, or other utensil before washing. Inspect dishware during washing so that cracked, chipped, or unusable items can be discarded. Often, a presoaking process is required to properly prepare for washing heavily soiled dishware.

- Dishware should be washed in a sink with at least three or four compartments. If a three-compartment sink is used, the procedures will involve washing, rinsing, and sanitizing. If a four-compartment sink is used, the normal process will involve prewashing, washing, rinsing, and sanitizing. Always follow local and other health codes.

- Use the proper type and quantity of dishwashing soap. Frequently, employees without training may not even use soap or they may use it in improper quantities. Determine the proper quantity of soap which should be used based upon information supplied by the manufacturer or supplier. Instruct employees accordingly and provide them with the proper equipment to measure necessary quantities of soap.

- Do not use dishcloths, dish mops, or soft sponges in the dishwashing operation. Also, do not use products made of metal spiral curls. The former are very difficult to keep clean; the latter can leave metal slivers in or on dishware being washed.

- Use plastic brushes with firm bristles for washing dishware.

- Frequently drain wash water and refill with clean, fresh, hot water.

- When manually washing dishware, the normal order should be: glassware, flatware, dishes, trays, pots, and pans.

- Wash glasses with a glassware brush.

- Place items in rinse baskets with the handles up after they have been washed.

- Rack glasses, cups, and bowls upside down in baskets. They should be placed in the racks so that water will reach all surfaces and they should not be crowded.

- Fill rinsing sink with clean water at approximately 100°F.

- Change rinse water frequently.

- Remove all detergent from dishes before placing them in the rinse sink.

- There are two ways to properly sanitize dishware when it is washed manually: with hot water or chemical sanitizing agents.

Hot water. Use water above 180°F. This normally requires using either a booster heater or an electrical heating element which is immersed directly in the water. Energy costs to keep water at this temperature can be expensive. Since employees cannot remove items from 180-degree water with their hands, they must use tongs or other devices.

Chemicals. It is frequently more practical to use a chemical sanitizing agent. When used properly, water does not need to be excessively hot, and the sanitizing process can be just as effective as when hot water is used. It is important to use proper chemical sanitizing agents in the correct amount. As with soap, determine the quantities to use and provide proper training and measuring utensils to employees.

Machine Cleaning. Even small food and beverage operations frequently use an automatic dish machine. Small operations may just use the dish machine for dishes and flatware; pot and pan sinks are often used to wash kitchen utensils. Sanitary practices for using a dish machine include the following:

- Inspect the dish machine before using it. Remove any soiled food, broken glass, flatware, or other foreign objects. Ensure that spray arms are working properly and that they are clean.

- The dish machine should always be operated according to the manufacturer's instructions. Carefully follow procedures for using automatic detergent dispensers, wetting agents, etc.

- Turn on booster heaters if they are used. They must be "sized" with the dish machine so that ample quantities of hot water are always available. Booster heaters are used to raise the in-line water temperature to the proper rinse temperature (180°F) in dish machines utilizing heat, rather than chemicals, to sanitize dishes.

- Temperature gauges for wash and rinse water must be working and must be accurate.

- Rinse dishes and flatware before running them through most machines. Rack them properly so that all surfaces are properly exposed to wash and rinse water.

- Wash water temperature must normally be between 150°F and 160°F.

- If a hot water rinse is used, the water temperature must be above 180°F for a certain number of seconds (normally specified by local sanitation codes). If chemical sanitizing is used for the rinsing process, it is important to follow the manufacturer's recommendations for usage, plus applicable local regulations.

- Air-dry dishware after washing; never use towel-drying which can recontaminate sanitized items.

- Handle clean dishes and utensils with plastic gloves or clean hands; be careful not to recontaminate clean dishes.

Procedures for Handling Garbage and Refuse

Every food service operation must use sanitary procedures for handling garbage and refuse. Use easily cleanable containers that are insect-, rodent-, and leak-proof. Thoroughly clean them on a routine basis to prevent odors and to protect the environment from rodents, insects, and germs. Cover all containers used in food preparation areas; there should be a sufficient number of containers to hold all garbage that accumulates.

Proper cleaning is a must. Use hot water, detergent, and/or steam and clean both the inside and the outside of containers. Provide a suitable space for the cleaning process to be undertaken.

Refuse must be removed on a regular, routine basis. Regular removal and other special precautions are necessary so that insects and rodents will not be attracted and will not have a place to live and reproduce. Filthy containers that are kept outside a food service entrance can attract rodents and insects which can then enter and infest the building environment. The areas outside the facility used to store garbage until pickup should be kept clean, and the lids on outside refuse containers should be closed. Place all garbage in these containers; they should be dumped frequently for the reasons cited.

Review of Sanitary Food Handling Procedures

Figure 9.9 reviews common food handling procedures which should be avoided, explains problems caused when these activities are permitted, and suggests alternate activities which comply with basic sanitation practices. Figure 9.9 is an effective review of procedures which should be consistently followed as employees work with and around food.

Concerns about proper food handling procedures relate more to attitudes than they do to the need to memorize an extensive list of "do's and don'ts." If you and your employees understand, first, the need to be careful around food and, second, the basic procedures which should be followed, many of the specific rules become more a matter of common sense. It is less difficult and more effective to become aware of the need

Figure 9.9 Food Handling Procedures

Employee Activity to be Avoided	Reason for Avoidance	Suggestion
1. Don't leave inventory on the loading dock.	Spoilage of perishable goods through bacterial growth.	Count inventory immediately and store in proper area, refrigerators, freezers, and dry storage.
2. Don't store food on the floor.	Food is easily contaminated by dirt on floor.	
3. Don't store food against the wall.	Prevents air circulation.	Food should be two inches away from the wall to ensure circulation.
4. Don't leave leftover food out.	To avoid contamination.	Refrigerate food as soon as possible.
5. Don't hold food in temperatures between 45-140°F.	To avoid contamination.	
6. Don't refreeze food.	Quality decreases, bacterial count increases.	Use completely or store after product is cooked.
7. Don't cook food incompletely.	To avoid contamination.	Heat food without interruption.
8. Don't taste suspicious-looking food.	Preservation of employee's health.	If it looks suspicious, throw it out.
9. Don't serve unwashed fruits or vegetables or open cans with unwashed tops.	To avoid contamination.	
10. Don't leave food particles on equipment, glasses, flatware, or dishware.	To avoid contamination.	Clean all equipment after use and inspect glasses, flatware, and dishware before service.
11. Don't use cracked or chipped glasses or dishware.	Bacteria can grow in the cracks.	
12. Never handle glasses by the rim, utensils by the eating portion, or tops of plates.	Transfer of bacteria from hands to dishware.	Touch dishes only by the edge, cups by handles, glasses near the base, and utensils by the handles.
13. Never place soiled dishes on the same tray with food that is to be served.	Possible contamination.	Use buspersons or clear the table with a separate tray.
14. Don't allow food to stand on the service counter.	Cooling food increases chances of bacterial growth.	Serve it at once.
15. Never sit on counters or tables; don't lean on tables.	Contaminants on clothing are transferred to tables.	
16. Don't have hair loose.	Hair falls in food and causes contamination. It is also not appetizing.	Wear hairnets or hats.
17. Keep your hands away from your face and hair and out of your pockets; do not touch money unless necessary.	Possible contamination.	If you must do any of these things, wash hands thoroughly afterward.
18. Never chew gum or anything of a similar nature.	It can spread infection.	
19. Never carry the check or pencil in your mouth. Don't put a pencil in your hair.	Bacteria can be spread.	Check should be carried in your hand; pencil in your pocket.
20. Avoid sneezing, yawning, or coughing.	Spreads infection.	If unavoidable, be sure to turn away from food or guests and cover your mouth.

Adapted from material originally developed by Jeanne Picard, School of Hotel, Restaurant and Tourism Administration, University of New Orleans, 1980.

Employee Activity to be Avoided	Reason for Avoidance	Suggestion
21. Do not spit.	Spreads infection.	
22. Don't eat or nibble on the job; never eat from bus trays or soiled dishes.	Disease can spread.	Eat at designated break times and wash hands thoroughly when finished.
23. Never smoke on duty.	The nicotine virus can be transferred as well as disease.	Smoke in designated areas during breaks; wash hands thoroughly afterward.
24. Never use your apron as a towel.	Clean hands are contaminated on a dirty apron.	Use disposable towels.
25. Never work with dirty hands.	Possible contamination.	Wash hands using warm, soapy water. Lather well and rinse with clear water. Dry hands with disposable towels.
26. Never handle clean dishes if hands have not been cleaned after touching soiled dishes.	Possible contamination from soiled dishes.	Wash hands thoroughly between these two stages. This is for all personnel — dishwashers, servers, and buspersons.
27. Never touch or pick up food with hands.	Spread of infection from the skin.	Use the proper serving tool or gloves.
28. Don't report to work in soiled clothes.	Soil can harbor infection.	Always wear a clean uniform and apron.
29. Avoid excessive jewelry.	Food particles can collect and cause contamination.	Wear a minimum of jewelry.
30. Don't arrive at work needing a bath.	To avoid bacterial contamination.	Bathe and use deodorant daily.
31. Never use the same knife and cutting board for meats and vegetables without washing.	Salmonella and other very small organisms can spread.	Use a different knife and board, or wash board and use a sanitizer.
32. Don't report to work if sick.	Increases the chances of spreading the illness.	Call in so a replacement can be located.
33. Don't work with exposed wounds.	Increases risk of wound infection and of spreading it.	Always keep wounds covered with the proper type of bandage.
34. Don't report to work if your health card has expired.	Prevents the spread of communicable disease, tuberculosis, and venereal disease.	Keep track of the expiration date and renew it immediately.
35. Never wash hands in sinks used to prepare food.	Contamination of food.	Use designated handwashing sink.
36. Never taste food with your finger.	Contamination of food by saliva.	Use a tasting spoon and only once.
37. Never re-serve food.	Handling of the food by guests can spread disease.	Throw food away; avoid giving an excess of rolls, etc., when serving.
38. Never serve pork rare.	To prevent trichinosis.	Cook pork until done to kill trichina organisms.
39. Never leave racks of glasses bowl-side up.	Airborne illness can collect.	Store glassware inverted.
40. Never store food in an open container.	Airborne particles can contaminate foods.	Always store food in sealed containers.
41. Don't leave prepped food out.	Possible contamination.	Prepare just prior to cooking or serving.
42. Never dry dishware, glasses, utensils, or cooking equipment with a towel.	Possible bacterial contamination.	Let air dry or dry in dishwashing machine's cycle.
43. Don't store garbage with food.	Increases chances of infection.	Have the proper places for each.

for proper sanitation and to incorporate this concern into the development of standard operating procedures for handling food than it is to memorize a number of rules without understanding the need for them.

Implementation of Sanitation Program

Merely knowing proper sanitary food handling techniques is, of course, not enough. Ongoing sanitation programs must be designed, implemented, and consistently followed. A self-inspection program is usually at the heart of any property's effort to ensure that sanitation procedures are consistently complied with.[3] You can develop checklists which focus attention on equipment, facilities, food handling practices, and food service employees as well. The responsibility to develop and conduct these self-inspection programs should be that of the management staff in each area of the food service operation.

Employee Training

Employee training is also part of a sanitation program. Not only must you provide sanitation guidelines, but employees must realize that there is a need to consistently follow these guidelines as work is performed. The success of any sanitation program rests with employees. Develop and incorporate proper sanitary food handling procedures into work which is to be performed. Then train your employees in these procedures with an emphasis on sanitary aspects of their work.

After employees have been trained in specific sanitation procedures for their jobs, you may want to give them additional training in general sanitation procedures. For example, use a safety inspection checklist and share it with your employees during general training sessions. Perhaps you could discuss specific sections of the checklist at employee staff meetings. Employees, themselves, may have suggestions about ways to improve the checklist and the resulting inspection program. With experience, employees could even be responsible for conducting parts of the inspection program.

It is unwise to train employees in sanitation only when time permits or when you get around to it. Rather, sanitation priorities should be included in both the orientation and the training which new employees receive and in the ongoing supervision and staff development/training programs provided for experienced staff members.

Notes

1. This discussion is based upon U.S. Department of Agriculture, Child Nutrition Programs, *Principles and Practices of Sanitation and Safety in Child Nutrition Programs* (Washington, D.C.: U.S. Government Printing Office, undated).

2. *Sanitation Operations Manual* (Chicago, Ill.: National Restaurant Association, 1979), p. iii.

3. For additional information readers are referred to Ronald F. Cichy, *Sanitation Management: Strategies for Success* (East Lansing, Mich.: Educational Institute of the American Hotel & Motel Association, 1984).

10
Food Service Safety

Management Challenges

As a result of studying this chapter you will:

1. understand why management must be committed to ongoing safety programs designed to protect customers and employees.

2. be aware of the part that employees play in ongoing safety programs.

3. be able to minimize and prevent food service accidents.

4. know general safety procedures which should be followed when food service equipment is operating.

5. recognize the need for accident inspection programs and know how to develop and implement them.

6. be able to implement and evaluate ongoing safety inspection programs.

7. understand Occupational Safety and Health Administration requirements which affect food service operations.

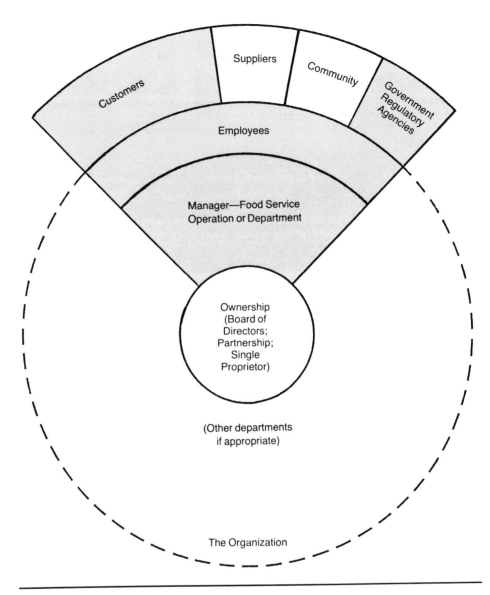

Suppliers

Community

Customers

Government
Regulatory
Agencies

Employees

Manager—Food Service
Operation or Department

Ownership
(Board of
Directors;
Partnership;
Single
Proprietor)

(Other departments
if appropriate)

The Organization

Focus on the
Food Service Publics

Chapter 10 is about safety programs. As was true in our discussion of sanitation, safety concerns are vital in the relationship between the food service staff (both management and employees) and the customers. As a food service manager, you have a professional responsibility to make safe working conditions and equipment available for employees. Facilities must be designed and maintained so that they do not contribute to accidents. You must be committed to training and inspection programs and work with employees on a continual basis to prevent accidents. When accidents occur, carefully investigate them to ensure that they do not happen again. You have a professional, personal, and often legal obligation to ensure the safety of employees and customers as they work at and visit the food service operation.

Does safety mean accident prevention for employees? Or for customers? How about personal health and accident concerns due to severe weather, fires, bombs, or bomb threats? For the purpose of this chapter, safety is defined as the prevention of accidents which can bring harm to customers and employees.

An accident is an unplanned or unforeseen event; most accidents are caused by someone's carelessness. This suggests that most accidents can be prevented. The issue then becomes what you, as a food service manager, can do to help protect customers and employees from danger or injury while they are at your property. Of course, your immediate concern should be about any personal injury, but it is also important to think about the possibility of damage or loss to your food service operation or to its equipment. (For example, a fire can injure an employee or a guest *and* can cause damage to the property.)

It is true that your primary concern rests with the safety of the customer and the employee. However, even as you focus attention on people's safety, it is also possible to, at the same time, implement action plans which can protect the operation.

Importance of Ongoing Safety Programs

Your primary concern in developing and implementing an effective safety program is, of course, to protect employees and customers. There are professional concerns about reducing losses of revenue, equipment, and property as well. In many ways, the development of ongoing safety programs really begins with the attitude that safety is important and that there are things you can do to improve the safety of guests, employees, the equipment, and your property. In other words, there must be a commitment from management and food service staff that safety programs include the following:[1]

- Management takes an active role in helping to reduce the possibility and occurrence of accidents.

- Management ensures that safety concerns take priority over convenience; safe practices are incorporated, whenever possible, into all operating procedures.

- Management urges the active participation of all staff members in ongoing safety programs.

**Management
Responsi-
bilities**

In many food and beverage operations, managers play an active part in ongoing safety programs. For example, they: (1) help develop work procedures which recognize safety concerns, (2) train employees in work procedures that incorporate safety concerns, (3) inspect food and beverage departments to ensure that both the equipment and the facilities are safe, (4) complete accident reports, assist in accident investigations, and do whatever is necessary to ensure that problems which cause accidents are quickly corrected, (5) whenever necessary, assist in treatment and seek medical assistance for injured employees or guests, (6) report needed repairs or maintenance, changes in work procedures, or other conditions which are potential causes of accidents, (7) conduct ongoing safety meetings and other safety activities, and (8) ensure that customer conduct is conducive to safety.

**Employee
Responsi-
bilities**

Food service employees also have responsibilities in ongoing safety programs. For example, they should observe and closely follow required work procedures. This includes using personal protective equipment and following all requirements for the safe operation of equipment at all times. It also includes ensuring that work areas are kept in approved condition, reporting any problems requiring repair and/or maintenance as soon as they are observed, and promptly notifying supervisors of any accidents no matter how minor they might appear.

It should be obvious that all members of the food service staff—top management, supervisors, and employees—are members of the operation's "safety team."

Food Service Accidents: Their Causes and Prevention

Let's look at some of the most common types of accidents which occur in food service operations. Special attention will be paid to precautions which employees should take to help protect themselves and other people from these accidents.

Burns

Many accidents in food service operations are caused by burns. Precautions that can be taken to prevent burns include the following:[2]

Use dry potholders. When handling hot pots and pans, never use an apron, towel, or dishcloth. A wet or damp potholder can cause a steam burn.

Open pots carefully. Always open pots (such as small equipment on ranges or lids for steam kettles) by raising the back of the lids so that steam will escape away from your face and body.

Treat hot water with respect. Always turn on hot water faucets cautiously.

Turn handles away from busy areas. Keep handles of pots and pans which are on cooking equipment out of traffic aisles.

Follow recommended procedures. Always follow the manufacturer's instructions when using any cooking equipment or when lighting gas equipment.

Use good judgment when filling containers. Avoid filling pots, pans, or kettles too full.

Do not spill. Avoid spattering, splashing, or allowing food to boil over.

Stir food carefully. Always stir food with long-handled spoons or paddles.

Plan ahead. Always have a place prepared for hot pans before removing them from a range or oven. If you know where you're going to put a hot pan before you pick it up, the time you spend holding it will be minimized. Do not hesitate to ask for assistance when handling hot and heavy containers.

Use appropriate pans. Don't use pans with loose handles (they can break off) or rounded bottoms which can tip.

Do not reach into hot ovens. Use a puller or other proper tool to bring pans to the front of the oven.

Cool equipment. Allow equipment to cool before you try to clean it.

Know how to put out fires. If food catches on fire, spread salt or baking soda on the flame; do not use water. Know how to use fire extinguishers and other safety equipment.

Be careful with matches. Put used matches into a tin or glass container.

Use safety measures with deep fat fryers. Always be careful when filtering or changing shortening in deep fat fryers; using gloves is recommended.

Prohibit horseplay. Do not allow running in the food service facility. Accidents (burns for example) can result.

Train employees. Food servers should be trained to properly pour coffee and other hot liquids.

Post caution signs. Counter surfaces below heat lamps can get very hot; warn employees with proper caution signs.

Clean appliances regularly. Prevent the buildup of grease on stove tops and in ventilation hoods.

Close oven doors. Keep oven doors closed when they are not being used.

Muscle Strains and Falls

Muscle strains are another frequent cause of accidents in food service preparation and storage areas. Always have a firm footing before attempting to lift a heavy object. Remember to keep your back straight; do not bend forward or sideways. Bend your knees to pick up low objects. The weight of the lifted object should be on your leg muscles, not on your back muscles. Food service employees should not try to carry too many or too heavy items at one time. When carrying a heavy load, ask for help or use a cart.

There are some common-sense rules which can be used to help prevent falls. Next to traffic accidents, falls kill more people than any other kind of accident. You may be interested to learn that most falls are from slips or trips at floor level and not from high places.[3] Some special precautions to help prevent falls include the following:

Clean floors. Keep floors clean and dry at all times. Wipe up spills immediately.

Remove hazards from floors. Keep hazardous objects such as boxes, mops, brooms, etc., off floors at all times. Replace loose or upturned floor tiles as soon as they are noticed.

Be careful with ladders. Use a sturdy stepladder to remove items from high places.

Open and shut doors carefully. Always walk, never run, and use caution when going through swinging doors.

Wear appropriate shoes. Food service employees should wear low heels and properly fitting shoes that have non-skid soles. Never wear shoes with thin soles, worn-out shoes, slippers, high heels, tennis shoes, or sandals. The heel and toe of the shoe should be completely enclosed. Keep shoestrings tied to prevent slipping.

Keep areas free of snow and ice. Always remove snow and ice from entrances and walkways.

Make sure that side entrances are safe. Frequently clean areas such as side entrances. Keep floor mats or other protective devices in good and clean condition.

Avoid slippery conditions. Utilize "slip-resistant" floor waxes.

Post safety signs. Use "Caution" or "Wet Floor" signs when appropriate.

Repair stairs. Replace stair treads that are cracked or worn.

Keep areas well-lit. Provide adequate lighting in stairwells or other places that are not frequently used.

Cuts   Cuts are constant hazards for food preparation employees. Precautions that can prevent cuts include the following:

Store sharp objects properly. Keep knives, cleavers, saws, and other sharp tools in racks or special drawers when they are not being used. Don't just throw them into a drawer or put them in a dangerous place.

Use safety procedures when cutting. Always place objects on a table or on a cutting board. Cut away from your body when slicing; the food item should be firmly grasped and sliced by cutting downward. When chopping food with a knife, bend your fingers and hold the item with your hand. Keep the point of the chopping knife on the block. Use the correct size of cutting tools and make sure they have the proper blade. In addition, discard or repair knives with loose handles.

Keep knives sharp. You may be surprised to learn that dull knives cause more problems than sharp knives because dull knives require employees to exert more pressure and slippage problems are more likely to occur. When using sharpening steels, be sure that there is a fingerguard between the handles and the steel.

Wash all sharp objects separately. Collect all sharp tools on a special tray; wash them separately. Never throw knives or other sharp tools into sinks filled with water.

Prohibit horseplay with knives. Never play with knives or sharp equipment and don't try to catch a knife which is falling.

Concentrate. Always be alert when using a knife, slicer, or similar equipment.

Don't leave knives on the edge of the counter. Push them back so they cannot fall on the floor or on someone's foot.

Minimize the use of glass in the kitchen. Clean up broken glass immediately; use a broom and dustpan to sweep up broken china or glass. Never use your fingers. If glass is broken in a dishwasher, drain it first and pick up bits of glass with a damp cloth. Always place broken glass or china in a separate refuse container.

Utilize safety features. Use safety guards and any other safety items which are provided on equipment.

Be careful with grinders. Use the feeder/tamper in the hopper of a meat grinder.

Unplug equipment. Always unplug any equipment before cleaning it.

Clean blades with caution. Use a folded heavy cloth to clean the blades. Work slowly and carefully from the center of the blade to the outside cutting edge. Make sure that the blade is in the position recommended for cleaning.

Always use appropriate tools. Never use knives as substitutes for screwdrivers or can openers. Don't use knives to open cardboard cartons; use the proper container-opening tool.

Electrical Equipment Accidents

Electrical equipment accidents are common causes of problems in most food and beverage operations. Special precautions which can help prevent electrical equipment accidents include the following:

Familiarize employees with equipment. Employees should be instructed in the proper way to disassemble, reassemble, and use all electrical equipment.

Use preventive maintenance. A qualified electrician should inspect all electrical equipment, wiring, switches, etc., on a regular basis as part of an ongoing preventive maintenance program.

Ground equipment. All electrical equipment must be properly grounded.

Follow recommended procedures. Carefully follow the manufacturer's instructions whenever operating electrical equipment.

Use caution when touching equipment. Never touch metal sockets and electrical equipment when your hands are wet or you are standing on a wet floor.

Replace electrical cords as needed. Never use an electrical cord which is worn through to the wire. Always use oil- and water-resistant cords.

Unplug equipment. Remove the plug from the outlet before cleaning any electrical equipment.

Avoid overloading circuits. Never use unauthorized extension cords; circuits should never be overloaded.

Fire

Another very common cause of accidents in food service operations is fires. These can be prevented by taking the following precautions:

Be sure there is adequate fire extinguishing equipment. Personnel should know where it is located and how to use it. Consult local fire authorities about the purchase, use, and inspection of the correct fire extinguishing equipment.

Install fire detection devices. Consider using authorized and frequently tested fire detection devices. These may be specialized equipment items which can detect smoke, flames, and/or heat.

Consider using automatic sprinkler systems. They are a very effective way to automatically control fires. Sprinkler systems may be required by local fire ordinances, but even if they are not, they may be a very wise investment. Special fire extinguishing equipment under ventilation filters is frequently required by local ordinances. Regardless of the type (dry chemical, carbon dioxide, or chemicals in special solutions), this equipment can only be effective if it is professionally designed, installed, and maintained.

Detailed information about fire prevention is beyond the scope of this chapter.[4] However, it is important that all local/municipal fire ordinances be followed. Contact fire department personnel for specific help in designing fire protection and emergency procedures for your operation. Employees should know where all emergency exits are located, and fire drills should be conducted so that they know what to do when there is a fire or other emergency. Make sure that all doors to the property open out and that fire exits are kept clear at all times. Fire department telephone numbers should be located in a handy place near the telephone.

How to Put Out Fires

There are three common types of fires that can occur in a food service operation: (1) **Class A fires** which involve ordinary combustible materials (wood, paper, plastics, etc.); (2) **Class B fires** which occur in flammable substances such as gas and grease; and (3) **Class C fires** which involve electrical equipment.

Small fires can normally be put out with portable fire extinguishers. Make sure they are located close to the most probable source of fires and that they are properly inspected and maintained. Also, it is important to train all food service employees in the correct use of fire extinguishing equipment.

There are many types of specialized fire extinguishing equipment. Frequently, a multi-purpose dry chemical fire extinguisher can be purchased which can be used to fight the three types of fires noted above.

Most portable fire extinguishers are easy to operate, but it is important that employees be trained to use the specific equipment available in the property. Usually, a safety pin must be pulled out before the fire extinguisher can be used. When applying a multi-purpose chemical, it is important to coat all burning areas with the chemical in order to minimize sources of reignition.

Large operations such as hotels and hospitals may have organized standard operating procedures for fire emergencies which use communications programs, fire brigades, etc. Food service employees should be an integral part of these fire prevention and detection programs.

Food Service Equipment and Safety Procedures

There are many equipment items which are an immeasurable help in producing the large quantities of food needed in food service operations. These equipment items, while very beneficial to the operation, can also be potential causes of many safety problems. Always follow the manufacturer's instructions very carefully when working around any potentially dangerous food service equipment. It is a good idea to place the instructions on or near dangerous pieces of equipment so that employees can constantly refer to them. The following general safety precautions should be used by all food service employees whenever they work with food service equipment:

Make sure that lighting is sufficient. Use good lighting—at least 30 footcandles in all work areas. (One footcandle of light is the energy falling on one square foot of surface one foot from a standard candle.)

Make sure that ventilation is sufficient. Use adequate ventilation (hood and filters) for all working equipment.

Inspect equipment. Conduct regular and detailed inspections of all food service equipment as an integral part of ongoing preventive maintenance programs. These inspections should be made by people from the equipment supply company or by utility service personnel.

Make sure that all equipment conforms to codes. Ensure that when purchases are made all electrical equipment and connections conform to the national electrical code requirements and other state and local requirements. Likewise, all gas connections should conform with national, state, and local regulations. Electrical equipment should, where applicable, bear the seal of approval of the Underwriters Laboratories. Gas equipment should bear the seal of approval of the American Gas Association and both electric and gas ranges and ovens should meet requirements of the National Sanitation Foundation. Figure 10.1 illustrates the approval seals that you should look for whenever purchasing food service equipment.

Figure 10.1 Seals of Approval

By permission of the National Sanitation Foundation, Ann Arbor, Michigan; the American Gas Association (the seal is the registered trademark of the Association), Arlington, Virginia; and Underwriters Laboratories Inc., Northbrook, Illinois.

Cool equipment. Normally, cool cooking equipment before cleaning.

Be careful with gas equipment. Use special precautions when lighting gas cooking equipment.

Properly maintain equipment. Improper maintenance can lead to unsafe working conditions.

Disconnect equipment. Equipment should be disconnected from power sources before cleaning whenever possible.

Follow correct equipment operation procedures. Do not take short-cuts when operating potentially hazardous food service equipment.

Train new employees. They should be carefully supervised during orientation and early training periods to ensure that proper procedures are followed and that they are not using shortcuts which violate basic safety procedures. Employees should know how to use, maintain, and clean equipment.

Accident Inspection Programs

All employees should be trained to know what to do immediately after an accident occurs. It is also very important that management personnel learn from any accidents to help ensure that they will not happen again. While state laws may differ, workers' compensation and federal OSHA regulations (which are described later in the chapter) do require the reporting of many accidents. Figure 10.2 illustrates the type of information which must be reported for workers' compensation purposes in one state. Copies of the form may be sent to the insurance company and the employee; of course, you should keep a copy for the food service operation's records. As a result of this report and, perhaps, investigations by state labor officers or insurance company investigators, a settlement consistent with the applicable state compensation laws will normally be made.

It is very important that the form be completed carefully and accurately since information contained in the report will have a bearing on the cause of the accident. This will be reflected in subsequent insurance premiums which the food service operation will need to pay.

As noted above, you can learn much from accidents. Develop procedures designed to prevent their recurrence. In addition to information contained in the required workers' compensation report, you may be interested in developing inspection reports and/or procedures which will specifically help your operation. Figures 10.3 and 10.4 illustrate internal forms which can be used to report employee and customer injuries, respectively.

Figure 10.2 Employer's Basic Report of Injury

Form 100
Rev. 1-82

DEPARTMENT OF LABOR

Bureau of Workers' Disability Compensation

OSHA
Case or File No. _____

EMPLOYER'S BASIC REPORT OF INJURY

COPIES TO BE DISTRIBUTED

Yellow and Green — Bureau of Workers'
Disability Compensation, Lansing, Mich.
Blue — Insurance Company
Pink — Employer File
White — Employee

Employers must report to the Bureau on Form 100 all injuries, including diseases, which arise out of and in the course of the employment and cause: 1. Seven(7) or more days of disability not including Sundays or the day of injury. 2. Death. 3. Specific Losses. In case of DEATH also file immediately an additional report on Form 106.

1. **INJURED EMPLOYEE** _____ Soc. Sec. No. __/__/__
2. Address _____ Telephone No. _____
3. Birthdate - Month ____ Day ____ Year ____   If under 18, date working permit issued _____
4. Sex: ☐ Male ☐ Female   Number of injured employee's children under age 16 living with injured _____
5. Marital status: ☐ Married ☐ Single   If married male, is wife living with him? ☐ Yes ☐ No
6. Number of other family members or relatives at least 50% supported by injured _____
7. **DATE OF INJURY** _____ Last day worked _____ Did employee die? ☐ Yes ☐ No   If yes, date _____
8. Location of Injury   City _____ State_____ County _____
9. Was place of accident or exposure on employer's premises? ☐ Yes ☐ No
10. Name and address of physician _____
11. If hospitalized, name and address of hospital _____

12. DESCRIPTION OF ALLEGED INJURY (Complete and specific information needed for each category)

A. Describe the injury or illness
   Examples: Amputation, Burn, Cut, Fracture, Sprain, etc.

B. Part of body - The part of body directly affected by the injury or illness.
   Examples: Head, Arm, Leg, Circulatory system,etc.

C. Describe the events that caused the injury. Examples: Fell, Operating machinery, Exposure to chemicals, etc.

D. Name the object or substance which directly injured the employee.
   Examples: Knife, Band Saw, Acid, Floor, Oil, Punch Press, etc.

13. Occupation of injured employee (be specific) _____
14. Department _____ Foreman or supervisor _____
15. Total Gross Wages - Highest 39 of 52 weeks preceding date of injury
    Total Gross Weekly Wages $ _____ No. of weeks used in calculation _____
                        Average weekly wage $ _____
16. Complete the following only if the injured employee received wages from a second employer.
    Name of second employer _____
    Mailing address _____
17. Date returned to work _____ or estimated lost time from work _____

18. IS EMPLOYEE CERTIFIED AS VOCATIONALLY HANDICAPPED?   ☐ Yes   ☐ No

19. IS EMPLOYEE RECEIVING UNEMPLOYMENT INSURANCE BENEFITS?   ☐ Yes   ☐ No

20. **EMPLOYER**   MESC. No. _____
    A. _____   Federal ID No. _____
    B. _____
21. Location (if different from mail address) _____
22. **TYPE OF BUSINESS** _____
23. **INSURANCE COMPANY (Not agent)** _____ Carrier ID No. _____
24. **HAS WHITE COPY OF THIS REPORT BEEN GIVEN TO EMPLOYEE?**   ☐ Yes ☐ No

   Questions or errors should be immediately reported to the employer representative indicated below

Date of Report _____ Prepared by _____
                                    Signature (in ink) **Employer** or Representative   Tele.#

Source: Michigan Department of Labor.

Figure 10.3 Report of Employee Injury

REPORT OF EMPLOYEE INJURY

Name_____

Job Classification_____

Department_____Supervisor_____

Date of accident_____Location of accident_____

What happened?_____

_____

_____

Length of disability_____

Why did it happen?_____

_____

_____

Classification of Cause

____Defective equipment   ____Unsafe practices   ____Poor supervision

____Improper working conditions   ____Lack of housekeeping   ____Inattention

____Lack of protective equipment   ____Lack of training   _____

What should be done to prevent a recurrence?_____

_____

_____

What has been done to date?_____

_____

_____

Report completed by_____
                        (name)   (date)

Source: Safety Operations Manual *(Chicago: National Restaurant Association, 1981), p. B-11.*

The goals of any accident investigation should be to (1) assess exactly what happened, (2) determine why the accident occurred, (3) discover what should be done to prevent recurrences, and (4) note exactly what has been done to date. It is important that top management see all investigation reports and that they follow up to ensure that necessary precautions are taken to prevent a repeat of the accident.

You should be just as concerned about your customers as you are about your employees. Figure 10.5 lists some information you might not be aware of.

Figure 10.4 Report of Customer Injury

NRA

REPORT OF CUSTOMER INJURY

Injured Person:

____
(name)

____
(address)

____
(city, state and zip code)

Age________ Sex________ Telephone______________________

Nature of injury______________________
____
____

Medical Treatment Provided______________________
____
____

Accident Information:

Time______________________ Date________________

Location______________________
____

Condition of Accident Location______________________
____

Description of Accident______________________
____

Probable Cause of Accident______________________
____

Property Damage______________________
____

Witnesses:

____
(name) (address) (telephone)

____
(name) (address) (telephone)

____
(name) (address) (telephone)

Report completed by______________________ Date______________

Source: Safety Operations Manual, *p. B-13.*

First Aid Is Important

Immediately after an accident occurs, first aid is the primary concern. However, it is very important that someone trained in the proper first aid procedures apply any necessary treatment. People without proper first aid training normally should not attempt any first aid other than "common-sense" procedures: making the person comfortable, giving necessary information for accident reports, and urging the victim to see

Figure 10.5 Facts about Accidents

1.	Massive insurance claims can result from a customer's injury.
2.	Get information in advance from the insurance company so that you will know exactly what should be done if an accident occurs.
3.	After an accident occurs, contact the insurance company and follow their instructions very carefully.
4.	Approximately one-third of all customer claims arise from falls. Therefore, keep aisles free from obstructions, floors clean and dry, interior and exterior areas well-lighted, and snow and ice removed from outdoor walk areas.
5.	Approximately one-third of all claims are made due to injuries from foreign substances in food. This emphasizes the need for you to have an effective program of quality assurance when purchasing, preparing, and serving food.
6.	Food poisoning is a potential problem. Although it is not specifically an "accident" type of injury, massive settlements can result (see Chapter 9 for information about sanitation procedures).

Source of numbers 4 and 5: Safety Operations Manual , p. B-8.

a physician if it is a less serious accident. Some significant things to know about first aid include the following:

Encourage first aid training. The American Red Cross provides excellent first aid training throughout the United States. Employees at all organizational levels should be encouraged to avail themselves of these and related educational opportunities. The information they receive can prove invaluable in both their professional and personal lives. If at all possible, training should be given to several employees so that someone with first aid training is at the food service operation constantly.

Provide first aid equipment and supplies. First aid equipment and supplies should be available on-site. Frequently, state labor departments, municipal regulatory agencies, insurance companies, and other groups have requirements which may need to be met by your operation when first aid equipment is selected and made available. Because cuts, burns, sprains, and contusions are the leading types of injuries in restaurants, supplies to treat these injuries should be available and plentiful. Keep first aid equipment and supplies in convenient areas. In large operations, particularly those with more than one floor, several first aid kits probably will be needed.

Display first aid information. Post various types of medical and first aid posters (available from several sources) throughout your food service operation. Figures 10.6-10.9 illustrate the type of information which is available and give you information about first aid concerns. Study the material carefully, order it, and place it in your own operation.

Figure 10.6 Emergency Treatment of Wounds

CUTS, WOUNDS AND ABRASIONS

Immediately cleanse wound and surrounding skin with soap and warm water, wiping away from wound.

Hold a sterile pad or clean cloth over the wound until the bleeding stops.

Replace sterile pad or clean cloth and bandage lightly.

If hand injury, raise hand above the level of the heart.

DO NOT put mouth over a wound

DO NOT breathe on wound

DO NOT allow fingers, used hankerchief or other soiled material to touch the wound

DO NOT use an antiseptic on the wound

WHEN TO SEEK MEDICAL ATTENTION

1. If there is spurting bleeding (this is an emergency).
2. If slow bleeding continues beyond 4 to 10 minutes.
3. If there is foreign material in the wound that does not wash out easily.
4. If the wound is a deep puncture.
5. If the wound is long or wide and may require stitches.
6. If a nerve or tendon may be cut (particularly in hand wounds).
7. If the wound is on the face or wherever a noticeable scar would be undesirable.
8. If the wound is of a type that cannot be completely cleansed.
9. If the wound has been in contact with unclean material.
10. At the first signs of infection (pain, reddened area around wound, swelling).

SHOCK

Shock will be present with many injuries.

A person in shock will be cold, pale, perspiring and may pass out.

TREATMENT

1. Telephone for emergency ambulance or doctor.
2. Treat for shock by:
   Placing patient in prone position with feet elevated unless contraindicated.
   Covering only enough to prevent loss of body heat.

   Do not give any fluids.

   Do not administer any drugs.

   Do not give alcoholic beverages.

OTHER INJURIES

BRUISES

Apply ice bag or cold compress for 25 minutes. If skin is broken, further treatment is the same as for a cut.

BLISTERS

Keep clean with mild soap and water and protect from further irritation. If blister has broken, treat it as an open wound. If infected, seek medical assistance.

FOREIGN BODY IN EYE

If particle is located—do not rub eye. Gently touch with point of clean moist cloth and flush eye with water. If unsuccessful or if pain persists, refer to physician.

Do not attempt to remove foreign object by inserting a match, toothpick or any other instrument. Do not use dry cotton around the eye.

REPORT ALL INJURIES TO YOUR MANAGER OR SUPERVISOR

Source: Safety Operations Manual, *p. F-7.*

Safety Inspection Programs

You have learned that the food service operation's safety program must begin with an awareness and a concern for protecting the health and well-being of both employees and customers. You should develop safety procedures and follow up with training programs to teach employees about them. As a food service manager, you have a further obligation to conduct ongoing safety inspection programs to ensure that employees

Figure 10.7 Emergency Treatment of Burns

EXTENSIVE BURNS

If over 15% of body is burned, WASTE NO TIME Give appropriate first aid and get patient to hospital immediately!

SHOCK

SHOCK WILL BE PRESENT IN MANY BURN CASES

A person in shock will be cold, pale, perspiring and may pass out

TREATMENT

1. Telephone for emergency ambulance or doctor
2. Treat for shock by:
   - Place patient in prone position with feet elevated unless contraindicated
   - Cover only enough to prevent loss of body heat

DO NOT GIVE ANY FLUIDS
DO NOT ADMINISTER ANY DRUGS
DO NOT GIVE ALCOHOLIC BEVERAGES

3 RD DEGREE BURNS **SEVERE BURNS**
Involve entire skin layers. Burns are deep, charring the skin. (Includes electrical burns because these are deeper than they appear.)

TREATMENT

1. Protect burned area by covering with **clean dry** cloth
2. Treat for shock
3. Get patient to hospital or doctor IMMEDIATELY!

DO NOT APPLY BUTTER, LARD, FAT OR BURN OINTMENT

DO NOT REMOVE ADHERED PARTICLES OF CLOTHING

REPORT ALL BURNS
TO YOUR MANAGER OR SUPERVISOR
BURNS CAN BECOME INFECTED
AND CONTAMINATE THE FOOD

BURNS INVOLVING EYES

Needs IMMEDIATE First Aid Attention and Medical Assistance

IF SPLASHED BY HOT OIL OR GREASE—

Flush with a slow stream of cool water for at least 15 minutes

IF BURNED BY FLAME OR EXPLOSION—

Apply cold, wet towel or other cold pack

DO NOT APPLY OIL OR OINTMENT

1. Place sterile dressing over eyes to immobilize the lids
2. Take patient to doctor or hospital

CHEMICAL BURNS

- Immediately wash away chemical with large quantities of running water for at least five minutes.
- Remove victim's clothing from areas involved.
- Then treat as for any similar heat burn.

2 ND DEGREE BURNS **BLISTERS FORMED**
Shock likely with extensive 2nd degree burns.

TREATMENT

1. Immerse burned area in cold water bath—or under cold running water—or apply ice water soaked **clean** cloths until pain subsides.
2. Blot dry and apply **clean dry** cloth or dressing and send to doctor.

DO NOT OPEN THE BLISTERS

DO NOT APPLY BUTTER, LARD, FAT OR BURN OINTMENT

1 ST DEGREE BURNS **MINOR BURNS**
Skin is reddened

TREATMENT

Apply cold water applications to the affected area or submerge the burn area in cold water. (A dry dressing may be applied.)

DO NOT APPLY BUTTER, LARD OR FAT

Source: Safety Operations Manual, p. F-9.

practice safe working habits and to ensure that the equipment and the facility will not contribute to accidents. You can address both procedural and equipment/facility concerns in an inspection program. The objectives of an inspection program include: (1) to determine how safe the existing equipment and procedures are and (2) to decide what can be done to make them safer.

Figure 10.8 First Aid for Choking

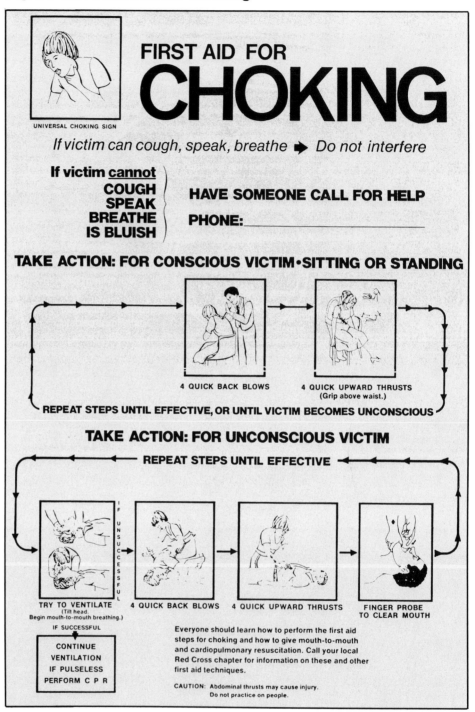

Source: Safety Operations Manual, *1981, p. F-11.*

Safety Inspection Forms   It may not be necessary to develop extensive safety inspection forms; several very good inspection forms are already available and are included in this chapter. You can review these forms and modify them

Figure 10.9 CPR in Basic Life Support

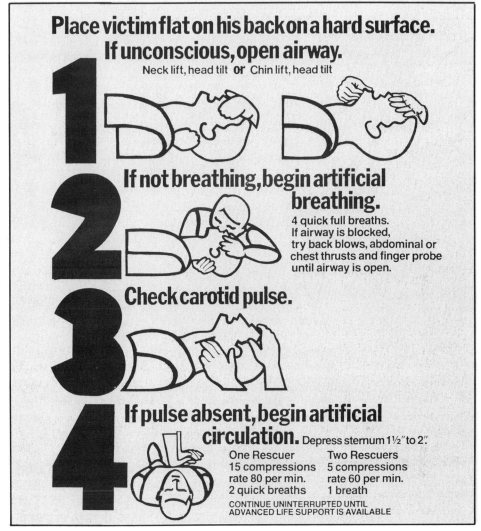

Courtesy of Chicago Heart Association.

to suit your specific needs. Likewise, people with special knowledge (insurance safety representatives, state or local fire inspectors, municipal and state agency personnel, the local safety council, etc.) can help you either modify the forms or contribute to safety inspections.

How often you make safety inspections depends, in part, on how well your property "measures up" during the first inspection. A complete inspection should be made at least once every month. However, you should also conduct daily inspections of specific work station areas, equipment, and facilities that are used every day.

A primary reason to conduct safety inspections is to correct hazards and potentially dangerous conditions which are found. You should do this promptly; alert management to any problems so that funds, if necessary, can be made available. If any time elapses before a problem is corrected, inform employees of any possible hazards and instruct them to be especially careful. Perhaps you can modify standard procedures until the problem is resolved.

Employee Safety Training Programs

Safety inspection forms can be used as an integral part of employee safety training programs. These programs should be held frequently and are important for all staff members: experienced employees with many years on the job and new employees who really don't understand the potential hazards which exist in a food and beverage operation.

It might be possible, for example, to identify the most potentially hazardous items on the safety checklist. These could be the topic of initial employee safety training sessions. Alternatively, you could literally start at the beginning and, using the modified safety checklist as a guide, conduct training sessions which address all areas covered by the forms.

An advantage of employee safety training sessions is the possibility that employees will be able to generate additional areas of concern which can be "policed" by using a safety inspection program. After all, employees who work with equipment and in specific work areas daily may have many good ideas about potential problems and ways to resolve them which top management might be less likely to consider.

Don't forget follow-up! You have already learned that problems which have been identified by safety inspections should be promptly corrected. However, it is not reasonable to assume that instructions to take care of things will always be followed. Make sure that corrective action is, in fact, taken.

Retain safety inspection report forms. They will give you an indication of the long-range effectiveness of safety inspection programs. Also, if any safety problems occur (lawsuits or inspections by safety agencies), the forms will be evidence of your interest and effectiveness in maintaining a safe food and beverage operation.

Figure 10.10 is a safety checklist developed by the National Safety Council. It reviews each area of the food service operation and addresses other areas of possible concern. Figure 10.11 is a guest safety checklist focusing on dining areas. These forms, if used together, can be useful tools in an ongoing safety program.

Occupational Safety and Health Administration and Food Service Operations

You have probably heard of the Occupational Safety and Health Administration (OSHA). It is an agency of the U.S. Department of Labor which was created in 1970 to help make working conditions in businesses of all sizes safer for their employees. OSHA has:

- developed a general duty requirement which states that employers should furnish employees with jobs and places of employment that are free from recognized safety hazards.

Figure 10.10 Food Service Safety Checklist to Locate Hazards

To Locate Hazards			
The following checklist covers both physical factors in the property and work practices of your personnel. During your inspection be as aware of unsafe acts as you are of unsafe conditions.			

Area	Yes	No	Comments
Receiving Area:			
Are floors in safe condition? (Are they free from broken and defective floor boards? Are they covered with non-skid material?)			
Are employees instructed in correct handling methods for various containers, etc., that are received?			
Are garbage cans washed daily in hot water?			
Are garbage cans always covered?			
If garbage disposal area is adjacent to a part of the general receiving area, is there a program that keeps floors and/or dock areas clear of refuse?			
Is there a proper rack for holding garbage containers? Are garbage containers on dollies or other wheel units to eliminate lifting by employees?			
Are adequate tools available for opening crates, barrels, cartons, etc. (hammer, cutter, cardboard carton opener, and pliers)?			
Is crate, carton, and barrel opening done away from open containers of food?			
Storage Area:			
Are shelves adequate to bear weight of items stored? Are employees instructed to store heavy items on lower shelves and lighter materials above?			
Is a safe ladder provided for reaching high storage?			
Are cartons or other flammable materials stored at least two feet from light bulbs?			
Are light bulbs provided with a screen guard?			
Is a fire extinguisher located at the door?			
Are employees carefully instructed in the use of detergents to prevent agitation of dermatitis, etc.?			
Do you have a program for disposition of broken glass or china?			
Where controls are in a passageway, are they recessed or guarded to prevent breakage or accidental starting?			
Are dish racks in safe condition (if wooden, free from broken slats and smoothly finished to eliminate splintering; if metal, free of sharp corners that could cause cuts)? Are these racks kept off the floor to prevent tripping?			

Adapted with permission from National Safety Council, Chicago, Illinois, no date.

Area	Yes	No	Comments
Serving Area:			
Are steam tables cleaned daily and maintained regularly (are gas or electric units checked regularly by a competent serviceperson)?			
Is safety valve equipment operative?			
Are serving counters and tables free of broken parts and wooden or metal slivers and burrs?			
Do you have regular inspections of: Glassware? China? Silverware? Plastic equipment?			
If anything breaks near the food service area, do you remove all food from service adjacent to breakage?			
Are tray rails adequate to prevent trays from slipping or falling off at the end or corners?			
Are floors and/or ramps in good condition (covered with nonskid material, free from broken tile and defective floor boards)?			
Are these areas mopped at least daily and waxed with nonskid wax when necessary?			
Is there effective traffic flow so that customers do not collide while carrying trays or obtaining foods?			
Dining Area:			
Are floors free from broken tile and defective floor boards? Are they covered with nonskid wax?			
Are pictures securely fastened to walls?			
Are drapes, blinds, or curtains securely fastened?			
Are chairs free from splinters, metal burrs, broken or loose parts?			
Are floors "policed" for cleaning up spillage and other materials?			
Is special attention given to the floor adjacent to water, ice cream, or milk stations?			
Are vending machines properly grounded?			
If customers clear their own trays prior to return to dishwashing area, are the floors kept clean of garbage, dropped silver, and/or broken glass and china?			
If dishes are removed from dining area on portable racks or bus trucks, are these units in safe operating condition (for example, are all casters working, all shelves firm)?			
Soiled Dish Processing Area:			
Are floors reasonably free of excessive water and spillage?			
Are floor boards properly maintained and in safe condition (free from broken slats and worn areas that cause tripping)?			

Area	Yes	No	Comments
Are all electrical units properly grounded?			
Are switches located to permit rapid shutdown in the event of emergency?			
Can employees easily reach switches?			
Pots and Pans Room or Area:			
Are duckboards or floor boards in safe condition (free from broken slats and worn areas which could cause tripping)?			
Are employees properly instructed in use of correct amounts of detergent and/or other cleaning agents?			
Are adequate rubber gloves provided?			
Is there an adequate drainboard or other drying area so that employees do not have to pile pots and pans on the floor before and after washing them?			
Do drain plugs permit draining without the employee placing hands in hot water?			
Walk-in Coolers and Freezers—(Refrigerators):			
Are floors in the units in good condition and covered with slip-proof material? Are they mopped at least once a week (and whenever spills occur)?			
If floor boards are used, are they in safe condition (free of broken slat and worn boards which could cause tripping)?			
Are portable and stationary storage racks in safe condition (free from broken or bent shelves and set on solid legs)?			
Are blower fans properly guarded?			
Is there a by-pass device on the door to permit exit if an employee is locked in (or, is there an alarm bell)?			
Is adequate aisle space provided?			
Are employees properly instructed in placement of hands for movement of portable items to avoid hand injuries?			
Are heavy items stored on lower shelves and lighter items on higher shelves?			
Is the refrigerant in the refrigerator nontoxic? (Check with your refrigerator service manual.)			
Food Preparation Area:			
Is electrical equipment properly grounded?			
Is electrical equipment inspected regularly by an electrician?			
Are electrical switches located so that they can be reached readily in the event of an emergency?			
Are the switches located so that employees do not have to lean on or against metal equipment when reaching for them?			

Area	Yes	No	Comments
Are floors regularly and adequately maintained (mopped at least daily and waxed with nonskid wax when necessary; are defective floor boards and tiles replaced when necessary)?			
Are employees instructed to immediately pick up or clean up all dropped items and spillage?			
Are employees properly instructed in the operation of all machines?			
Are employees forbidden to use equipment unless specifically trained in its use?			
Are machines properly grounded?			
Don't Overlook:			
Lighting—is it adequate in the: 　　Receiving Area? 　　Storage Area? 　　Pots and Pans Area? 　　Walk-in Coolers and Freezers? 　　Food Preparation Area? 　　Cooking Area? 　　Serving Area? 　　Dining Area? 　　Soiled Dish Processing Area?			
Doors—do they open into passageways where they could cause an accident? (List any such locations.)			
Are fire exits clearly marked and passages kept clear of equipment and materials? (List any violations.)			
Stairways and Ramps:			
Are they adequately lighted?			
Are the angles of ramps set to provide maximum safety?			
If stairs are metal, wood, or marble, have abrasive materials been used to provide protection against slips and falls?			
Are pieces broken out of the casing or front edge off the steps?			
Are clean and securely fastened handrails available?			
If the stairs are wide, has a center rail been provided?			
Ventilation–is it adequate in the: 　　Receiving Area? 　　Storage Area? 　　Pots and Pans Area? 　　Walk-in Coolers and Freezers? 　　Food Preparation Area? 　　Cooking Area? 　　Serving Area? 　　Dining Area? 　　Soiled Dish Processing Area?			
Other Safety Concerns:			
Do employees wear good shoes to protect their feet against injury from articles that are dropped or pushed against their feet?			

Area	Yes	No	Comments
Is employee clothing free of parts that could get caught in mixers, cutters, grinders, or other equipment?			
Are fire extinguishers guarded so they will not be knocked from the wall?			
If doors are provided with a lock, is there an emergency bell or a by-pass device that will permit exit from the room should the door be accidentally locked while an employee is in the room?			
Is there a pusher or tamper provided for use with the grinders?			
Are mixers in safe operating condition?			
Are the mixer beaters properly maintained to avoid injury from broken metal parts and foreign particles in food?			

- established mandatory job safety and health standards.

- developed an enforcement program.

- constructed reporting procedures which deal with job injuries, illnesses, and fatalities.

- created and implemented many procedures to help improve working conditions.

- implemented programs to encourage employers and employees to reduce hazards in the workplace.

OSHA regulations usually apply to every employer who has one or more employees. Restaurants and food service operations in hotels and institutions of all types are generally covered. In the past, OSHA has received publicity—and criticism—because it developed many standards which were allegedly impractical. Nevertheless, it is true that the "spirit and intent" of the act is important: ensuring safe and healthful working conditions for employees.

OSHA permits states to develop programs for occupational safety and health which are at least as effective as federal programs. In effect, federal standards indicated by OSHA become minimum plans. They are either applicable to a state or form the foundation for a state-administered plan.

There are several major components of OSHA laws that affect food service operations.

Inspection   Federal, state, and local inspectors may visit your operation and are likely to look for potential safety hazards such as those outlined in Figures 10.10 and 10.11. After an inspection, officials hold a closing meeting to discuss and review any violations. Plans for remedial action, if this is necessary, are covered at these meetings. Follow-up inspection may also be part of the process.

Figure 10.11 Guest Safety Checklist

Date of Review: _____

Review By: _____

Check (x) to indicate that no problem is observed.

_____ 1. Parking lots and sidewalks are well-defined, well-lighted, and well-maintained.

_____ 2. Steps, ramps, and other passages leading to exterior doors are well-marked and well-lighted, and are in good repair.

_____ 3. Steps have nonskid strips or other devices to prevent slips and falls, and are in good repair.

_____ 4. Bannisters and rails are available and well-secured.

_____ 6. Exterior light fixtures and building ornamentations are firmly attached.

_____ 6. Snow is removed promptly; salt or sand is spread over shoveled sidewalk areas to prevent slipping and falling.

_____ 7. Mats, abrasive strips, or other devices are used in entrance areas where water may be tracked in during times of inclement weather; they are in good repair.

_____ 8. Outdoor lighting at ground level is protected with grills or other devices to prevent finger burns by children and trespassers.

_____ 9. Tree limbs which overhang parking lots or sidewalks are not in danger of falling.

_____ 10. Signs, lights, or other devices are used to alert guests to steps or ledges in areas between parking lots and the building.

_____ 11. Safety decals, drapery, or other devices/materials clearly indicate large panels of glass.

_____ 12. Emergency door-opening devices are in good working order.

_____ 13. Fire alarms, emergency lighting, fire extinguishers, and similar equipment are in good working order.

_____ 14. All furniture is in good condition; tables, chairs, and stools are checked frequently for damage; chairs are checked for loose legs, arms, and backs; *damaged seating equipment is not used.*

_____ 15. All interior steps are clearly marked/lighted; bannister rails and other devices are securely mounted.

_____ 16. Coat racks are in no danger of collapse and/or are securely fastened to the wall or other support.

_____ 17. All light fixtures, other ceiling attachments, pictures, and other wall decorations/attachments are securely fastened and in no danger of falling.

_____ 18. Ceiling and wall attachments are located to prevent/minimize the possibility of guests bumping heads on the attachments.

_____ 19. No equipment has frayed or damaged electrical cords or is otherwise unsafe to operate.

_____ 20. Carpeting is not frayed or torn; exposed edges, if any, are secured to prevent slipping and falling.

_____ 21. No items stick out of floor or carpet (nonflush nails, wooden splinters, improperly laid bricks, etc.).

_____ 22. Nothing is placed either permanently or temporarily on steps or in guest traffic aisles.

_____ 23. Emergency exit areas are not blocked by tables, chairs, or other obstacles; they are adequately marked and easy to locate.

_____ 24. Elevators, if any, are routinely checked and properly maintained.

_____ 25. There are no sharp or protruding edges on tables or on decorative or other furniture and equipment.

_____ 26. Food server tray stands are placed in areas where guest cannot bump into them, and where spillage and dropping will not affect guests.

_____ 27. Aisles between tables or booths are wide enough to prevent accidents from employees/guests running into each other.

_____ 28. Food/beverage servers are trained in proper service procedures to minimize the possibility of spilling food and beverages on guests.

Source: Jack D. Ninemeier, Food and Beverage Security: A Systems Manual for Restaurants, Hotels and Clubs *(Boston: CBI, 1982), pp. 152-153.*

Citation   If your food service operation does not comply with OSHA requirements and fails to take remedial action along guidelines agreed upon by these officials, citations are possible. There are several types of violations which range from major problems (a substantial probability of death or serious harm) to relatively minor violations which have a less direct impact on job safety and health. Procedures for penalties, appeals, and posting of job safety and health protection information are also required by OSHA.

Recordkeeping Requirements   OSHA requires employers with 11 or more employees at any time during a calendar year to maintain certain records. Smaller operations may also need to provide additional information. There are two basic forms required by OSHA, but neither of them has to be submitted to OSHA. However, both forms must be available if a compliance officer makes an inspection. One form deals with reporting occupational injuries and illnesses while the second form lists additional information which is required for injuries or illnesses that are reported.

Safety Concerns   As already noted, the intention of OSHA is to provide safe working conditions and environments for employees. Regardless of the bureaucracy and paperwork associated with compliance efforts, the safety procedures and information which are the result of OSHA are commendable. Safety inspection programs, employee training activities, and seeking assistance (often free) from officials with safety expertise are all part of a common-sense approach to recognizing the need for safety and then doing something about it. There are some businesses, including food and beverage operations, which may not be concerned about safety-related matters. However, the majority of businesses, including food and beverage operations, *are* concerned about the health and well-being of their employees and customers. Therefore, minimum requirements for some operations become helpful guidelines for others.

The attitude that safety-related information can help improve a food service operation is much more enlightened than the attitude, "I'll do what I have to, but not more, and only when I'm supposed to do it." If you address the concerns highlighted in this chapter and apply them, you will have done just about everything possible to provide safe working conditions for your employees and for your customers.

NOTES

1.   This section is based on *Safety Operations Manual* (Chicago, Ill.: National Restaurant Association, 1981), pp. A1-A4.

2.   Information about accident prevention in this chapter is based on U.S. Department of Agriculture, *Sanitation and Safety Practices for Child Nutrition Programs* (Washington, D.C.), pp. 85-96, and *Safety Operations Manual* (Chicago, Ill.: National Restaurant Association, 1981), pp. A24-A29.

3.   *Safety Operations Manual*, p. A27.

4.   For additional information see *Safety Operations Manual*, pp. H1-H23.

PART III

Satisfying Customer Expectations

After reading this far, you should have a good idea about the food service industry and what it involves. You are aware of the customers' importance and how the food service operation has to meet their wants and needs through the products and services it offers. But how are these products and services delivered? We will begin our study by looking at food and beverage serving procedures—the first activities which bring the customer in contact with the operation.

In order to be served, food products must pass through a series of steps, beginning with purchasing and continuing through receiving, storing, issuing, and production. We will look at each of these steps in some detail.

Many operations also offer beverage service. Chapter 15 provides an overview of many of the activities and concerns necessary to provide efficient and quality beverage service to the customer.

11

Serving the Customer

Management Challenges

As a result of studying this chapter you will:

1. understand how important food service and serving are to customer satisfaction.

2. know the tasks that are performed by expediters and food servers.

3. recognize special problems that can occur at the time of food service and know how to prevent and resolve them.

4. be able to identify and describe possible types of service styles and know when each should be used.

5. know basic procedures which should be used with cafeteria, banquet, and other types of service.

6. be able to develop basic dining room operating procedures.

7. understand the importance of service standards.

8. know how to practice selling techniques while serving the customer.

9. be familiar with sales income control procedures that can be used to reduce employee theft in the dining room.

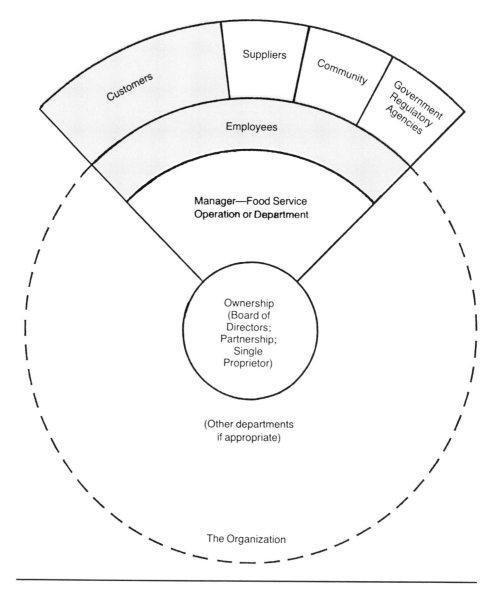

Customers

Suppliers

Community

Government
Regulatory
Agencies

Employees

Manager—Food Service
Operation or Department

Ownership
(Board of
Directors;
Partnership;
Single
Proprietor)

(Other departments
if appropriate)

The Organization

Focus on the
Food Service Publics

Chapter 11 focuses on food serving procedures and on the relationship between the customer and the food service operation employees. Ironically, it is often the lowest-paid and least-prepared employee (food and beverage server) who most frequently comes in contact with the customer. Obviously, the customers' attitudes toward the operation will be influenced by the servers. In many ways, the future, the reputation, and the success of the food service operation rest with the servers. Whatever the customer wants and needs will, in most operations, be delivered by these employees. They are critical to the success of the operation and attention to their training is crucial.

After the customer is greeted and seated, the activity of providing food and beverage service becomes important. Two processes must occur and the way in which they do has a dramatic effect on the success or failure of your food service operation:

1. **The food service process**—the transfer of food and beverage products from production personnel (cooks and bartenders) to serving personnel (food and beverage servers).

2. **The food serving process**—the delivery of food and beverage products to the customers.[1]

The way that these tasks are performed will have long-lasting effects. What happens if a food server turns in an order with a note for one serving of "SP"? Does that mean seafood platter or shrimp plate? And when the cook guesses wrong, who do you think suffers? The food service operation does because time as well as the incorrect order is wasted. But even worse, the customer suffers. The order is not served on time or it is served at an inadequate temperature, so the mix-up negatively affects the customer's impression of the operation.

As another example, let's assume that the food server communicates effectively with the cook and the food service is efficient, but the server mixes up orders with customers, practices poor sanitation or safety habits, and is impolite. Problems with food serving, from the customer's perspective, are also very serious. Inadequate food service or serving means that the customer does not have an enjoyable experience. Does the customer blame the untrained/incompetent food server or the operation itself? Usually, the operation—not the individual employee—must assume the responsibility.

Providing an Enjoyable Experience for the Customer

As the manager of a food service operation, you have a responsibility to provide an enjoyable experience for your customers. When this does not occur (for whatever reason), you cannot delegate the responsibility to someone else. It is management's responsibility to select, orient, and train the very best possible food serving employees. Management should also properly supervise food servers and develop effective standard operating procedures which provide an enjoyable experience for the customer.

The examples presented so far in this chapter have related to commercial food service operations such as those found in restaurants and hotels/motels. You can see how these examples would relate to drive-in or walk-up counter service in fast-food operations. But what about institutional food service operations in schools, hospitals, nursing homes, etc.? Throughout this book we have indicated the many similarities between commercial and institutional food service operations. The similarities extend to the service of food and to the recognition that the customer's wants and needs must be met at thetime of service as well as during menu planning and production.

You can use marketing techniques to address the way service and serving are undertaken. Marketing can be defined as "business from the perspective of the customer" (see Chapter 5). What can the employees in either a restaurant, hotel, or institutional operation do to create an enjoyable atmosphere and provide efficient service for the customer/patient?

The answer to this question can perhaps be arrived at by analyzing what you like about food service operations that you frequent. However, if you do not have the same wants and needs as the people being served, this self-analysis will be wasted. Customers or patients are the ones who must be considered when you plan and implement your food service operation.

Before looking at specific aspects of food service and serving, one additional point should be made. In many types of food service operations, the employee who has the most direct, lengthy contact with the customer is the lowest-paid, most poorly trained, and most inadequately supervised employee in the entire operation. Unless the food server is motivated to do a good job, he/she will probably not have the same concern about the customer as you do. You can develop customer-oriented procedures for food servers, but you should understand why a food server might instead use different procedures based on the attitude of doing "what's easiest for me." There is an obvious need to standardize procedures and to effectively train employees in all areas of the food service operation. This need is certainly great in the front of the house service area.

A Close Look at Food Service

As you know, food service involves getting food from the production personnel to the service staff. In a traditional table service operation, concerns about how food is ordered and picked up after production are important. Many operations use a standard list of abbreviations to eliminate the communication problem noted earlier in this chapter. Service staff should be aware of the amount of lead time needed between ordering a product and having it prepared and available for serving to the customers. You can establish procedures for assisting cooks with garnishes, cleaning up food spills, and perhaps bringing some items to the serving line for them. However, when the kitchen is busy, communication and coordination problems can still arise, so cooks and food servers must be trained in the exact procedures to use for ordering and picking up food items.

Expediters   Some operations use an expediter during busy times. Expediters aid communication between production and service personnel. This employee, who is often a manager, controls the process of turning in orders and picking up food items. In some operations, the server gives the order to the expediter. The expediter punches the order into a time recorder which indicates when orders should be picked up. The expediter serves a valuable function by monitoring production times, resolving disputes about when the order came in, and giving order information to cooks for servers. In addition, the expediter coordinates order pickups to ensure that the entire order is ready at the same time and that the food server picks up the order as soon as it is ready. The expediter can also check portion size and appearance and make sure that all items on the food server's tray are recorded on the check. The expediter can even verify item prices on guest checks when precheck registers are not used.

Food Checkers   Another employee who assists at the time of food service is the food checker. This employee helps control product quality and costs at the time of service. Today, there is a trend toward eliminating this position. In many operations, however, this employee can be cost justified. The food checker examines each tray before it goes into the dining area. In addition to checking plates for appearance, portion size, and related concerns, the checker is also an important part of the operation's sales income control system. The checker may, depending on the system, collect a copy of the guest check and compare items on the check with those on the plate or ring sales information on a by-server basis into a precheck register (a precheck register is discussed in greater detail later). In some operations, the checker may also be the cashier. Service personnel give the money collected from the customer to the checker who confirms that the amount of the bill is correct. Then the checker matches the ticket or ring-out from the precheck register with the value of food items that left the kitchen.[2]

Special Concerns   Since there are many production and service employees who must work together at the time of food service, favoritism is a potential problem. This, of course, will not help either your operation or the customer; close supervision is required to make sure that orders "come up" in reasonable time for all employees.

Other concerns are associated with food service. For example, there should be a sufficient backup supply of plates, napkins, and many other items and, of course, space must be available to store them until they are needed. Layout and equipment design (see Chapter 17) also affects the ability of production employees to get items ready on a timely basis.

Quality of Food. Quality of food at time of service is a paramount concern. The need to prepare the item as close as possible to the point of service is discussed in Chapter 14. Temperature, appearance, and flavor concerns must be carried through from production to the point of service.

Sanitation. Also consider the importance of proper sanitation procedures. What happens if potentially hazardous foods (see Chapter 9) are kept within the temperature danger zone for long periods of time during service? Food quality can suffer and serious sanitation problems can arise.

Portion Control Tools. These tools, which should be an integral part of your operation's food cost control program, must be used consistently at the time of service. Frequently, pictures of menu items are posted in service areas so that all employees can see portion sizes and how items are to be located in relation to each other on plates, in bowls, etc.

Appearance of Food. To a great extent, customers "eat with their eyes" so the appearance of the food is very important. Creative garnishes and the use of color, texture, and flair when the menu is initially designed can all help the food's appearance when it is served.

You should now know that many factors affect the service of food in table service operations. Do these concerns extend to other types of food service operations? Of course they do. Many of the same concerns become important when food is ordered by counter staff in fast-food operations and when food is prepared for pickup and service in buffet and cafeteria operations. While some food in cafeteria operations may be transported to the cafeteria line in bulk, other items are preportioned and placed on individual plates, in bowls, etc., in production areas before being moved to service lines. Hot and cold "pass-throughs" (i.e., heated or refrigerated passageways in the wall) also can expedite the transfer of food from production to service areas in cafeteria operations.

Banquet Procedures. Consider banquet service. In many respects, banquet service procedures are similar to those used to prepare items for service in hospitals and nursing homes. In hospitals and nursing homes, food items must often be preportioned and transported to remote locations (such as wards) for later service. In banquet operations, food items must also be preportioned onto plates. Decisions must be made about how plates are to be kept warm and about how preportioned food is to be kept at proper serving temperatures. Decision-makers must determine how preportioned plates are to be transported to banquet areas and what type of transport equipment is to be used. These and many other decisions all focus attention on food service—the act of transferring the food from production to service personnel.

One of the common ingredients for successful food service relates to the need for effective planning. Standard operating procedures detailing exactly what must be done and how it should be done as food is prepared for serving to the customers are necessary. We have already noted the relationship between available supplies, equipment, layout, standard operating procedures, trained and motivated employees, etc. These and other factors are very important and should not be overlooked when food service activities are designed and supervised.

Determining Your Customers' Wants and Needs

There are many ways that food can be provided to customers. The type of service style an operation uses should be based on the answer to this question: What do my customers want and need and how best can the food service operation satisfy them? The answer may involve using service styles other than the most prevalent or traditional ones. As stated throughout this book, your primary goal should be to find out what your customers want, then use the best available methods to provide it for them.

You should ask yourself what type of customer your operation is trying to reach. How would this customer like to be served? What is the cost incurred with each type of service style and how can it be passed on to the customer? For example, table service is a broad description for many types of food serving where the customer is seated, a food server attends to him/her, and the customer consumes the food at the table. Do families with children prefer table service since it is hard for young children to be supervised while passing through a cafeteria line? Or should a cafeteria line system be used with tray attendant service (where cafeteria employees transport trays for families, elderly people, handicappers, etc., to the dining room tables)? Frequently, table service is associated with a slower serving speed than is cafeteria or buffet service. If time is an important concern, then table service may not be the best style to use.

What will the check average be? Do customers like to pay a high price for food and then have to help themselves? Usually, as the check average gets higher, not only must table service be provided, but some tableside preparation may be offered, such as salads and flaming entrees or desserts.

What about the atmosphere in the dining area? Is your customer buying service and atmosphere—in other words, a total experience—in addition to food? Does a cafeteria line fit in with your operation's theme or atmosphere?

You can look at the factors just mentioned from the opposite viewpoint: When may a self-service cafeteria operation be called for? Your operation could be a good candidate for cafeteria service if it has a low check average, serves customers who don't mind helping themselves, and caters to people who want a speedy meal instead of a dining experience.

"All you can eat" buffets, salad bars, sandwich and dessert stations, etc., are popular in many areas. As inflation hurts the customer's purchasing power, value becomes a primary concern. For example, some customers equate lots of food and low cost with value. A self-service buffet may be just what is needed to satisfy these customers. They would rather help themselves and get a larger portion of food than transfer some of the purchase price to employees providing table service.

There is often a market for buffets. They are similar to cafeteria operations because guests serve themselves by walking through a service line. However, there are some differences. Cafeterias frequently have service employees who portion out food to customers. By contrast, buffets feature more "help yourself" items. Both cafeteria lines and buffets have service employees who carve meat for sandwiches, prepare omelets made to order, and perform related tasks. However, items offered on buffets are frequently much more lavish. Presentations (ice carvings, centerpieces, and related culinary art) are often elaborate with buffet service. The customer who desires a lot of food, a wide selection, untimed service, or something "a little different" may enjoy buffet service. Even operations with traditional dining room service may offer a buffet. For example, a luncheon buffet could offer items that would not normally be on the menu through table service.

You should note that banquet service meets specific needs. When many people need to be served at the same time, banquet service and buffet service often provide the only good choices. Lavish buffets can be assembled for many people, but the time required for buffet service is greater than effectively scheduled banquet service. Banquet service, where preplated food is brought to guests seated at tables, is often more formal and has a wider variety of menu items than buffet service. Modern equipment (some of which is discussed in Chapter 17) makes high-quality banquet service very practical and attainable today.

Types of Food Service Styles

Now that you have some understanding about factors which should be considered as a particular service style is selected, let's look at some common types of dining room service. We will begin with table service and then briefly discuss cafeteria service, buffet service, banquet service, and several other types of service styles.

Table Service

As you know, table service involves the customers being seated at a table with food servers waiting on them. Three basic types of table service are used in the United States:

French Service. This service style is used in some dining rooms which feature elegant atmosphere, gourmet foods, and a high check average. A common characteristic is that many food items are partly or completely prepared at tableside. For example, food is brought to the table on a cart and is quickly prepared to the customer's satisfaction by using some type of heating unit. Steak Diane, flaming desserts and drinks, and Caesar salads are some popular items that are prepared at tableside. Experienced employees are needed for effective French service. In addition to knowing recipes for items to be prepared, the service staff must know how to bone and carve fish, poultry, and meats. Specialized personnel are also normally used for food preparation, table service, table setting, and clearing activities. Since carts are needed in the dining room, aisle space must be wide. This means that fewer tables are used and therefore fewer customers are served.

Russian Service. This style of service is not used very often in the United States. Carving and finishing of food products are done in the kitchen where portions are attractively arranged on platters and garnished to provide effective presentation. The food server carries the tray directly to the table and after showing (presenting) it to the customer, serves portions onto plates which are in front of each customer. While it is not as labor intensive as French service, skill is required. Russian service also requires more employees than traditional American service.

American Service. American service is the most frequently used style of service in the United States. With this type of service, food is portioned onto plates in the kitchen and full plates are brought to the table by the food server. Food is often placed and removed from the left with the left hand and beverages are usually served and removed from the right with the right hand. This style is fast, and food servers—while needing some special training—need not be as skilled as those attempting French or Russian service. Portioning, plating, and garnishing can be done under the supervision of a professional chef.

Cafeteria Service

In cafeteria service, customers pass through serving lines and receive food items from service staff. In some operations, cafeteria service is similar to buffet service; customers help themselves to many items. In most cafeterias, however, service staff are available to portion at least the most expensive and hard-to-serve items. Traditionally, the cafeteria operation has been one in which customers enter the serving area, pass down a "straight-line" serving counter, and pay for their meals at the far end of the counter or as they exit the dining room past a cashier's stand.

Recently, however, "scramble" cafeteria layouts have evolved. With this plan, customers enter the cafeteria line area and can bypass each other, going to mini-serving stations, each of which has separate food items. For example, there may be a salad bar, soup station, hot and cold sandwich area, entree center, etc. There is less of a "waiting in line" feeling when the scramble system is used. Customers can go through the cafeteria line area without feeling that they are holding up customers behind them. With the advent of scramble systems have also come creatively designed cafeteria areas. The stainless steel islands and sterile serving lines which have been associated with cafeterias are becoming a thing of the past.

Buffet Service

Traditional buffet service involves arranging food on platters which are then placed on large tables. Often, a separate table is used for each course. Plates, silverware, and other necessary service items are conveniently located so that people can help themselves.

There are many different types of buffets. Some operations offer buffet service on a continual basis; there is no other type of service. Others have special buffets on weekends, holidays, or at lunch. Still other properties offer a combination of table service and buffet. Appetizers, salad ingredients, and, perhaps, breads and soups are offered buffet style; the entree with accompaniments is served at the table by a server. Some operations may have buffet tables set up only for appetizers or desserts. As you can see, buffet service is versatile and can lend itself to almost any type of meal being served.

Banquet Service   As we have noted, banquet service is used to provide large numbers of people with meals in a relatively short period of time. Service is often at the table, but buffets or a combination of buffet/table service are other possibilities. Banquets can be a very profitable part of your food service operation. However, banquets can also be a great problem both in terms of filling banquet space on a day-to-day basis and in developing procedures which guarantee that satisfied customers will want to return. In large operations, the marketing/sales department may be responsible for selling banquets. In fact, this department may also be responsible for food service at banquets and special catered events. While you can debate the advantages and disadvantages of one organizational plan over another, the need for effective, ongoing communication between everyone who has a role in the banquet operation is essential.

Knowing Your Markets. Concerns about marketing—looking at what potential customers want and need and finding ways to satisfy them—are just as much a part of banquet service as they are of the regular dining operation. Many properties with a large banquet service develop a variety of banquet menus over a range of prices for prospective customers. There are special concerns that you should be aware of when developing banquet menus. For example, there might be equipment and personnel limitations due to the large quantities of the same menu item which must be prepared for service within a relatively short time period. You may have to modify established banquet menus to meet the specific needs of your prospective customers. Be careful that such changes do not sacrifice quality and other requirements established for the customer's benefit.

Communication and Cooperation. It is critical that production, service, and sales staff know what each other is doing. What exactly will be on the menu? What exactly is the cut-off point for the total number of customers to be served and when will it be known? Proper setup of the banquet areas is important. While this is often not the responsibility of the food service staff, they must be concerned about it. If tables are hastily and incorrectly arranged because of problems with setup crews, this reflects on the food and beverage department. Banquet service illustrates the concept of "interdepartmental cooperation," which means that all departments work together in order to attain the entire operation's goals (this should be true in all areas of the operation).

Scheduling and Timing. In Chapter 14 you will learn that foods must be prepared and preportioned as close as possible to the point of service. In banquet service, even when things go well, there are time lapses between when food is preplated and when it is served. With banquet service, foods are placed in mobile equipment for transport to the banquet area. While this may not be a problem for items that need to be kept cold (they can be preportioned and stored in refrigerated units until the point of service), it can be a serious problem for hot food items. If food is kept at the appropriate hot temperature, it can quickly deteriorate in quality. If it is kept at a lower temperature, it may not be palatable to customers and sanitation problems can occur. Therefore, carefully scheduled and timed banquet service is an absolute necessity.

Supervision and Control. With large banquets, captains often supervise and control service in specific areas of the dining area. Many food servers are necessary to serve large numbers of people at one time. Often, transport racks which contain eight or more plated items can be used to hasten service. In some operations, tray stands are used in much the same manner when service is conducted in dining areas. Regardless of the plan, it is important to consider the personnel and service techniques that will be needed to provide food to people on a timely basis.

Cleanup. When several courses are being served, soiled flatware, plates, and other items are normally removed before the next course is served. Adequate transport equipment to move soiled items from banquet service areas to dishwashing areas must be available. If the operation is properly laid out, service corridors, freight elevators, and other nonpublic access spaces will facilitate this task. Make sure there is adequate space in dishwashing areas for transport equipment that is being unloaded and for moving large quantities of serviceware through the dishwashing process.

Other Types of Service

While table, cafeteria, and buffet service are among the most commonly used types of service, there are other styles. For example, family style (similar to English service) involves presenting large quantities of food in large bowls or on large platters. The bowls and platters are then passed to the customers who help themselves. Some operations market their family-style service and use it with special and family-oriented themes. Other operations may use family service only on holidays. For example, whole turkeys can be roasted if orders are placed ahead of time, and the turkeys can then be carved and passed by the customers at their tables.

Tray service has been traditionally associated with institutional food service. For example, meals may be preplated, put on trays, kept hot or cold by special transport carts, and moved from preparation/preplating areas to service wards as needed. A variation of tray service is now used in the airline industry. All items except the hot entree are placed on individual trays and kept chilled. After the entree is warmed, it is added to the entire tray of food items which is then presented to the passenger.

Some operations use a combination of service styles. Consider the American-style restaurant which offers Caesar salads, flaming desserts, or after-dinner drinks in an attempt to increase the check average.

Organizing the Dining Room

In the past, a wide variety of positions has been required for dining room operation. For example, a maitre d'hotel would be in charge of all dining rooms and, perhaps, all food service functions. In a large prop-

Figure 11.1 Front of House Position: Banquet Captain

Position:	**Banquet Captain**
Reports to:	**Banquet Service Manager**

The Captains must set an example with their leadership. Never let down in your supervisory capacity. Insist on efficiency, neatness, and adherence to all policies at all times.

1. **TIMING:** Arrive two hours before a function (or earlier as required).

2. Read menus and all memoranda carefully and check out all arrangements such as the coatroom, programs, amplification, etc.

3. Check the seating diagram. Make sure the setup is no more than 5% above the guarantee. If it is more, check immediately with the Banquet Service Manager.

4. Go to the function room and check all the lights in the room, the physical condition of the room, the carpeting on the platforms, etc.

5. Check the menu with the chef. Tell the chef how many tables there are if there are a large number of "12's," or if there are all "8's" or "10's."

6. Look at the food the chef has prepared and check it against the menu.

7. Make a sample setup for food servers to follow.

8. Most important, be in the room when the people in charge of the function arrive. Introduce yourself and offer assistance in any way that is needed. Assure the host or hostess that you are at their disposal for the remainder of the function.

9. Find out where the person in charge and any other important guests(s) are seated. Staff these tables with good servers and make sure special attention is provided.

10. During the function, go from table to table and inquire about the food and service. Take care of any requests the guests may have. Always remember to avoid any controversy with the guest, regardless of who is right or wrong.

11. Do not rush service. Many times there is a tendency to rush when we have more than adequate time to serve.

12. After the meal is served, remain in the room for the remainder of the function. If you must leave the room, assign someone to stay, but advise this person where you can be located. If an emergency should arise, we will then be covered.

erty, assistant maitres d'hotel would be available to supervise individual dining areas. Directors of service, supervisors of dining room sections, food servers, assistant food servers, bus personnel, wine stewards, cashiers, and other personnel would round out the dining room staff.

Staffing Pattern

Today, however, with rising labor costs and less need for formal service in many operations, a modern staffing pattern has evolved. There may be a host or hostess whose primary duties involve taking reservations and "meeting and greeting" the guests. In large dining rooms, other personnel (sometimes called captains) are used to manage the service and seating in specific areas of the dining room. Captains may assume many of the responsibilities of the host/hostess, making sure that menus are available, that all table settings are correct, and, perhaps, assisting with beverage service. In formal dining rooms, food servers are necessary to take orders and to deliver food. Buspersons may be required to set and clear tables and to assist the food server with food and beverage service as needed.

While every dining room is unique, all have basic tasks that must be done by someone. Figures 11.1 and 11.2 illustrate possible job descrip-

Figure 11.2 Front of House Position: Busperson

Position:	**Busperson**
Reports to:	**Manager of Dining Room**

Basic Functions:

1. **Duties**
   a. Assist servers in servicing their stations.
   b. Make sure chairs, tables are clean and set.
   c. Deliver supplies from storerooms, as requested by hostess.
   d. Supply ashtrays, china, glasses, silverware, and ice.
   e. Supply Danish, rolls, butter, milk and cream.
   f. Keep floor clean around tables and buffet.
   g. Report to supervisor on arrival and before departure.

2. **Service**
   a. Set up table with linen, silverware, salt and pepper, sugar tray, ashtrays.
   b. When guests are seated, provide ice water, basket of bread and butter.
   c. Service tables with guest requests — more coffee, tea, condiments, bread, butter.
   d. Keep ashtrays clean and water glasses filled.
   e. Remove dishes when guests are finished.
   f. Reset table with fresh linen.
   g. Reset table with clean silverware and china, using a tray at all times.
   h. Dirty silverware, china, and glasses are to be segregated in the dishwashing area; china to one area, glasses to another, and silverware into sterile bath.

3. **Appearance**
   a. Black pants, well-polished shoes, and black socks.
   b. Hotel provides special uniform jacket.
   c. Must be cleanshaven, well-groomed, practice good personal hygiene.

tions for typical front of house positions. (A job description is a written list of all tasks, responsibilities, and other basic information for a position.

When you consider the tasks required to provide proper service in operations other than those offering traditional table service, you can see that other positions and, therefore, additional job descriptions, are necessary. Figures 11.3 and 11.4 show, respectively, abbreviated job descriptions for a tray assembly line worker in a hospital food service operation and a room service ordertaker in a hotel food service operation.

Service Standards

In all types of food service operations, management must:

1. Look at the activity from the customer's perspective.

2. Define exactly what must be done and the standards of performance to indicate when required work has been effectively accomplished.

3. Develop standard operating procedures.

4. Practice supervision techniques and follow-up evaluation.

Figure 11.3 Job Description: Tray Assembly Line Worker (Hospital)

Job Title: **Line Aide**

**Department
Name:**   **Dietetic Services**

General Functions

Responsible for preparation and portioning of cold food items; all patient tray setup; service of gourmet dinners; utilization of approved sanitation and safety techniques under direction of dietetic supervisor.

Specific Duties

1. Sets up and works assigned position on patient trayline.
2. Prepares, portions and wraps cold food items as assigned.
3. Cleans and sanitizes assigned work areas and all involved equipment daily.
4. Wraps patient silverware and straws in napkins for trayline.
5. Sets up, serves, and cleans up gourmet dinners.
6. Employs highest standards of safety in all aspects of work.
7. Performs other related duties as assigned.

Education and Training

Must be able to read and write basic English.

Experience

No experience is necessary.

Supervision

Works under the direction of Dietetic supervisor. Not responsible for supervising other employees.

Contacts and Working Relationships

Constant contact with other department personnel. Some contact with patients and public.

Mental Demands

Most tasks are routine in nature, but require attention to detail.

Physical Demands

Includes pushing food carts, lifting light objects, and being constantly on feet.

Working Conditions

Works in cheerful, well-lighted, air conditioned department with hazards typical of any institutional kitchen.

Courtesy of St. Lawrence Hospital, Lansing, Michigan.

We are talking, of course, about establishing minimum quality standards which must be consistently followed by all employees in front of house areas. You have already learned that you cannot rely on the employees' common sense to do the right thing at the right time. Planning is necessary to identify required tasks and to develop procedures for effectively performing them.

It is at this point that you should carefully consider the customer; recall from our previous discussion that the type of service provided should be that which is best from the customer's perspective. What does

Figure 11.4 Job Description: Room Service Ordertaker

Position: Ordertaker
Reports to: Room Service Manager/Captain on Duty

Basic Functions
1. Takes telephone orders from guests.
2. Verifies and repeats orders, room numbers, and name of guest.
3. Time stamps order to keep track of delivery time.

Standards of Performance
1. Knows the menu and special daily items.
2. Has a clear, friendly voice; always uses a guest's name.
3. Repeats order, guides guest through ordering, and suggests extra items such as wine, beer, juices, etc.
4. Keeps working area clean and orderly.
5. Keeps all time orders in secure place for early-morning shift.

Sequence of Ordertaking
1. "Good morning (Good evening), this is room service. (x) speaking, may I help you?"
2. Inquire room number and name of guest. Address the guest by name from this moment on.
3. Take order, repeat order and room number, offer the daily newspaper (compliments of the hotel). Use salesmanship to promote extra sales. For example, offer orange juice in the morning and wine/cocktails in the afternoon/evening.
4. Always specify time for delivery and call back even if it appears to take "just a few minutes longer."
5. Thank guest, close with "Have a nice day."

the customer/patient desire and how can the operation best provide for these wants and needs?

This question must be answered by each operation. While it is not possible to develop generalizations that apply to all properties, there are many principles addressed in this chapter that can be used to develop consistent procedures for all front of house employees. Supervision is necessary to ensure that shortcuts are not used which violate standard operating procedures. When you view the operation from the customer's perspective, questions to ask should center on, "If I were a customer, what things would I like or dislike about the serving procedures?" When these questions are answered, you have an idea about what procedures should or should not be used. The answers to these questions also govern the development of standard operating procedures; they indicate where and even how training programs to teach required activities should be conducted.

Now put yourself in the customer's place:

_____

You enter a traditional table service restaurant which you have never visited before. A sign indicates that you should wait to be seated. A food server who is passing by notices you and says, "The host will be with you in just a moment. Thanks for waiting." (In most operations, this never happens unless service staff are trained.) In a moment, the host meets and greets you and makes you feel welcome.

As you are being taken to your table by the host you notice things around you. The dining room appears to be clean, and the tables have been bused. Customers who are already seated appear to be satisfied.

Now you are seated. First, you notice that the table, chairs, and table settings are clean. While you wait for the menu, the busperson brings you ice water. When the menu arrives, you notice that it is clean and attractive. The server asks if you would like a cocktail or other beverage, then answers all your questions about the menu. It is obvious that the food server is trying to do a good job of suggestive selling.

Your order is delivered on a timely basis by the food server. The food is effectively presented and has a pleasing aroma, temperature, and flavor. The service during the meal is attentive, but not overbearing. Any problems, regardless of how minor, are quickly attended to. You observe that consistent serving procedures are being used: every customer who orders the same item is served the same size portion in the same type of serving dish or glass.

It is time to pay the bill. It is delivered quickly and procedures are used which make you confident that the arithmetic is correct and that all of your orders, but no others, are accounted for (a calculator tape which you compare with the handwritten total is included). The food server tells you that she will take your payment. Payment is processed promptly and, as you leave, the "thank you's" which you receive appear genuine and warm.

The above scenario, of course, does not cover every occurrence in dining room service. You could have peeked through glass doors into kitchen areas and noted sanitation procedures. The point is that service standards must be established and they should be based on the customer's wants and needs. Every reasonable concern that a customer might have should be addressed in the required procedures for dining service which are taught to all service staff. The old saying that "the customer is always right" may or may not be true. However, from the perspective of the servers, this observation represents the proper attitude. What is needed in many operations is not expensive equipment and elaborate atmosphere. Rather, an attitude of concern for the customer and the use of consistent service procedures will be a good first step toward having effective front of house serving procedures.

Figure 11.5 notes procedures which can be used to define minimum requirements for quality service, products, atmosphere, cleanliness, etc., in an operation. After considering the necessary components of an acceptable dining experience from the customer's perspective, you can develop objective performance standards. (For example, customers should be greeted by the host/hostess within one minute of their arrival and restrooms should be cleaned at least each half-hour.)

You can use this report to evaluate your food service operation. It can also be supplied to "shoppers" (people hired by management to pose as customers and to report their experiences at the operation). Alterna-

Figure 11.5 Food Service Operation Report

Required Procedures

Seating

Performance Requirements

A. Customers are greeted as they enter the dining room.

B. The host/hostess is neat and clean.

C. The table is available at the reservation time.

D. No dirty dishes or ashtrays are on the table when customers are seated.

E. Good judgment is used when selecting the table for customer seating.

F. A nonsmoking section is available.

G. Chairs/booths are:
- comfortable
- in good repair
- clean

H. The host/hostess distributes menus after customers are comfortably seated.

I. The host/hostess tells customers the server's name.

J. The host/hostess informs customers about special or additional items not noted on the menu.

K. Other seating procedures: _____
_____
_____

Cleanliness

Performance Requirements

A. The dining room is clean.

B. Tables/booths are clean.

C. Napkins and tablecloths are free from spots.

D. Flatware, dishes, and glasses are clean.

E. Public restrooms are clean.

F. The dining room area is clean.

G. Other cleanliness procedures: _____
_____

Atmosphere

Performance Requirements

A. The dining area is conducive to conversation.

B. There is sufficient lighting.

C. The temperature is comfortable.

D. Background music is not too loud.

E. There is adequate privacy.

F. The decor is pleasant.

G. The decor, menu, employees' uniforms, etc., are in agreement with the general theme of the operation.

H. Other atmosphere requirements: _____

_____

_____

Service   **Performance Requirements**

A. The server arrives at the table promptly.

B. The server greets the customer and identifies himself/herself.

C. The server is neat and clean.

D. The server is cordial.

E. The server is familiar with all menu items.

F. Suggestive selling is used.

G. Selling is done courteously.

H. Food and beverage items are served promptly.

I. The server is aware of which customer has ordered each item.

J. After serving the meal, the server asks if any additional items are desired.

K. The water glasses are refilled promptly.

L. Empty dishes and glasses are removed promptly.

M. Other service requirements: _____

_____

_____

Food and Beverage Products   **Performance Requirements**

A. Food and beverages are delivered to the table as they are described in the menu.

B. All the items on the menu are available.

C. Hot foods are served hot and cold foods are served cold.

D. The food looks appetizing and is placed on the plate in an appealing manner.

E. The quality of food and beverages meets customers' expectations.

F. Portions are appropriately sized.

G. There is a variety of specialty drinks.

H. Special brands for drinks are available.

I. Drinks are appealing in appearance.

J. Drinks are palatable.

K. Other product requirements: _____

_____

_____

Check Handling   **Performance Requirements**

A. Service staff complies with all sales income control procedures.

B. Checks are given to customers at the correct time.

C. The server promptly presents the customer with a check upon completion of the meal.

D. The check is readable.

E. The check is correctly totaled.

F. The correct change is returned.

G. The customer receives the check stub.

H. The server courteously invites the customers to return.

If payment is at the register:

I. The amount of purchase is quoted.

J. The cashier works with the register drawer closed.

K. The sale is recorded immediately.

L. The price is repeated when change is given.

M. The cashier says, "Thank you."

If payment is at the table:

N. The server informs the customer that he/she will return to collect the payment when the customer is ready.

O. The server takes customer payments directly to the cashier.

P. The server brings the customer's change directly from the cashier's station.

Q. The server makes change from his/her pocket.

R. The server returns the correct change.

S. The server thanks the customer.

T. Other payment requirements: _____

_____

_____

tively, some of your regular customers can complete the report and receive a complimentary meal for their efforts.

Suggestive Selling   There are some items on the menu that are more profitable to the operation than others. According to the menu engineering concept, all items on the menu can be classified into four types:[3]

1. **Stars**—items which are both popular and profitable

2. **Plow horses**—items which are low in profit but high in popularity

3. **Puzzles**—items which are high in profitability but low in popularity

4. **Dogs**—items which are neither profitable nor popular

If menu items can be classified according to the above types (the menu engineering concept provides easy procedures to do this), your operation will have identified the items it wishes to sell: stars and puzzles. You can then design menus, implement effective menu pricing and food costing plans, train service staff, and enact related strategies which will help your operation maximize economic objectives while addressing issues that are of concern to the customer.

One objective of suggestive selling has just been identified: to sell those items which are most profitable to the operation. However, there is one additional objective that should be noted. It relates to increasing the check average (check average refers to the total dollars of food sales divided by the total number of customers consuming a meal). Additional sales income can be generated by having the same number of customers spend more, thereby increasing the check average, or by more customers coming into the dining room and spending, in total, more than previous customers spent.

The food server is probably the employee with whom the customer comes into the most contact. The person who occupies this position is the most critical element in your food service operation's plan for financial success.

Suggestive selling embraces a variety of techniques that can be used by food servers to encourage customers to buy certain menu items. You can imagine the need for tact and training as these efforts are practiced. The primary objective of your food service operation is to provide customers with the food service and atmosphere which they desire. When customers know what they want, absolutely no effort should be made to change their minds. However, many customers do not know what they want as they are ordering and would appreciate some assistance from food servers. When this is done, both the customers and the operation can benefit.

Increasing Sales of Profitable Items. Let's look first at suggestive selling which is aimed at increasing sales of profitable menu items. The food server can draw the customer's attention to these items when the menu is presented and make recommendations. This technique works especially well when the operation has planned its menu around the items it wants to sell. For example, items which head a list, are boxed, have written descriptions, or are located in specific areas of the menu may sell with greater frequency than other items.

Increasing the Check Average. Also consider how the check average can be increased by using suggestive selling techniques. Food servers should ask questions which cannot be answered no. For example, "Our strawberry shortcake is fantastic and the chef's own special cherry pie just came out of the oven—which would you like?" Or, "You probably noticed all of the tableside flaming we are doing this evening. The customers really like our cherries jubilee and flaming crepes—which would you like for dessert?" The second example illustrates another important concept of suggestive selling: customers are influenced by what they see being consumed around them. If a customer sees a Caesar salad being prepared at tableside, this may be a powerful incentive to order the salad.

Some final points about suggestive selling should be made. Suggestive selling can be applied to cafeteria service as well as to dining room table service; a serving line attendant can make suggestions to customers as they pass through the serving line. Suggestive selling also has implications for buffet service. Obviously, only those items which management wants the customers to have should be offered on the buffet line. The way in which items are presented through placement on the buffet line, use of garnishes, etc., will affect the customers' desire to take portions of the menu items.

Dining Room Operation

We have looked at some aspects of dining room service from the customer's perspective. Let's now look at the dining room area from the operation's perspective. We will begin with the activity of inspecting, which should be done on a scheduled, routine basis. (Some of the tasks in the dining area must be done daily before the dining room opens.)

Inspect Facilities

Inspect facilities to ensure that any problems with room temperature, lighting, etc., are identified and referred to the appropriate maintenance personnel promptly. Safety hazards such as rips in carpeting, loose banisters, and wall decorations which are not securely fastened should also be identified and promptly corrected.

A safety checklist can be used to help remind you about these and related potential problems (see Chapter 10). Additional inspection is necessary for sanitation purposes. Have the dining and public areas been properly cleaned? Are the tables set correctly? Are the chairs clean? Are the tables wobbly? Are all the tables set in the configurations needed for confirmed reservations? Again, sanitation checklists can be used to ensure that all potential problems are reviewed before the dining room opens.

Some dining areas can be viewed from the street. You should walk through the dining room and walk past the building from the exterior to look at things from the customer's perspective. You might ask yourself, "If I were a customer, would the dining room and adjacent areas be attractive to me?"

Assign Food Server Stations

Several other activities must be performed before the dining room opens. For example, food server stations must be assigned. A station is a certain number of tables for which each food server is responsible. In some operations, especially traditional dining rooms, stations may not be assigned. Rather, tables are assigned to food servers in turn. This means that food servers are waiting on customers all over the dining room simultaneously. Normally, this procedure is not recommended. The number of tables assigned to a food server should depend upon:

- the number of seats,

- the frequency with which seats turn over,

- the experience of the food server,

- the distance to the kitchen, and

- the number of food servers scheduled for a specific meal period.[4]

Of course, you must consider your specific operation. For example, a food server may only be able to properly serve six or seven seats in a busy coffeeshop counter operation even though the distance to the food service pickup counter is only a few feet. By contrast, in a dining room with moderate turnover, a food server may be able to serve 16-20 customers.

In many operations, stations are rotated between service staff. This is an especially useful procedure when specific stations are the first to open. Since specified setup duties must be performed by the first scheduled food servers, it is often fair to rotate employee schedules so that no employee performs the same setup duties every shift. Because the amount of cleanup duties which can be done early in the shift is usually minimal, the closing of stations with associated cleanup duties can also be rotated between employees.

Convene Food Server Meetings

Convene short food server meetings before the dining room opens. You will need this time to review work stations, explain daily specials, answer specific questions, review menu prices, and properly plan so operating problems will be minimal. You can also use this time to conduct ongoing tasting of new dishes and to provide training in exactly how menu items are made. This information can be very helpful to food servers as they use suggestive selling techniques.

Check Food Server Supply Stations

Finally, before the dining room opens, check food server supply stations to ensure that they are properly stocked. A final discussion with the chef and opening service staff will confirm that everything is ready and that the dining room can be opened.

Seat Customers to Their Satisfaction

When seating customers, particular requests should be satisfied if possible. Requests for special tables, help for handicapped people, seating for smokers and nonsmokers, etc., should be attended to. The person responsible for seating should provide the best available table. For example, tables in traffic aisles, next to kitchen doors, or near servers' supply stations may be less desirable than other tables. Perhaps they will not need to be used or, at least, can be held until there are no preferred seats/tables available.

Distribute Workload Evenly

The host/hostess (or other person responsible for seating) should work closely with servers to ensure that the workload is evenly distributed. It does little good to seat a customer at an empty table in a work station which is the responsibility of an already very busy food server. The customer will not receive timely service and problems may arise

Figure 11.6 Schedule of Side Work Tasks

Task	Days of Week						
	Mon.	**Tues.**	**Wed.**	**Thur.**	**Fri.**	**Sat.**	**Sun.**
Fill Table Condiments	Mary	Dan	Jackie	Dave	Stacey	Susan	Paul
Fix Butter Chips	Susan	Mary	Stacey	Paul	Jackie	Dave	Dan
Set Up Salad Bar	Dave	Paul	Susan	Dan	Mary	Jackie	Stacey

which could easily have been avoided if the customer had been seated elsewhere. This can happen, for example, if the food server is busy with a large party of customers at a table. There is a fine balance between rotating tables so that all food servers get a fair chance at tips and providing quality service to the customers.

Train Employees to Avoid Costly Mistakes

Much breakage occurs in operations using washable items; theft of these items also can contribute to higher than necessary supply costs. What can you do? To reduce breakage, you can train buspersons to properly stack soiled dishes (bus boxes can be used). The decoy system can also help reduce dish breakage in dishwashing areas. With this system, the dishwasher places one serviceware item in a specified area of a soiled dish counter. Buspersons then stack each type of soiled serviceware item in the appropriate area. Also, make sure that racks for glasses, cups, and other items are always available. To reduce theft, you can train servers to remove soiled glasses, flatware, and other items as fresh portions are provided. In addition, you can offer glassware and other items for sale; this gives people an opportunity to buy the items instead of taking them.

Linen costs can be excessive as well. Do not use table linens for rags or food service towels. Train service staff to carefully check table linens as they are being placed on tables. If they are torn or soiled, they should not be used. This linen should be kept separate from other linens so that you can make arrangements for credit (if you have a contract with a commercial laundry) or plan for additional purchases.

Emphasize Importance of Side Work

We have already noted that the setup and cleanup work must be done before and after dining rooms are opened. These activities are referred to as "side work." Food service employees usually realize that the work must be done, but because tips are not provided, they may object to doing it. This is why side work tasks might best be rotated between service personnel so that no employee consistently gets the "easy" or "hard" assignments. Examples of side work tasks might include supplying server stations, filling salt and pepper shakers, preparing butter chips, filling bun warmers with rolls, watering dining room plants, or polishing table tops. You can use a simple plan to identify and schedule employees to do required tasks (see Figure 11.6).

You and/or the dining room manager should emphasize the importance of doing required side work. The dining room must be readied for service. If the work is not done, there is an increased likelihood that supplies will be needed at the busiest times and service staff will be unavailable to do the work. If side work is de-emphasized, safety and sanitation (which are highlighted during the preopening inspection) will eventually become problems. Teach new employees that side work is an important part of their jobs and, with proper supervision, you can reduce or eliminate problems that many operations have in keeping up with side work.

Sales Income Control Procedures

You must, of course, be concerned about procedures which are used to control sales income during food service. Simply put, procedures must be implemented to help ensure that income is received for all items that go out of the kitchen. There are many basic procedures that you can incorporate into sales income control systems in your operation.[5]

Guest Check System. When this system is used, no order for a food or beverage product is taken from the customer without listing each item on the guest check. At the same time, no food or beverage order is prepared if it is not on the guest check. When a guest check control system is used, numbered guest checks are issued to food servers and become their responsibility. The amount of sales income which should be collected is represented by the sales totals on all guest checks after they are accounted for.

Duplicate Guest Check. Many properties use duplicate guest checks. The soft copy is given to production employees and can, at a later time, be compared with the hard copy given to the customer and retained by the cashier.

Precheck Register. A precheck register is like a cash register except that no operating cash drawer is used. The food server takes the guest order, writes it on the guest check, and goes to the precheck register. The check is inserted into the machine, a clerk key (signifying which server is using the machine for this transaction) is depressed, and information is entered into the machine. With some models, a preset key is used. For example, if a steak has been ordered, all the server needs to do is press a key labeled "steak." The steak order is automatically printed on the guest check and, at the same time, the amount of money that is due the operation from the sale is tallied on a by-server basis. Use of the precheck register authorizes the order noted on the guest check to be prepared. The order is taken to the kitchen, perhaps given to an expediter, and then prepared. Before the server is "checked out" at the end of the shift, the precheck register is totaled to assess the amount of sales income due from his/her food sales. Guest checks are accounted for and the totals from each guest check are added together and compared with the total from the precheck register.

A running balance of the number of steaks sold can also be kept with a precheck register. Control of these expensive items therefore becomes easier. The number of steaks issued to the production station at the beginning of the shift, less the number of portions sold (from the precheck register count), and any necessary adjustments due to burned or returned products should equal the number of steaks remaining in work station storage at the end of the shift.

Income Collection Systems. There are two basic income collection systems which you can use. With the food server banking system, the food server keeps all income collected from customers until the end of the shift. With the cashier banking system, the cashier operates a cash register, collects tickets and cash (from either the customer and/or the food server), and retains the funds until the end of the shift. The amount of sales income due from food server sales is determined by totaling and comparing precheck register totals with guest check totals. Then this amount of money is collected from the food server (if a food server banking system is used) or from the cashier (if a cashier banking system is used).

Protecting Your Operation

There are many ways that dishonest food servers can attempt to "beat the house." As the manager, you have a responsibility to ask the following question: "If I were a dishonest food server and wanted to steal from this operation, how would I do it?" To the extent that you can answer this question, possible problems have been identified. You must resolve them. Do not make the assumption that your employees are honest and would never steal. While the majority of employees may be honest, there are likely to be others who are not. Procedures to control sales income should be an integral part of the entire management control system used by your operation. This concern, of course, should also extend to procedures for banking sales income, writing checks to pay bills, and managing other aspects of back of house recordkeeping and physical systems. Embezzlement is just as much a problem in the food service industry as it is in any other business. Therefore, don't think that just because the money gets to the bank, everything is all right. While this discussion is directly related to control of income from food servers, it illustrates a fundamental concern. You must control all resources (including income) at any point in the system where they can be lost to your operation.

What You Should Know

We have noted the importance of knowing your customers' wants and needs. Let's see how these wants and needs are met. Viewed from an operational perspective, serving is the final activity in a sequence which begins with menu planning and continues with:

- Purchasing

- Receiving

- Storing

- Issuing

- Preparation

- Production

The following chapters explain these activities and how they all fit together.

NOTES

1. William W. Kahrl, *Introduction to Modern Food and Beverage Service* (Englewood Cliffs, N.J.: Prentice-Hall, 1976), pp. 129 and 147.

2. Jack D. Ninemeier, *Planning and Control for Food and Beverage Operations* (East Lansing, Mich.: Educational Institute of the American Hotel & Motel Association, 1982), p. 109.

3. Michael Kasavana and Donald Smith, *Menu Engineering* (East Lansing, Mich.: Hospitality Publications, 1982).

4. Carol A. King, *Professional Dining Room Management* (Rochelle Park, N.J.: Hayden, 1980), p. 32.

5. Ninemeier, *Planning and Control*, Chapters 12 and 13.

12
Purchasing and Receiving Procedures

Management Challenges

As a result of studying this chapter you will:

1.   recognize goals which all purchasing programs should have.

2.   know how to determine purchase needs.

3.   know how to assess quality needs at time of purchase and understand how to determine quality requirements.

4.   be able to determine quantity of products required at time of purchase.

5.   understand basic purchasing documents and their role in the purchasing process.

6.   understand basic security concerns that must be incorporated into purchasing procedures.

7.   realize the role that ethics plays in purchasing.

8.   know the role of the receiving clerk's daily report and understand how to complete and use the form.

9.   recognize the importance of marking and tagging incoming products.

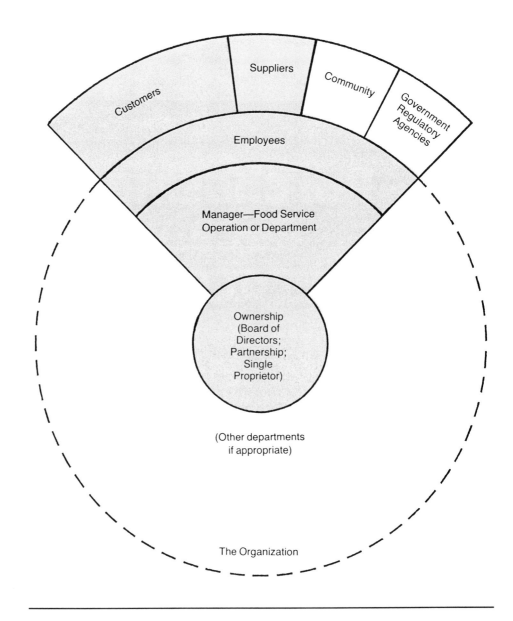

Customers

Suppliers

Community

Government
Regulatory
Agencies

Employees

Manager—Food Service
Operation or Department

Ownership
(Board of
Directors;
Partnership;
Single
Proprietor)

(Other departments
if appropriate)

The Organization

Focus on the
Food Service Publics

All products must be purchased and received. This process involves a relationship between the food service manager (who establishes purchasing and receiving procedures) and the external supplier. The relationship between the manager and food service employees must also be examined. Since these procedures affect profit (or minimum cost levels), owners and customers are involved in purchasing and receiving relationships.

The food service manager must be involved in many activities that are not directly concerned with meeting and greeting guests or producing food and beverage products. We have come to the point in our introduction to food and beverage operations where we must focus on the flow of food and beverage products through the operation. Special emphasis is given to the review of basic management procedures that should be used at each step along the way.

Managers of small food and beverage operations sometimes believe that basic management techniques are necessary only for large operations. While some sophisticated management procedures require extensive labor or specialized equipment like computers to complete records and collect information, there are many less sophisticated or demanding procedures that are are worth the time and effort needed to practice them.

The flow of products through the property begins with purchasing. Let's look at some of the basics of an effective purchasing system, see how it works, and learn fundamental procedures that can be used to manage a food and beverage operation.

Goals of a Purchasing Program

As with any management activity, purchasing programs must be planned. These programs often evolve based upon what has and has not worked in the past. A better approach is to consider the goals of purchasing and how they are best achieved. In discussing the goals of a purchasing program, remember that at their most basic level these goals are of concern to any property—large or small. Whether purchasing is done by a staff purchasing specialist or by a line manager, the basic goals and procedures to attain them are similar.

Goals of an effective purchasing program are:[1]

Obtaining the right product. The purchase specification determines what is "right" for the operation. There are, for example, many different types of green beans, shrimp, and even flour. What exactly is the product that the food and beverage operation desires?

Obtaining a quality product. The food and beverage operation must receive the proper quality of purchased products. This, by the way, is not always the highest quality that is available. Consideration of the product's quality isn't possible until its price is examined.

Obtaining the right price. The purchaser is responsible for obtaining a quality product at the best price. The relationship between the purchaser and supplier should not be adversarial.

Obtaining products at the right time. There is an optimal time when products should be purchased and received. If they are purchased too early, there may be larger quantities than needed in inventory. If products are purchased too late, stockouts and customer dissatisfation can occur.

Obtaining products from the right supplier. As will be discussed later, there are many suppliers that can deliver products to the property. Which one is best? Why?

These five primary goals indicate some reasons why purchasing is important. There are others as well. For example, the manager can obtain much information from suppliers that will be helpful in making decisions. What new products are available? What kind of products does a supplier have that might help resolve some operating problems? Since supplier representatives visit many properties to make sales calls, they may be able to give some practical advice to the manager about ways other properties have solved problems.

In addition to general information, very specific advice also can be received. What will the price of shrimp be next week? Should we buy a large quantity now because the price is going up, or should we wait because prices will be dropping? Suppliers can review the property's purchase specifications (discussed below) to make suggestions that will enable the property to get the products it wants.

Why Is Purchasing Important?

Purchasing is necessary in order to bring products into the property for processing and sale. But this is not the only reason that purchasing is important. The property's efforts to control costs begin with developing and implementing effective purchasing procedures. Neither can commercial operations maximize profits nor can institutional operations minimize expenses unless the purchasing tasks are closely examined. Simply stated, money can be made or lost based on how well the purchasing process works for the property. When 40% or more of all sales dollars generated by a commercial operation and 50% or more of all costs incurred by an institutional operation are used to purchase products and services, the importance of the purchasing task is evident.

Purchasing also is important because it affects cash flow. Purchased products must be paid for, generally within 30 days. Money must be available to pay these bills when due, and managers must be concerned about the flow of cash through the operation. Continuity and supply concerns are also important. Internal operating procedures are disrupted and customers/patients are disappointed when products are not available. Purchasing personnel should store products in proper quantities so that these types of disruptions are minimized.

The importance of purchasing can be noted in one simple point: purchasing affects the bottom of the budget line. Every dollar that can be saved through effective purchasing increases a property's profit by one dollar. Whether the food service manager is trying to increase profits or reduce expenses, these economic goals will be harder to attain without the best possible purchasing system.

Determining Purchasing Needs

As you will see, purchasing is much more than picking up the phone and calling in an order. Planning is important. To achieve the goals of a purchasing program, the purchaser must first determine what is needed.

Chapter 4 indicated that the menu determines what needs to be purchased. Simply put, if ground beef is required for some menu items, then this product must be purchased. Questions about the type of ground beef, quantity, delivery, the meat supplier, and cost are important.

Purchase needs also are dictated by the standard recipe. If the menu says that beef stew will be served, then a standard recipe for beef stew must be developed. The recipe will suggest what kind of and how many vegetables will go into the stew. Since the recipe will reflect the property's quality requirements, quality aspects of purchase specifications also will be dictated by the standard recipe.

Assessing Quality Needs at Time of Purchase

How are quality requirements for the property determined? The relationship between price and quality is referred to as value. The concept of value, of course, applies to the property as it purchases products and services and to the property's customer, who will be purchasing products and services from the property. Top management at the organization must establish the basic parameters in which the business will operate. In the case of a multi-unit chain, the market is determined at the corporate—not individual unit—level. While some properties are price-conscious and want the least expensive items available, other properties are concerned only about receiving the highest possible quality products because they know the market will pay for them. Other properties fall between these two extremes. Therefore, decisions must be made about the quality, the availability of products, and how these will or will not fit into the "package" that the property is making available to the guest.

This relates not only to commercial food and beverage operations, but to institutional operators as well. They must think about their market—whether they be patients in a hospital, children in a school, or inmates in a correctional facility. The needs of these "customers" of the food and beverage operation must be considered when purchase decisions are made.

Within a specific property, decisions about product and service needs are likely to be made by the food service manager and perhaps the chef for food products, and the beverage manager for beverage products. Even in large operations with purchasing agents, the actual decision to purchase the products which the operating department desires should still rest with the line department managers, not with staff purchasing officials.

Overview of Purchasing Process

You have learned that purchasing involves more than calling in an order. The many activities which make up the purchasing process can best be illustrated by Figure 12.1. As shown in the figure, the food or beverage department, as it produces and serves menu items, needs food products. Products should be requested from the storeroom through a

Figure 12.1 Overview of Purchasing Process

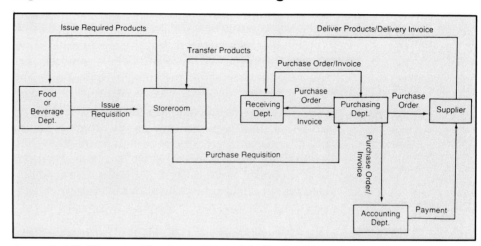

Source: Jack D. Ninemeier, Planning and Control for Food and Beverage Operations *(East Lansing, Mich.: Educational Institute of American Hotel & Motel Association, 1982), p. 61.*

formal requisition process. Normally, the storeroom has ample supplies of these products and merely issues them to the food and beverage department. At some point, however, the storeroom will need to replenish its inventory, and does this by developing a purchase requisition which alerts the purchasing department that more products must be ordered. The purchasing department, through either a formal purchase order system or informal purchase record system, orders products from the supplier. The supplier delivers products to the receiving department which transfers the products to the proper storage areas. The receiving department provides the purchasing department with the delivery invoice and other documents. After initial processing, the accounting department is alerted that the supplier can be paid for the products which were delivered.

While the actual procedures and forms used for purchasing may vary among properties, these basic steps generally are followed. While accounting aspects of the purchasing system will be discussed later, you should understand that several departments and people with differing responsibilities are required to ensure that user departments (food and beverage) have the products that they need.

An important concern that must be addressed prior to making a purchase is an assessment of the quality and quantity requirements for the purchase.

Determining Quality Requirements

You have already learned that it is important for the property to purchase the right quality product. How is this done? To answer this question, you must first understand what quality is. The term "quality" refers to the suitability of a product for its intended use. The closer that a product comes to being suitable, the higher the quality. For example, a super colossal olive represents a quality product for garnish or salad purposes. It may not, however, represent the proper quality if the item is to be chopped for a salad bar topping. Quality, then, refers to a product's

Figure 12.2 Purchase Specification Format

(name of food and beverage operation)

1. Product name: _____

2. Product used for:

> Clearly indicate product use (such as olive garnish for beverage, hamburger patty for grill frying for sandwich, etc.)

3. Product general description:

> Provide general quality information about desired product. For example, "iceberg lettuce; heads to be green, firm without spoilage, excessive dirt or damage. No more than 10 outer leaves; packed 24 heads per case."

4. Detailed description:

> Purchaser should state other factors which help to clearly identify desired product. Examples of specific factors, which vary by product being described, include:
> - Geographic origin
> - Variety
> - Type
> - Style
> - Grade
> - Size
> - Portion size
> - Brand name
> - Density
> - Medium of pack
> - Specific gravity
> - Container size
> - Edible yield, trim

5. Product test procedures:

> Test procedures occur at time product is received and as/after product is prepared/used. Thus, for example, products to be at a refrigerated temperature upon delivery can be tested with a thermometer. Portion-cut meat patties can be randomly weighed. Lettuce packed 24 heads per case can be counted.

6. Special instructions and requirements:

> Any additional information needed to clearly indicate quality expectations can be included here. Examples include bidding procedures, if applicable, labeling and/or packaging requirements and delivery and service requirements.

Source: Jack D. Ninemeier, Purchasing, Receiving and Storage: A Systems Manual for Restaurants, Hotels and Clubs *(Boston: CBI, 1983), p. 60.*

ability to do what it is supposed to do. Quality requirements are incorporated into purchasing by developing purchase specifications which indicate the minimum quality standards for a product. Managers must define what products they need, quality requirements must be established, and specifications to represent these needs must be developed.

Quality characteristics can be described by brand names. For example, a manager may decide that a specific brand meets his/her quality requirements. Purchase specifications, grades, samples, and trial orders can be used to define and establish minimum quality requirements.

Figure 12.2 illustrates a purchase specification format. Managers should develop this type of information for each of the most expensive products purchased. Note that the purchase specification illustrated in Figure 12.2 requires the following information:

- Name of product.

- Name of food service operation for which the specification is written.

- Product use.

- General description of the product.

- Specific quality. Detailed factors should be identified to avoid any communication problems resulting from lack of clarity in the product's general description.

- Product test procedures. This section should tell what procedures will be used to ensure compliance with quality factors noted in the purchase specification.

- Special instructions and requirements. Any additional, special requirements that must be met by the products being provided should be noted in this section.

When the purchase specification is being developed, the food service manager should obtain help from the supplier. The supplier can tell what products are available, what products other food service operations use, and what new products are or will be available.

In large operations with staff purchasing agents, user department personnel must be involved in developing purchase specifications. These officials should help find what product is needed, develop the purchase specification, and suggest which suppliers should be contacted for price quotations. User department staff also should evaluate, sample, and trial-order products.

In addition to the purchase specification, which lists quality specifics, other information must be provided as orders are placed. For example, instruction as to days and times for delivery, general information about bidding (if this system is used), and qualifications for suppliers who would be eligible to do business with the operation.

As individual orders are placed, the quantity, weight, and count of products being ordered must be stated. Likewise, the agreed price of the product should be noted and the purchase unit size (for example, a case of six #10 cans, #10 bulk, 16-ounce bottle, etc.) should be stated.

Once developed, the purchase specification should be given to suppliers. When you request price information for future orders, the supplier will pull the quality requirements of the property and be better able to quote a price for the desired product.

Determining Quantity Requirements

You have already learned that there is a need to purchase the proper quantity of products. If too many products are purchased, cash flow problems, theft and pilferage, and spoilage can take place. When inadequate supplies of products are purchased, stockouts may result and more frequent orders will have to be placed.

Many factors affect the quantity of products that should be purchased. Some of these factors are:[2]

1. Schedule needs. As larger volumes of products are produced, a greater quantity of items must be purchased.

2. Changing price concerns. Information about rising or decreasing costs may affect the quantity to be purchased.

3. Available storage facilities.

4. Storage and handling costs.

5. Waste and spoilage concerns.

6. Theft and pilferage concerns.

7. Concerns about emergency needs. Quantities purchased may include a "safety" factor which allows for possible delivery delay or runs on specific items without resulting stockouts. (See Figure 12.3 for an illustration of the minimum/maximum order system which incorporates safety factors.)

8. Market conditions. For example, some items may be in limited supply.

9. Level of available inventory.

10. Quantity discounts, if any.

11. Minimum order requirements imposed by suppliers. If, for example, suppliers will not "break cases," it may be necessary to purchase in "case lot" quantities only—which may be more than the optimal quantity desired.

12. Transportation and delivery problems.

13. Order costs. Costs to initiate and process an order can be high. If so, larger, less frequent orders should be placed.

Products can be purchased for either immediate use or inventory. Perishable products—such as fresh produce, bakery goods, and dairy items—must be purchased in quantities that can be used in a short period of time. These goods are often purchased and received several times a week. Management generally knows the usage rates for these types of products. In a two-day purchasing cycle, for example, 12 dozen eggs and 15 gallons of milk might be used. The quantity of perishable products to be purchased can be assessed by counting the number already on hand and subtracting this quantity from the amount needed. Figure 12.4 illustrates how to assess the quantities to be purchased and how to select the supplier. Note, for example, that six cases of spinach

Figure 12.3 Minimum/Maximum Order System

Example 1. Assume:

Purchase unit = case

Usage rate = 2 cases per day

Order period = monthly (30 days)

Monthly usage rate = 2 cases/day × 30 days = 60 cases

Lead time = 4 days

Lead time usage rate = 4 days at 2 cases/day = 8 cases

Safety level = 4 days at 2 cases/day = 8 cases

Order point = lead time + safety level

8 cases + 8 cases = 16 cases

Maximum level = usage rate + safety level

60 cases + 8 cases = 68 cases

When ordering at the order point, the quantity to order is the monthly usage rate. This is shown by the following calculation.

Order point	16 cases
Monthly usage rate	60 cases
Total cases available	76
Lead time usage rate	−8 cases
Maximum level	68 cases

So the maximum level is maintained.

Example 2. When placing an order before the order point is reached, such as when putting together an order for price quotations from suppliers, first determine the number of cases in storage, then subtract the order point from the amount in storage.

Amount in storage	25 cases
Order point	16 cases
Excess over order point	9 cases

The amount to order is the usage rate minus the number of cases in excess of the order point:

60 cases − 9 cases = 51 cases

The decision to order 51 cases can be proved.

Cases ordered	51
Amount available	25
Total	76
Lead time usage rate	−8
Maximum level	68

Again, the maximum inventory level is maintained.

Source: Ninemeier, Planning and Control, *p. 68.*

Figure 12.4 Perishable Product Quotation/Call Sheet

Item	Amount			Supplier		
	Needed	OnHand	Order	A & B Co.	Green Prod.	Local Supplier
1	2	3	4	5	6	7
Spinach	6 cs	2½ cs	4 cs	22⁰⁰/cs = 88.00	14⁸⁵/cs = 59.40	21⁷⁰/cs = 86.80
Ice. Lettuce	8 cs	1 cs	7 cs	17⁰⁰/cs = 119.00	16⁷⁵/cs = 117.25	18¹⁰/cs = 126.70
Carrots	3-20#	20#	2-20#	14⁷⁰/bag = 29.40	13⁹⁰/bag = 27.80	13⁸⁰/bag = 27.60
Cabbage	2 sacks	½ sack	2 sacks	18⁶⁰/sack = 37.20	18⁰⁰/sack = 36.00	18¹⁰/sack = 36.20
			Totals	861.40	799.25	842.15

Source: Ninemeier, Planning and Control, *p. 65.*

are required for the period covered by the order. Inventory count reveals that two and a half cases are available. Four cases, however, may need to be ordered if the supplier will not break cases. After the quantity for all perishable products is determined, three suppliers are called. Each is asked to quote a current price for the items needed. (Remember that each supplier has copies of the required purchase specifications so that each is quoting a price for the same quality of product.)

After all suppliers are contacted and prices are obtained, the purchaser has two choices. He/she can give the order to the supplier with the lowest total price on all products, or the order can be awarded on an item-by-item basis. That is, if one supplier has quoted the lowest price for several items, the orders for these and no other products are placed with that supplier. Orders for other products are given to the suppliers quoting the lowest price for those items. You should be aware, however, that suppliers often place minimum poundage and/or dollar restrictions on orders to be filled. Therefore, it may not be possible to award one item (such as 10 bags of radishes) to one supplier since it is unlikely that he/she will make the delivery.

As noted earlier, some products may be purchased for inventory. The minimum/maximum system of inventory management is useful to determine the quantity of these products purchased. Since some time and arithmetic are needed to calculate quantities to purchase under a minimum/maximum system, it is wise to consider the "80/20" rule (which states that, for the average operation, 80% of all purchase dollars are used to obtain 20% of the items purchased) and give first priority to developing an effective purchasing system for the relatively few high cost items.

Basically, the minimum/maximum order system works as follows:

- Minimum quantity. The manager must determine the minimum inventory levels for each item.

- Maximum quantity. Inventory levels above which items should not rise must be indicated.

- Usage rate. The quantity of products used during an order period must be assessed.

- Lead time. The quantity of products withdrawn from inventory between the time the order is placed and is delivered must also be calculated.

- Safety levels. The quantity of products that should remain in inventory at all times must be known.

- Order point. The quantity of products which should be in stock when an order is placed must be assessed.

Figure 12.3 illustrates how this system can be used to determine the quantity of items to be purchased according to varying inventory levels.

The Right Purchase Price

An objective of effective purchasing is to obtain desired products and services at the best price. Purchasing is based, in part, on how badly the buyer needs the products. If the product is on the menu, it must be available to the buying public. If products are being purchased for a "special," higher than desired prices might be avoided by a substitution for a lower priced item.

When price is viewed from the seller's perspective, there is a minimum limit to what the seller will accept. This is affected by prices charged by other suppliers of similar items, whether the buyer is price-conscious, the supplier's operating costs (overhead and profit requirements), and the extent to which the supplier controls the market. Prices may be established by supply and demand or by suppliers charging what the market will bear.

There are several procedures buyers can use to reduce prices while maintaining quality. These include:[3]

1. Negotiate with the seller. Bargaining over the price is a well-established practice in the hospitality industry.

2. Consider purchasing lower quality products. If the quality of products has not been researched and described in formal purchase specifications, this may be a very reasonable alternative.

3. Evaluate the need for the product. Some products that are purchased can be made "from scratch."

4. Discontinue some suppliers' services. The price you pay for a product includes more than the product cost. For example, costs of such services as delivering, extension of credit, technical assistance, etc., may be included in the price. If some or all of these services are not needed, prices might be lowered.

5. Combine orders. If fewer suppliers are used and each supplier gets a larger volume of the purchaser's orders, prices may be decreased through volume purchases.

6. Purchase in larger quantities. Volume purchases might result in lower per-unit prices.

7. Reevaluate the need for high cost items. If prices for certain garnishes increase because they are out of season, these items might be replaced with other, less expensive garnishes.

8. Pay cash when possible. The dealer experiencing cash flow problems may well offer a lower price for cash transactions.

9. Speculate about price trends. If you anticipate prices to decrease as products come into season, lower quantities should be purchased until the price stabilizes at a lower rate.

10. Change the purchase unit size. Product cost per unit may be less as larger purchase units are received. For example, one pound of flour may cost less when purchased in a 100-pound sack than when it is purchased in a 10-pound sack.

11. Be innovative when buying. Cooperative (pool) purchasing or competitive bidding procedures are ways to reduce prices.

12. Negotiate creative price agreements. Suppliers may agree to a price markup based on changing wholesale market prices.

13. Take advantage of promotional discounts.

14. Bypass the supplier. Purchase directly from a distributor, manufacturer, or grower.

The prices which you pay for products are affected by the method of payment. Bills should be paid when due. If they are paid late, the property will lose its negotiating ability as it attempts to receive lower prices. Conversely, if bills are paid too early, cash flow problems may result. If the supplier offers a discount for prompt payment, this option should be studied. If cash flow permits, there may be advantages to this payment plan.

Generally, payment terms should be negotiated after an agreement is reached on the price. Managers should work out payment problems with the supplier, since most suppliers will cooperate with the property that is honest about difficulties in paying bills when due.

Now that you understand the importance of the right price in the purchase decision, remember that price cannot be assessed without considering quality. Many items besides the product are purchased when an agreement is made between the supplier and the property. For example, many food service managers would pay a higher price knowing that a certain supplier will consistently deliver. Often, as lower prices are paid there is a gamble that the product may not be received or may not be of the proper quality. Always consider quality when establishing purchasing price.

Some managers believe that they should buy from the supplier that gives them the lowest price. Experienced managers realize, however, that other factors besides price should be considered when a supplier is selected. A "good" supplier from the perspective of the food service operation will (a) offer products at a fair price, (b) consistently provide the quality and quantity of desired products, (c) develop a relationship that will benefit the operation, and (d) work with the property as day-to-day business transactions occur.

Factors to consider when selecting a supplier include:[4]

1. Supplier's location. A close location shortens delivery time.

2. Supplier's facilities. A visit can help the manager determine sanitation levels, procedures for processing, and the desirability of conducting business with the supplier.

3. Financial stability. Financial soundness of potential suppliers should be investigated.

4. Technical ability of supplier's staff. Good salespersons do more than just take orders. They know their products and are able to help managers understand how best to use them.

5. Reasonable prices. The price, relative to quality, makes the offer by the supplier reasonable and fair.

6. Compatible attitudes. A working relationship between the manager and supplier is very necessary.

7. Honesty and fairness. The business practices of the supplier—as monitored through effective receiving procedures (discussed later)—can reveal these qualities.

8. Reciprocal purchasing. Food service managers may trade food products for prepared meals and beverages. Suppliers may, at times, wish to entertain customers.

Figure 12.5 Purchase Requisition

Needed By: _____ (Department)			Requisition Number: _____	
Date Needed: _____			Date: _____	

Item	Purchase Unit	Number of Unit	Specification Number

_____
(Signature of authorizing staff member)

Source: Ninemeier, Purchasing, Receiving and Storage, p. 301.

9. Local purchasing. Many managers desire to purchase from local sources when possible because they believe that this fosters good will and improves community relations.

Essentially, food service buyers want four things from suppliers: prompt delivery, adequate quality, reasonable prices, and service. Each potential supplier should be evaluated before an order is placed on a continuing basis to ensure that these concerns are addressed in the buyer/seller relationship.

Purchasing Documents

Since there are several parties involved in the purchasing process, effective communication channels must be established. This is best done by using such purchasing documents as:

• Purchase requisitions (see Figure 12.5). These forms can be

Figure 12.6 Purchase Order

Purchase Order Number: _____		Order Date: _____

(form reproduction)

Purchase Order Number: _____   Order Date: _____

Payment Terms: _____

To: _____   From/Ship to: _____
        (Supplier)   (Name of Food Service)

_____   _____

_____   _____
        (address)   (address)

                                  Delivery Date: _____

Please Ship:

Quantity Ordered	Description	✔	Units Shipped	Unit Cost	Total Cost

Total Cost _____

IMPORTANT: This Purchase Order expressly limits acceptance to the terms and conditions stated above, noted on the reverse side hereof, and any additional terms and conditions affixed hereto or otherwise referenced. Any additional terms and conditions proposed by seller are objected to and rejected.

_____
Authorized Signature

Source: Ninemeier, Purchasing, Receiving and Storage, *p. 307.*

used by storeroom personnel to alert purchasing staff of the need to order additional quantities of goods.

- Purchase orders (see Figure 12.6). These documents can be used by large food and beverage operations to solicit prices and make purchase commitments with suppliers.

- Purchase records (see Figure 12.7). These forms can be used by small food and beverage operators to record information about products, purchase unit size, and cost as they order products from supplier representatives.

Figure 12.7 Purchase Record

Date Ordered	Item Description	Unit	Price	No. of Units	Total Cost	Invoice No.	Comments
(supplier)							

Source: Ninemeier, Planning and Control, *p. 71.*

Copies of the purchase order (Figure 12.6) or purchase record (Figure 12.7) should be provided to the receiving department staff so they will know what products are to be delivered. These documents are an important part of the receiving process.

Make or Buy Decisions

There is an increased use of convenience food products today. The term "convenience foods" refers to food products which have some or all of the labor built into them that otherwise would have to be provided by the food and beverage operation. For example, sliced bread is a convenience food when compared with the alternative of purchasing flour, shortening, yeast, etc., and making the bread on-site.

The choice to make or buy relies on objective decision-making about whether and to what extent convenience food products should be used. Traditionally, there has been a negative impression about convenience foods—perhaps stemming from the frozen TV dinners which were introduced many years ago. But today, there are many high-quality convenience food products available that may be acceptable for many operations. Also, make or buy decisions are generally not "all or nothing." In other words, few properties use either all or no convenience foods. More frequently a property uses some convenience foods and produces some items on-site.

An important consideration in a make or buy analysis is that quality requirements be met. If an adequate quality product is not available, there is no sense in spending time and effort developing an objective cost analysis. On the other hand, if the quality of available convenience food products is acceptable, further study (make or buy analysis) may be advantageous.

There are several possible advantages to on-site production. If only small quantities of an item are needed, their production might be integrated with other ongoing work tasks. Quality standards might be better maintained if production stays in the control of the property. Items prepared on-site may be less expensive. In addition, there may be an assurance of continued supply because of on-site preparation which also may help the property better utilize existing equipment and labor. Employees frequently resist the use of convenience foods since they may perceive this as threatening their job security. House "specialty" items may need to be produced on-site for marketing reasons. If there is only one supplier of these convenience foods, price increases may be less "bargainable."

Each of the possible advantages to on-site production can be countered with advantages of using convenience food products. For example, less space, equipment, and capital are needed when convenience food products are used. Lack of skilled personnel will favor the use of these products. In addition, productivity may increase, and menu variety can be enhanced and maintained when convenience foods are used. Product waste can be decreased when portion control items are used. In fact, convenience foods may be less expensive than items prepared on-site when all costs are considered.

Food service operations can best be improved if officials maintain an open attitude toward the use of convenience foods. Deciding whether to use convenience foods depends on the specific product and food and beverage operation. An objective make or buy analysis is an important consideration.

Make or buy analysis includes the following steps:

- Define the problem. Personnel must know why convenience foods are being considered.

- Measure the quality. Quality requirements cannot be sacrificed when make or buy decisions are made.

- Assess the costs for all alternatives. Figure 12.8 illustrates how costs are considered and how a make or buy analysis is implemented.

Security Concerns During Purchase

In small properties where the owner/manager is responsible for purchasing, there is less concern about theft. As properties get larger and more people become involved in purchasing concerns, however, the chances of theft increase.

Figure 12.8 Example of Make/Buy Analysis

The food service operation is considering quality and cost differences between purchase of a commercially prepared Bloody Mary Mix and the preparation of a product on-site.

A group comprising the property's food and beverage directors, beverage manager, "head" bartender, and several cocktail waitresses sampled several prepared mixes and, almost unanimously, determined that one product is of extremely good, and, hence, acceptable quality. In fact, there will not be a need to add any other ingredients on-site to yield a product to meet the quality/taste preference requirements of the officials and staff members making the selection decision. The selected mix costs $21.00 per case of 12 quart bottles. There is a 5% reduction when the product is purchased in 5 case lots. It is very acceptable to purchase in this quantity and thus the per quart cost is $1.66 ($21.00 - 5% [$1.05] ÷ 12 bottles).

The facility has been making its own product. Identified costs are:

a) Product Costs. The current costs of ingredients used in the standard recipe (which yields two gallons) is $10.45. The product cost per quart is, therefore, $1.31 ($10.45 for 2 gallons ÷ 8 quarts).

b) Labor Costs. A time study suggests that the bartender (who prepares the mix) spends approximately 15 minutes in assembling the 2 gallons of mix. First an issue requisition must be completed, approved, and carried to the storage area. The ingredients (tomato juice, lemon juice, Worcestershire sauce, etc.) must be assembled (while the bartender waits). The ingredients are then carried back to the bar area and are combined according to the recipe. The various utensils and the work area must be cleaned after the product is prepared.

The bartender is paid $4.25 per hour with approximately 15% additional fringe benefits. The actual hourly labor cost is, therefore, $4.89 ($4.25 + 15%). The labor cost for 15 minutes to prepare the two gallons of mix is $1.22. Since 2 gallons of mix are prepared, the labor cost per quart is 15¢ ($1.22 ÷ 8 quarts). The total estimated product and labor cost to prepare one quart of Bloody Mary Mix on-site is

Product Cost	$1.31
Labor Cost	.15
Total Cost	$1.46

The final step in the make-buy analysis is to compare estimates of costs when the product is prepared on-site or in convenience (prepared) form.

Cost of on-site production	$1.46 per quart
Cost of purchased product	1.66 per quart
Estimated savings per quart with use of product prepared by the facility	$ .20 per quart

The study done above suggests that 20¢ per quart can be saved if the facility prepares its own product. While the unit (quart) savings may not seem significant, the savings of $.80 per gallon is equal to $1.60 daily (since 2 gallons are used). This is equal to a weekly savings of $9.60 ($1.60 per day x 6 days) or an annual savings of $499.20 ($9.60 per week x 52 weeks).

Source: Ninemeier, Purchasing, Receiving and Storage, *pp. 144-145.*

Theft can take place in several ways at the time of product purchase.[5]

1. Kickbacks. Kickbacks occur when the purchaser works in collusion with an employee from the supplier's company. Products are purchased at higher than usual prices with the difference in cost pocketed by the purchaser and supply company representative. There are many variations to this scenario. The

result is that food and beverage operations spend more money than necessary for purchasing products.

2. Fictitious companies. Fictitious companies can be used by dishonest purchasers to "sell" nonexistent products to food and beverage operations. Normally, checks are sent to a post office box address.

3. Processing theft. Processing thefts occur when suppliers request payment for an invoice more than once.

4. Credit memo problems. Credit memo problems occur when personnel in the receiving department sign delivery invoices for items not received. Often there is a promise that "we'll deliver it next time and not charge you."

5. Delivery invoice errors. Intentional delivery invoice errors, such as problems with arithmetic, short weights or counts, etc., must be guarded against.

6. Quality substitutions. Quality substitutions occur when a price is quoted for the proper quality item but a lower quality product is delivered. The food and beverage operation ends up paying a high price for a low-quality product.

Each of the above purchasing problems can be prevented, or their incidence reduced, by using effective payment and purchasing procedures.

Ethical Concerns in Purchasing

There must be sound and ethical relationships between the partners in the purchasing task: the food and beverage operation and the supplier. Food and beverage operations should establish and monitor policies that ensure that the purchasing staff meets ethical obligations imposed by management. Purchasing policies can be developed for such matters as acceptance of gifts, favoritism to suppliers, permission of personal purchases, or reciprocal purchases. Figure 12.9 offers some guidelines for professional purchasers.

To ensure ethical purchasing procedures, good relations with supplier representatives must be maintained. As noted throughout this section, the purchaser and suppliers should be partners, not adversaries. Figure 12.10 suggests ways that food service officials should relate to suppliers.

A Close Look at Product Receiving

You have learned in this chapter that the procedures used to purchase products and services have a dramatic impact on the marketability and economic goals of the property. Development of effective proce-

Figure 12.9 Sample Code of Ethics

As a professional purchaser I accept the following obligations as I go about my work:

1. To give primary concern to the best interests of my company.

2. To try to obtain maximum value for each dollar that I spend.

3. To be active in professional groups which help improve my profession.

4. To desire and accept as necessary advice from colleagues, top management, and suppliers.

5. To be fair and honest in all my dealings with management, fellow employees, and supplier representatives.

6. To practice effective, ethical procedures which enhance relations with suppliers.

7. To learn as much as possible about all products and services which are needed and purchased.

8. To honor all my obligations and to be sure that all commitments are consistent with good business practice.

Source: Ninemeier, Purchasing, Receiving and Storage, *p. 166.*

dures for receiving products is as important as development of purchasing plans.

In many operations, the receiving task is done by whomever is closest to the back door when products arrive. Yet, receiving requires a knowledgeable person who follows specific operating procedures to ensure that the property gets what it orders in terms of quality, quantity, and price.

Why are knowledgeable receiving personnel important? Staff members who receive products must (a) recognize whether incoming products meet the quality specified in purchase orders, (b) understand how to handle products that are received and know what to do when problems are uncovered, and (c) perform all required receiving tasks including the completion of receiving reports.

In small operations, the same person—generally a manager if not the owner—is responsible for purchasing and receiving the products. When this person is the owner, there is clearly little reason to worry about theft. As another person assumes both of these tasks, however, an absentee owner may have reason to be concerned since the possibility of theft increases.

As operations grow, purchasing and receiving duties are split into two departments. In some properties, purchasing is handled by a separate purchasing department while receiving and storage become the responsibilities of the accounting department. Responsibility for the product does not rest with the production department until the products are issued.

Figure 12.10 Principles of Good Supplier Relations

- Suppliers are told about applicable purchasing policies.

- Suppliers are informed about potential volumes of product purchases required by the food and beverage; estimates are reasonable.

- Suppliers are given suitable time to prepare responses to request for price quotations.

- Suppliers are informed about preferred visiting/calling times.

- Suppliers are thanked when advice is given.

- Suppliers' advice is solicited.

- Sales managers are informed when salespersons provide "extra" service and assistance.

- Salespersons are given a courteous reception; their time is not unduly wasted.

- Salespersons are promptly told if there is not time for a visit; if there will be a wait they are told how long it will be.

- Suppliers are interviewed in their proper turn.

- Appointments with salespersons are promptly kept whenever possible.

- Supplier ideas for changes in purchase specifications are considered.

- All suppliers are notified when there are changes in purchase specifications.

- All eligible suppliers are invited to quote prices.

- Suppliers who unsuccessfully quote prices are told why they did not obtain the order.

- Rush and emergency orders are kept to a minimum.

- Some tolerance is allowed when "extenuating circumstances" occasionally affect the supplier's ability to comply with all requirements of an order.

- Vendors are given suggestions about how their products can more closely meet specification requirements.

- Complete honesty is an integral part of all relationships with all suppliers.

- All procedures enhance the operation's reputation for fairness.

- Vendors are not "taken advantage of" even in times when it is "legally" possible to do so.

- It is recognized that vendors have a right to a fair profit.

- All agreements with all suppliers are honored.

Adapted from J. Bedford, "How to Improve Vendor Relations," Purchasing, February, 1953, p. 81.

Space and Equipment Concerns

In some operations, the receiving area is little more than a wide space in a hallway. But, sufficient space normally is required to permit proper review of all incoming products. When possible, the receiving area should be located near the delivery door in order to restrict access of the supplier to other areas.

Some space is necessary to house receiving equipment. An accurate scale is needed in every food service operation to confirm the weight of incoming products. A principle of receiving is that every incoming product should be weighed, counted, and measured, which requires an accurate receiving scale.

Other equipment needed in receiving areas includes mobile transport equipment to move products to storage, a desk and/or file cabinet to house receiving documents, a calculator to check order calculations, and small items such as a thermometer, clipboard, and marking and tagging supplies, etc.

The Receiving Process

There are six steps to follow when receiving products.

Step One. Inspect incoming products against a purchase record (used at small properties) or a purchase order (used at large properties). Copies of the purchase record and purchase order are shown in Figures 12.6 and 12.7. It is important for the employee who receives the goods to confirm that the property does not (a) accept items it did not order, (b) take partial orders, and (c) accept items of unacceptable quality.

Step Two. Inspect incoming products against the purchase specifications. A primary responsibility of the receiving clerk is to confirm that the quality of the incoming products meets minimum standards established by purchase specifications.

While this step is very critical, it is frequently overlooked. How does the receiving clerk know if "fresh" fish actually is fresh or if it has been frozen and thawed before delivery? What if "frozen" chicken is thawed on the surface or meat patties that are delivered weigh four ounces instead of five ounces? How do we know if "choice" meat is the proper grade? The only way to know is to learn by seeing the proper quality product and remembering what to look for as products are received. Of course, this is easy to say, but it illustrates that a property which purchases several hundred products needs a knowledgeable and trained staff.

Step Three. Inspect incoming products against the delivery invoice (see Figure 12.11). The supplier's delivery invoice accompanies the products being delivered. The supplier's bill to the operation will be based on the invoice. If the delivery invoice states that 75 pounds of ground beef were delivered, this should be confirmed by weighing the meat to be sure that 75 pounds were, in fact, received. In some operations, the price per unit and the arithmetic extensions are to be verified by the receiving staff. In other properties, these tasks are assumed by management, accounting, and/or purchasing department employees. Sometimes, a check of products against the delivery invoice will indicate a problem. If the receiving

Figure 12.11 Delivery Invoice

Acme Produce Company
Phone (000) 000-0000

1101 Hentschel

New York, New York 10111

Sold to:

Date: _____

Sold By:

C.O.D.
Cash

(circle)
Charge

Driver/Route:

Lot	Amt.	Unit	Item	Price/ Unit	Total Amount

Changes must be made day goods are received. All amounts due Monday after purchase date.

Inv. #: _____   Received: _____

clerk notices that products are, for example, short weight or short count, a credit memo should be completed to adjust the amount of the delivery invoice. Figure 12.12 is a sample credit memo. This document should be completed by the receiving clerk and signed by the delivery representative. The copy belonging to the food and beverage operation should be attached to the delivery invoice. Special precaution should be taken during payment processing to ensure that the adjusted—not original—amount on the delivery invoice is paid.

Step Four. Accept the products. After steps one through three have been completed, the receiving clerk should accept the product for the operation by signing the delivery invoice. At this point the responsibility for products rests with the property, not with the supplier.

Figure 12.12 Credit Memo

(prepare in duplicate)	Number: _____

From: _____ To: _____
(supplier)

_____ _____

_____ _____

_____

Credit should be given on the following:

Invoice Number: _____ Invoice Date: _____

Product	Unit	Number	Price/Unit	Total Price

Reason: Total: _____

_____ _____
(delivery person) (authorizing signature)

Source: Ninemeier, Planning and Control, p. 75.

Step Five. Move products to storage for quality and security reasons. Normally, it is a very poor practice for the supplier's delivery personnel to place items in storage. A separate receiving area that is close to the receiving door should be used instead. After the delivery person leaves, the receiving clerk or other employee of the property can quickly move items to secure storage areas.

Step Six. Complete the receiving clerk's daily report (see Figure 12.13). Let's see how this report is used.

First of all, information taken from the delivery invoice is used to complete the report. Note, for example (line one) that Ajax Meat Company delivered six ten-pound units of ground beef. The price for each ten-pound bag was $28.50, making a total cost of $171. Note that the total cost of the ground beef ($171) is listed in column 9 (stores). While a detailed discussion about calculation of daily food costs is beyond the scope of this text, you should know that "stores" are items that are received and entered into storage. Food costs for these items are incurred when items are issued. By contrast, "directs" (see column 8 in Figure 12.13) are items—mainly perishable products—that are received and charged to food costs on the day they are received. These two components, stores and directs, represent the elements in calculating daily food costs.

Likewise, the receiving clerk's daily report allows the employee in receiving to separate incoming beverages into their type (liquor, beer,

Figure 12.13 Receiving Clerk's Daily Report

Receiving Clerk's Daily Report

Date: 8/1/00   Page 1 of 2

Supplier	Invoice No.	Item	Unit	No. of Units	Unit Price	Total Cost	Food Directs	Food Stores	Beverages Liquor	Beverages Beer	Beverages Wine	Beverages Soda	Transfer to Storage
1	2	3	4	5	6	7	8	9	10	11	12	13	14
AJAX	10111	Gr.Beef	10#	6	28.50	171.00		171.00					Bill
ABC LIQUOR	6281	B.Scotch	cs(750)	2	71.80	143.60			143.60				Bill
		H.Chablis	gal	3	8.50	25.50					25.50		Bill
B/E Produce	70666	Lettuce	cs	2	21.00	42.00	42.00						
						Totals	351.00	475.00	683.50	—	102.00		

Source: Ninemeier, Planning and Control, p. 74.

wine, soda), which is useful in calculating the value of purchases (costs of goods sold) for the income statement. At the end of the day, the four types of receiving documents which have been generated (purchase order, delivery invoice, credit memo, and receiving clerk's daily report) should be collected and forwarded to the person responsible for processing payment. In many operations, these documents are routed to the food service manager and then to the purchasing department. They eventually will reach the accounting office where they are prepared for payment. These steps taken at the time of payment can help ensure that invoices are not submitted twice for payment. They also serve as a control device to monitor the type, quantity, and price of items that are received.

Other Receiving Tasks

In addition to the series of steps just described, receiving activities include:

1. Marking and tagging. The process of marking and tagging items helps assure proper stock rotation and aids in the inventory evaluation process. If, at the time of delivery, the date and

price are written directly onto the shipping container or other packaging units before being placed in storage, it will be easier to withdraw the oldest products from inventory. When requisitions must be completed, the purchase price of products taken from inventory can be assessed easily. When the value of the entire inventory must be calculated, the cost of items as noted on storage containers will make this task easier.

2. Refusal procedures. Effective receiving procedures will indicate reasons for refusing to accept incoming products. Products may be refused, for example, because they were not ordered or were not delivered on time. Or, their quality could be inadequate or their price incorrect. While specific procedures for product refusal vary by property, common practices do exist. For example, the receiving clerk may be aware of a potential problem and will contact the buyer, chef, or other official for a second opinion. If only a partial order is delivered or products are on back order, a management official in the property may need to be contacted so that necessary decisions can be made.

In any event, credit memos should be completed to ensure that the signed invoice accurately reflects the exact quantity and price of products for which payment is requested.

NOTES

1. The goal statements noted here are adapted from Jack D. Ninemeier, *Purchasing, Receiving and Storage: A Systems Manual for Restaurants, Hotels and Clubs* (Boston, Mass.: CBI, 1983), pp. 6-8.

2. Ninemeier, *Purchasing, Receiving and Storage*, pp. 69-70.

3. Ninemeier, *Purchasing, Receiving and Storage*, pp. 84-86.

4. Ninemeier, *Purchasing, Receiving and Storage*, pp. 102-105.

5. Ninemeier, *Food and Beverage Security: A Systems Manual for Restaurants, Hotels and Clubs* (Boston, Mass.: CBI, 1982), pp. 91-92.

13

Storing and Issuing: Getting Ready for Production

Management Challenges

As a result of studying this chapter you will:

1. be able to practice basic security procedures at the time of food product storage.

2. know that food quality deteriorates if products are kept too long or under improper storage conditions.

3. understand the relationship between inventory and accounting.

4. know how to maintain physical and perpetual inventory systems.

5. be able to describe three basic procedures for assigning value to products in storage.

6. know six ways to reduce inventory costs.

7. be able to use basic product issuing procedures.

8. be able to use basic preproduction procedures.

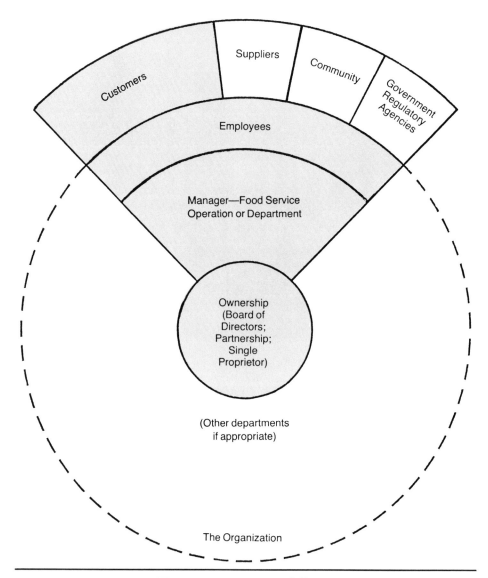

Customers

Suppliers

Community

Government Regulatory Agencies

Employees

Manager—Food Service Operation or Department

Ownership
(Board of
Directors;
Partnership;
Single
Proprietor)

(Other departments
if appropriate)

The Organization

Focus on the
Food Service Publics

Chapter 13 focuses on storing and issuing procedures. Storing and issuing concerns relate, in part, to management control and to the relationship between you and your employees. Since storing and issuing procedures affect costs—and hence the profitability of the food service operation—your relationship with the owner is also involved. Excessive costs usually are passed on to the customer, so there is even a spin-off relationship between you, your employees, and the customers. A storeroom is much more than just a place to hold products after delivery, and issuing is more than just taking products from the storeroom to the kitchen. This chapter will discuss professional procedures that you can incorporate into your operation's storing and issuing activities.

After food items are purchased and received, they must be stored. Even perishable products which are purchased for almost immediate use should be placed in proper storage areas; most perishable products require refrigeration. Though "stores" (items which are less perishable) can remain in inventory for longer periods of time, they too must be stored properly.

You should carefully develop and implement policies relating to the storage of products after receipt. In far too many operations, storage control means little more than putting items in storage areas and having an "open-door policy" so that it is convenient for employees to get products needed for production at any time. As you will learn, this is not a good strategy. The concern for quality and cost effectiveness which begins with purchasing and continues through receiving must now extend to storing activities.

As you develop inventory and storage policies, three primary areas must be reviewed: (1) security aspects of storage, (2) quality concerns in storage, and (3) recordkeeping procedures. Each of these three topics will now be discussed.

Security Aspects of Storage

Consider the storeroom to be a bank vault and products kept on storage area shelves to be money. In many operations, there are thousands of dollars' worth of products that are kept in storage areas. Ask yourself, "If I had a roomful of money, how would I safeguard it?" The answer that you develop should give you an idea about how food products in storage areas should be controlled.

Controls   Some security procedures which you should incorporate into storage controls include:[1]

Limited Access. Allow only authorized personnel to enter storage areas. This policy is best met by keeping storage areas locked except when products are being issued. A management staff member with access to keys should retrieve items in locked storage which are needed during the shift.

Lockable Storage Areas. It should be possible to lock the freezer, dry storage, and liquor storage areas. Cages, compartments, or sections of walk-in refrigerators should also be available for lockable storage.

Precious Storage. Keep very expensive items locked in special cabinets or compartments within storage areas (this is referred to as "precious" storage).

Effective Inventory Control Procedures. Control expensive and "theft-prone" items by using a perpetual inventory system.

Central Inventory Control. At the end of the shift, items in work station storage areas should be put back in central inventory control. For example, issue portion-cut meat items to work station refrigerators based upon estimated need. At the end of the shift, return the remaining steaks to central storage areas and adjust perpetual inventory records.

Design and Security. Design the storage areas with security in mind. For example, walls should extend to the ceiling and doors should be properly constructed and lockable. Make sure it is impossible to enter the storeroom through the ceiling (when removable ceiling tiles are suspended between rafters, people can enter the storeroom from adjacent locker areas). There should be no windows.

Lighting and Monitoring. Adequate lighting is necessary in storage areas. In addition, many operations use closed-circuit television systems to monitor storage areas.

In many instances, common sense will help you identify potential problems and can provide practical, inexpensive ways to resolve them.

Quality Concerns in Storage

Naturally, your food service operation requires products of suitable quality. The effort you make to develop and use purchase specifications and to check the incoming products against purchase specifications during receiving will likely be wasted if you do not safeguard the quality of products by using proper storage procedures.

The term "quality" means more than just ensuring that food will not spoil. Spoiled items, of course, must be discarded (resulting in food cost increases). However, products which deteriorate even slightly in quality can cause problems for your food service operation. For example, what happens when produce is just a little too ripe or when ground beef has taken on a bit of an odor? The use of such products might help control food costs but only at the expense of customer dissatisfaction—an expense no food and beverage operator can afford. These types of problems can be minimized with just a little common sense and by applying basic storage procedures.

Storage Procedures   Basic procedures to help maintain the proper quality of food products in storage include the following:

Purchase Proper Quantities. Items must be purchased in the proper quantities. A major problem with the purchase of larger-than-necessary quantities is that products often remain in storage areas for long periods of time. This additional time is frequently accompanied by a deterioration in quality.

Rotate Food Stocks. Items which have been in storage the longest should be used first. This concept is referred to as first-in, first-out (FIFO). It is important to minimize the time that products remain in storage. The FIFO rule is easier to follow when incoming products are placed in back of or underneath the products already in storage. Marking and tagging receiving dates on products as they are placed in storage is also useful. It is then easy to see which products have been in storage for the longest time.

Store Foods at the Proper Temperatures. Use accurate thermometers in storage areas to ensure that: (1) refrigerated storage temperatures are kept between 32°F and 45°F, (2) dry storage areas are kept between 50°F and 70°F, and (3) frozen items are kept in freezers with temperatures of 0°F or below.

Clean Storage Areas. Foods must be kept in clean storage areas. Routine, scheduled cleaning of all storage areas is necessary.

Ensure Proper Ventilation and Air Circulation. Keep items off the floor and away from walls to permit air circulation. Normally, items should be stored in their original packing containers. Items which absorb odors (such as flour) should be kept away from items which give off odors (such as onions). Store food in air-tight containers or in covered containers.

The above examples are among many that were noted in Chapter 9. The point being made is that proper handling of products during storage does affect quality levels.

Recordkeeping Procedures

The third general concern about storage of products relates to recordkeeping procedures. The value of products in inventory is used to calculate the cost of goods sold when income statements are developed (see Chapter 16). When you want to determine daily food costs, the value of products withdrawn from storage each day must be assessed. This cannot be done unless you keep records of these items.

In addition to helping with food and beverage costing procedures, there are other reasons recordkeeping procedures should be implemented. These include the need to control theft. It is difficult to identify a theft problem unless you can see differences between what should be and what actually is in storage. Recordkeeping techniques also help determine when additional quantities of products should be purchased.

Unfortunately, in many operations the inventory control system involves merely placing items in storage, taking them out when needed, and ordering more when necessary. However, planned, systematic procedures are necessary for proper control of items in storage. This control requires effective recordkeeping.

There are two basic systems for determining quantities of products in inventory: physical inventory and perpetual inventory.

Physical Inventory System

When a physical inventory system is used, the actual amount of each product in inventory is counted periodically (usually monthly) to provide information necessary to calculate food and beverage costs. This system is very simple to use and it does not take much time.

However, many food and beverage operations do not bother to count inventory. Instead, management staff assumes that since the amount of products purchased during each month is relatively stable, the amount of products in inventory stays the same throughout the month. When this assumption is made, the operation must use a cash accounting system (see Chapter 16). The food or beverage costs for the month equal the value of purchases. This method is, at best, inaccurate because values of inventory do not stay the same on a month-to-month basis. Without close checking of inventory, it is impossible to determine whether theft and pilferage are occurring.

To use a physical inventory system, you must first determine what products need to be counted in inventory. Is inventory considered to be just the products in the central storeroom and walk-in refrigerator? What about items that are in process, in work station storage areas, or in broken case rooms? (A broken case room is a room sometimes used to store opened and partially used cases or boxes of goods.)

Second, you have to decide what items are to be counted. Frequently, managers assume that the value of low-cost items (such as spices and seasonings) and the amount of products in opened containers (such as flour in mobile bins or the remaining salad oil in a five-gallon container) "average out." That is, the value of these types of items remains approximately the same during the month. When this assumption is made, the "constant value" of low-cost items and items in opened containers that are not counted can be added to the total cost of inventory items that are counted in order to assess the inventory value.

In Figure 13.1 (a format for determining the amount and value of food products in inventory), the cost of inventory items is assessed by multiplying the number of purchase units of each product by their cost.

You can more easily complete the physical inventory form by listing the products to be counted in the order in which they are stored. For example, in Figure 13.1, applesauce might be located next to green beans. This procedure reduces or eliminates the time spent in having to locate the item being counted on the inventory form.

Figure 13.2 is an example of a physical inventory form for beverage products. Notice that it shows the amount of beverages both in central storage areas and in opened and unopened bottles behind the bar. Unlike inventories for food, which may exclude the value of products in work station areas, many food and beverage operations do consider the value of unopened bottles of liquor in bar areas. The physical inventory form for beverages provides an easy way to do this.

Perpetual Inventory System

A perpetual inventory system allows you to keep track of items in storage on a continuing basis. It is possible to keep a running balance of the amount of products in inventory when a perpetual inventory system is used. The concept is identical to the way a checkbook record is main-

Figure 13.1 Physical Inventory Form

Type of Product: _____				Month: _____		Month: _____	
Product	Unit	Amount in Storage	Purchase Price	Total Price	Amount in Storage	Purchase Price	Total Price
1	2	3	4	5	6	7	8
Applesauce	6 #10	4⅓	15.85	68.63			
Green Beans	6 #10	3⅚	18.95	72.58			
Flour	25# bag	3	4.85	14.55			
Rice	50# bag	1	12.50	12.50			
			Total	486.55			

Source: Jack D. Ninemeier, Purchasing, Receiving and Storage: A Systems Manual for Restaurants, Hotels, and Clubs *(Boston: CBI, 1983), p. 282.*

Figure 13.2 Beverage Inventory Card

Beverage Item	Storage Unit	Quantity Available		In Storage	Total	Cost Per Storage Unit	Total Cost
		Bottles Behind-Bar					
		Open	Unopened				
1	2	3	4	5	6	7	8
Bar Scotch	750 ML	3/4	3	12	15¾	5.72	90.09
Bar Gin	750 ML	½	3	24	27½	4.81	132.28

Source: Ninemeier, Planning and Control for Food and Beverage Operations *(East Lansing, Mich.: Educational Institute of the American Hotel & Motel Association, 1982), p. 87.*

Figure 13.3 Perpetual Inventory Form

Date	In Carried Forward	Out	Balance _15_	Date	In Carried Forward	Out	Balance ___
1	2	3	4	1	2	3	4
5/16		3	12				
5/17		3	9				
5/18	6		15				
5/19		2	13				

Product Name: _Applesauce_   Purchase Unit Size: _Case (6#10)_

Source: Ninemeier, Purchasing, Receiving and Storage, *p. 285.*

tained. As money (food) enters the checking account (storeroom), the running balance increases. As checks are written (food is withdrawn), the running balance decreases. Therefore, at any time, you know what amount of money (food) is in the checkbook (storeroom).

Even large food and beverage operations may not be able to justify keeping a perpetual inventory for small-use and inexpensive items. However, frequently used expensive items (such as liquor and meats) should be kept under closer control in both large and small food and beverage operations.

Figure 13.3 shows how you can keep a running balance of items under the perpetual inventory system. As items are brought into storage, the quantity of goods on hand increases (storage information can be obtained from the receiving clerk's daily report). As items are issued from storage, the running balance decreases. Note that only one item can be recorded on each perpetual inventory form. It is also possible to use 5" x 7" index cards, separate pages in notebooks, or other procedures to record the information.

When a perpetual inventory system is used, you will have one item of information that is not available when only a physical inventory is taken. The perpetual inventory system will indicate the quantity of each product which *should* be available. This amount can then be confirmed by a physical count. Any discrepancy between what should be in inventory and what is actually in inventory helps to determine whether theft, pilferage, poor recordkeeping, or another problem exists.

By contrast, a physical inventory system indicates only what *is* available. How can you know what should be available? It is for this reason that even small food and beverage operations often use a perpetual inventory system for expensive items.

For control purposes, the person who takes a physical inventory count to verify the accuracy of perpetual inventory information should not be the same person who is responsible for initially recording inventory information. Often, for example, someone from management or the accounting department along with the chef (for food) and the head bartender (for beverages) may actually take the physical inventory.

As with the physical inventory system, perpetual inventory forms should be arranged in the same sequence as the items kept in inventory. One employee can then count the number of items available and the second employee can compare the quantity counted with the quantity noted on the perpetual inventory form. Note that the physical inventory forms (Figures 13.1 and 13.2) can be used to take the physical count to confirm the accuracy of perpetual inventory records.

Bin Card System

Before leaving the topic of inventory control, you should be familiar with the use of bin cards (see Figure 13.4) which are sometimes used to provide extra control over expensive items. When this system is used, small cards are actually attached to the shelves where special control items are stored. As items are moved into or out of storage, the balance shown on the bin card is adjusted. When this plan is used, management staff who are in the storeroom for other purposes can quickly and randomly verify the accuracy of items in storage. This is also a double-check on a perpetual inventory system. This system is rather cumbersome for small food and beverage operations, but may be used by some large properties or those with special inventory control problems.

Value of Items in Storage

As you have learned, it is necessary to assign values to products in inventory in order to accurately complete financial statements. For example, what do you do when there are cases of applesauce in storage which cost one price because they were purchased three weeks ago, and there are other cases of applesauce purchased at different times and different prices?

Methods of assigning value to products in inventory include:[2]

1. **First-in, first-out (FIFO).** The value of products in inventory is represented by the price paid for the products in inventory which have been purchased most recently (since the first products placed in storage are used first). For example, if a case of applesauce in storage was purchased three weeks ago and costs $22.50, but a case of applesauce in a more recent delivery is valued at $23.75, then cases of applesauce in inventory are priced at the rate of $23.75.

Figure 13.4 Bin Card

Name of Item: *Bar Bourbon*				Minimum Number *12*			
				Maximum Number *24*			
Forward: *16 Bottles*				Forward:			
Date	In	Out	Balance	Date	In	Out	Balance
8/14		3	13				
8/15		3	10				
8/18	12	2	20				
8/19		4	16				

Ninemeier, Purchasing, Receiving, and Storage, *p. 289.*

2. **Last-in, first-out (LIFO).** The value of products is represented by the price paid for the product which has been in inventory the longest. In the example above, a case of applesauce would be valued at $22.50.

3. **Weighted average.** This method considers the actual cost of products in storage. If there are three cases of applesauce at $22.50, and five cases of applesauce at $23.75, the value of a case of applesauce is $23.28 (three cases at $22.50 + five cases at $23.75 ÷ eight cases = $23.28).

Because the method used to assign inventory values affects financial statements, you should consult an accountant about tax implications and other inventory-related concerns.

Reducing Inventory Costs

Cash flow problems can occur when inventory levels are kept too high. The following procedures are among those you can use to reduce inventory costs:

● If volumes of products kept in storage are too large, reduce the quantities of products that are purchased.

- Reduce requirements for lead time and stock-out safety levels. For example, if you establish shortened delivery times and decrease minimum stock requirements, the quantity of products carried in inventory can be reduced.

- Obtain more frequent deliveries and then purchase smaller quantities of necessary items. This can sometimes be done by negotiating with suppliers.

- Be sure that required levels of inventory are correct. In other words, periodically examine the ways that minimum levels of inventory are established.

- Standardize the types of products that you carry. For example, perhaps you only need two or three—rather than four or five—different sizes of shrimp. The inventory could be reduced accordingly.

- Refuse to accept early deliveries. You will have to pay for these products sooner than you would have to if they were delivered as originally scheduled.

Product Issuing Procedures

You have now learned about some procedures that you can use for purchasing, receiving, and storing food and beverage products. The next step in the product control cycle is that of issuing required products from storage to production areas.[3] In many operations, the task is no more complicated than walking back to storage areas and getting what you want. However, as noted in our discussion about storage concerns, only authorized personnel should have access to storage areas; at the very least, expensive items should be kept under lock and within an inventory recordkeeping system. There are several objectives to consider when you design effective issuing procedures:

- Limit access to storage areas to authorized personnel only.

- Match items removed from storage with actual production needs.

- Assess quantities and cost of products removed for recordkeeping purposes.

Large food and beverage operations may have one or more full-time storeroom employees. These employees may also receive goods. When this approach is used, items in storage are accessible throughout the entire workshift. Small properties usually do not have full-time employees who are responsible for this work.

Whenever possible, you should use a food issue requisition form (see Figure 13.5) to identify the type and amount of food products re-

Figure 13.5 Food Issue Requisition Sheet

					Employee Initials	
					Approved	Withdrawn
Item	Purchase Unit	No. of Units	Unit Price	Total Cost	By	By
1	2	3	4	5	6	7
Tomato Paste	cs-6#10	2½	28.50	71.25	JC	Ken
Green Beans	cs-6#10	1½	22.75	34.13	JC	Ken

Storage Type (check one):
Refrigerated _____
Frozen _____
Dry _____✔_____

Date: _____
Work Unit: _____

Source: Ninemeier, Planning and Control, *p. 90.*

moved from storage areas. Each item needed for production is entered onto the requisition form (column 1). The size of purchase unit (column 2) and number of purchase units needed (column 3) are also listed. Approval from an authorized official such as the chef or the assistant manager is required (column 6) before items are removed. Depending upon the system, the unit price (column 4) and the total cost (column 5) can be completed by either the storeroom clerk or someone in the accounting office. Note that the unit price information (column 4) can be easily obtained if, at the time of receiving, prices are marked on the cases of items as they enter storage areas. The total cost (column 5) of food issues for the day is an integral part of a daily food cost calculation.[4] When items are issued, they should be promptly taken to the appropriate production area(s).

The food issue requisition form shown distinguishes between products from refrigerated, frozen, and dry storage areas. Smaller operations, of course, may not need this information. Note that total cost informa-

tion (column 5) does not need to be completed before products are issued. Issue requisition forms can be retained throughout the day and
these calculations can be made as time permits.

When all daily issues are finished, you, the storeroom clerk, or other
staff may use the forms to update perpetual inventory records (see Figure 13.3). At the end of the day, the food issue requisition forms can be
forwarded to you or to the secretary/bookkeeper for review and calculation of daily food cost information. If total cost (column 5) has not been
completed, it can be finished at this time. If it has been calculated by storage employees, other personnel should still verify the calculations to ensure accuracy of daily food cost records.

Beverage   Basic procedures for issuing food can also be used for issuing bever-
Issuing   ages. There are some additional concerns since, by their very nature,
beverages are very susceptible to employee theft. Special precautions
which you can incorporate into beverage issuing can help reduce the
possibility or frequency of theft.

First of all, beverages should only be issued in quantities which are
necessary to re-establish bar par inventory levels. A bar par is a pre-es-
tablished number of bottles of each type of liquor and wine (some operations may also set bottle beer pars) which are always kept in behind-the-
bar storage areas. To establish a par, note the number of bottles of each
type used on a busy shift. For example, if an average busy bar shift uses
four bottles of house scotch, the scotch bar par may be set at five bottles:
four full bottles and one open bottle in speedrail or back-bar display
areas.

The number of empty bottles at the beginning or end of the shift
(preferably the end) determines the number of full bottles needed to replenish the bar par. If the bar par requires five bottles of house scotch
and two bottles are empty, then two bottles should be issued to maintain
the five-bottle bar par. An important rule is that empty bottles must be
presented before full bottles are issued. A beverage issuing process may
typically include the following steps:

1.   At the end of each shift, the bartender places bottles emptied
     during the shift on top of the bar.

2.   The bartender completes a beverage issue requisition form (see
     Figure 13.6). The name of each type of empty liquor or wine
     bottle (column 1), the number of empty bottles (column 2), and
     the size of the bottle (column 3) are recorded. Depending upon
     the specific operation, the bartender may also record the unit
     cost (column 4). Information for this column is obtained from
     costs marked on the bottle (see below).

3.   The beverage manager checks the number and type of empty
     bottles on the bar against the information on the beverage
     issue requisition form. If there are no problems, he/she signs
     or initials the "ok to issue" section on the form.

Figure 13.6 Beverage Issue Requisition Sheet

Shift: _AM (Lunch)_   Date: _8/1/00_

Bar: _Main_   Bartender: _John Smith_

Liquor	Number of Bottles		Unit Cost	Total Cost
---	Number	Size		
1	2	3	4	5
B. Scotch	3	750 ML	5.72	17.16
B. Gin	2	750 ML	4.81	9.62

Total Bottles: _12_   Total Cost: _82.15_

OK to issue: _gn_

Issued by: _GC_

Received by: _JS_

Check one:
- ☐ low price
- ☑ reg. price
- ☐ high price

$82.15 ÷ $410.75 = 20%
(cost)   (sales)   (beverage percent)

Source: Ninemeier, Planning and Control, *p. 92.*

4. You or the bartender then take the empty bottles and the beverage issue requisition form to the beverage storage area where the empty bottles are replaced with full bottles on a bottle-for-bottle basis.

5. Empty bottles are broken or otherwise disposed of according to local or state laws.

6. Total cost calculations (column 5) are then made by the storeroom clerk, assistant manager, bookkeeping staff, or other personnel. When possible, a double-check on these calculations is helpful.

7. Information from total cost calculations can be used to determine beverage cost percentages (see the bottom of Figure 13.6). This information can be used to determine an actual daily beverage cost percent.[5]

The concept of bottle marking was noted above. This refers to placing the bottle price and an identifying mark on the bottle before it is issued. Note that the price can easily be placed on the bottle when products are received and entered into storage. The mark (perhaps an adhesive-backed label or a special hard-to-remove ink stamp) is used to identify the bottle as house property. This helps ensure that all bottles behind the bar do indeed belong to your operation. There is less likelihood that the bartender can bring in bottles to circumvent your operation's income control system.

Since liquor is a highly theft-prone item, it is important that all liquor behind the bar be kept locked when a bartender is not present. Central storage areas are generally more secure than behind-bar areas so it is important that the bar par levels be kept as small as possible without frequent runouts that require bartenders to leave bars during busy shifts. (Small bar pars are also important because normally there is limited behind-bar storage space for liquor or any other supplies.)

A Practical Approach to Storing and Issuing Procedures

You can imagine that each of the storing and issuing procedures discussed above requires some time. If it takes a *lot* of time, however, it loses some practicality. Is there any compromise between the all-too-common practice of leaving storage areas open and allowing people to get items on an as-needed basis and the systems such as those discussed in this chapter which tighten control? The answer is yes. You can use procedures which recognize that some control may be necessary for the most expensive items while reduced control may be practical for less expensive items. This concept recognizes that perhaps 20% of all items purchased cost approximately 80% of all purchase dollars. Let's see how you can maintain control over the expensive items and, at the same time, be practical while doing it.

Whenever possible, liquor should be stored by itself and not with food or other products/supplies. With this procedure, there is no reason to keep liquor storage areas unlocked. Management can be available when needed to issue beverage products so there is no need for access to this area at other times. If separate liquor storage is not practical for your operation, perhaps the "precious" storage concept mentioned earlier can be used. With this plan, liquor and other expensive items are locked in cabinets, shelving units, or even closets which are constructed in storage areas. Personnel can then have access to less expensive items on an as-needed basis, but a key—and therefore a manager—is needed to gain access to the liquor.

The same procedure can be applied to the storage of expensive refrigerated items. It is usually not practical to lock walk-in or reach-in refrigerators since there is often a need to enter these areas; however, this may be possible when there is ample refrigerated space in work station areas. Again, expensive items needing refrigerated storage, such as fresh meats, seafood, wines being chilled, etc., can be locked in special units purchased or constructed for use in refrigerated walk-ins. Alternatively, one or two compartments in a reach-in refrigerator could be used to store these items. They, of course, would also be kept locked.

There is less need for production personnel to consistently enter freezer spaces. Perhaps these can be kept locked at all times. If this is not practical, it may be wise to purchase or construct lockable storage areas in a walk-in freezer or to use one or more compartments in a reach-in freezer unit.

If the preceding procedures are used to control expensive items during storage, how you simplify the issuing process? One procedure is to try to obtain all the products needed for production at one time. Not only does this help control, it also increases employee productivity (time is lost when employees must constantly leave production areas to retrieve items from storage which could be picked up during one trip). When emergencies occur during production hours which require removal of items from storage, this may suggest that employees are not thinking ahead. Perhaps a management staff member can be present during the early morning and prior to lunch and dinner preparation periods to supervise the withdrawal of items from storage areas and to unlock rooms or equipment which store expensive items. Alternatively, the chef or other official could have a key for this purpose.

Not all of the procedures suggested for storing and issuing beverage products are useful in small food and beverage operations. Normally, though, even small operations will benefit from (a) keeping beverage products under locked storage, (b) requiring that perpetual inventory systems be used with expensive items, and (c) ensuring that products are issued only under supervised conditions. Unfortunately, it is true that product and income losses in beverage areas can be expensive. The wise food and beverage manager recognizes this and counters it with basic control procedures such as those noted throughout this chapter.

Preproduction Procedures

Production personnel do not begin production tasks without some planning efforts. You have already learned that the menu dictates many of the production needs. Therefore, when you plan a menu, you begin the task of planning for production. During the time of preproduction planning—and at all other times as well—it is important to remember the quality concerns which must be built into products as they are prepared.

Standard recipes indicating ingredients needed for production of menu items, purchase specifications noting minimum quality requirements for ingredients needed by standard recipes, and items such as scales, scoops, and ladles are among the tools needed to incorporate required quality standards into production activities. Standards cannot be attained unless they are known by and made the goals of staff members trained in the proper procedures. Management staff, as part of their routine supervisory activities, must constantly ensure that required standards are being met.

It is necessary for you to develop procedures which must be undertaken before production actually begins. Only then can you be certain that your operation is equal to production demands. In some operations, especially smaller ones, preproduction planning may be done by the manager. In larger operations, preproduction planning is a formal task undertaken at weekly production meetings attended by various personnel in order to coordinate production needs.

Advantages to preproduction planning include the following:

- Assurance that the required food and beverage products, personnel, and equipment will be available in necessary quantities when they are needed.

- A greater likelihood that resources such as products, labor, and equipment are not over- or under-utilized because coordinating activities are undertaken between different departments.

- A reduction of potential problems with economic and marketing implications. For example, planning can reduce costs to required minimums and, at the same time, help ensure that customers are satisfied with the products and services they receive.

While preproduction planning sessions need to be tailored to meet the needs of your specific operation, there are several common denominators. For example, you should schedule meetings on a regular basis (at least once weekly). Likewise, use sales history records to guide estimates for production needs during the week. Figure 13.7 indicates the type of information which can help you make preproduction decisions. Note that the weather, total meals served, and notations about any special activities are listed for each day in the week. If you keep this type of information over time for regular dining rooms (special banquets and catered events should not normally be included on this form), it can help you estimate production needs for the upcoming week.

Large food service operations may take information generated from sales history records and expand it into a master food production planning worksheet (see Figure 13.8). This worksheet can be a useful tool to tell production personnel the exact number of portions needed each day

Figure 13.7 Sales History Record

Date	1/23	1/24	1/25	1/26	1/27	1/28	1/29
Day	Mon	Tues	Wed	Thurs	Fri	Sat	Sun
Weather	Mild	Snow	Very Cold	Mild	Mild	Rain	Rain
Total Meals	250	270	265	290	315	330	200
Special Activities	—	—	Sales in Shopping Center	Same	Football	Football	—
Menu Item							
Seafood Appetizer	15	18	19	23	42	38	14
Soup d'Jour	35	45	40	21	35	43	20
Chef's Salad	10	6	10	12	31	19	10

Figure 13.8 Master Food Production Planning Worksheet

Day Tuesday
Date 8/1/00

Master Food Production Planning Worksheet

Local Weather Forecast: Cloudy & mild
Special Plans Party of 15 — steaks

Items	Standard Portion Size	Forecasted Portions — Customers	Forecasted Portions — Officers	Forecasted Portions — Total Forecast	Adjusted Forecast	Requisitioning Guide Data — Raw Materials Requested	State of Preparation	Remarks	Number of Portions Left Over	Actual Number Served
Appetizers										
Shrimp Cocktail	5 ea.	48	X	48	51	12 lbs. of 21-25 count	R T C		—	53
Fruit Cup	5 oz.	18	1	19	20	See Recipe for 20 Portions			—	19
Marinated Herring	2½ oz.	15	1	16	16	2½ lbs.	R T E		—	14
Half Grapefruit	½ ea.	8	—	8	8	4 Grapefruit			—	9
Soup	6 oz.	30	3	33	36	Prepare 2 Gallons			5	32
Entrees										
Sirloin Steak	14 oz.	28	X	28	29	29 Sirloin Steaks (Btchr.)	R T E		—	28
Prime Ribs	9 oz.	61	1	62	64	3 Ribs of Beef	R T C	Use Re-heat if necessary	out at 10:45 p.m.	62
Lobster	1½ lb.	26	X	26	28	28 Lobsters (check stock)				26
Ragout of Lamb	4 oz.	24	2	26	26	12 lbs. lamb fore (¾" pcs.)		Recipe No. E.402	1+	25
Half Chicken	½ ea.	34	2	36	38	38 halves (check stock)			—	39
Vegetables & Salads										
Whipped Potatoes	3 oz.	55	1	56	58	13 lbs.	A P		2-3	56
Baked Potatoes	1 ea.	112	3	115	120	120 Idahos			out at 11:10 p.m.	120
Asparagus Spears	3 ea.	108	X	108	113	8 No. 2 cans			2	110
Half Tomato	½ ea.	48	4	52	54	27 Tomatoes			2	52
Tossed Salad	2½ oz.	105	3	108	112	See Recipe No. S.302			—	114
Hearts of Lettuce	¼ hd.	63	2	65	67	18 heads			—	69
Desserts										
Brownie w/ice cream	1sq./1½oz.	21	2	23	26	1 pan brownies			—	24
Fresh Fruits	3 oz.	10	—	10	11	See Recipe No. D.113			—	10
Ice Cream	2½ oz.	35	3	38	40	Check stock			—	43
Apple Pie	1/7 cut	21	—	21	21	3 Pies			out at 10:50 p.m.	21
Devils Food Cake	1/8 cut	8	—	8	8	1 cake			1	7
Total No. of Persons		173	5	178	185					180

Abbreviations: AP — as purchased; RTC — ready-to-cook; RTE — ready-to-eat.

Adapted from Carl H. Albers, Food and Beverage Cost Planning and Control Procedures, *rev. ed. (East Lansing, Mich.: Educational Institute of the American Hotel & Motel Association, 1981), p. 68.*

(the number of portions to prepare would equal the number needed from Figure 13.8 less the number which are on hand at the beginning of the

Figure 13.9 Special Event Notice

Event:			
Date: _____		Date of Notice: _____	
No. of Guests: _____			
Special Requirements: _____			

The following items are needed for the above event:

Item	Purchase Unit	Quantity	Estimated Price

Source: Ninemeier, Planning and Control, *p. 103.*

workshifts). Also note that the worksheet allows you to provide special requisitioning information; likewise, the actual number served (last column) can be used to complete your sales history record (see Figure 13.7).

In addition to considering the quantity of each menu item to be prepared, preproduction planning meetings serve other purposes. For example, after you have estimated the number of meals, it is possible to schedule labor and equipment.[6] If there are special events such as banquets or other catered functions scheduled for the upcoming week, you will need to plan, communicate, and coordinate to ensure that no problems result. Following the preproduction planning meeting, you will know the required number of each menu item. Therefore, issue requisitions might be completed, at least partially, for some days or items. Forms might even be completed for catered events when these costs are to be charged to separate revenue/cost centers.

Purchasing systems generally consider the amount of each product used during regular order cycles. Unless the preproduction planning meeting indicates that the volume of food to be prepared is greater or less than normal, no special changes in purchasing procedures are required. However, if production volumes are judged to vary significantly from normal patterns, changes in quantities of items to be ordered may be necessary. If there are special events being planned which require menu items not normally carried in inventory, you must consider this information in the preproduction planning meeting. Figure 13.9 is an example of a notice which can be used to alert purchasing staff to the need for special purchase requirements.

Much of the preceding information about preproduction planning does not relate specifically to beverage production service. If adequate bar par inventory levels have been established, and if there is an effective minimum/maximum inventory system used in central storage areas, little preproduction planning for the beverage operation is usually necessary. Preproduction planning must, however, focus on employee scheduling and on expediting, when necessary, to maintain constant supplies of required brands of liquors and wines. If a special event requires beverage products that are not normally carried , a notice similar to the Figure 13.9 example can be used to alert purchasing staff.

NOTES

1. Jack D. Ninemeier, *Food and Beverage Security: A Systems Manual for Restaurants, Hotels, and Clubs* (Boston, Mass.: CBI, 1982), pp. 96-99.

2. Ninemeier, *Purchasing, Receiving and Storage: A Systems Manual for Restaurants, Hotels and Clubs* (Boston, Mass.: CBI, 1983), p. 290.

3. Ninemeier, *Planning and Control for Food and Beverage Operations* (East Lansing, Mich.: Educational Institute of the American Hotel & Motel Association, 1982), pp. 88-94.

4. Readers who are interested in details for calculating actual daily food costs are referred to Ninemeier, *Planning and Control*, pp. 128-131.

5. Readers who are interested in details for calculating actual daily beverage cost percents are referred to Ninemeier, *Planning and Control*, pp. 131-137.

6. Readers interested in details for scheduling labor and/or equipment are referred to Ninemeier, *Planning and Control*, pp. 181-191.

14
Producing What the Customer Wants

Management Challenges

As a result of studying this chapter you will:

1. know fundamental principles of cooking and the secrets of successful food production.

2. understand basic methods of cooking.

3. be familiar with procedures for preparing fresh fruits and vegetables, dressings and garnishes, and fruit and vegetable salads.

4. understand basic principles for cooking vegetables and fruits, meat, poultry, and seafood.

5. know preparation procedures for eggs and dairy products, baked goods, coffee, and tea.

6. recognize that food quality is a constant concern in food production.

7. recall basic control procedures which should be followed during food production.

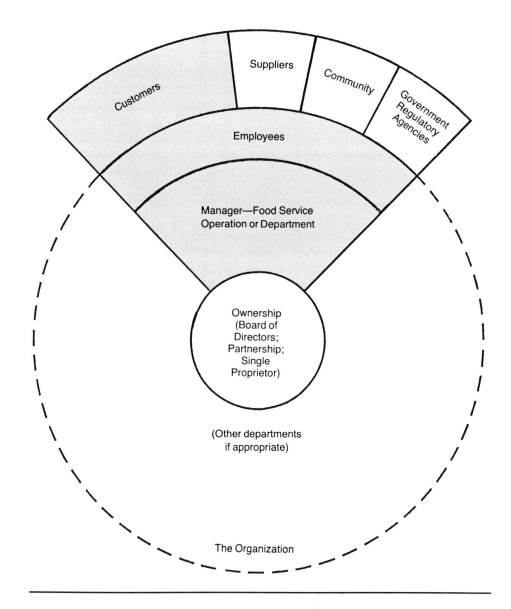

Focus on the
Food Service Publics

Chapter 14 focuses on the food production process. Since food service must deliver quality food that meets the customer's wants and needs, the production of food that conforms to minimum standards is crucial. While many customers visit a property for reasons other than obtaining quality food, it is still a component of the package that is purchased. A property that has excellent service, ambience, and cleanliness won't be successful if food production procedures do not incorporate basic food preparation principles. Therefore, the relationship between the food service employees—especially production staff members—and the customer is paramount. Food production personnel must appreciate the sometimes difficult role they play in marketing the food service operation. You, as the manager, must explain and defend this role so the food production staff will realize the importance of their relationship with the customer.

Much has been written about food preparation; as an introduction to food and beverage operations, this text cannot provide extensive details about the subject. However, the basic information included in this chapter will be helpful if you are ever employed in a position that requires food or beverage production skills. In addition, almost all management personnel in food and beverage operations should have a fundamental understanding of food preparation. Therefore, the objective of this chapter is to introduce the concept of food production. As your career in food and beverage operations evolves, you will learn a great deal more.

Methods of Cooking

Many foods that we eat are cooked. There are several reasons why food is cooked: (a) to develop, enhance, and/or alter its flavor; (b) to improve its digestibility; and (c) to destroy harmful organisms. Too much cooking, however, can harm food. Overcooking can destroy vitamins, weaken the potency of proteins, and unfavorably change the flavor, texture, and color of food products. Therefore, foods should be cooked according to basic preparation principles (see Figure 14.1), some of which will be discussed in this chapter.

There are two basic cooking methods: dry heat and moist heat. The method to use depends on the characteristics of the food that is to be cooked.

Dry-Heat Cooking

Dry-heat methods involve the use of hot air to cook food. They include:

Baking. In baking, food is cooked by dry heat in an oven. Baked items include breads, vegetables, fish, fruit, macaroni, pastries, and some desserts. Some types of breads and rolls are baked with the use of steam. This produces a crisp and shiny crust.

Roasting. Roasting is essentially the same as baking. Food is cooked by dry heat in an oven. However, the term "roasting" popularly applies to meat and poultry. For roasting, meats should be placed with the fat side up in a rack in an open pan. This enables the meat to baste itself while cooking.

Figure 14.1 "Secrets" of Successful Cooking

1.	Develop a proper attitude toward cooking. Food must be treated creatively in order to bring out its best.
2.	Never be satisfied with a mediocre product. Always try to make it perfect.
3.	Begin with quality food, which is not necessarily the most expensive.
4.	Make sure food is clean.
5.	Be sure that food is properly handled.
6.	Properly season the food.
7.	Use the right techniques and equipment when cooking.
8.	Standard recipes are an absolute must.
9.	Imagination is often the "magic ingredient." Don't cook without thinking.
10.	Cook food in as small a quantity as possible.
11.	Timing is important. Serve food as soon as possible after preparation.
12.	Remember the "rule"—serve hot food hot and cold food cold.
13.	Food must be served well. Make every food presentation something special.
14.	Be sure that all items being served complement one another.

Broiling. When food is broiled, it is placed on a rack that is located above, below, or between heat sources. The temperature is governed by the size of the food product or the fattiness/tenderness of the product being broiled. With most broiling equipment, the rack can be moved closer to or farther from the heat source. This, of course, determines the amount of time required to broil the product. Thick food items may be placed farther from the heat so that the product can be cooked thoroughly without burning the exterior surface.

Barbecuing. This method involves broiling while basting with a sauce. Barbecuing also may involve roasting in a covered pit. Smoke that is created by this process adds flavor to the product. With traditional barbecuing methods, temperatures are kept quite low and barbecuing time is increased. However, you can barbecue at a higher temperature for a shorter length of time.

Grilling. When items are grilled, they are cooked on a hot surface that is generally coated with melted fat to keep the product from sticking. The process of grilling is very similar to that of frying and sauteing. The product is cooked or browned on one side and then it is turned over for cooking on the second side. Items such as eggs, french toast, potatoes, fish, and hamburgers are often grilled.

Ovenizing. When foods are ovenized, they are placed on greased pans and baked in the oven. Normally, high temperatures (above 325°F) are used. The finished product often looks like fried foods. Ovenizing is a popular cooking method used in quantity food operations—especially those without deep-fryers.

Frying. There are several popular frying methods. When foods are *pan-fried*, the items are cooked in a shallow pan. Generally, just enough fat to prevent the food from sticking to the pan is used. Pan-frying is commonly used with seafood, vegetables, and eggs. When items are *sauteed*, food is cooked in a pan with a small amount of fat. The product is turned and browned on each side as it cooks. When products are *deep-fried*, the food is totally immersed in hot fat (the temperature is above 300°F). Deep-fried items are frequently dipped in a batter or breading mixture. Items such as fish, onion rings, and chicken are popular examples. *Pressure-frying* is increasing in popularity. In this method, the deep fryer has a tight-fitting cover. Pressure is created and the cooking process yields a product that often is more juicy and flavorful than when common deep-frying methods are used. With pressure-frying, food is cooked more quickly and there is less absorption of grease.

Moist-Heat Cooking

Moist-heat methods involve cooking with water, milk, juice, wines, and broth. Common methods of moist-heat cooking include the following:

Boiling. The boiling process involves cooking food by submerging it in water at a temperature of 212°F. In Chapter 8 you learned that cooking in water can destroy water-soluble vitamins. The problem worsens when the water used in cooking is thrown out rather than being used in preparing the product.

Blanching. When foods are blanched, they are submerged in boiling water for a very short time. For example, peaches and tomatoes may be blanched so removal of the outer skin is easier. Blanching also can help in freezing fruits and vegetables. Vegetables are often blanched as a preliminary process in cooking. Then just before serving, blanched items may be cooked by another process. Foods can also be parboiled, which is similar to blanching. This process involves immersing products in water for a longer period of time until they are partly cooked. This may be done in preparation for roasting, etc.

Braising. Braising is a cooking method in which meat is browned in fat and then simmered in a covered pan with a little liquid. Browning may be used to give meat color. This is done by placing the meat in a small quantity of fat and turning it frequently until the product is well-browned. Some foods may be coated in flour before being braised. (It is not necessary to add liquid to fish, meat, or poultry as part of the braising process because these products make their own liquid.)

Poaching. Poaching involves cooking the food in liquid below the boiling point of water. The food itself may or may not be covered with liquid. Normally, the liquid is at least halfway up the side of the food being poached. Fish and eggs are examples of foods commonly poached. This moist-heat cooking method can increase the flavor, moistness, and tenderness of food. It is even possible to "poach-roast" a product. For example, turkey parts may be placed skin-down in pans, partially covered with a stock, and then poached in an oven.

Simmering. Simmering also involves cooking food in a liquid which is below 212°F. Frequently, the liquid to be used is brought to a boil, the food to be simmered is added, and the product is then held at a simmering temperature (185°-205°F) until it is cooked. Alternatively, both the liquid and the product can be slowly heated to the desired temperature and then held. Products that have been simmered are often tenderer, juicier, and more flavorful than products that have been cooked with a dry-heat method.

Steaming. This cooking method involves using water converted to an invisible vapor or gas by heating it to the boiling point. This method is often favored because it helps retain nutrients. Vegetables are usually steamed, although almost any type of food can be cooked with this process. Special equipment can be used for steaming. Steaming is useful because it preserves the form and flavor of food and helps reduce shrinkage. Steaming also can be used to reheat foods and to thaw frozen foods prior to cooking by another method.

Stewing. Stewing is a process in which small cuts of poultry and/or meat are simmered in a liquid. Essentially, stewing is the same as braising except that the latter involves whole or sliced meat. Stewing also differs from braising in that an item being stewed is completely covered with the liquid. The stewing process involves thickening the liquid and serving it along with the cubed or chopped food as a one-course dish such as a stew or casserole.

Preparing Fresh Fruits and Vegetables

A heightening of nutritional awareness is leading Americans to consume an increasing quantity and variety of fresh fruits and vegetables. The quality of these products is constantly improving. Excellent choices of fresh fruits and vegetables are available—often on a year-round basis—because of the diverse climates in the United States. Technology also has improved storage and transportation systems which make the availability of fresh fruits and vegetables less of a problem for food service managers.

Fresh Fruits

The term "fruit" refers to the matured ovary of a flower which includes the seeds and adjacent parts. In other words, it is the reproductive body of the seed plant. Different structures of fruit are based upon the kinds of flowers from which they develop. For example, pears develop from one blossom, while pineapples and figs represent multiple blossoms.

As you learned in Chapter 8, fruits are high in carbohydrates and water. They are excellent sources of minerals and vitamins.

The colors of fruits are caused by pigments. Unless fruits are properly processed, these colors can be lost. Cellulose is material that makes up plant cell walls. Cellulose holds water and when these walls are broken (for example, in eating), the water escapes and the structure is altered.

Normally, only ripe fruit is good for food production purposes. Changes during maturation are caused by enzymes that cause not only ripening, but eventual spoilage. When fruit is ripe, (a) it is at full size, (b) the tissue becomes soft and tender, (c) the color is good, (d) the taste is better because starch in fruit has turned to sugar, and (e) aroma has developed.

The cost of fruits is affected by:

1. **Perishability.** Fruits are liable to spoil or deteriorate quickly.

2. **Pesticides.** These expensive chemicals are used for killing insects, weeds, etc.

3. **Weather conditions.** Early frost can kill plants, make fruit relatively unavailable, and generate high prices.

4. **Consumer preferences.** Large fruit is often more desirable to the customer and is therefore more expensive.

5. **Cost of packaging.** Storage and distribution can add significantly to the purchase price.

6. **Amount of processing.** Processed fruits such as frozen orange juice and bottled lemon juice are often less expensive than their fresh counterparts.

There are many food preparation principles which should be followed when working with fresh fruit. For example, careful washing is a must. Fresh fruit should be handled as little as possible in order to avoid bruising. Citrus fruit is easier to peel after it has been steamed (for example, in a compartment steamer). After cutting, low acid fruits turn dark because exposure to oxygen causes browning. To prevent this, place the cut fruit in orange or lemon juice—the acid slows the browning process—or cover the cut fruit with a sugar solution to prevent contact with oxygen.

Remember that fresh fruits are often more palatable and nutritious than their cooked counterparts. Therefore, try to be creative and find innovative ways to serve fresh fruits.

Usually, fresh fruits are best stored in the refrigerator. Bananas are an exception. Bananas should be purchased for immediate use because they are highly perishable (enzymes in the fruit continue the maturation process even after picking). Several weekly deliveries of this fruit are much better than infrequent deliveries.

Fresh Vegetables

The term "vegetable" refers to any plant that is grown for an edible part (except the ovary—which is classified as fruit). Generally, vegetables have less sugar and more starch than fruits. Color in vegetables comes from the same pigments that are found in fruits. The structure of a vegetable, which is formed by cellulose, can be maintained only when water remains in the cell. Vegetables shrink and wilt as they dry up.

Vegetables are classified by the part of the plant from which they come:

- **Roots**—sweet potatoes, beets, carrots, and turnips

- **Tubers or underground stems**—potatoes

- **Bulbs**—onions, garlic, and leeks

- **Stems**—celery, rhubarb, asparagus

- **Leaves**—lettuce, spinach, and cabbage

- **Vegetable fruits**—tomato, eggplant, squash, pumpkin, okra, pepper, and cucumber

- **Flowers**—cauliflower, broccoli, artichoke, and sweet corn

- **Pods and seeds**—green beans, peas, and lima beans

- **Sprouts**—soybeans and alfalfa

Vegetables are very rich in minerals and vitamins. Vegetables generally cost less when they are in season and when there is an abundant supply.

Careful washing is an important first step when preparing fresh vegetables. Wilted vegetables can be soaked in cold water to help regain crispness; however, this doesn't restore lost nutrients. Covering vegetables with ice will also help restore crispness. Improper processing of fresh vegetables can cause much waste. Therefore, you should be careful as you clean lettuce (don't throw away usable leaves), pare potatoes (nutrients as well as the edible product are lost when peelings are thickly cut), and cut celery (often outer stalks are thrown away or are not effectively used).

As with fresh fruits, vegetables should be purchased only for immediate consumption and should be stored in a cool, well-ventilated space. Generally, refrigerated storage is best for vegetables except roots and tubers. The tops on fresh carrots should be removed before storing. When receiving fresh vegetables, it is necessary to remove spoiled products since one spoiled item will contaminate the remaining items.

**Dressings,
Marinades,
and Garnishes**

Dressings are frequently served with fresh fruits and vegetables. There are many types of dressings, but they usually contain acid, fat, and/or seasonings as basic ingredients. Generally, lemon juice or vinegar is used as the acid. Oils of various types are the main ingredient.

Emulsions. In order to learn about salad dressings, you must know what an emulsion is. The most common emulsion is made from oil and water. Water forms a continuous structure and separates tiny particles of oil. The original french dressing is an unstable emulsion; the oil and water separate when standing. It is usually made by adding two parts of oil to one part of an acid. Vigorous shaking or mixing breaks up the fat and surrounds it with water. Emulsifiers such as eggs, egg yolks, starch, and gum can be used to keep a temporary emulsion from breaking down. Homogenization—a process to break up fat—helps disperse the fat throughout the liquid. Whipping also is used to help disperse the oil in the liquid.

Mayonnaise is an example of a stable emulsion; that is, one that does not separate when standing. Mayonnaise is semi-solid (does not flow) and has a yellowish sheen, a smooth texture, and a distinct tart flavor. According to federal standards, a product termed "mayonnaise" must contain at least 50% oil. Vinegar and egg yolk also are ingredients.

Several factors affect the stability of an emulsion.

Temperature. Temperature ranges of 60°-70°F favor the formation of the emulsion. By contrast, freezing and heat break emulsions.

Mechanical factors. Unless special equipment is used, products containing more than 15% vinegar will normally break down. To form an emulsion, place an emulsifier such as egg yolk in a bowl and beat it. Then add vinegar and seasonings along with small amounts of oil. After the emulsion is formed, add the remaining oil more rapidly. To re-form a broken emulsion, place a liquid or emulsifier in a bowl, pour in the broken emulsion, and beat.

Chemical factors. Excess salt can break an emulsion. Salt may be added to the liquid ingredient (e.g., vinegar) in order to dissolve it. Dissolved salt is less likely to break an emulsion.

Another type of dressing is one that is cooked or boiled. Generally, it is a mixture of liquids and seasonings that has been thickened with starch or egg. The oil content of commercial cooked or boiled dressings is approximately 35%.

Marinades. Marinades usually are mixtures of oil and acid. Examples of acids which are used include wine, vinegar, and fruit juices. Spices may also be added. The flavor of meat, fish, or vegetables can be enriched by soaking the product in a marinade.

Garnishes. Garnishes frequently are made of fresh fruits and vegetables. They must be edible and should contribute form, color, and/or texture to the foods with which they are served. The varieties of garnishes are end-

Figure 14.2 Color in Fruits and Vegetables

Color in fruit and vegetables results from the presence of one or more chemical compounds:		
Color	**Chemical**	**Examples**
Green	Chlorophyll	Green peas, green beans, broccoli, asparagus, and green grapes
Red and Blue	Anthocyanin	Red cabbage, red onions, beets, red and blue plums, red grapes, red apples, blueberries, and strawberries
Yellow and Orange	Carotenoid	Carrots, sweet potatoes, yellow corn, peaches, and apricots
White	Flavone	Yellow onions and cauliflower

less. Garnishes range from the traditional lemon wedge served with fish to an orange slice served with alcoholic beverages to a creative array of sieved egg whites, rose radishes, vegetable flowers, chocolate curls, and gumdrop slices. There are many popular books that provide examples of easy-to-make, low-cost garnishes. Recall the principle noted throughout this chapter that every food item should be "something special." The use of garnishes can contribute to a food's uniqueness.

Fruit and Vegetable Salads

Fruits and vegetables to be used in salads should be fresh and have fine flavor and color (see Figure 14.2). Salads may be served on a plate with an entree, as part of a salad bar, or as meals in themselves, such as a chef salad. There are many variations of salads, ranging from simple accompaniments to full-course meals. Salads may be classified as follows:

Tossed Salads. Tossed salads can be made with one kind of salad green or a combination of salad greens. Examples include iceberg, romaine, Boston, and Bibb lettuce, escarole, endive, and chicory. Parsley and spinach also are greens frequently used in salads.

Cabbage Slaws. Chopped or shredded green and/or red cabbage perhaps mixed with cucumbers, mixed fruit, marshmallows, nuts, cheese, and onions are examples of cabbage slaws.

Fruit Salads. Fruit salads can be tossed, layered, frozen with whipped cream, or have a cream or cottage cheese base. They can be diced and served with other complementary foods or served as fruit halves or sectioned fruit.

Hot Vegetable Salads. Common examples are hot potato or German potato salad and wilted lettuce or spinach salads.

Molded Salads. Molded salads generally have a plain gelatin or gelatin dessert base. They can be served layered with fruit, vegetables (cooked or raw), meat, fish, cheese, or even a milk or cream base.

Protein Salads. Salads made with meats, poultry, seafood, and dairy products (especially cheeses) are commonly used entrees.

Some techniques for preparing salads are listed in Figure 14.3.

Figure 14.3 Techniques for Preparing Salads

1. Make salads light and refreshing.

2. Balance the flavor, texture, and color with other foods the salad accompanies.

3. Use a pleasing pattern.

4. Use distinct ingredients in bite-sized pieces.

5. Use fresh, ripe, and clearly colored products.

6. Use varied textures—crisp, soft, and smooth combinations are good. Foods should not be mushy.

7. Use delicate flavors instead of harsh or bland flavors.

8. Begin preparation as close to the serving time as possible.

9. Use good tools such as clean vegetable brush, sharp knives, and special cutting board.

10. Wash salad ingredients with special care since they will be eaten raw.

11. Freshen vegetables in very cold water, but only until crisp. Drain vegetables well before using them. Do not place sliced or diced vegetables in water.

12. Chop or cut salad ingredients in pieces of uniform size. Take care when cutting and chopping fruits and vegetables so they won't get crushed.

13. Handle prepared salad ingredients gently. Toss mixed salads together lightly.

14. When arranging salads on chilled plates, do so neatly. Use an assembly line method for speed.

15. Add salad dressings to salads just before serving since dressings may wilt the vegetables.

16. Use dressing that will complement the salad. Use only enough dressing to bind together the ingredients.

17. Keep salad ingredients and finished salads refrigerated at all times except during actual serving.

Fruit and Vegetable Cookery

A major concern with cooking fresh fruits and vegetables is minimizing nutritive losses. Palatability (how it tastes) also is affected by cooking. Do you like mushy, off-colored fruits and vegetables? Probably not—and neither do the people for whom you will be preparing the products.

Reasons to cook fruits and vegetables include the following:

- To make the product more appetizing

- To soften the product

- To improve the product's texture

- To increase the product's digestibility

- To add variety

Properly prepared products enhance customer and patient acceptance. Normally, only a small amount of water should be used in cooking. Products should be cooked until tender and firm, but not soft. Be careful not to overcook fruits and vegetables since this destroys many valuable nutrients and distorts their color, flavor, texture, and shape. As with any product, preparation should be scheduled as close to the serving time as possible.

Cook fruits and vegetables in pieces as large as possible. Vegetables such as potatoes and carrots should be cooked without peeling to save nutrients. When peeling any fruit or vegetable, care must be taken to minimize excessive loss of the edible material for both economic and nutritional reasons.

When possible, cook fruits and vegetables by steaming. (Use a perforated pan with a compartment steamer.) Vegetables that are prepared in this manner normally should be salted and seasoned **after** they are cooked.

Batch cooking, in which small quantities of products are prepared immediately before serving, requires that all fruits and vegetables be cooked simultaneously.

General principles for cooking fruits and vegetables are based on common sense and are simple to learn and practice. The goals are to retain the maximum amount of nutrients, to yield a high level of palatability, and to produce a product that is tender, firm, colorful, and flavorful.

The color of green vegetables is affected by long cooking periods and by minerals and acids (such as vinegar) that are present during cooking. Discoloration can be minimized by boiling vegetables in a pot or pan without a cover. Cooking at high heat levels, especially when acids and minerals are present, can turn vegetables a brownish color. Baking soda (or any other alkaline chemical) deepens the green color of vegetables, but it also can cause a loss of vitamin C. Therefore, proper handling and cooking procedures—not the use of baking soda—should be used when processing green vegetables, which are a main source of vitamin C.

Overcooking may cause yellow vegetables to become a pale color. Red vegetables such as beets may lose color when cooked in water. Alkalies that are present in hard water can cause vegetables to turn a bluish color. Acids such as lemon juice make the color brighter. White vegetables (for example, cauliflower) turn yellow in alkaline or hard water. The color of white vegetables can be enhanced by using covered cooking vessels.

Before fresh vegetables are cooked, they may need to be washed, torn, trimmed, cut, or soaked. Clean vegetables deteriorate less in storage. Therefore, fresh produce should be cleaned and stored as soon as possible after delivery, especially if the products are to be held for several days or more. Some vegetables such as potatoes and carrots may require scrubbing while other products such as greens will need to be soaked. Naturally, water used to clean vegetables should not be reused.

When processing canned vegetables, remember that the products already have been fully cooked as part of the canning process. Therefore, only a very short heating time is needed. Canned vegetables lend themselves to batch cooking methods. As always, the heating time for these products should be scheduled so they can be served as soon as possible after being heated. Canned vegetables should be cooked in their own liquid.

Applicable cooking methods include:

Baking. Products such as potatoes, squash, eggplant, apples, and tomatoes have enough water in them to form steam. Therefore, a dry-heat method should be used.

Boiling. When boiling nongreen vegetables, bring the water to a full boil, add the vegetables, cover the cooking vessel, bring the water to a boil again, and then turn down the heat to a gentle boil. The same process should be used for boiling green vegetables except that the cover should be left off for a few minutes after the vegetables are added. This allows volatile acids to escape and helps preserve color.

Steaming. Compartment steamers have low-, high-, or room-pressure compartments into which steam is injected. The direct application of steam quickly cooks the food while maintaining high quality and nutritional levels. The instructions from the equipment manufacturer should be followed closely.

Pan Cooking. When preparing mild-flavored vegetables on top of the range, cook them in a covered pan. However, strong-flavored vegetables such as cabbage and brussel sprouts are best cooked in an uncovered container. Vegetables such as cabbage, spinach, and string beans can be shredded or cut into small pieces and then placed in a pan with a small amount of fat or oil. These products should be cooked in pots or pans with tight covers. The moisture in the vegetables will create their own steam.

French Frying. Potatoes, eggplants, and onions should be rinsed and dried before frying. Tempura is a method of french frying in which products are parboiled, dried, and breaded, usually in a flour and water batter. Then they are deep-fried.

Microwave Cooking. Vegetables to be cooked in a microwave oven should be placed in a pan with a very small amount of liquid, and then the pan should be covered. Since vegetables cook quickly, timing is critical to prevent overcooking.

Meat and Poultry Cooking

Meat is the edible portion of animals. Popular meats are beef from cattle, pork from pig, mutton from lamb, and poultry from chicken, turkeys, and ducks.

There are four parts to the structure of meat products:

Muscle Fiber. Muscle is made up of fibers which are held together by connective tissue. The thickness of the fibers, the size of fiber bundles, and the amount of connective tissue will determine the grain of the meat.

Connective Tissue. Connective tissue, which holds muscles together, determines the tenderness of the meat products. This tissue covers the walls of muscle fibers, binds fibers into bundles, and surrounds the muscles as a membrane. Tendons and ligaments that attach the muscle to the bone are composed of connective tissue. Less tender meat cuts have more connective tissue. The type of connective tissue determines the method used to cook meat.

Fat. Fat is distributed inside of meat in small layers called marbling. Fat contributes to the tenderness and flavor of meat products. Exterior layers of fat cover the muscle.

Bone. Bone is not edible. A high proportion of meat to bone is favorable since there is a lower cost per edible unit. The shape of bone helps identify the meat cut. Bones are used in stocks to give flavor.

Tenderness of Meat

The meat's tenderness is important to its selection, preparation, and service. The more connective tissue that is present, the tougher the meat will be. There are two types of connective tissue: (1) collagen (white) which breaks down into gelatin when heat is applied, and (2) elastin (yellow) which does not break down when heated. The tenderer meat contains collagen instead of elastin.

Fat and age also affect tenderness. The more fat that is present, the tenderer the meat will be. Young animals yield tenderer meat. The location of the muscle affects tenderness, too. The least-used muscles (for example, loin and rib cuts) are tenderer than fully developed muscles such as chuck and round.

In addition, temperature affects tenderness. The higher the temperature that is used, the tougher the meat, especially if it is overcooked. Grinding, pounding, and other techniques can be used to tenderize meat. Aged meat, which is hung in a refrigerator during the time of post mortem changes, will be tenderer. Enzymes, which can be injected into the meat before or after the slaughtering process, are also tenderizers.

Goals of the meat cooking process include improving flavor, changing color, tenderizing the product, and destroying harmful organisms. Cooking at a low temperature for longer periods of time is better than using a hot temperature for shorter cooking times because there will be less weight and nutrient loss.

The two basic heating methods (dry-heat and moist-heat) can be used for preparing meats and poultry. You should know something about how each method applies to cooking meat.

Figure 14.4 Techniques for Proper Roasting

1. Select the right pan. The pan used for roasting should be made of a heavy material. The pan should also be the correct size: deep enough to permit turning of the food without spilling juices and fat.

2. The meat should cover the pan bottom and should not leave space for drippings to burn.

3. Do not add salt until the browning, at least, is completed.

4. When turning a roast, do not pierce the lean flesh. Insert a fork in the fatty tissue or roll the meat with a fork.

5. Do not use liquids or cover the pan.

6. Insert the thermometer in the center of the meat's largest muscle.

7. Place meat in a preheated oven at 300°F. Maintain this temperature during the roasting period.

8. Allow the meat to stand for 15 to 30 minutes before carving. Internal temperatures will rise 15°F or more when the meat stands. If the meat is held on a hot food counter, such as for sandwich carving, leave the pan cover off. Reduce the heat so that the meat will not continue to cook.

9. When carving, cut against the grain in thin slices.

Dry-Heat Cooking Methods

Dry-heat methods can be used to cook tender meat cuts.

Roasting. Roasting in an oven is a common dry-heat method (see Figure 14.4) of cooking meat. Meat to be roasted should be placed on a rack with the fat side up so it will baste itself. A meat thermometer should always be used by inserting it in the thickest part of the muscle, but not so it is touching bone. Do not rely on charts that list minutes per pound or other roasting factors. While these can be used as a guide, careful use of the meat thermometer is always best.

Figure 14.5 indicates internal meat temperatures that are critically important when meat is being prepared. Your customers will have different preferences about how their meat is prepared. Some people prefer meat that is well-done (no pink color; gray throughout). Others like rare meat (browned surface with a red interior). Still others like their meat between these stages (a thicker layer of gray surface with a pink interior). Popular cooking references vary in the recommended interior temperatures necessary to attain these different stages. Experienced cooks have their own standards. Food service managers should work with chefs to develop cooking procedures that will meet food quality standards established by the operation.

Remember that meat continues to cook after it is removed from the oven. Therefore, it should be removed when the product is a few degrees cooler than the desired temperature.

Figure 14.5 Meat Cooking Guide

Stages	Internal Temperatures
Very Rare	140°F
Rare	
Medium Rare	
Medium	160°F
Medium Well	
Well	170° F

Pork should always be cooked until it is well-done (an internal temperature of at least 150°F). This prevents trichinosis, a disease characterized by a type of tapeworm present in the meat because of improper care of the animal before slaughter or poor sanitary practices after slaughter.

Broiling. As you know, broiling is a cooking method that uses direct radiant heat. Meats should be approximately half-cooked when turned with tongs or a spatula. Normally, broiling heat should be kept at a temperature between 300°-350°F for the best product.

Pan Broiling. When this technique is used, the meat is broiled in a heavy fry pan and cooked slowly. The pan should not be covered and usually it is not necessary to add water or fat. Fat generated during cooking should be poured off as it accumulates.

Frying, Pan Frying, Sauteing. With these cooking methods, a small amount of fat is used in the cooking vessel.

Deep-Frying. When this cooking method is used, the meat is submerged in fat.

Moist-Heat Cooking Methods

Moist-heat methods are used for cooking less tender cuts of meat.

Braising. Braising is a process in which meat is browned in a small amount of fat and then a little liquid is added. The meat is then cooked slowly in a covered cooking vessel (see Figure 14.6).

Simmering. The meat is cooked in a small amount of water or broth in a covered pan until it is tender. The temperature of the water should be below the boiling point.

Pressure Cooking and Steaming. Meats can be cooked under pressure in a compartment steamer or steamed in an oven. This process is used when meats are covered with aluminum foil before cooking to prevent moisture loss. Trapped moisture is turned to steam which is then used to cook the meat.

Figure 14.6 Techniques for Braising

1.	Meat may be floured before braising; this is needed if browning is to occur.
2.	Add enough fat to cover the bottom of the pan (about one-eighth to one-quarter inch deep).
3.	Bring temperature to approximately 350°F and add the meat.
4.	Add moisture when the meat is richly browned.
5.	Simmer meat slowly until tender.
6.	Vegetables, if any, are added late in cooking so they will remain unbroken, bright in color, and cooked only until "crisply tender." Vegetables can be cooked separately and then served with the meat.
7.	Braising must be done in a covered cooking vessel.
8.	When meat is tender, the cover of the cooking vessel may be removed and the liquid can be reduced to the desired level.
9.	Braising also can be done in steam-jacketed kettles. The kettle is heated with the cover down. Fat is added and melted, meat is added and turned until all sides are browned. The kettle cover is left up during this process.
10.	After browning, seasonings and a small quantity of liquid can be added.
11.	The cover is placed on the kettle, steam is reduced, and the meat product is simmered until tender.

Other Cooking Procedures

Some meats, such as portion-cut items, can be cooked from their frozen state. If done properly, there is little difference in tenderness, juiciness, and flavor of frozen or thawed meats. When frozen meats are cooked, they should be processed at a lower temperature for a longer period of time.

Meat stocks are often an important ingredient in preparing many meats and other products. Stocks are made from cracked bones, cut meat pieces, and other ingredients. These products are covered with water, simmered for several hours, and then vegetables and spices are added. After cooking, the substance is strained, chilled, and degreased. Further processing can be done at this time. If a brown stock is desired, the bones are roasted before simmering. If a white stock is needed, the bones are not roasted. Bouillon is a brown stock that has been clarified by adding egg whites.

Despite much experimentation, microwave cooking has not proven to be a generally useful technique for processing meats. While the cooking time is much faster, the product often is much drier and there is more shrinkage. Unless special heating elements are used in microwave cooking, no surface browning occurs on the meat.

Most of the principles for cooking meats which have been discussed also apply to processing poultry. Moist-heat methods are not suitable for tender cuts of either meat or poultry. However, dry-heat methods can be used for less tender cuts if ample time for cooking is allowed. The total weight loss from drippings, water evaporation, and other volatile substances generally is greater when moist heat is used than when dry-heat is used.

Preparing Seafoods

There are many species of fish ranging in size from less than one-half of an inch to more than 50 feet in length. Some fish may live for only a few weeks or months; others live from 10-20 years. There are two types of edible fish: (1) finfish that have bony skeletons and come from salt or fresh water, and (2) shellfish that don't have bony skeletons and come mainly from salt water. There are two types of shellfish. Mollusks have hard-hinged shells (oysters, clams, scallops, mussels) and crustaceans have segmented shells (lobsters, shrimp, crabs).

The fat content of seafood can range from less than 1% (such as in cod and haddock) to more than 25% (such as in salmon, mackerel, and lake trout). The fat content of the seafood product being prepared is an important factor in determining the cooking method. The nutritive value of seafood is generally quite high. Seafood is a good source of protein and, therefore, presents a good alternative to meat protein. Fish also are a good source of minerals. Seafoods with a higher fat content provide a good vitamin source as well.

Cooking Seafoods

Since there is relatively little connective tissue, compared to meats and poultry, shorter cooking times are possible with seafoods. Seafoods should be cooked at a moderate temperature long enough for flavor to develop, for the breakdown of the small amount of connective tissue that is present, and for protein to coagulate.

Seafoods should not be overcooked because they become tough. The flesh is cooked sufficiently when it falls into clumps or flakes when tested with a fork. If the cooking is not stopped at this point, the product will become tough, dry, and flavorless. Because fish that is cooked well breaks up easily, seafoods should be handled carefully during the cooking and serving process.

Fish can be cooked without using heat. Recall learning about the marinating process in which proteins can be coagulated with an acid such as lemon or lime juice. The flesh of fish that has been sufficiently marinated will coagulate and turn white. Marinated products such as pickled herring are well-liked by many customers.

Popular cooking methods for seafoods usually involve dry-heat techniques such as broiling, baking, and frying although moist-heat methods such as poaching and steaming also can be used. Low-fat fish may require some fat in the cooking process. However, fat normally will not be needed when a high-fat fish product is prepared.

Shellfish can be cooked by plunging the product into simmering salt

Figure 14.7 Techniques for Preparing Seafoods

1. Remember that seafoods are fairly tender. Therefore, moist-heat methods generally are not used to make fish tender, but only to create variety.

2. The chief problem in preparing fish is to retain the form of the fish. Products must be handled carefully.

3. When cooking fish in a liquid, use cheesecloth or parchment to prevent the product from falling apart.

4. Cook fish until it is done.

5. When broiling fish with skin, put the skin side down.

6. When baking fish, place it in a shallow, uncovered pan; baste it frequently to keep the skin from becoming hard.

water. Shrimp is usually baked, char-broiled, or deep-fried. For further tips on preparing seafoods, see Figure 14.7.

Preparing Eggs and Dairy Products

Eggs   Eggs are a very versatile product and a good source of vitamins and minerals. They are used in food preparation for many meals. Eggs can be served alone in various styles or used as an ingredient in other menu items. Contrary to popular opinion, there is no relationship between the color of the eggshell (brown or white) and the quality or taste of egg products.

When eggs are heated, the protein in the yolk will coagulate. This factor makes eggs useful for thickening agents and for coating food material. When heat is applied to egg white, it changes from being transparent to a soft white color. When sugar is added to any egg mixture, higher heat is necessary to coagulate the product. By contrast, when salt is added to an egg product, a lower temperature is needed for coagulation to occur. When an acid such as lemon juice is added, the temperature for coagulation is also lowered and a fine gel is produced.

Cooking Uses. As we have mentioned, there are many different ways to use eggs in cooking. For example:

Binding and coating. Eggs help make the ingredients stick together in products such as meat loaf and in batters for deep-fried products.

Leavening. Beaten egg whites create a foam which is air bubbles surrounded by thin layers of egg-white film. When the foam is incorporated into a mixture and heated, the air bubbles expand and the film hardens. This process is useful when preparing omelets, souffles, and sponge cakes. Egg whites should be beaten only until the peaks stand straight. If they are overbeaten, the volume of the foam will be reduced. If sugar is added to egg whites while being beaten, the resulting foam will be

Figure 14.8 Techniques for Cooking with Eggs

1.	Eggs to be cooked soft in the shell should be cooked for no longer than one to three minutes.
2.	Hard-cooked eggs should be cooked no more than 15 minutes. When preparing eggs in the shell, don't boil them because they become rubbery. Put eggs in boiling water and then turn down the water to simmer, or take them off the heat.
3.	Prevent green yolks by immersing eggs in cold water or by peeling immediately after taking them out of the water.
4.	Poached eggs are prepared out of the shell in just enough water to cover them. The temperature of the water should be close to—but not at—the boiling point (212°F).
5.	When frying eggs in a pan, fat is needed to keep them from sticking.
6.	When egg is used as a thickening agent, avoid directly adding the egg to any hot mixture. Instead, stir a small portion of the hot liquid into the egg before it is added to other ingredients. Then add it to the main mixture, stirring continuously while the egg is coagulating.
7.	Cook eggs at the lowest possible temperature to avoid toughening.
8.	Use eggs as soon as possible after purchasing. Flavor and appearance decrease with age.
9.	Remember the best rule for cooking with eggs: don't overbeat or overheat.

more stable. Greater volume and faster beating times occur when whites are whipped at room temperature rather than at refrigerated temperatures. However, stability may not be as great.

Egg yolks can also be used as a leavening agent: when heated, they increase in size. However, because of the presence of fat, yolks are less effective leavening agents than egg whites.

Emulsifying agent. Our earlier discussion of salad dressings pointed out that oil and vinegar separate unless the oil droplets are coated with egg or some other emulsifier to prevent the separation. Egg yolks are also used as an emulsifier in mayonnaise, ice creams, cakes, and other products.

Interfering substance. Eggs prevent ice crystals from combining to create a larger mass (as sometimes, for example, in ice cream).

Clarifying agent. When egg protein coagulates, it traps particles in the substance so they can be removed. This makes liquids clear and free from impurities. Broths, for example, are clarified with egg whites.

Techniques for cooking with eggs are reviewed in Figure 14.8.

Dairy Products   Milk is the single most naturally nutritious product. Milk is often pasteurized and homogenized. Pasteurization is a process of controlled heating which destroys bacteria. The process makes milk safe to use. Homogenization is a process which breaks up fat particles in the milk so that they will remain suspended. Homogenization prevents milk from separating into fat and liquid parts.

Milk, along with products containing large amounts of milk, is used in cooking. However, milk is delicate. It can curdle (separate into protein and liquid particles), it scorches easily, and it is highly perishable. While there are many types of milk available, basic cooking procedures are the same regardless of which product is used.

Cooking with Milk. Acids such as lemon or tomato juice and vinegar can cause milk to curdle. This is a frequent problem since these ingredients are used together in many recipes. To prevent curdling, heat should be kept as low as possible during cooking, and salt should be withheld until the product is served. Acid should be kept out of the product until it must be added to the recipe.

Some recipes require milk to be added to a product containing an acid such as tomato juice. To prevent the product from curdling, the milk can be warmed or some of the product can be added to the milk base, the mixture can be blended, and then poured back into the main mixture containing the acid. This process is much more effective than adding the milk directly to the product that could cause curdling.

Scorching is another problem that can occur in milk cooking. To prevent this, milk should be heated in a double boiler, a steam-jacketed kettle, or a steamer. When milk is heated, its flavor and odor can be hurt by prolonged cooking or a surface skin can form. The latter can be prevented by covering the milk, stirring it, or by placing a bit of fat such as butter on the surface of the milk. Low heat and frequent stirring are two of the most important preparation principles that should be followed when you cook with milk.

Cooking with Cheese. These basic cooking procedures are also important when working with cheese. There are many varieties of cheese and, like milk, it is a very nutritious food. Expensive cheeses are not necessarily higher in food value. The extra expense is due to the cost of popular flavoring techniques and the "supply and demand" characteristics of the marketplace.

Remember that cheese protein coagulates with heat. Cheese can become tough and rubbery when it is overheated. This can occur when it is heated for too long and/or at too high of a temperature. Fat in cheese is solid at room temperature. As it warms, it softens and when it is heated, the fat melts.

Cream cheese is frequently used in cooking since it is so easy to blend. Cheddar is the most popular cheese used in cooking and should be chopped or grated before being added to a sauce or cooked dish. This increases the surface area and hastens the melting process.

Figure 14.9 Techniques for Bakery Production

1.	Maintain high sanitation standards.
2.	Properly use all the equipment and tools.
3.	Use tested standard recipes.
4.	Use high-quality ingredients.
5.	Weigh and/or measure everything. Weighing is always more accurate than measuring. Professional bakers, for example, will even weigh water and other liquid ingredients.
6.	Use recommended mixing techniques.
7.	Practice proper portioning.
8.	Maintain and check proper oven temperatures.
9.	Prepare bakery products as close as possible to serving time.
10.	Constantly evaluate finished bakery products.

Preparing Baked Products

Many food service operations bake all, or at least part, of their bread and dessert products. Bakeshop production, especially, is an art and a science (see Figure 14.9). Sometimes it is difficult—even with the best recipes—to develop quality bakery products. The moisture content of the specific flour being used and the humidity in the air affect the amount of liquid that must be added to baked products as they are produced. Even the altitude can affect the action of yeast which is used to leaven many bread products. Let's look at some of the ingredients commonly used in baking.

Common Baking Ingredients

Flour. Flour is made by grinding and sifting wheat, rye, barley, or corn. Flour also can be made from rice, potato, and soy products. Wheat is the most popular cereal from which flour is made and it is classified by "hardness." For example, "hard" wheat flour has a higher protein content and produces a larger volume and finer texture of bread product. By contrast, "soft" wheat flour has a lower protein content and is used to make cakes, pastries, and cookies. The highest protein of all is found in durum wheat which is used to make macaroni and similar products. There are many types of wheat flour; some of the most popular are noted in Figure 14.10.

Leavening Agents. Leavening agents are used to make dough light and porous. Dough products can be leavened by incorporating air or by forming gas. For example, air can be incorporated into dough products by beating eggs or by creaming fat and sugar. Water vapor (steam) can be

Figure 14.10 Types of Wheat Flour

Whole wheat graham flour—this wheat flour contains the entire wheat kernel.

Bread flour—high in protein content, this flour is used for yeast breads. The protein ingredients develop into gluten which gives the bread structure, elasticity, and strength.

All-purpose flour—made of blended wheats with a lower protein content than bread flour. All-purpose flour has less strength and elasticity and is used for pastry, cookies, and homemade bread.

Pastry flour—this type of flour has a lower protein content than all-purpose flour and is used in the commercial baking industry for pastries and cookies.

Cake flour—cake flour has very low protein content and is very finely ground. It is bleached white and, as the name suggests, is used in cake production.

Instant flour (quick mixing)—this type of flour does not need to be sifted and creates no flour "dust."

Self-rising flour—a leavening agent such as baking soda is added to self-rising flour.

Gluten flour—this flour is very high in protein content (approximately 41%) and is used for special bakery purposes.

Enriched flour—enriched flour has B vitamins and iron added. Other ingredients are added as well.

incorporated into flour mixtures that contain water which turns to steam. Examples of products leavened entirely by steam include popovers and cream puffs. Carbon dioxide (CO_2) is a gas which is created by the action of yeast on sugar. Pressed yeast (in which live cells are pressed into a cake) and dry yeast (where yeast is dried in granular form) are packaged in metal foil to avoid contact with the air. These are the types of yeast most commonly used for baking purposes.

Carbon dioxide can also be produced by using baking soda with water. Baking powder (which is made of dry acid, baking soda, and starch or flour) is another popular leavening chemical. Whenever baking powder or baking soda is used, it should always be added with the dry ingredients so that the gas-forming reaction can be delayed until necessary.

Fat. Fat creates a tenderizing effect. It coats flour particles and prevents them from coming together. The term "plasticity" refers to a fat's ability to be molded. More "plastic" fats—those that have a waxy texture—tend to hold their shape in a batter or dough, have a high melting temperature, and have greater shortening power. Shortening power refers to the ability of shortenings to surround flour particles and other ingredients, lubricating them so that they cannot stick together.

Liquids. Liquids are used for several purposes in bakery production. For example, they can be used to hydrate (add water to) starch and gluten. Liquids are also used to dissolve salt, sugar, and baking powders. In addition, liquids can be used to moisturize baking powders and sodas to start carbon dioxide production.

Eggs. Eggs are used to incorporate air into batter as well as to add flavor and color. Since egg proteins coagulate, eggs add rigidity to the structure of baked products.

Sugar. Sugar serves several purposes in baked products. It adds sweetness, it creates a browning effect, and it serves as a yeast food. Sugar also tenderizes by interfering with development of the gluten in the flour, and helps contribute to the fine texture of bakery products.

There are several methods of mixing batter and dough. When the muffin method is used, dry ingredients are sifted together first and then eggs are beaten. Liquid and fat are added to the eggs, and this liquid is then blended with dry ingredients. When the pastry method is used, dry ingredients are sifted together and fat is blended with the dry ingredients. The liquid is added last. When the conventional cake method is used, fat and sugar are first creamed together and then eggs are added. Dry and liquid ingredients are alternatively blended with the fat/sugar/egg mixture.

Flour mixtures can be classified as either dough or batter. Dough products such as pie or bread dough are thick enough to be kneaded on a board. By contrast, batter can be poured, as in cake-making, or dropped, as in cookie preparation.

Preparing Beverages

Coffee   Chapter 15 will provide general information about preparing and serving alcoholic beverages. However, you must know something about the preparation of nonalcoholic beverages. Coffee is one of America's most popular beverages. Coffee can mean the difference between a "good" and a "bad" dining experience (see Figure 14.11). Blends of coffee used in quantity food service operations are specially designed to maintain quality for relatively long periods of time.

Coffee normally is made in an urn or in an automatic coffee maker. When an urn is used, ground coffee is placed in a cloth or metal container through which boiling water flows or is poured. The brew that drips through the coffee grounds is caught in a receptacle and can be drawn for serving. One typical recipe calls for one pound of ground coffee for each two and one-half gallons of water.[1] Half of the brew is poured back into the urn after the coffee grounds are removed. Then, approximately ten minutes is allowed for the coffee to "set" before being served.

When using an automatic coffee maker, measure the amount of coffee accurately. Spread the coffee evenly over the filter and add fresh boiling water. Pour the water in a slow, circular motion and immediately re-

Figure 14.11 Techniques for Coffee-Making

1.	Use a high-quality coffee.
2.	Make sure that the coffee stock is rotated; the oldest coffee should be used first. Store coffee in a cool, dry place since heat and moisture can cause quality deterioration.
3.	Follow the manufacturer's suggestions for the proper use of equipment.
4.	Use the proper grind for the coffee maker.
5.	Do not let the urn bag come in contact with the brewed coffee.
6.	Rinse the urn with boiling water after each coffee batch to remove the old coffee film.
7.	Rinse urn bags and coffee filters in hot water to remove coffee deposits.
7.	Store cloth filters in cold water when not in use to keep them "fresh" for their next use.
9.	Maintain coffee at approximately 185°F.
10.	Make frequent batches of coffee. When possible, coffee should not be kept for longer than one hour.

move the grounds. Then mix the brew. "Heavy coffee" at the bottom of the batch should be poured back into the brew after the grounds are removed. Coffee should be held at approximately 185°F; it should never be allowed to boil.

Tea   Tea is another popular beverage used in quantity food service operations. There are usually 200 individualized tea bags—with or without holding tags—per pound. When making tea, the water should be close to or at the boiling point when it is poured over the tea bag. The tea pot or tea cup should be kept hot and the tea should be allowed to steep for no more than five minutes. Iced tea used in quantity food services is often prepared with one-ounce tea bags which are immersed in water that has reached the boiling point. The normal proportion is two ounces of tea to one gallon of water. Like hot tea, iced tea should steep for five minutes and then be poured into a glass with ice. When this is impractical, tea should be precooled and ice should be added to the glass when it is served. Since ice will dilute the tea, the product is generally prepared in a stronger solution than that used for hot tea.

Hot Chocolate   Hot chocolate and similar drinks are also popular in quantity food service operations. Many properties use a powdered mix containing cocoa, powdered milk, and sugar. Hot water can be added at the time of service. Machines which premeasure and mix water with cocoa and other ingredients also are available.

Food Quality Is Constant Concern

Regardless of the type of food product being prepared, the proper food quality is a constant concern. It is useless for the food service operation to make special efforts to purchase, receive, store, and issue food products if attention is not given to food quality at the time of production. The management staff must first define the minimum acceptable quality in each product being prepared. Then, constant supervision and evaluation are needed to ensure that these quality requirements are met.

Color   Let's look at quality from the customer's perspective. When you think of particular food items, don't you think of certain colors? You have learned that food can change color during cooking. Some changes are desirable (for example, searing of steaks and browning of cookies). However, other color changes are not desirable. Olive green or brown colors in "fresh" green vegetables are an obvious example. Manufacturers may add coloring agents to products to enhance food colors. Bakers may add an egg-colored tint to baked goods to give them a rich egg color.

Texture   Texture also relates to the quality of the product. Do you like soft crackers, stringy vegetables, gritty butter, soggy french fries, or tough meat? Probably not, and neither will your customers.

Flavor   Flavor is another consideration and it may be the most important one. As with other quality determinants, a perception of what constitutes a "good" flavor may vary between individuals. Flavor is actually the total impression received from the taste, smell, texture, and touch of food items.

There are really only four taste sensations: sour, salty, bitter, and sweet. In order for a product to have "taste," food must first be dissolved in a liquid. The liquid may be in the food itself or in the saliva in a person's mouth. This solution of food and liquid stimulates our taste buds.

As a manager, you must be concerned about the quality of food prepared in your food service operation. The quality must be built into the product at the time the recipe is standardized. The marketing concern which views the finished products from the customer's perspective is an important measure of whether the recipe and the finished product will or will not meet the property's quality requirements.

Control During Food Production

The primary concerns of managers during the time of food production are (1) to make quality food ingredients available for food production, and (2) to develop procedures that will ensure the property's quality requirements are met. However, there are other basic management concerns that must be addressed at times of food production. These include the following:[2]

- Consistently require that all standard cost control tools (standard recipes, standard portion sizes, etc.) be used.

- Ensure through proper supervision that only the amount of food actually needed for production is issued.

- Train personnel to constantly comply with required food production procedures.

- Minimize wasted food.

- Monitor and control employee eating and drinking practices.

- Make sure that items taken out of storage which are not used in production are put back in secure storage areas.

- Inspect and approve items to be discarded because they spoiled in storage or weren't properly prepared.

- Match production records with sales records to assess which products generated income dollars.

- Study and resolve bottlenecks that may arise during production.

- Make sure that weighing and measuring tools are available and always used.

- Carefully study systems for managing equipment, layout and design, and energy usage. Implement any procedures that can reduce costs without sacrificing quality standards.

- Evaluate the effectiveness of communication and coordination activities between different work sections and departments.

- Maintain production records and use them for revising quantities of items to be produced in the future. This can cut down on the amount of leftover food.

- Make sure that labor-saving convenience foods or equipment items are, in fact, reducing labor costs.

- Recruit, train, and use personnel who are genuinely concerned about preparing and offering high-quality products that meet the property's standards. Management concerns about "good" food will enhance quality control.

We have not provided details about basic food preparation procedures in this chapter because entire books are devoted to this topic. However, you should understand that it does little good to design quality standards into other phases of the food service operation without following through to the point of actual food production. As an integral part of the supervisory task, it is important to ensure that standard recipes are consistently followed. When this is done, you can be confident that the same procedures will be used even if food items are prepared by employees without extensive culinary backgrounds.

NOTES

1. John W. Stokes, *How to Manage a Restaurant or Institutional Foodservice*, 3rd ed. (Dubuque, Iowa: Brown, 1977), p. 238.

2. This section is adapted from Jack D. Ninemeier, *Planning and Control for Food and Beverage Operations* (East Lansing, Mich.: Educational Institute of the American Hotel & Motel Association, 1982), pp. 104-105.

15

Beverage Service Procedures

Management Challenges

As a result of studying this chapter you will:

1. understand the importance of aggressive beverage sales in the attainment of financial goals of commercial food service operations.

2. learn basic background information about beverages.

3. understand basic procedures of purchasing, receiving, storing, issuing, producing, and serving alcoholic beverages.

4. understand many of the specific activities for which the bartender is responsible.

5. be able to apply basic sales income control procedures to minimize theft by employees at time of beverage production and service.

6. know how to develop and use a shopper's service to monitor bartenders.

7. be able to develop sales and service programs to increase the sale of these products.

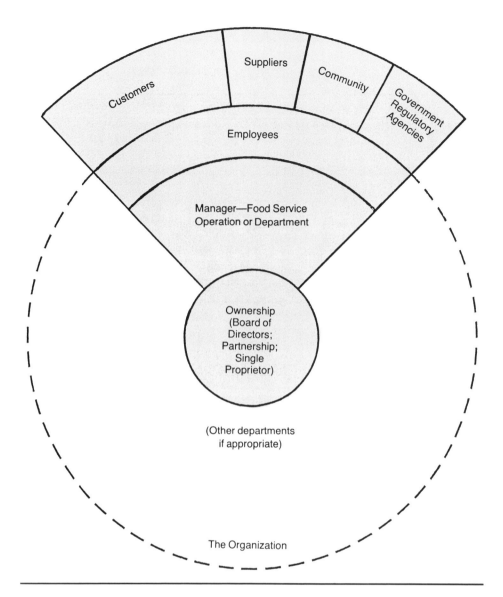

Suppliers

Customers

Community

Government Regulatory Agencies

Employees

Manager—Food Service
Operation or Department

Ownership
(Board of
Directors;
Partnership;
Single
Proprietor)

(Other departments
if appropriate)

The Organization

Focus on the
Food Service Publics

Chapter 15 focuses attention on the management of alcoholic beverages in the commercial food service operation. Properly used, beverages can complement the dining occasion of guests. Since the financial structure of the food service program is affected by beverage sale and control, the chapter looks at the relationship between the owner, food service manager, and employees. Also, the community in which the food and beverage operation is located has a concern that alcoholic beverages are properly used. There are local, state, and federal regulations applying to the sale of beverage products that affect both the operation and its suppliers.

In this chapter (as in the hospitality industry generally), the term "beverage" refers to drinks containing alcohol. When this definition is used, common beverages often served with food—such as coffee, tea, milk, soft drinks—are frequently classified as "food" for management, control, and other purposes.

References to beverage services have been made throughout this book to illustrate how planning and management principles that specifically apply to food services can be adapted to beverage operations. This chapter will focus on beverage services—primarily operations working with food services in hotels and restaurant properties. Remember that much of what is said about commercial properties will apply to institutional operations as well. For example, some hospitals provide wine and liquor service at special receptions and other functions given for medical staff and boards of directors. Some hospitals also provide wine service with their meals as a treat for new parents after a child is born.

Two special concerns should be noted as you study beverage operations. First, beverages are items that are prone to theft. Remember that beverage theft occurs not only when entire bottles are removed from facilities, but when a lack of proper beverage controls provides opportunities for employees with drinking problems to nurture their habits while on the job. Second, there is an opportunity to significantly increase sales and generate large contribution margins when beverages are aggressively marketed.

Beverages must be controlled. If they aren't, theft is likely. Beverage operations are an integral aspect of the entire food and beverage program in many restaurants and hotels. Before we examine beverage service in depth, one more point must be made: it is more difficult to control sales income generated by beverages than it is for food. Consider the complexity of a bar where the bartender may be responsible for taking orders, preparing drinks, collecting income, ringing up sales, and even ordering beverages, stocking production areas, and performing other tasks which would be separated among several employees in a food service operation. In studying procedures for effectively managing beverage service, these special concerns about product and income theft must be considered in addition to maximization of revenues from the sales.

This is a difficult job. There are, however, basic priniciples of beverage control that, when combined with food service management principles, can give your management staff a competitive edge over colleagues in other operations that do not have command of these skills.

Background on Beverages

The history of wine dates back more than 10,000 years.[1] The Bible, of course, mentions wine frequently throughout the Old and New Testaments. References are made to wine production and consumption in Mesopotamia and Asia (6,000 B.C.), Egypt (3,000 B.C.), Greece (2,000 B.C.) and throughout Europe and North Africa at least 2,000 years ago.

Beer is a liquor fermented from cereals and malt that is flavored with hops. Beer dates back as far in history as wine.

The process of distilling (obtaining alcoholic beverages from the distillation of alcohol-containing liquids) dates back at least to ancient Greece. In Scotland and Ireland, whiskey already was being produced by the middle ages. Cognac brandy was available in England by the late 1600s, and the distillation process has been known in America since the time of the early settlers. By the 1800s, procedures for distillation had improved so that it was possible to develop a much clearer and purer spirit than was possible before that time.

It appears that, throughout the ages, alcoholic beverages have been made from whatever products were most abundant. If it was the grape, wine resulted. If it was grain—as found in Scotland—whiskey was made. Beer has been made from rice in Japan and from barley in Europe and North and South America. Figure 15.1 illustrates the wide variety of alcoholic beverages available.

A Closer Look at Wine, Beer, and Spirits

Wine   Wine is a beverage that is fermented from grapes or other fruits and plants. Grapes are by far the most popular base and our discussion focuses exclusively on wine as a grape product. There are four general types of wine: (a) appetizer—before dinner and with appetizers, (b) table wine—red or white wine consumed with foods during a meal, (c) dessert wine—served after dinner, with sweets, or any time that sweet dishes are served, (d) sparkling—champagne and related wines which can be served at any time.

The quality of the wine relates to the grape that is used, general environmental conditions, soil, and the skill of the wine maker. The quality of the grape is the single most important factor. After grapes are harvested, they are crushed. The color of the wine depends partly on how the grapes are handled and partly on their color. Color is extracted from the skin—not the juice. That is, a red grape can have clear juice. White wine, therefore, can be made from white or red grapes. The difference is that red grape skins are carefully kept out of the juice being fermented for white wine. Red wine can only be made from grapes with red skins and fermentation is done "in the skins."

Fermentation is a very complex series of reactions. Essentially, it involves the interjection of yeast into the grape juice, causing a reaction with sugar in the juice. The result is, in part, alcohol.

The alcoholic content of most wines ranges from 11 to 13%. If there is not sufficient sugar content in the grape mixture being fermented, it is sometimes necessary to add sugar to the grape mixture. The alcoholic content of wine is limited because once a certain point is reached, the concentration of alcohol will be high enough to kill the yeast. When this occurs, fermentation ceases. If there is any sugar remaining that has not been converted to alcohol and other by-products, the wine will be naturally sweet.

Yeasts do not cause fermentation, but release enzymes that make the reaction possible. Yeast grows best at specific temperatures, and

Figure 15.1 Classification of Alcoholic Beverages

I. Fermented

  A. Grapes

   1. Natural
   2. Sparkling
   3. Fortified
   4. Aromatized

  B. Other Fruits

  C. Grain

   1. Beer
   2. Ale
   3. Stout
   4. Porter
   5. Saki

  D. Miscellaneous

   1. Pulque
   2. Kava

II. Fermented and Distilled

  A. Grain

   1. Whiskey, also Whisky

    a. Rye
    b. Bourbon
    c. Blend
    d. Irish
    e. Scotch
    f. Canadian

   2. Vodka

  B. Sugar cane and molasses (rum)

  C. Tequila

  D. Fruit brandy

   1. Grape

    a. Cognac
    b. Armagnac
    c. California brandy
    e. Spanish brandy
    f. Greek brandy
    g. German brandy

   2. Apple

    a. Calvados
    b. Applejack

   3. Cherry

    a. Kirsch
    b. Silbowitz

   4. Plum

   5. Apricot

III. Compounded Spirits

  A. Gin

  B. Liqueurs or cordials

Source: Donald A. Bell, The Spirits of Hospitality, *(East Lansing, Mich.: The Educational Institute of the American Hotel & Motel Association, 1976), pp. 4-5.*

these must be maintained as fermentation takes place. Wine generally is aged before being sold so that changes in flavor and bouquet, which are caused by slow oxidation, can develop. There is disagreement over whether there are differences between products aged in wooden barrels and those aged in glass bottles.

Beer

Yeast is also important in the production of liquors and beer, again because it gives off enzymes which react with sugar to yield alcohol. When grains are used—such as in liquors and beer—starches that are present must first be converted to sugar so that the enzyme reaction can occur. The quality of finished beer products is determined by:

1. **Water.** Finished beer contains 85%—or more—water.

2. **Barley malt.** Malt is germinated barley. By controlling the treatment of the malt, the brewer can control the type of beer being produced.

3. **Hops.** Hops are plants that are specially grown for brewing.

4. **Additional ingredients.** Corn and rice are the most commonly used.

5. **Yeast.** Special strains of yeast are used for the fermentation process.

6. **Sugar.** Sugar used in brewing is manufactured from specially treated cane sugar.

The brewing process requires that malt and other grains be crushed and mixed with water. After several other procedures are completed, the hops and sugars (if desired) are added and the mixture is boiled. When this step is completed, the fermentation process begins and takes from eight to eleven days. After fermentation, the beer is aged and clarified. One of the last procedures that must be done before the beer is packaged in kegs, bottles, or cans involves pasteurization—the heating process that kills any yeast which remains in the beer.

Spirits

The procedures used to make distilled spirits are similar to those used for making beer. First, the grain must be mashed with water and cooked. After other treatments, yeast is added to the product (called mash). The resulting product is placed in special equipment to be distilled. Following this process, the product is diluted with water, aged, and diluted again to the desired proof before being bottled. The procedures just described are greatly simplified, and actual techniques for producing distilled spirits vary depending on the product being manufactured.

The procedures just outlined for manufacturing wines, malt beverages, and spirits are quite involved. Fortunately, detailed information is not necessary to effectively manage day-to-day operations in the beverage department. Nonetheless, some background is helpful in understanding quality factors for alcoholic beverages. For example, the quality of beers and wines can be affected by the type and length of storage. Exposure to air and sunlight can be detrimental. Concerns over storage and handling refer more often to wines and beers than to distilled spirits. As with any product, concern for the product at each step of the production/service cycle is always in order.

Beverage Management Cycle

Effective management of the beverage operation begins with planning. Remember that developing an operating budget requires that an estimate of income, profit, and expenses be developed separately for food and beverage operations. Concerns about the beverage operation must carry into the pricing structure, the standard recipes, portion sizes, and costs. Managers must plan for the control systems that are used to protect property from product or income abuse and must know how to correct deviations from standard quality that have obvious marketing implications. Management systems are needed to protect the operation and the customer from dishonest employees. Protecting the customer is both an ethical and a practical concern. The customer normally will, with justification, blame the whole operation—not the dishonest employee—if problems of any type detract from the enjoyment of the visit to the property.

After extensive planning, it does little good to develop and implement procedures to achieve objectives unless management officials work—through constant supervision and reevaluation of standard procedures—to ensure that the beverage operation is doing what is it supposed to do.

Let's look at each of the management subsystems of the beverage production/service cycle. We will point out concerns especially applicable to management of beverage products.

Purchasing   In many states, laws and other restrictions regulate the purchase of alcoholic products. For example, some states operate "state stores" from which all alcoholic products must be purchased. Definite requirements about alcoholic beverage licenses—required in order for these products to be purchased for resale—must be met. Prices for many beverage products may be set, making negotiating and shopping for better values pointless. Since many alcoholic beverages are purchased by brand name and only one wholesaler in an area may carry this product, there may be less of a need for a property to develop purchase specifications. If a particular brand of product is desired, it may have to be purchased from a specific supplier.

Still, there are frequent opportunities to save money in purchasing. For example, some suppliers may discount prices as increasing quantities of products are purchased. How do you tell when it is worth the investment in adding to the stock in order to reduce purchase unit prices? How do you determine the types of house liquor—the brand of beverage product served when no special brand is requested—that should be purchased? These and related purchase decisions will depend on the goals of the individual property. There are a number of concerns which purchasers may consider when selecting brands.[2]

1. Supplier services.

2. Supplier discounts, if any.

3. Reciprocity between supplier and purchaser.

4. "Opportunity" buys.

5. Product availability.

6. Type (reputation) of establishment.

7. Price structure of operation.

8. Owner's preference.

9. Proof of liquor. ("Proof" is the alcoholic content of the liquor. It refers to twice the percentage of alcohol in the product. For example, a 100 proof whiskey is 50% alcohol by volume. Normally the rest of the product is water—except for a tiny amount of other ingredients and impurities.)

10. Result of taste tests.

11. Brands used by competing operations.

12. Suggestions made by competent individuals.

13. Supplier payment plans, where laws permit options.

14. Reputation of label.

15. Clientele preference.

16. Friendships with suppliers.

There are clearly many factors that can be considered. Attitudes of beverage managers can range from: "Don't use anything you wouldn't be proud to display on the back bar" to "Use the least expensive. Let the customer pay extra for a premium brand." In practice, a middle-range brand—neither the least nor the most expensive—is generally used for house liquor. Quality and value are major factors in determing house brands.[3]

The selection of call brands—specific brands of beverages that are named by the customer when an order is placed—is also a marketing decision. Sometimes, beverage operations make the mistake of trying to please everyone. They try to offer a wide variety of liquors, each of which must be ordered, stored, issued, and controlled. Beverage operations would be more efficient if they had a selection of liquors available to meet most needs of the regular customers instead of trying to satisfy everyone's particular tastes. Not everyone can be pleased all the time. If one call brand is not available, there usually is a reasonable substitute that can be offered. Of course, if one type of liquor is ordered by a regular customer, consideration should be given to adding it to the list of products that are routinely purchased.

When making purchase decisions, a manager should be aware of deals that are offered by suppliers. Examples include per bottle or case discounts when specified volumes are purchased. These discounts can effectively reduce beverage costs. However, the manager must consider: (a) How much cash should be tied up in inventory? (b) Will cash flow be affected negatively? (c) Will the greater risk of theft and pilferage warrant the purchase? (d) If deals are for brands not normally carried by the property, will customers accept the change? (e) Can bartenders and beverage service personnel "keep up" with frequently changing brands purchased to take advantage of deals? (f) In areas where property taxes must be paid on items in storage, will increased inventory taxes eliminate much of the savings from the deal?

The minimum/maximum ordering system discussed in Chapter 12 is applicable to the purchase of beverage products. While it is difficult to generalize about the quantity of beverage products that should be kept on hand, remember that inventory turnover is faster for food products than for beverage products. This is because food products generally are more perishable than are beverage items. For example, a property's food inventory may turn over 26 times per year—the value of goods on hand equals the approximate amount of products used during a two-week period. By contrast, a property's beverage inventory may turn over only 12 times per year—the amount of beverage inventory on hand approximately equals the cost of products purchased for one month's use.

Receiving   In addition to the principles of receiving noted in Chapter 12, several common principles apply to beverages:

1.   Since beverage products are prone to theft, check that all incoming products noted on the delivery invoice (for which payment will be requested by the supplier) were, in fact, received. Be sure there are no shortages. Cases should be opened and bottles should be checked. Cases that are wet or appear to have been damp must be opened to ensure there was no breakage. Some properties weigh incoming cases of liquor to confirm that all bottles are present.

2.   After products are received, they should be moved immediately to secure storage areas. The longer products remain in unsecure receiving areas, the greater the chance of theft.

3. Purchasing and receiving tasks should be separate for beverage products—unless both tasks are assumed by the owner/ manager in a small operation. Even when these tasks are separate, the possibility of collusion between purchasing and receiving staff—ever present in the purchase of food products— must be guarded against.

Storing

Each of the special concerns about storage noted in Chapter 13 should be re-emphasized. Prevention of unauthorized physical access, the need to keep effective records, and concern for sanitation in storage are equally important.

In addition to a central beverage storage area, many beverage production units (bars) also have back-bar storage. These areas should be locked when the facility is not open. Otherwise, cleaning staff and other personnel will have access to these products. Generally, quantities of beverages in behind-bar or other noncentral storage areas should be minimal since security controls are less effective in these areas. The main concern is to establish correct bar "pars"—the number of bottles that should be on hand behind the bar.

When possible, wines, beer, and other refrigerated beverages should be stored away from refrigerated food items. If this is not possible, locked storage areas should be provided.

Each of the recordkeeping procedures that keep track of on-hand products are necessary. Calculations of costs for goods sold must be consistent and follow recognized accounting practices. A close monitoring of the beverage inventory is critical for effective control. Normally, all alcoholic beverages can be kept under perpetual inventory; quantities should be verified by physical count at least monthly.

Issuing

Beverages should be issued on a bottle-for-bottle basis to replenish bar pars. Normally, beverage products should be issued once each shift—preferably at the end. If there are frequent "run outs" of beverages behind the bar, this suggests the need to re-examine the established bar levels.

As beverages are issued, bottles should be marked in order to:

1. Identify a bottle as coming from the property's central storage, which reduces the chance of bartenders bringing in and selling from their own bottles.

2. Indicate the date of issue. Management personnel might question why a bottle of fast selling liquor is at the bar for a long time period.

3. Identify to which bar, when a property has several, a bottle has been issued.

Managers also may wish to put the purchase price directly on the bottle label. When done inconspicuously, this can be a definite aid in completing issue requisitions for beverage products (see Figure 13.6).

When bottles of liquor are to be used for tableside flaming of food or when bottles of wine are to be served at the table, this labeling practice may be impractical.

Empty liquor bottles should be turned in as part of the issuing process. These bottles then must be broken or disposed of in compliance with local or state ordinances.

Managers sometimes believe that the key to the locked beverage storage area should be kept at the bar. They reason that if a bottle runs out during a busy shift, the bartender can quickly retrieve another. This practice, however, lessens management's control over issuing. To avoid this, inventory par levels behind the bar should be checked. Control is more effective if management staff retrieves the bottles as they are emptied.

Managers sometimes are concerned that no additional liquor can be issued if no one who is working has a key to the central beverage area. If this is the case, a storeroom key should be behind the bar. The key can be sealed in an envelope. Lines should be drawn in ink across the envelope flap, which is then taped shut. The bartender still can get into the storeroom by tearing open the envelope, but management staff will be able to tell that this occurred. The amount of liquor in the storage area then should be verified with the amount noted on perpetual inventory records.

Producing

Production procedures for beverages must ensure that quality is maintained and that drink costs are reasonable. Both of these objectives can be achieved by complying with standards established for the beverage operation. For example, there should be standard recipes available for drinks that are frequently prepared. As noted earlier, this does not mean that the bartender must refer to each recipe before making a drink. Rather, this means that the procedures and quantities dictated by the standard recipe should be followed when drinks are prepared. Beverage production personnel must be trained so they will know exactly what their job involves and how to perform it properly. On-the-job training programs and using bar backs (assistant bartenders who perform back-up tasks while learning bartending procedures) are two training methods. After bartenders are trained, they must be well supervised to ensure that procedures are followed.

Effective procedures for beverage production should be developed to best fit the needs of the specific operation. Examples of these procedures involve policies regarding preparation of beverage mixes, the handling of check and charge transactions, the ring-up of cash sales, preparation of garnishes, and availability of bar supplies.

Beverage management personnel must closely analyze beverage production during busy periods. Then they can assess where, if any, production bottlenecks exist. Managers should talk with bartenders and beverage service personnel so they can work together to resolve production problems. As alternatives are considered, take time to test these options to discover how they might affect beverage quality and control of sales income. Such a study often reveals other areas where unproductive motions waste time that otherwise could be spent in beverage production and/or control tasks.

Special security concerns are important during beverage production:

1. Bartenders should be responsible for maintaining beverage par levels during the shift. At the beginning of the shift, the bartender should check that the required number of bottles of each alcoholic beverage is available in behind-bar inventory. With this check completed in the presence of a management official, the bartender becomes responsible for inventory. At the end of the shift the proper number of bottles (full and empty) should be available. The issuing process will then be used to replenish supplies to the required par level.

2. Bartenders should not be permitted to drink or accept drinks from customers while working. They also should not give drinks to other employees.

3. All returned drinks should be shown to management before they are discarded.

4. Shot glasses, jiggers, proper glassware, and other portion control devices should be used at all times.

5. Records of sales information should not be made or kept by bartenders. This information is the responsibility of management staff.

6. Policies on employee visiting or drinking at the bar before or after work should be strictly enforced.

7. A system to account for all beverages sold at the bar versus those dispensed for service in the lounge or restaurant should be established and used consistently.

8. Only management staff should determine drink selling prices.

9. Shoppers—i.e., people hired to pose as customers and evaluate the performance and honesty of bartenders—should be used routinely and randomly.

10. All procedures detailing the use of the cash register should be followed consistently.

11. Policies covering "drinks on the house" should be strictly followed.

Service and Serving

The distinction made in Chapter 11 between service (getting products from production staff to service staff) and serving (moving products from service staff to customers) applies to the beverage operation. Some drinks are prepared and served by one staff member—the bartender.

Other drinks are prepared by the bartender and given to the service staff who give the drinks to the lounge and restaurant guests.

Let's look first at the bartender preparing and serving drinks at the bar, which involves income control as well as other management concerns. First of all, bartenders should be provided with guest checks. When a customer at the bar orders a drink, it can be recorded on a guest check. After the drink is served, the guest check is placed face down in front of the guest. When the guest pays, the money and the guest checks are taken to the cash register. Guest checks can become cumbersome when a large number of customers must be served at the bar in a short period of time. While some operations use the guest check system at all times, others do not. Rather, they use shoppers to monitor bartender performance.

When drink orders are taken by food servers in the restaurant, orders should be written on a guest check. (In some properties, special beverage servers whose only responsibility is to take orders and serve drinks in the restaurant may also be used.) When a precheck register is used, sales information should be entered into the precheck register. In some operations, precheck registers are "tied" to remote printers. With this system, the order is automatically transferred to a printer that is located in the bar area. (Remote printers can also be used to transfer orders for food by the food server from the precheck register to production personnel in the kitchen.) This method is especially appropriate in large and busy operations with bars where a bartender prepares drinks for the service staff who take them to customers in the lounge or restaurant.

Whether the drink order is physically or electronically transmitted to the bar, the beverage must be picked up by the server. Many operations use a type of "cancellation" system in which the bartender draws a line, punches a hole in the ticket, or makes a mark to confirm that drinks recorded on the guest check have, in fact, been served. This eliminates the possibility for a dishonest server to return for a second round of drinks without having entered the information on the guest check. When beverages are served in the restaurant area, usually no money changes hands. Some cash registers in bars have an "accounts receivable" function on the register. With this, the guest check from the food server is inserted into the machine and the sale is rung up on an accounts receivable key. A separate "clerk" key often is used for each food server so that drink sales can be tracked by server.

When drinks are ordered by service personnel working in the lounge area, the same basic procedures can be used. However, money coming through the lounge area can be handled by a server banking system or a cashier (bartender) banking system. For example, some beverage servers actually pay for drinks when they pick them up from the bartender. From the bartender's perspective then, this is a cash sale. He/she will take the guest check and the money and ring it up on the register just as if a customer had purchased a drink. When the beverage server provides the drink to the guest and collects money for the sale, the money received replenishes the beverage server's bank. Alternatively, the beverage server may collect money from the guests and take it and the guest checks to the bartender to be rung up. In either event, a guest check con-

Figure 15.2 Job Description: Bartender

A. Basic Responsibilities
1. prepare drinks for food and beverage service personnel at service bar
2. prepare and serve drinks to patrons at public bars
3. ensure that all sales income control procedures including use of cash register are consistently followed
4. prepare basic drink mixes
5. stock bar
6. perform necessary sanitation and clean-up duties

B. Specific Duties:
1. prepare necessary drink garnishes
2. stock bottle drinks in refrigerator
3. ensure that opening and closing bar pars are available
4. prepare drinks according to standard recipe procedures
5. operate cash register
6. complete guest checks (drinks served at public bar) and audit guest checks (drinks prepared for service staff)
7. wash glassware
8. maintain cleanliness of behind-bar, counters and above other floor areas
9. complete required sections of beverage issue requisition form
10. comply with cash bank counting and protection procedures
11. notify supervisor of any necessary repair/maintenance
12. clean draft beer dispensing equipment according to required procedures
13. perform other tasks as required by head bartender

C. Supervises
1. bar backs (assistant bartenders)

D. Supervised by:
1. head bartender

E. Equipment used:
1. automated beverage dispensing equipment
2. electronic cash register
3. draft beer dispenser
4. blender and other beverage preparation equipment

F. Other:
1. must be tactful and courteous when dealing with the public
2. must be able to work under busy (rushed) conditions and must be able to effectively interact with food and beverage servers

trol system must be used and there must be an accounting of all guest checks. The total sales from guest checks represents the amount of beverage income which should be collected and rung into the cash register or otherwise collected from beverage servers.

Figure 15.3 Receipt of Cash Bank

By signing on the last unsigned line below, I acknowledge receipt of cash in the amount of $ ____ to be used as a cash register bank. The total amount is due and payable before checking out at the end of the shift.

Name	Date of Shift	Returned (Signature of Manager on Duty)

Focus of Bartender

The bartender is unique within the food and beverage operation. What other position is responsible for taking and preparing orders for guests, determining the amount of money that should be collected from guests, collecting sales income, and ringing up money that is collected into the cash register? Frequently, there is no practical way to separate all of these tasks, though some properties do hire cashiers who are responsible for collecting income and ringing up sales applicable to drinks prepared by the bartender. While many properties find this labor cost difficult to justify, a cashier might well be worthwhile in large volume beverage operations.

Figure 15.2 indicates some of the tasks performed by a bartender. While the job description must be modified to fit the needs of the specific operation, it provides an illustration of the type of work that a person in this position must perform. Bartenders must serve guests at the bar and at their tables when service personnel are absent. A bartender may also be responsible for serving food, depending upon the property. This practice generally is not practical because the bartender should not leave the bar in order to place or pick up food orders.

When the bartender begins work, many tasks must be done. For example, garnishes must be readied and mixes for drinks such as Bloody Marys and specialty drinks must be prepared. Disposable supplies must be stocked and inventories for liquor, wine, and beer must be checked.

The bartender must be given a cash bank. In many properties, a form similar to Figure 15.3 must be completed. When this is done, the bartender certifies that the cash bank has been received and that he/she is responsible for the amount of cash in the bank until it is returned at the end of the shift. The manager, in the presence of the bartender, might ring out the register at the beginning of shift to assure the bartender that there are no sale ring ups on the register for which he/she will be responsible.

Figure 15.4 Guest Check Number Log

Date	Shift	Type Ticket		Server Name	Guest Check No.		Signature
		Food	Bev		Start	End	

As already noted, bartenders may have to receive guest checks. If so, the guest check number log (see Figure 15.4) might need to be signed.

There are certain procedures that are performed at the end of each shift. In addition to completing the obvious cleaning duties, the bartender must account for all beverage guest checks which have been assigned to him/her. The amount of money in the cash register must be verified with tallies of guest checks, precheck register totals, and a review/verification of sales rung for each food and beverge server. Details of bartender closing procedures are beyond the scope of this chapter. You should be aware, however, that managers must have at least a double check, if not a triple check, on the amount of beverage income that should be collected and rung up on the machine. Use of precheck registers and guest checks along with sales journal tapes located in the cash register provides information to verify the amount of sales income for which the bartender is responsible. Issuing procedures are also an important part of the bartender's closing procedures. Management should ensure that the amount of liquor the bar—either full or empty bottles—equals what was available at the beginning of the bartender's shift.

Supervision of the bartender is difficult, especially when the property is busy. Nevertheless, managers must take at least some time to observe what the bartender is doing. The manager can ask the bartender questions, such as: "Why is the cash register drawer open?" "Why are you (the bartender) not using a shot glass/jigger?" "What are you (the bartender) drinking?" Managers should routinely walk behind the bar and question everything that is seen. Common thefts include working from the tip jar instead of the register and not ringing up drinks that are served. When "no rings" occur, the bartender must keep track of the number of "no sale" ring-ups, which represent money deposited in the cash drawer but not accounted on the register. Swizzle sticks kept in a separate glass, small piles of marischino cherries, bent matches, a slip of paper with several tears, etc., are common methods that bartenders use to keep track of unrecorded drinks which represent cash they can collect at the end of the shift. Managers should occasionally go behind the bar, "x" the machine (this term refers to reading the amount of sale that is rung on the machine without returning the tally to a zero balance), and replace the cash drawer out of which the bartender is working with a new cash drawer. The amount of money in the drawer should equal the original cash balance plus the amount of sales that have been rung on the machine since the beginning of the shift. More money than this may represent income that was deposited because of "no rings."

Automated beverage equipment has made supervision of the bartender less difficult. Some automated systems contain metering devices that count the number of drinks that has been rung through the meter head. More sophisticated and computerized systems are available which—at the push of a button—make the drink, add any mixture, print tickets, and ring up sales income information on sales journal tapes. Still, despite automated beverage systems, there are many ways that a creative bartender can "beat the house." While supervising the bartender, the manager must ensure that basic sales income control procedures are in effect and used.

Sales Income Control Procedures

We have consistently pointed out the need to use income control procedures which make it difficult for one person working alone to steal from the operation.

Figure 15.5 Cash Register Operating Procedures

Each of the following register operating procedures should be consistently followed.

1. The cash drawer is to be closed when not in use.

2. Each ticket must be rung up separately. At no time should two or more tickets be totaled in the bartender's head and run as a total. Each ticket will be closely checked to ensure that the printed ring-up agrees with the total charge due from the guest.

3. At no time is the bartender's tip jar to be near the cash register. A place for keeping tips should be located away from the cash register. This measure will eliminate the possibility of the bartender making change from the tip jar, and will prevent removal of money from the register into the tip jar.

4. Bills over $20 should be placed under the currency tray. Bills collected from the customer should remain on the register shelf until the transaction is acceptable to the guest. When making change, count from the amount of the sale up to the amount of money given by the customer. Call the manager on duty if there are any questions regarding cash collection or change making.

5. Only the bartender or cashier should have access to the register. No employee other than the one with responsibility should use, enter, or otherwise have any contact with the cash register for any reason whatsoever. Management may, of course, do spot audits of tapes and currency as necessary.

6. The appropriate department key must be depressed to record the type of transaction represented by the guest check being rung up. All procedures in register ring-up should be designed to provide sales information on a department basis for greater accuracy in financial accounting.

7. Separate cash drawers (or separate cash registers) should be used by each person having access to the cash register.

8. The register user should not be able to read or total the machine. Information regarding sales should not be made known to the cashier/bartender.

9. Cashiers/bartenders should begin each shift with a new bank.

10. Each register user should have a separate key to the register. A separate identification number should be used to identify transactions on cash register tapes.

11. Each sale must be rung up in proper sequence, in proper amount, and without "bunching" or totaling tickets. Each ticket or transaction must be rung separately.

12. Each register user should have a written copy of procedures for use of the cash register.

13. Register users, when practical, should call out the price of items being run on the register.

14. The cash drawer should only be opened by depressing the sales price or "no sale" key. It should not be possible to enter the machine by use of a lever or other mechanical device, except in case of power outage.

15. Detail tapes should be replaced *before* they run out (there is generally a colored strip or other marking which becomes noticeable as the tape supply diminishes).

16. Registers should be empty, unlocked, and left open when not in use (or drawers should be removed) to prevent damage to machine during theft attempts.

17. Void overrings. Other problems should be reported to management immediately after they occur.

18. Surprise cash register audits, including counting money in the drawer(s), should be made randomly.

19. Management should watch the cash register and its operation closely as part of its ongoing supervisory responsibilities.

20. Detail tapes should be studied on a random basis to uncover possible fraud.

21. Cashiers are not allowed to accept postdated checks or IOUs in payment or as collateral for loans.

22. Only a minimum number of supervisory personnel should have access to cash register keys.

23. Register banks should be counted and exchanged at each change in cashiers; cash register tapes are read or totaled and cleared at this time.

24. All checks accepted from employees are immediately marked "FOR DEPOSIT ONLY."

25. Forms should be available to record, by shift, sales from each register (point-of-sale) for food and beverage service for the entire day (or other period).

Source: Jack D. Ninemeier, Food and Beverage Security: A Systems Manual for Restaurants, Hotels and Clubs *(Boston: CBI, 1982) pp. 224-225.*

You should be aware of common theft methods that bartenders and beverage servers can use and precautions that can be taken to protect against such thefts.[4] Common bartender thefts include the following:

1. Violating procedures used in cash register operation, including bunching sales, no rings and working out of the tip jar. **Precaution**—Specific register operating procedures should be developed. The tip jar should not be near the register. Supervision is necessary to ensure that all required procedures are followed consistently. See Figure 15.5 for a brief list of standard

procedures that the bartender should use when operating the cash register.

2. Underpouring or diluting drinks and pocketing cash from the sale of the "extra drink." If drinks are underpoured by one quarter ounce, for example, sales of every fifth drink can be pocketed by the bartender without affecting the established beverage cost percentage. **Precaution**—Managers should require that a shot glass or jigger be used when preparing all drinks. Prepouring drinks should not be permitted.

3. Bringing in personal bottles of liquor, preparing drinks from these bottles, and keeping the money. **Precaution**—Mark bottles and use a visual inspection program to eliminate this practice. The stamp of the bottle should be secured so that employees cannot misuse the bottles.

4. Accumulating drink sales from liquor served from the entire bottle, recording a "bottle sale" (usually at a lower sales price than the drinks) and pocketing the difference. **Precaution**—Use shoppers, implement effective cash register operating controls, supervise employees closely, and establish a rule that all drinks served be tallied on guest checks to help control this type of theft.

5. Selling drinks for cash and recording drinks as spilled, returned, or complimentary. **Precaution**—No drinks should be served without charge except as approved by managers. Returned drinks should not be discarded without the manager's approval. Bartenders who spill excessively or display evidence of high pouring costs should be retrained and closely supervised.

6. Serving and ringing up a low quality brand but charging full price when a call brand is requested. The bartender pockets the extra cash resulting from the substitution. **Precaution**—All drink orders should be written on a guest check. The amount rung and printed on the guest check should equal the total charge on the check.

7. Bartender working in collusion with cocktail service so that drinks are served but income is not received. **Precaution**—Employees should be rotated. The manager should be aware of gossip about employee relationships. Control systems should be used to monitor beverage cost percentages.

8. Lowering sales income value written on the guest check and rung into the register (undercharging). **Precaution**—Routine audits of guest checks should be made to insure that pricing errors do not occur.

9. Trading liquor with the cook for food products. **Precaution**—All eating and drinking policies should be enforced. Managers should be aware of signs of employees eating and drinking such as plates and glasses from the restaurants or other items hidden in the work station.

10. Using stolen checks to replace cash. **Precaution**—No checks should be accepted without the manager's approval.

11. Using counterfeit guest checks to collect sales income. **Precaution**—The property should use unique, hard to duplicate guest checks.

12. Using old bottle stamps or other identification tags to mark personal bottles. **Precaution**—Properties should use unique, hard to duplicate bottle stamps. Identification tools and supplies should be kept in a secure place.

13. Using a personal jigger to aid in over/underpouring. **Precaution**—Managers should check the portion control tools that are used as part of their supervisory duties. Only portion tools provided by the property should be used.

14. Taking cash from cash drawer. **Precaution**—A basic sales income control system should be used to determine exactly how much money should be in the cash drawer. The bartender should be liable for all cash shortages, if this is allowed under local or state laws.

15. "Borrowing" from cash bank. **Precaution**—The amount of cash in the bank should be checked at the beginning and the end of the shift.

16. Giving away drinks to friends or to promote a bigger tip. **Precaution**—No complimentary drinks should be given without manager's approval. Guest checks must be in front of each guest at all times. Shoppers can be used to spot these and similar problems.

This is only an abbreviated list of the many ways that dishonest bartenders steal money and products from the property and customers. Effective control sytems must be implemented and managers must ensure that all procedures are followed consistently. There is no truth in the idea that managers can "tell" a good bartender from a bad bartender, or that honesty is obvious. Bartenders, as with all other personnel in the property, should be subjected to operating procedures that protect the staff from allegations of problems, the property from theft, and the customer from quality substitutions or errors that ultimately affect the guest's impressions about the property.

Beverage servers also can manipulate beverage products and/or money in order to steal from the property. Common types of theft include the following:

1. Receiving beverages from the bar without recording it on the sales check. **Precaution**—No beverages should be given to personnel without a copy of the guest check unless, in the case of a beverage server, cash is paid for drinks when they are picked up.

2. Collecting cash from the customer without a sales check and pocketing the cash. **Precaution**—Same as above.

3. Reusing paid checks or collecting cash from one customer with the sales check that has already been presented to another guest. **Precaution**—All sales checks given to the beverage server should be recorded by number and matched with duplicates. Servers must not take the beverage out of the preparation area without submitting a check.

4. Collecting cash and destroying sales check. **Precaution**—Same as above.

5. Under-adding checks or omitting items for friends or in order to influence the amount of the tip. **Precaution**—Guest checks should be audited to check arithmetic. Original and duplicate copies should be matched.

6. Providing high priced items to friends and recording them at a lower price. **Precaution**—Use and match duplicate checks to ensure that items picked up from the bar were, in fact, the items for which payment was received.

7. Collecting cash with counterfeit guest checks. **Precaution**—Sales checks should be unique to the property.

8. Collecting sales income from guests and alleging that a customer walked out without paying. **Precaution**—Close supervision of all customer areas will minimize walk outs. A record of walk outs should be kept for all beverage servers. Any server with more than an infrequent rate of walk outs should be retrained and closely supervised.

9. Collecting income, destroying the check, and arguing that the claim ticket was lost while turning in the allegedly correct amount. **Precaution**—Where legal, servers should be assesed and charged for lost checks. Records of lost checks should be kept and servers with more than an infrequent rate of lost checks should be retrained and closely supervised.

10. Collecting sales income for a check, deleting items because of alleged returns and pocketing the cash. **Precaution**—All returns should be reported to managers as they occur.

11. Serving guests, collecting sales income, deleting items (for example, a guest allegedly didn't have a drink) and pocketing the cash. **Precaution**—Original and duplicate copies of the check can be matched on a routine but random basis.

12. Eating food and drinking beverages. **Precaution**—All policies regarding employee eating and drinking should be enforced.

These examples of server theft are only a brief sample of ways that dishonest employees can steal from the property and/or guests. By now, you are beginning to realize that there are significant opportunities in a food and beverage operation for theft to occur. You, as a professionally trained and effective manager, must know these methods and be able to develop a control system to protect against them. If not, the property will probably not be able to attain its economic objectives. You may never know the number of customers who did not return because of the bad treatment they received due to dishonest acts of your employees.

Shopper Services for Bartender Control

Several of the methods to prevent theft which were noted earlier include the use of shopper services. A shopper's service involves hiring a person to pose as a guest in order to observe the beverage operation. Shopper services may be used primarily for detecting bartender theft, but the service also can be used to look at the entire operation with the aim of making improvements.

Recall that Figure 11.6 illustrates a form for collecting required information. Principles in using a shopper service include the following:[5]

1. The bartender should not know or recognize the shopper. The person chosen could either be a friend of the management staff or could represent a professional shopping service. Such services are available in larger metropolitan areas.

2. Bartenders should be told when hired that shoppers will routinely be used to assess effectiveness of the operation's sales income control and other systems.

3. Shoppers should meet with management staff before they visit the operation in order to get acquainted with all cash registers, drink preparation, sales income collection policies, and any other pertinent procedures and systems. If there are special problems, such as procedures used to collect income from appetizers served in the lounge or the way income is transferred from the beverage server to the bartender, these concerns can be highlighted to the shopper during the initial meeting.

4. New bartenders or persons that the managers have reason to suspect because of high beverage cost or negative attitudes should be shopped. All bartenders, however, should be checked as a routine part of the control system.

5. During the shopping review, the shopper-guest should order

a drink and carefully observe all procedures that are used to take the order, prepare, serve, and collect cash for the drink. Cash register operating procedures should also be viewed. The shopper can remain at the bar and casually observe the various transactions and interactions. Using this process, shoppers often catch problems with register ring up, free drinks to service or other personnel or guests, prepouring, etc.

6. During the shopper's visit, he/she can also visit the restrooms, look over other public areas, and react as a guest to the total experience.

7. At the conclusion of the visit, the shopper should report all findings to the manager.

During the shopper's visit, he/she probably will not witness bartender theft. The shopper, however, may observe signs of dishonesty, such as misuse of the cash register, pouring free drinks, suspicious conversations between the bartender staff members and guests which might suggest a potential problem. With this information, the manager can learn of a possible problem and take precautions to ensure that management control procedures effectively deal with the problem.

Developing Beverage Sales and Service Programs

The sale of alcoholic beverages can be of great economic value to food and beverage operations. Contribution margins are high from beverage sales. After the product's cost is subtracted from the income that is generated, there is significant income "left over" to contribute toward property profits. What can be done to increase sales of these products? Many techniques can be used; this section will focus on in-house merchandising programs.

Beverage pricing is a special concern when in-house merchandising programs are developed. Remember that beverages are one product that can be made as well at home as in the restaurant. Therefore, customers readily compare prices they pay in a retail grocery or liquor store with those prices being charged in a food and beverage operation. Even though the customer realizes that he/she is paying for atmosphere and ambience, that customer normally is not willing to place a significant monetary value on these things. In fact, many customers resent pricing structures that appear to take advantage of them. Therefore, marking up wine by a formula two times the cost of the wine plus $1 is unrealistic. A better approach would be to consider the actual cost of the wine plus other associated costs and then add a reasonable amount of profit.

To effectively sell beverages, the following points are important:

1. Service personnel should know exactly what products a restaurant has to sell.

2. Service staff should know something about all drinks that are served and should be able to make suggestions.

3. Food service staff should know what wines to suggest with various menu items.

4. When wine is sold, service personnel should know how to present, open, and serve the product. When you consider the price paid by the customer for wine, you'll see why many customers enjoy the "pomp and circumstance" associated with the serving of wine. Contrast this with an all-too-common practice of the bartender opening the wine at the bar or, worse yet, presenting screw-top bottles of wine to guests who are expecting a premium wine.

A well-rounded wine list is very important. Entire books have been written on the topic.[6] A good wine list should include dry and sweet wines, white and red wines, and champagne (sparkling wine) at low, medium, and high prices. These wines and special wines that complement the food items served by the property can go a long way toward meeting the needs of many customers.

There is much that can be done to merchandise wine. The wine list, for example, is an important marketing tool. Descriptions of the wine—even if it is only two or three words—can be of great help. Wines that are recommended with each menu item can be listed on the food menu.

Wine displays set up around the dining room, wine tasting stations (where customers can sample various wines at no cost), table tent cards, and menu riders may also help sell beverage products.

Many of these same techniques can be used for the in-house merchandising of other beverage products. Part of the "secret" of selling beverages is for them to be expertly prepared and attractively presented. Standard recipes and techniques used to ensure that products always taste the same are an important first step. Selection of attractive glassware and appropriate garnishes also helps in the suggestive selling of these products.

Some operations specialize in certain beverage products. They might have a reputation for preparing an exotic tropical drink, a flaming drink, or other product. If so, the manager should be sure that proper in-house merchandising is done so that all customers know about the availability of these special products.

Seasonal drinks are relatively easy to sell. Tom and Jerry drinks during the Christmas season, green beer during the week of St. Patrick's Day, and special fruit punch drinks during summer months are examples of seasonal drinks.

The manager also should provide menus for drinks, table tents, and other in-house devices to make the guests aware that special beverages are available. The service staff must then reinforce these messages. The manager can help motivate the staff by noting that as more beverages are sold, check averages increase and so do tips.

Importance of Glassware in the Beverage Operation

Glassware is an important ingredient in the operation's beverage program because it helps to convey the image, theme, and decor of the property. The customer's first impression of the drink being served is affected by the glassware. Appropriate glassware helps to merchandise beverage products. A glass can make a simple drink look good and can contribute immeasurably to the offering of exotic and specialty drinks.

Glassware must also be durable. Use of expensive, fine crystal may be appropriate in certain dining establishments, but since the glasses will be abused and frequently handled in the beverage operation, careful selection is important.

Normally, there should be a relationship between the price of the drink and the cost of the glass. As the selling price of the drink increases, the elegance of the glassware often becomes a factor in the customer's perceived value.

Basic procedures should be used to maintain glassware properly. Glasses frequently break or chip because they are washed improperly. Improper racks, hand washing, stacking of glassware, or contact with other objects can cause damage. Glassware also is affected by fast temperature changes. When a cold glass is put in hot dishwater or when ice is put into a hot glass, the sudden temperature changes can cause cracks.

Glasses should never be used to scoop ice because this contact with the ice can chip the glass and lead to potential safety problems for the customer. On the other hand, glasses used for hot drinks should be tempered with hot water before adding hot coffee or other liquid.

An adequate supply of glassware is important because it eliminates the need for service personnel to hurriedly clean soiled glasses—a haste that can lead to more chipping and breaking.

Some properties can increase sales of wines and other drinks by offering them by the pitcher, half pitcher, carafe, or other unit of measure besides the typical glass. Entire in-house merchandising campaigns about "pitchers of martinis," "yards of beer," or other drinks can be very successful if they are properly developed.

Contests between service staff also can help boost beverage sales. Rewards of free meals for a service staff member and his/her guest, a free bottle of wine, or other incentives can provide reasons for the service staff to emphasize beverage sales.

Some properties use a wine steward (called a sommelier) who is very knowledgeable about wines. He/she can suggest wines to discriminating customers that they will enjoy with their meals.

Suggestive selling techniques can be tools for increasing beverage sales. Suggestions about the guest ordering a second drink before dinner, wine to be served with the dinner, or an after dinner drink are possibilities. To do this effectively, service staff must be trained. Training is important from the staff's as well as the property's viewpoint. Pleasing the guests and increasing check averages, both of which can contribute to higher tips, are important reasons for the food service staff to be encouraged to increase beverage sales.

As a final thought, a concern emphasized throughout the book must be noted: always consider and try to meet the customer's wants in the type of products, service, and atmosphere the property provides. If you can find some special way to distinguish your product from that of the competition—or from the product the customer can make at home—you have come a long way toward generating increased business from sales of beverages in your food and beverage operation.

NOTES

1. This section is adapted from Donald A. Bell, *The Spirits of Hospitality: An Overview of the Origin, History and Service of Alcoholic Beverages* (East Lansing, Mich.: Educational Institute of the American Hotel & Motel Association, 1976), chapters 1-5.

2. These general purchase and selection criteria were developed by F.A. Olschner in a class project for the University of New Orleans School of Hotel, Restaurant and Tourism during summer, 1980. This list was initially published in Jack D. Ninemeier, *Beverage Management: Business Systems for Hotels, Restaurants and Clubs* (New York: Lebhar Friedman, 1982), pp. 150-151.

3. This discussion and much of the remainder of this section is adapted from Ninemeier, *Beverage Management*, p. 150.

4. This section is adapted from Jack D. Ninemeier, *Food and Beverage Security: A Systems Manual for Restaurants, Hotels and Clubs* (Boston: CBI, 1982), pp. 75-79.

5. This section is adapted from Jack D. Ninemeier, *Planning and Control for Food and Beverage Operations* (East Lansing, Mich.: Educational Institute of American Hotel & Motel Association, 1982), p. 227.

6. An excellent reference on beverages is Harold J. Grossman, *Grossman's Guide to Wines, Beers, and Spirits*, 6th rev. ed., revised by Harriet Lemveck (New York: Scribner's, 1977).

PART IV

Planning Food and Beverage Operations

As a food service manager, you must efficiently deliver required products and services to the customers. To help you make meaningful decisions, you must have access to timely and accurate financial information. A discussion of financial management, focusing on the operating budget and financial statements generating fiscal information, is therefore important.

In addition, products and services cannot be effectively delivered unless the proper equipment is used in an effective layout and design location. This topic is discussed because it is of great concern to every food service manager.

16

Financial Management Practices

Management Challenges

As a result of studying this chapter you will:

1. understand how important proper accounting procedures are to the food and beverage operation.

2. recognize the characteristics of good financial information and understand the role of this information in management decision-making.

3. understand the basic procedures which should be used to assess profit requirements.

4. understand basic procedures which are important in developing and using an operating budget.

5. know the difference between cash and accrual accounting systems and recognize the importance of the latter.

6. understand basic principles important in developing and using an income statement and the balance sheet.

7. know how selected food and beverage operating ratios can help management decision-makers.

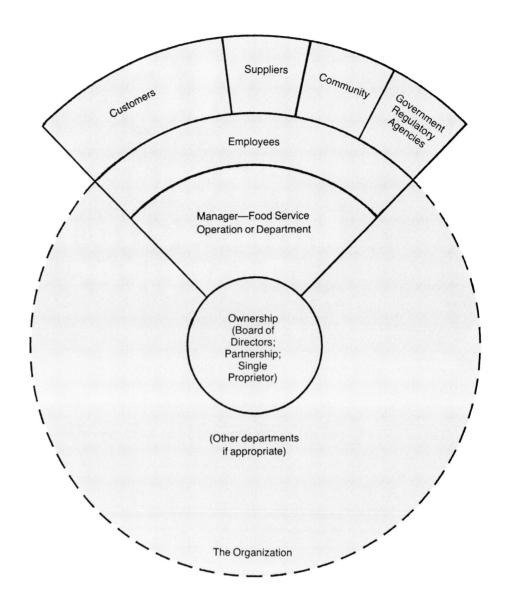

The Organization

Focus on the
Food Service Publics

Chapter 16 focuses upon the financial management of food service operations. Many groups both internal and external to the food service operation require financial information about the operation. For example, ownership has a definite interest in this information. The relationship between the manager and the owner is dramatically affected by "what the numbers say." Elements within the community such as banks and other lending institutions also have a concern about the financial status of the operation. Likewise, suppliers are interested in confirming that bills will be paid on a timely basis. Since financial information is the basis for reporting information to tax authorities, several government regulatory agencies are concerned with this information, too. The relationship between the food service operation and each of the external publics is affected by procedures used to develop, and information stemming from, financial accounting systems.

Other departments within the operation are also affected. For example, as the food service department meets financial objectives, there will be less drain on other departments within the operation. Likewise, if the food service department is expected to compensate for operating losses or reduced contribution margins from other departments, there is greater emphasis placed upon effective management. It can be seen, then, that each public has a concern about the way that the operation's financial accounting information is developed and used.

As the name implies, financial management deals with economic aspects of the food service operation. You already know that all resources available to the food service operation are in limited supply. Certainly this fact applies to money. There is no operation that has all of the money it would like to have to purchase desired resources. You cannot operate out of a cigar box or keep all the bills in a desk drawer and magically come out all right at the end of the month. The essence of financial management starts with planning—planning for profit, planning for selling prices, planning for expenses, etc.

Business has developed an effective system that consistently accounts for all revenues and expenses of any operation—those wanting to make a profit and those wanting to minimize expenses. This system is called "accounting."

Accounting can be thought of as the language of the hospitality industry. Through the development and implementation of effective accounting systems, financial information is gathered, put into meaningful terms, and used to make business decisions.

You must know where you are at all times as you plan strategies to achieve goals. Economic concerns—whether they deal with profit in a commercial food service operation or with cost minimization in an institutional program—are charted by using accounting systems.

The basic standards for accounting which are used in the hospitality industry are essentially established. Groups such as the American Accounting Association, the American Institute of Certified Public Accountants, and others establish rules and standards which are used by all businesses (including those in the hospitality industry) to report financial operating results.

In the hospitality industry, hotels and restaurants can use financial systems which have been developed by their respective organizations.[1]

As you can see, you do not need to "re-invent the wheel." Accounting systems that have been developed and tested over many years are widely used throughout the hospitality industry, and can easily be adapted to any type of food service operation.

Unfortunately, there is a common belief in the hospitality industry that accounting should be left to accountants. In other words, "the accountant is an expert; he/she should tell the food service manager what to do." At the least, this belief may mean that the manager will not contribute needed information to the design of accounting systems; at the extreme, it suggests that the accountant should make business decisions for the manager. In practice, the accountant should be in a staff/advisory relationship to you and should incorporate all financial information that will make the numbers more useful. After all, the major purpose of accounting is to generate accurate and timely information which can aid in business decision-making. If you do not know all the information that is necessary, how it was gathered, or what the information means, it is obvious that the usefulness of the accounting data will be diminished.

There are several specialized fields of accounting. In this chapter, we are concerned about financial accounting which relates to the general process of developing and using accounting information to make business decisions. Through a formalized process, business activities (sales, purchases, payrolls, etc.) are recorded and summarized, and financial statements are prepared.

Many parties besides yourself will be using the operation's financial information. Consider the following:

Owners—investors in the business want to know how well their operation is doing.

Board of directors—stockholders elect people to represent them in the management of a corporation's business. The members of the board of directors and the stockholders want accounting information in order to evaluate the managers who are hired to run the operation.

Creditors—people who lend money, products, or services to the operation want to know when they will be paid back.

Employee unions—financial information is used by union officials and others to assess the ability of the food service operation to meet wage and benefit demands.

Government agencies—since income is taxable by the federal government, most states, and many local governments, financial information becomes the base upon which tax assessments are made.

Characteristics of Financial Information

There are four very important characteristics which must be met in order for accounting information to be useful.

Accounting information must be relevant. The information must apply to the specific situation and to the decision being made.

Accounting information must be timely and current. Old data is generally not very helpful as decisions are made in today's fast-paced food service operation. Many food service operations select and analyze major costs and sales income information daily.

Accounting information must be accurate. The results must reasonably depict the financial aspects of activities which are measured.

Accounting information must be cost effective. The usefulness of the information must be worth the effort which is expended to generate it. It is possible to develop extremely accurate accounting information, but it may take a great deal of time which cannot be cost justified.

Financial Management and Decision-Making

We have already indicated that you should have relevant, timely, accurate, and cost-effective financial information. You can obtain various types of accounting information from several sources.

Historical information. Historical financial information can be of great assistance in monitoring the present and in planning for the future. This data is expressed in past financial statements, especially balance sheets and income statements.

Current information. Current financial information helps you know how your operation is performing. Examples of collecting financial information on a daily basis have already been noted.

Anticipated information. You can use anticipated financial information to look into the future. Operating budgets and pro forma income statements (which project revenue and expenses for new businesses) are examples.

Determining Profit Requirements

What is profit? You probably know that a formula for calculating profit is: revenue - expense = profit. However, when profit is viewed in this manner, it makes the act of profit planning very passive since profit is "what's left" after expenses are deducted from revenue.

A better view of profit is expressed by the following formula: revenue - required profit = allowable expenses. When this approach is used, the operation "pays itself first." Profit requirements are deducted from revenue and the remaining revenue is used to meet required expenses.

This text promotes the belief that you must know profit requirements and factor them into operating plans. By working with the accountant, you can then develop practical ways to measure the extent to which profit goals have been met. As you will see, even institutional food service operations—which do not have overt profit objectives—often need to generate revenue in excess of expenses. Therefore, you must also understand how profit is measured and how plans to generate required profit levels are developed and implemented.

If you were to ask food service managers how much profit they desire, the answers might be: "As much as possible," "At least as much as last year," or "At least as much as my competition is making." These answers, while popular, are neither realistic or useful. It is much better for food service managers to assess their own specific profit requirements.

While there are many ways to do this, two of the most popular methods are discussed in the following sections with a note of caution about a possible third method.

Return on Investment

This profit measure considers the amount of return which the food service operation wants to generate for the owner's investment. For example: the owner (a single investor, a partnership of two or more people, or stockholders in a corporation) has invested $50,000 in the food service operation. How much profit does the operation want to generate? Investors desire at least two things from investments they make:

1. They want to recover their original investment. As you know, the food service industry is one of very high risk. Ninety percent or more of food service operations that open may not exist five years later. Therefore, more risks may be associated with a food service business than with other investment opportunities which are available.

2. They want to generate a return on their investment. Not only does the investor want the original investment back, he/she also wants to be compensated for its use. It is at this point that the investor must determine "what the money is worth" so profit requirements can be established.

After considering the above two factors, assume that the owners desire a 15% return on their initial $50,000 investment. This means that, each year, the profit requirement of the food service operation is as follows:

$50,000   x   15%   = $7,500
(initial investment)   (desired return on investment)   (profit)

Therefore, the owner is hiring a manager—or is working in the business himself/herself—to generate $7,500 of after-tax profit.

Return on Assets

This common measure of profit considers the effectiveness with which the total assets (resources) committed to the food service operation have been utilized. For example, assets in the form of land, buildings, food and beverage inventories, cash, etc., must be used to generate profits. A simple formula can be used to calculate the return on average total assets: net income (profit) ÷ average total assets = percent return on assets. In this formula, average total assets are determined by adding the beginning and ending balances in the asset accounts and dividing by two. Consider the following example: (a) total assets (year one) equal $1 million, (b) total assets (year two) equal $2 million, and (c) net income (year two) equals $150,000.

Return on average total assets is calculated as follows:

($1 million + $2 million) ÷ 2 = $1.5 million
(total assets year one) (total assets year two) (years) (average total assets)

$150,000 ÷ $1.5 million = 10%
(net revenue year two) (average total assets) (percent return on assets)

In this example, the food service operation generated a return on assets which equaled 10%. This return can be compared with previous years or with applicable statistics from comparable operations to assess whether the utilization of assets was effective.

Return on Sales

Before reading on, you should be aware of one common measure of profit used in the hospitality industry which is dangerous. That method is return on sales. With this approach, the manager determines the percent of sales that should be represented by bottom line profit. For example, the manager may desire a profit equal to 10% of sales. The manager's effectiveness is judged to be "good" if this level is attained.

What is wrong with this method? We do not know how the 10% bottom line relates to investment requirements. There must be a rational way to relate profit requirements to the level of investments made. How was the 10% rate of return developed? Often, as noted above, the bottom line profit percent is determined by subtracting all estimates of expenses from revenue. In other words, the manager estimates that 10% will be left after expenses are deducted from revenue. Also, consider that, as sales increase or decrease, the amount of bottom line profit will fluctuate. Again, what if the investors are requiring a specified rate of return?

In order to get a return on sales, establish profit requirements according to one of the above procedures. Then, by dividing the profit requirements by estimated sales, a return on sales percent can be generated. This is a useful statistic when monitoring operating performance. For example, assume that the investors require a $20,000 profit and that sales are estimated to be $200,000. Then, you can calculate the return on sales as follows:

$$\frac{\$20,000}{\text{(profit requirement)}} \div \frac{\$200,000}{\text{(estimated sales)}} = \frac{10\%}{\text{(return on sales)}}$$

Procedures for determining profit requirements will differ in every type of commercial food service operation. For example, a restaurant may generate profit from the sale of food, beverages, and/or catering activities. A hotel—and its food and beverage department—may also have these activities along with, perhaps, room service, rental of lobby space, etc.

The procedures discussed above provide insight as to how profit for your operation can be assessed. You must use the budget process to determine the amount of profit which will become the responsibility of each department head. Normally, operating budgets for specific departments in a restaurant or hotel do not consider their bottom line profit. Rather, each department is responsible for estimating sales and levels of various direct allowable expenses (see the discussion about the budget process which follows). Other expenses which are not allocated to specific departments, and also profit requirements, must be paid for/generated out of the departmental contribution margins from each operating department. Therefore, department managers are responsible for generating income in excess of direct expenses. Higher levels of management are expected to manage indirect expenses (those not allocated to specific departments) so that income generated by operating departments will meet these indirect expenses. Finally, the highest levels of management— perhaps including ownership—are responsible for managing fixed costs such as taxes, insurance, etc., in order to attain bottom line profit requirements.

While the procedures just described might sound rather complicated, they really are not. They will become clearer as we discuss the development and use of operating budgets later in this chapter.

Profit in Institutional Operations

We have noted that the commercial food service operation's effectiveness can be measured by the extent to which its profit goals are attained. Profit becomes an overall measure of the effectiveness and efficiency of the food service operation. How, then, does an institutional (not for profit) food service operation measure its performance? By definition, the economic goal of an institutional food service operation is not to earn a profit, but to achieve financial goals such as minimizing expenses. For example, an institutional operation's performance might be judged on the extent to which it does not exceed its budgeted expense levels (this assumes that quality and other requirements of the operation are satisfactory).

At the least, then, institutional food service operations must meet their direct cost obligations. How is income generated? Perhaps from payments by consumers (there is a charge for many meals served in schools, colleges, and universities). Maybe income is generated through government reimbursements (this may be the case in government subsidized hospitals or community nutrition programs). Possibly, food service income is allocated from a central budget (when a hospital receives income from patient charges, insurance payments, government reimbursement programs, etc.).

There are many institutional food service operations which must generate income in excess of direct expenses. Some facilities may allocate overhead expenses to the food service operation. It might be necessary for a food service operation to pay its "fair share" of mortgage and debt expenses. Also, many institutional food service operations must generate income to purchase new equipment. Even if the facility uses a depreciation program to "match" the estimated amount of equipment use with the income generated during a period, this depreciation will not be sufficient. It will cost more to purchase a new dish machine than it did to buy an older model 15 years ago. Where does this additional money come from? Many institutional operations generate income in excess of direct operating expenses so funds are available to pay for these kinds of expenses.

Managing finances in commercial and institutional food service operations can be quite similar. Certainly, the principles of money management are identical. Commercial operations that want to generate a profit and institutional operations desiring to break even or attain other economic objectives must all be planned, organized, and managed in the same way. The financial management procedures discussed in this chapter—and other management concepts included in this book—are equally applicable to commercial and institutional food service operations.

A Budget Overview

The operating budget is a profit plan and a control tool.[2] Many food service managers, however, think of a budget as an obstacle to efficient performance. They develop budgets because they have to and, once developed, they do not look at the numbers until it is time to develop new budgets for the next year.

This is a poor philosophy that does injustice to the effective development of plans to attain required profit levels. You should not be satisfied with profit levels which are left after expenses are deducted from revenue. Instead, develop a profit plan that will help yield required profit levels by the end of the fiscal period. If you are an institutional food service manager, you must have economic information which will serve as a guide in attaining the operation's economic goals.

A budget is a financial plan that indicates how much revenue will be generated and how the revenue should be spent in order to meet required financial goals. There are many types of budgets, but the short-term or one-year operating budget which reviews items affecting the income (profit and loss) statement is most important. Operating budgets will constantly remind you about the amount of expected revenue and the allowable levels of expenses. By constantly reviewing this document, you will know if (and to what extent) economic goals are being attained.

The budget is an integral part of your operation's control system. Through the process of budgetary control, you will know how much should be spent (from the budget) and how much actually was spent (from the income statement). Problems can be identified by comparing these two documents and you can take timely, corrective action. The budget will also tell you how much money is left to be spent in each category of allowable expenses. Since all management personnel should be involved in developing the budget, it is an opportunity to improve coordination and communication so the entire management team will be aware of the "game plan."

The budget helps you consider alternatives while developing plans. For example, how can the operation generate increased sales? And if expenses are excessive, how can you reduce them? By reviewing accurate financial information in subsequent periods, you can assess the effectiveness of corrective action which has been taken. Finally, the budget helps pinpoint responsibility. Management personnel know the extent to which they are responsible for meeting income and expense goals. A budgetary control process yields objective information about their job performance for evaluation purposes.

Budget Development Process

When you develop a budget, first determine the expected levels of sales income. Then calculate the cost incurred to generate these sales. One of the "costs" assessed during the second phase is the profit requirement itself. You will learn later in this section how to treat profit as a cost.

In small food service operations, the manager/owner generally undertakes budget development. In larger operations, other staff members provide important help. For example, supervisors are judged by the extent to which they stay within budget limitations. They might budget expense levels for their areas of responsibility in consultation with senior management personnel or a budget committee may review department income and expense plans before a property-wide budget is approved.

Generally, annual operating budgets are developed before the beginning of a fiscal year by projecting income, profit, and expense information on a monthly basis. The months are then combined to develop the operating budget for the year. As the budget cycle evolves, the remaining months of the annual budget might need to be revised to account for unexpected situations. For example, a sales increase or decrease may make it necessary to readjust budgeted food and beverage costs. Steps in the budget development process include:

Step One: Calculate Projected Sales Levels. When possible, food and beverage sales information should be generated separately. Past sales levels can usually be obtained from monthly income statements. Computerized (and even many manual) systems list monthly, to-date statistics which can be useful. Factors to consider in developing sales estimates include:

- **Sales histories.** Past revenue levels can be analyzed. It may be possible to identify trends which will help in projecting sales for the new budget period.

- **Current factors.** New competition, street improvement projects, and other activities over which the operation has little or no control may affect sales levels for the new budget period.

- **Economic variables.** As inflation takes its toll, the public's habits and lifestyles change. This may affect repeat business or strategies that are used to counter economic problems.

- **Other factors.** Internal sales promotion plans, remodeling, and similar activities scheduled for the coming year may create a need to adjust sales trends.

Step Two: Determine Profit Requirements. Using the procedures described above, determine your profit requirements and factor them into the budget along with expenses. It may be easier to consider this problem if you view profit as an expense. Just as revenue must be available to pay for various categories of expenses, it also must be available to "pay the owner" for profit requirements.

Step Three: Calculate Projected Expense Levels. Many expenses are directly related to sales volume and will vary as volume changes. For example, food and beverage costs increase as sales increase because more food and beverage products must be purchased. Once sales volumes are known, you can estimate these types of expenses. There are additional expenses (fixed costs) which do not fluctuate according to sales volume. Examples include rent, depreciation, insurance, license fees, etc. These categories of expense must be considered when the budget is developed.

Planning Your Operating Budget

The following example illustrates how you can incorporate budget development procedures into an operating budget for the food and beverage program. Where applicable, completed sample budget worksheets and accompanying explanations review how to develop operating budget information. Although the focus is on developing a budget for the food operation, the same procedures are used to plan a beverage budget.

Figure 16.1 Budget Worksheet A: Sales History Analysis

	2 Years Ago			1 Year Ago			Current Year		
Month	Sales Amount	Difference (Previous Year)	%	Sales Amount	Difference (Previous Year)	% *	Sales Amount	Difference (Previous Year)	% *
	1	2	3	4	5	6	7	8	9
Jan.	12,550			12,975	425	3	13,995	1,020	8
Feb.	12,430			13,550	1,120	9	14,900	1,350	10
Mar.	12,220			13,375	1,155	9	14,750	1,375	10
Apr.	13,050			13,950	900	7	14,825	875	6
May	12,975			13,985	1,010	8	14,800	815	6
June	12,490			13,610	1,120	9	14,700	1,090	8
July	12,200			13,290	1,090	9	14,850	1,560	12
Aug.	12,950			13,975	1,025	8	14,800	825	6
Sept.	12,490			13,690	1,200	10	14,950	1,260	9
Oct.	12,420			13,590	1,170	9	14,875**	1,285	9
Nov.	12,310			13,495	1,185	10	14,800**	1,305	10
Dec.	12,300			13,550	1,250	10	14,775**	1,225	9
Totals	150,385			163,035	12,650	8%	177,020	13,985	9%

* Percents are rounded.

** Estimates (the operating budget is being developed in October for the coming calendar year).

Source: *Jack D. Ninemeier,* Planning and Control for Food and Beverage Operations *(East Lansing, Mich.: Educational Institute of the American Hotel & Motel Association, 1982), p. 48.*

Calculate Projected Sales Levels

Figure 16.1 shows monthly food sales that have been tallied from guest register tapes or guest checks. The worksheet reports sales for each month and the increase in dollars and percent over the same month in the preceding year.

To calculate the amount of sales increase in dollars, subtract January sales for the previous year (Column 4) from January sales for the current year (Column 7): $13,995 - $12,975 = $1,020. Sales have increased by $1,020 (Column 8).

To calculate the monthly percentage of sales increase, divide the increase of $1,020 (Column 8) by January sales from the previous year, $12,975 (Column 4). This percent (Column 9) is: $1,020 ÷ $12,975 = 8%.

Figure 16.2 Budget Worksheet B: Estimated Monthly Operating Budget

Month	Sales in Current Year	Increase By 10%	Estimated Sales: Operating Budget
January	13,995	1,400	15,395
February	14,900	1,490	16,390
March	14,750	1,475	16,225
April	14,825	1,483	16,308
May	14,800	1,480	16,280
June	14,700	1,470	16,170
July	14,850	1,485	16,335
August	14,800	1,480	16,280
September	14,950	1,495	16,445
October	14,875*	1,488	16,363
November	14,800*	1,480	16,280
December	14,775*	1,478	16,253
Totals	177,020	17,704	194,724

*Estimates

Source: Ninemeier, Planning and Control, *p. 49.*

The same calculation (increase in sales from previous year divided by sales from previous year) is used to calculate the total increase in sales on an annual basis.

In Figure 16.1, you can see that food sales in the second year of operation increased 8% over the first year (Column 6) while sales in the current year increased 9% over the second year (Column 9).

In addition to making these calculations, you should study the economy and other factors which were noted at the beginning of this chapter. Suppose you believe that the upward trend will continue and that sales will increase by 10% during the coming year. You can then make monthly food cost projections as shown in Figure 16.2. In Figure 16.2, these projections were made by adding 10% to each month's sales. Note that the total estimated sales for the operating budget ($194,724) is a 10% increase ($17,704) over food sales for the current year. The total sales income available ($194,724) is the base you would use to both generate expected profits and to meet expenses required to produce the sales income of $194,724.

Calculate Profit Required from Food and Beverage Sales

The second step in the budget development process is as follows:

a. Calculate total profit required by the food and beverage operations.

b. Determine profit which is required from food sales.

c. Determine profit which is required from beverage sales.

Total profit − food profit = beverage profit

In order to assess profit generated by the food and beverage operations, you must first understand how costs are allocated. While details of cost allocation are beyond the scope of this book, there are several basic principles you should understand:[3]

- Food and beverage costs should be charged, respectively, to food and beverage operations.

- Other large expenses should be prorated between the food and beverage operations according to how much expense each incurs. For example, labor costs could be prorated between operations according to salaries/wages paid to employees whose primary duties are generating food and beverage income. Wages for employees involved in both food and beverage operations (for example, the bookkeeper and the purchasing agent) could be prorated based upon the percentage of total sales generated by both. If 75% of the total food and beverage sales is generated by the food operation, then 75% of these indirect labor costs could be allocated to the food operation.

- Other smaller expenses, such as office supplies or equipment, can be allocated on the basis of a simple sales percentage. Figure 16.3 indicates the total amount (Column 2) of each cost (Column 1) identified in the restaurant's accounting system. Then each cost is allocated between the food and beverage operations according to the allocation method that has been chosen.

Figure 16.3 Budget Worksheet C: Recap and Allocation of Current Costs Between Food and Beverage Operations

Type of Cost	Total Annual Current Cost	Amount Prorated To			
		Food		Beverage	
		Sales =177,020	Percent of Sales	Sales =46,655	Percent of Sales
1	2	3	4	5	6
Food	61,957	61,957	35%	—	—
Beverage	12,000	—	—	12,000	26%
Payroll	48,985	42,485	24%	6,500	14%
Payroll Taxes and Employee Benefits	4,190	3,540	2%	650	1%
Direct Operating Expenses	11,101	8,851	5%	2,250	5%
Music/Entertainment	7,500	—	—	7,500	16%
Advertising	4,540	3,540	2%	1,000	2%
Utilities	9,851	8,851	5%	1,000	2%
Administration/General	9,080	7,080	4%	2,000	4%
Repairs/Maintenance	2,670	1,770	1%	900	2%
Rent	16,391	12,391	7%	4,000	9%
Real Estate/Property Taxes	2,670	1,770	1%	900	2%
Insurance	4,415	3,540	2%	875	2%
Interest Expense	7,780	7,080	4%	700	1%
Depreciation	6,811	5,311	3%	1,500	3%
Totals	209,941	168,166	95%	41,775	89%

$$209,941 = 168,166 + 41,775$$

Food Cost	61,957	Beverage Cost	12,000
Non-Food Costs	106,209	Non-Beverage Cost	29,775

Source: Ninemeier, Planning and Control, *p. 51.*

In Figure 16.3, current food sales of $177,020 (top of Column 3) is taken from Figure 16.2. Assume that current beverage sales are $46,655 according to another worksheet. Percent of sales (Columns 4 and 6) is calculated for each cost by dividing the amount of cost allocated to the operation by the total sales income for the operation.

The percent of sales for food (Column 4) is:

$61,957 (food costs, Column 2)	÷	$177,020 (total estimated food sales, top of Column 3)	=	35% (percent of sales for food, Column 4)

Profit before taxes is computed as follows:

(a) $177,020   + $46,655   = $223,675
     (food sales,   (beverage   (total food
     top of   sales, top   and
     Column 3)   of Column 5)   beverage sales)

(b) $168,166   + $41,775   = $209,941
     (total food costs,   (total beverage   (total food and
     bottom of   costs, bottom   beverage costs)
     Column 3)   of Column 5)

(c) $223,675   − $209,941   = $13,734
     (total food and   (total food and   (profit before
     beverage sales)   beverage costs)   taxes)

The profit percentage is determined by dividing the profit by total sales:

     $13,734   ÷ $223,675   =   6.1%
     (profit before   (total food and   (profit
     taxes)   beverage sales)   percentage)

If the $13,734 profit estimation of the food and beverage operations is not sufficient, ways to either increase sales and/or decrease costs must be considered. By developing the operating budget before the beginning of the fiscal period, management will have an idea about expected profit requirements. Then corrective action can be taken, if necessary, to bring financial plans for the operations in line with profit requirements.

Calculate Food Program Costs

At this point, you should know estimated food sales and the profit required from food and beverage sales. To project costs applicable to the food operation, multiply the current percentage of each cost listed in Figure 16.3 by the estimated sales income for the new budget period. This is done in Figure 16.4.

Note in Figure 16.4 that the estimated cost for next year's food service operation is $184,986. This estimate assumes that the percentage of total sales for each cost category remains the same for the budget year and for the current year. Now that you know the costs for the food service operation, subtract food-related costs from food sales to determine its profit:

     $194,724   − $184,986   = $9,738
     (food sales)   (food expenses)   (food profit)

Figure 16.4 Budget Worksheet D: Calculation of Food Program Costs For Budget

Category of Cost	Percent of Food Sales Income: Current Year	Estimated Sales Income: Budget Year	Estimated Cost: Budget Year
1	2	3	4
Food Cost	35%	$194,724	$ 68,153
Payroll	24%		46,734
Payroll Taxes/Employee Benefits	2%		3,894
Direct Operating Expenses	5%		9,736
Music/Entertainment	—		—
Advertising	2%		3,894
Utilities	5%		9,736
Administration/General	4%		7,789
Repairs/Maintenance	1%		1,947
Rent	7%		13,631
Real Estate/Property Taxes	1%		1,947
Insurance	2%		3,894
Interest Expense	4%		7,789
Depreciation	3%		5,842
Other (Specify):			
		Total Estimated Cost:	184,986

Source: Ninemeier, Planning and Control, *p. 53.*

Once you have made this calculation, you can determine the beverage sales profit by subtracting food sales profit from total required profit. If total required profit is $24,604, then the beverage profit needed is:

$24,604 (total required profit) − $9,738 (food profit) = $14,866 (beverage profit)

Figure 16.5 Budget Worksheet E: Food Program Operating Budget

Item	Budget Percent	Budget		Actual		Monthly Profit Calculation	
		Month	Year	Month	Year	Amount	%
1	2	3	4	5	6	7	8
Food Sales	100%	15,395	194,724	16,010	16,010	16,010	100%
Cost of Goods Sold							
Food Cost	35%	5,388	68,513	5,764	5,764	(5,764)	(36%)
Operating Expenses							
Payroll	24%	3,695	46,734	3,750	3,750	X *	X
Payroll Tax/Benefits	2%	308	3,894	325	325	X	X
Direct Operating Expenses	5%	770	9,736	870	870	X	X
Music/Entertainment	—	—	—	—	—	X	X
Advertising	2%	308	3,894	308	308	X	X
Utilities	5%	770	736	810	810	X	X
Administration/General	4%	616	7,789	550	550	X	X
Repairs/Maintenance	1%	154	1,947	110	110	X	X
Rent	7%	1,078	13,631	1,078	1,078	X	X
Real Estate/Property Taxes	1%	154	1,947	154	154	X	X
Insurance	2%	308	3,894	308	308	X	X
Interest Expense	4%	616	7,789	616	616	X	X
Depreciation	3%	462	5,842	462	462	X	X
Other (Specify)	—	—	—	—	—	X	X
Total Operating Expenses	60%	9,239	116,833	9,341	9,341	(9,341)	(58%)
Profit (Before Tax)	5%	768	9,738	X	X	905	6%

Month: *January*

*Indicates operating expenses are deducted in total ($9,341) below. Likewise, the total operating expense percent (58%) is deducted below.

Source: Ninemeier, Planning and Control, *p. 54.*

By using the budget information in Figure 16.5, comparisons between budgeted and actual financial information can be made each month. This worksheet is used to note the amounts of sales and expenses which were estimated when the budget was developed, and the actual amount of sales and expenses which were incurred. With this information on the same form, it is easy to see if corrective action is needed to bring operating results in line with the budget.

Let's see how this worksheet is used for the month of January:

Column 1 lists food sales, food costs, operating expenses, and profit in a format similar to an income statement (an income statement is discussed later in this chapter).

Column 2 lists the percent of food sales represented by each item.

$68,153	÷	$194,724	=	35%
(cost of goods sold: food cost)		(budgeted food sales)		(budget percent)

Column 3 lists budgeted sales and expenses by month (in this case for January). Food sales of $15,395 is taken from Figure 16.2. To calculate the amount of each expense listed in Column 1, multiply the budget percent (Column 2) by food sales of $15,395 (Column 3).

24%	×	$15,395	=	$3,695
(budget percent)		(food sales)		(monthly payroll expense)

Column 4 lists budgeted sales and expenses for the entire year. Food sales of $194,724 is taken from Figure 16.2. Each operating expense—for example, a payroll of $46,734—is obtained from Figure 16.4.

Column 5 lists the actual sales and expenses for the month. Data is obtained from the same source documents (invoices, payroll records, contracts, etc.) that are used to develop information for monthly accounting statements.

Column 6 tallies actual information on a year-to-date basis. Usually, Column 6 of the preceding month + Column 5 of the current month = Column 6 of the current month. However, since this is January, the first month of the budget year, Column 6 = Column 5.

Column 7 (carried forward from Column 5) lists information used to make monthly profit calculations. To find the monthly profit before taxes, simply subtract food and operating costs from sales:

($16,010	−	$5,764)	−	$9,341	=	$905
(actual monthly sales)		(actual monthly food costs)		(total monthly operating expenses)		(actual monthly profit before taxes)

Column 8 provides the same information in percentage and actual food sales. For example, the food cost percent is:

$5,764	÷	$16,010	=	36%
(food cost)		(food sales)		(food cost percent)

The information in Figure 16.5 shows (a) what food sales, costs, and profits should be, and (b) what food sales, costs, and profits actually are.

Figure 16.5 also gives you the following important information:

• **The actual food sales for January were greater than antici-pated:**

| $16,010 (actual food sales, Column 5) | — | $15,395 (planned food sales, Column 3) | = | $615 (increase in sales) |

• **Food costs were greater than planned:**

| $5,764 (actual food costs) | — | $5,388 (budgeted food costs) | = | $376 (increase in total food costs) |

While the increase in total food costs may be expected as a result of increased food sales, it may be noted that as a percentage of food sales (36% - Column 8), they were greater than planned (35% - Column 2).

• **Total operating expenses were $102 greater than planned:**

| $9,341 (actual operating expenses, Column 5) | — | $9,239 (budgeted operating expenses, Column 3) | = | $102 (increase in total operating expenses) |

• **Profit was also more than expected:**

| $905 (actual profit) | — | $768 (planned profit) | = | $137 (increase in total profit) |

When comparing budgeted and actual costs in Figure 16.5, it appears that direct operating expenses are somewhat out of line. A cost review and control process might begin with these expenses. Also, since food costs were slightly greater than anticipated, some analysis may be appropriate here. Bottom line profit is greater than planned, too, so it is probably reasonable to assume that the manager is effectively controlling operating costs and will take some action to generate food sales. However, it is difficult to generalize about budget costs after only one month. More accurate and meaningful analysis becomes possible with data from several months.

Overview of Accounting Systems

As our discussion of the operating budget has suggested, you must know how to make decisions regarding the economic aspects of today's food and beverage operation. You do this by developing and using recognized accounting systems to collect financial information in a meaningful way, and by analyzing the information as an integral part of the decision-making process. Some food service managers feel uncomfortable working with accounting information. They prefer to make decisions by using only intuition and experience. In their view, they do not need "the numbers," don't have time to develop or analyze financial information, and do not believe that judgments can be tempered with current financial information.

However, you should realize that good decisions are directly related to the accuracy and timeliness with which financial information is generated. You are not expected to be an accountant, but you must, at least, know the basic types of information needed to make effective decisions. You can then communicate these needs to accounting specialists who will design recordkeeping and accounting systems for you. What we are proposing is much different from the common industry observation that the accountant is the expert and you must do what he/she says. Instead, you and the accountant should be partners. When you tell the accountant what information is needed, the accountant should develop this information and help you analyze it to detect implications for future business decisions.

Cash and Accrual Accounting Systems
There are two basic types of accounting systems that you can use. With the cash accounting system, an accounting transaction is recognized when cash comes into or goes out of the operation. If a restaurant operates under a cash accounting system, revenue is considered to be earned when it is received; expenses are considered to be incurred when they are paid. This is a simple method to account for revenue and expenses, but it is not accurate or realistic for larger food service operations. Consider the following example: A restaurant has booked a banquet for the last week of the month. It orders and receives food and pays cash for it. The client is given several weeks to pay the bill. This means that the income statement for the month in which the banquet was held will not reflect accurate financial information. Expenses have been incurred (a check was written) and will appear on the income statement, but no revenue will have been received to offset them. Conversely, during the month after the banquet, expenses will be understated; revenue will have been received, but not offset against the expenses which were incurred.

The accrual accounting system has evolved to resolve these types of problems. With this system, revenue is recognized during the period in which it is earned (not received). Also, expenses are considered to be incurred when they have been used to generate revenue—not when they have been paid for. The accrual accounting system matches revenues with expenses. At the close of any accounting period, the system allows you to evaluate the profit or loss of the property during that particular period.

An in-depth study of accounting principles is beyond the scope of this book.[4] However, you should realize now that the food service manager must understand details of financial accounting systems and be able to use information which they generate to make meaningful management decisions.

Two specific statements are developed as a result of accounting systems—the income statement and the balance sheet. The following sections will briefly explain what these statements are and how you can use them.

Income Statement

The income statement indicates revenues and expenses (profit or loss) over a period of time. Generally, an income statement is prepared at the end of each month to review profit or loss during both the preceding month and the year-to-date. Sometimes, however, operations establish fiscal periods other than monthly ones; for example, some properties use 13 four-week periods in their fiscal year. Financial information that is reported on income statements is developed through a bookkeeping process in which various categories of revenue and expense are identified. As transactions occur during the fiscal period, bookkeeping entries are made in each account. At the end of the month, trial balances and various types of adjusting entries are made to ensure that account balances accurately reflect the activity which occurred during the month.[5]

In small food service operations, the manager may keep the books. Often, a bookkeeping service may be utilized for this activity. As food service operations become larger, staff accountants and other employees skilled in this specialization may be retained. In either event, you must know how the accounting systems work and must thoroughly understand how they are used.

Uniform System of Accounts The hospitality industry has developed uniform systems which provide recommendations for the design of accounting systems and procedures. This information enables managers wanting to learn more about accounting and operators who are "inheriting" an existing system to gain useful ideas about how accounting systems for the industry can be developed and implemented.

Figure 16.6 shows what an income statement might look like. It follows an accepted industry format with the percentages closely approximating the actual percent of sales income figures reported by restaurants in 1980.[6] (Dollar figures are *not* national averages; they are used for illustrative purposes only.)

As you review the income statement, recall that the actual amounts should be compared with those of the operating budget which indicates a standard (allowable) amount for each cost. Control procedures should be implemented when actual costs differ significantly from budgeted amounts.

Food and Beverage Sales. The food department generated 71.9% of all sales; only 28.1% of total sales were from the sale of beverages.

Figure 16.6 Sample Income Statement

<table>
<tr><td colspan="3">Brandywine Restaurant
Income Statement
Month Ended January 31, 19XX</td></tr>
<tr><td>Sales</td><td>Amount ($)</td><td>Percent</td></tr>
<tr><td> Food</td><td>533,250</td><td>71.9</td></tr>
<tr><td> Beverages</td><td>208,500</td><td>28.1</td></tr>
<tr><td>   Total Food and Beverage Sales</td><td>741,750</td><td>100.0</td></tr>
<tr><td>Cost of Sales</td><td></td><td></td></tr>
<tr><td> Food</td><td>217,033</td><td>40.7</td></tr>
<tr><td> Beverages</td><td>58,172</td><td>27.9</td></tr>
<tr><td>   Total Cost of Sales</td><td>275,205</td><td>37.1</td></tr>
<tr><td>Gross Profit</td><td></td><td></td></tr>
<tr><td> Food</td><td>316,216</td><td>59.3</td></tr>
<tr><td> Beverages</td><td>150,328</td><td>72.1</td></tr>
<tr><td>   Total Gross Profit</td><td>466,545</td><td>62.9</td></tr>
<tr><td>Other Income</td><td>8,250</td><td>1.1</td></tr>
<tr><td>Total Income</td><td>474,795</td><td>64.0</td></tr>
<tr><td>Controllable Expenses</td><td></td><td></td></tr>
<tr><td> Payroll</td><td>203,981</td><td>27.5</td></tr>
<tr><td> Employee Benefits</td><td>35,604</td><td>4.8</td></tr>
<tr><td> Direct Operating Expenses</td><td>48,214</td><td>6.5</td></tr>
<tr><td> Music and Entertainment</td><td>6,676</td><td>0.9</td></tr>
<tr><td> Advertising and Promotion</td><td>14,093</td><td>1.9</td></tr>
<tr><td> Utilities</td><td>18,544</td><td>2.5</td></tr>
<tr><td> Administrative and General</td><td>40,055</td><td>5.4</td></tr>
<tr><td> Repairs and Maintenance</td><td>12,610</td><td>1.7</td></tr>
<tr><td>   Total Controllable Expenses</td><td>379,777</td><td>51.2</td></tr>
<tr><td>Profit Before Occupation Costs</td><td>95,018</td><td>12.8</td></tr>
<tr><td>Occupation Costs</td><td></td><td></td></tr>
<tr><td> Rent, Property Taxes and Insurance</td><td>35,604</td><td>4.8</td></tr>
<tr><td> Interest</td><td>6,676</td><td>0.9</td></tr>
<tr><td> Depreciation</td><td>17,060</td><td>2.3</td></tr>
<tr><td> Other Additions and Deductions</td><td>(2,967)</td><td>(0.4)</td></tr>
<tr><td></td><td>56,373</td><td>7.6</td></tr>
<tr><td>Net Income Before Tax</td><td>38,645</td><td>5.2</td></tr>
</table>

Format adapted from Uniform Systems of Accounts for Restaurants, *4th ed. (Chicago, Ill.: The National Restaurant Association, 1968), p. 19.*

Food and Beverage Costs. Food costs were $217,033. This represents 40.7% of all food sales ($533,250). Similarly, beverage costs were $58,172. This represents 27.9% of total beverage sales ($208,500). These cost percents are very common ratios in the food service industry.

Total cost of sales percent. The total cost of sales ($275,205) is the sum of the total cost of sales for the food and beverage departments. The total cost of sales percent (37.1%) is calculated by dividing the total cost of sales by the total food and beverage sales.

$275,205	÷	$741,750	=	37.1%
(total cost of sales)		(total food and beverage sales)		(total cost of sales percent)

With the exception of food and beverage costs—which are calculated separately according to food and beverage sales—all other expenses in the income statement are normally calculated as a percent of total food and beverage sales.

Gross Profit. Gross profit equals the total sales for the food and beverage departments less the cost of sales (product costs) for each department. For example, gross profit for food is calculated by deducting the cost of sales (food) from the total food sales.

$533,250	−	$217,033	=	$316,217
(total food sales)		(cost of food sales)		(gross profit for food)

Total gross profit. The total gross profit represents the sum of the gross profit for food and the gross profit for beverages.

$316,217	+	$150,328	=	$466,545
(gross profit for food)		(gross profit for beverages)		(total gross profit)

Gross profit percent for food. The gross profit percent for food is calculated by dividing gross profit for food by the total food sales.

$316,217	÷	$533,250	=	59.3%
(gross profit for food)		(total food sales)		(gross profit percent for food)

Gross profit percent for beverages. A similar calculation for beverages is determined by dividing the gross profit for beverages by the total beverage sales.

$150,328	÷	$208,500	=	72.1%
(gross profit for beverages)		(total beverage sales)		(gross profit percent for beverages)

You should now see a very obvious fact: There is generally more profit from the sale of beverages than there is from the sale of food. Note that the gross profit (total product sales minus total product costs) is 72.1% for beverages and only 59.3% for food. Even by reading only this far in the sample income statement, you should realize the importance of separating food sales and costs from beverage sales and costs. Since each profit center requires its own budget, you should consider revenue and costs separately and also develop accounting systems which enable information to be collected separately for each profit center.

Other Income. In Figure 16.6, the food and beverage operation has generated other income of $8,250. This could represent sales of recipe books, gift items in a novelty shop, or proceeds from vending machines and pay telephone concessions, etc.

Controllable Expenses. Note the types of controllable expenses in Figure 16.6. Controllable expenses refer to those which are generally within the restaurant manager's control. Depending upon the management procedures that are utilized, expenses such as payroll, employee benefits, music and entertainment, repairs and maintenance, etc., are more or less within the restaurant manager's control. Occupation costs such as rent, interest, and depreciation are generally fixed and are not within the restaurant manager's control.

Payroll. These costs represent total wages and salaries paid to employees of the property. Large properties may break down these types of expenses between profit centers (food and beverage), but they usually only post totals to the income statement.

Employee benefits. These are various types of costs which the property incurs to support employees. Examples include the employer's share of social security, unemployment taxes, health insurance, life insurance, and miscellaneous employee-related expenses such as awards and prizes, training, parties, etc.

Direct operating expenses. Each property's accounting system requires a different degree of detail, but direct operating expenses can be put into expense categories such as uniforms, laundry, linens, china and glassware, bar supplies, flowers and decorations, etc. Direct operating expenses in Figure 16.6 represent the total expenses charged to these types of accounts during the month covered by the income statement.

You should now know how important it is for you to work with the accountant as the accounting system is designed. Shouldn't you know what categories of expenses are included in "direct operating expenses" in order to control these costs? If they exceed the amount allowed by the budget, the types of charges included in this expense category must be identified so that they can be reviewed.

Music and entertainment. These expenses are generally self-explanatory. If "live" entertainment is provided in the restaurant or lounge, these costs must be assessed. Likewise, royalties may need to be paid to licensing companies and expenses for jukeboxes, etc., may be incurred.

Advertising and sales promotion. These costs refer to newspaper, magazine, direct mail, radio, television, and related types of expenses required to promote the business. Donations and entertainment costs can also be charged to these accounts.

Utilities. These costs refer to electric, gas, waste removal, and related expenses incurred by the property.

Administrative and general. These expenses include a wide variety of items such as office stationery, printing and supplies, postage, telephone, collection fees, etc. As is true with direct operating expenses, managers must work closely with their accountants to determine the need for detail when the accounting system is developed.

Repairs and maintenance. These are costs incurred for painting and decorating, fixing any type of equipment in the property, building alterations which are not an improvement, etc.

Profit Before Occupation Costs. Note that of the total revenue generated ($750,000—$741,750 from food and beverage sales + $8,250 other income), there is only $95,018 remaining after the total cost of sales ($275,205) and controllable expenses ($379,777) are deducted. This is classified as "profit before occupation costs" and these fixed expenses— rent, property taxes, insurance, interest, and depreciation—must also be deducted. Definite, consistent procedures must also be established to identify expenses to be charged to these accounts. You should understand how these costs are assessed so that management plans can be established and corrective action taken as part of the budgetary control process.

Net Income Before Tax. Finally, we arrive at the bottom line—net income before tax. In Figure 16.6, there is $38,645 (5.2% of sales) which has been generated in January that is not needed to meet the cost of sales, controllable expenses, or occupation costs. Federal, state, and perhaps other taxes must be paid based upon this net income figure.

Hospital Financial Report

Figure 16.7 illustrates a financial report utilized by a hospital. Let's look at some of the similarities between the type of information gathered by an institutional operation and its commercial counterpart:

1. Percent occupancy—also called census—(upper left-hand corner of Figure 16.7) is also a popular and useful statistic in a hotel.

2. The labor, food, and supply costs (boxes 11, 20, and 21, respectively) are calculated for the month and for year-to-date on a total and per meal basis.

3. Meal counts and expenses are separated by cost centers (patient and nonpatient in this hospital operation).

4. Comparisons are made between actual and budgeted costs.

Notice that there are several distinct differences between the hospital's food service performance report and a typical income statement utilized by a commercial operation.

First, there is no income generated from the service of meals to patients. The food service department does generate cash receipts from the

Figure 16.7 Food Service Performance Report

Potential Patient Days ______
Patient Days ______
% of Occupancy (Census) ______

Hospital ______
Month Ended ______
Prepared by ______

MEAL COUNT		Current Month	(7) = % of Total	Year to Date Meals
Patient Meals	(1)			
Cafeteria Meals	(2)			
Charge Meals	(3)			
Special Function Meals	(4)			
Other Meals	(5)			
Total Meals	(6)			

Total Full-Time Equivalents

(13) ______

LABOR COST		Patient Service	Non-Patient Service	Total Labor	Year to Date Labor
Pat. Serv. Direct	(8)				
Non-Pat. Serv. Direct	(9)				
Total Labor $	(11)				
Total Labor Hrs.	(12)				

FOOD AND SUPPLY COSTS

Food Cost

		Meat, Fish & Poultry	Fresh Produce	Frozen	Groceries	Milk & Dairy	Bakery	Total Food	Y-T-D Food
Beg. Inv.	(14)								
Purchases	(15)								
Ending Inv.	(16)								
Gross Cost	(17)								
					(18) Less Nourishments				
					(19) Less Transfers				
					(20) Net Food Cost				

Supply Cost

	Dispos-ables 580	Cleaning Supplies 450	Office Sup. 460	Uten./China 500	Other 590	Total Supplies	Year to Date Supplies
Sup. Trans.							
			(19a) Less Transfers				
			(21) Net Supply Cost				

Net Food Cost X ____% Patient Meals = Patient Food Cost = (22) ____ Net Supply Cost X ____% Patient Meals = Patient Supply Cost (23) $ ______

Remarks

RECAP

		PATIENT COST					NON-PATIENT COST				
		This Month	Cost Per Meal	Budget Cost Per Meal	Y-T-D Total	Y-T-D Cost Per Meal	This Month	Cost Per Meal	Budget Cost Per Meal	Y-T-D Total	Y-T-D Cost Per Meal
Labor	(24)										
Food	(25)										
Supplies	(26)										
Total	(27)										
Less Cash Rec.	(28)										
Net Cost	(29)										

Net Cost PPD ______ Patient Meals/Labor Hour ______ (30) Non-Patient Meals/Labor Hour ______ (31)

Source: Determination and Allocation of Food Service Costs, *by the American Society for Hospital Food Service Administrators, published by American Hospital Publishing, Inc., copyright 1975.*

sale of diet instructions and nutritional supplements to patients, as well as from such nonpatient sources as the cafeteria and catering/vending operations.

Second, costs incurred for food, labor, and supplies (lines 24, 25, and 26, respectively) are allocated between patient and nonpatient programs. Any cash received (line 28) is deducted from total costs (line 27) for each program. The cost of patient meals is used as part of the cost per patient day statistics when daily charges are established.

Third, information about meals/labor hours is generated. This statistic, routinely assessed in institutional operations, becomes a basic measure of productivity. It is not, however, a popularly used indicator in a commercial operation—perhaps because it is difficult to define the term "meal."

Fourth, there are other expenses such as utilities and fixed overhead costs that are not allocated to the food service operation. (With external and internal forces creating the need for cost containment efforts to more closely "match" income with associated costs—including food services—increased efforts to identify specific income and costs are likely.) Currently, however, many hospitals do not allocate income from patients, insurance payments, etc., to their respective cost centers.

Simply stated, then, income is assessed from all sources without identifying which is for the food service operation. Food service expenses are deducted from total institutional income along with those expenses incurred by all other departments. It is therefore important for you, the food service manager, to know the costs incurred by (but not the "income" allocated to) the operation.

Accounting Systems for Hotel Food and Beverage Operations

As is true with restaurants, a uniform system of accounts for hotels has evolved.[7] This system is, in many ways, more complicated than that used for restaurants since it must recap sales and expense information for all departments in the property—not just for the food and beverage department. Figure 16.8 reviews the type of expenses—and respective percentages of total food and beverage revenues—which can be expected. When reviewing this information, note the following:

- Like the restaurant income statement, food and beverage revenues are separated. The cost of food sales is also separated from the cost of beverage sales.

- Gross profits from beverage sales are greater than gross profits from food sales. For example, in properties under 250 rooms, gross profits for food sales are 63.7% and gross profits for beverages are 76.6%.

- Departmental expenses are identified as they relate to total food and beverage sales. It is at this point that accounting for food and beverage operations in a hotel differs from that of a

Figure 16.8 Sample Income Statement for Food and Beverage Department in a Hotel: 1980

Food and Beverage Department:						
Food Net Revenue	100.0%	100.0%	100.0%	100.0%	100.0%	100.0%
Cost of Food Consumed	40.1%	37.8%	35.2%	32.6%	38.3%	35.1%
Less: Cost of Employees' Meals	3.8	3.8	3.8	3.5	3.6	3.6
Net Cost of Food Sales	36.3%	34.0%	31.4%	29.1%	34.7%	31.5%
Food Gross Profit	63.7%	66.0%	68.6%	70.9%	65.3%	68.5%
Beverage Net Revenue	100.0%	100.0%	100.0%	100.0%	100.0%	100.0%
Cost of Beverage Sales	23.4	21.6	20.6	18.9	21.9	20.3
Beverage Gross Profit	76.6%	78.4%	79.4%	81.1%	78.1%	79.7%
Total Food and Beverage Revenue	100.0%	100.0%	100.0%	100.0%	100.0%	100.0%
Net Cost of Food and Beverage Sales	32.5	30.4	28.5	26.5	30.9	28.7
Gross Profit on Combined Sales	67.5%	69.6%	71.5%	73.5%	69.1%	71.3%
Public Room Rentals	1.8	2.9	2.0	2.1	2.7	1.9
Other Income	.4	1.1	2.2	2.7	1.0	1.8
Gross Profit and Other Income	69.7%	73.6%	75.7%	78.3%	72.8%	75.0%
Departmental Expenses:						
Salaries and Wages Including Vacation	32.8%	33.3%	34.5%	34.8%	31.8%	32.4%
Employees' Meals	1.4	1.5	2.0	2.4	1.4	1.6
Payroll Taxes and Employee Benefits	6.6	7.3	7.8	10.2	6.5	7.5
Subtotal	40.8%	42.1%	44.3%	47.4%	39.7%	41.5%
Music and Entertainment	3.3	2.4	3.2	1.1	2.8	2.3
Laundry and Dry Cleaning	.9	1.1	1.0	.8	.9	.9
Kitchen Fuel	.3	.3	.3	.4	.2	.3
China, Glassware, Silver and Linen	1.6	1.9	2.2	2.6	1.7	2.3
Contract Cleaning	.4	.2	.7	.9	.3	.5
Licenses	.3	.2	.1	.1	.2	.1
All Other Expenses	5.0	5.1	4.7	3.9	5.3	4.7
Total Food and Beverage Expenses	52.6%	53.3%	56.5%	57.2%	51.1%	52.6%
Food and Beverage Departmental Income	17.1%	20.3%	19.2%	21.1%	21.7%	22.4%

Source: Trends in the Hotel Industry, *U.S.A. ed. (New York: Pannell Kerr Forster, 1981), p. 25.*

restaurant. Although some properties allocate expenses such as administration, marketing, and energy costs to revenue-producing departments, these expenses are more typically detailed as part of a separate category called Undistributed Operating Expenses. If a property wants to charge its undistributed expenses to individual departments, allocation procedures must be established.[8] Any decision about how such costs are allocated will have a direct impact on the profit or loss of the food and beverage department.

In Figure 16.8, the bottom line of the income statement for the food and beverage department is "Food and Beverage Departmental Income." This represents the amount of income remaining after all expenses which are to be charged to the food and beverage department have been deducted from total food and beverage income. However, this amount does not represent profit to the hotel. Instead, this amount must be used to pay for expenses that have not been allocated to any department. General expenses which have not been allocated to the departments must be recovered from the departmental income generated by food and beverages, rooms, rental of public space, etc. Examples of expenses which may not be allocated between departments include those associated with parking lots, landscaping, and swimming pools. Fixed costs are often not allocated to departments either. Expenses such as licenses and permits, interest payments, and taxes must also be recovered. Therefore, as is true with restaurants, a relatively small amount of food and beverage income "falls" to the bottom line of the hotel's income statement.

Balance Sheet

The income statement which you have just studied summarizes the revenues earned and expenses incurred during a specific time period. The balance sheet reports the financial position of the food service operation as of the specific date on which the accounting period ends. It does this by reviewing three types of accounts:

1.   **Assets**—anything owned by the business.

2.   **Liabilities**—debts owed by the business.

3.   **Equity (net worth)**—the claims which the owners have to the assets of the business.

In effect, the balances in the assets, liabilities, and net worth accounts reflect the net accumulation of all accounting transactions which have occurred since the business began.

Using the Balance Sheet

As with the income statement, there are many people who use the firm's balance sheet. In this book, we are interested in you, the food service manager. You can use the balance sheet to determine inventory values, accounts receivable (money which is owed to the operation), accounts payable (money which is owed by the operation), the amount of available cash to pay debts, etc. By controlling these and various other items (all reflected in the balance sheet), you make sure that funds are available to meet current obligations, keep the operation going, and meet the investment requirements of owners.[9]

The balance sheet for a restaurant is similar to one for a hotel. The type of information that is categorized—such as assets and liabilities and the way in which equity is reported—will also be very similar. In Figure 16.9 note the following:

Current Assets—cash and other resources which will be converted to cash in one year or used to generate revenues within a year.

Noncurrent Assets—resources that benefit the business for longer than a year. In Figure 16.9, "Investments and Advances" relates to investments in affiliated companies and amounts due from them after one year's time. Fixed assets (property and equipment) are usually shown at cost on the balance sheet. Since, in inflationary times, the value of land, buildings, etc., increases, valuing fixed assets at cost generally understates the worth of the business. Footnotes to the balance sheet are often used to provide additional information that is necessary to evaluate the financial position of the business.

Figure 16.9 Sample Balance Sheet

Assets

	Date	
	19____	19____
CURRENT ASSETS		
Cash	$	$
House Banks		
Demand Deposits		
Time Deposits and Certificates of deposit		
Marketable Securities		
Receivables		
Accounts Receivable — Trade		
Notes Receivable		
Other	____	____
Total Receivables		
Less Allowance for Doubtful accounts	____	____
Inventories		
Prepaid Expenses		
Other Current Assets	____	____
Total Current Assets	____	____
INVESTMENTS AND ADVANCES		
Affiliates		
Others	____	____
PROPERTY AND EQUIPMENT, at cost	____	____
Land		
Buildings		
Leasehold and Leasehold Improvements		
Construction in Progress		
Furniture and Equipment	____	____
Less Accumulated Depreciation and Amortization	____	____
China, Glassware, Silver, Linen, and Uniforms	____	____
OTHER ASSETS		
Security Deposits		
Cash Surrender Value of Life Insurance, Net		
Deferred Expenses		
Preopening Expenses		
Other	____	____
TOTAL ASSETS	$	$

Liabilities and Shareholders' Equity

	Date	
	19____	19____
CURRENT LIABILITIES		
Notes Payable	$	$
Accounts Payable		
Current Maturities on Long-term Debt		
Unearned Income		
Federal and State Income Taxes		
Accrued Liabilities		
Salaries and Wages		
Interest		
Taxes — Other than Income		
Other Current Liabilities	____	____
Total Current Liabilities		
LONG-TERM DEBT, LESS CURRENT PORTION		
OTHER NON-CURRENT LIABILITIES		
DEFERRED INCOME TAXES		

BALANCE SHEET *(continued)*

*SHAREHOLDERS' EQUITY

Preferred Stock, Par Value $ _____
   Authorized _____ Shares
   Issued _____ Shares
Common Stock, Par Value $ _____
   Authorized _____ Shares
   Issued _____ Shares
Additional Paid-in Capital
Retained Earnings

Less Common Stock in Treasury, at cost
_____ Shares 19 ; _____ Shares 19

   Total Shareholders' Equity

COMMITMENTS AND CONTINGENCIES

TOTAL LIABILITIES AND SHAREHOLDERS' EQUITY $ _____ $ _____

* If Partnership or Proprietorship:
   Partners' Equity (or Owners' Equity if Individual)
     A
     B

     Total Partners' Equity

See accompanying notes to financial statements.

Source: Uniform System of Accounts and Expense Dictionary for Small Hotels and Motels, *rev. ed.* (East Lansing, Mich.: *Educational Institute of the American Hotel & Motel Association, 1981), pp. 2-3.*

Current Liabilities—obligations that must be paid within the next 12 months. Examples include short-term debts and current portions of long-term debts, accounts payable to suppliers, employee-related liabilities, income tax liabilities, and other miscellaneous liabilities.

Noncurrent Liabilities—long-term liabilities include money that is owed and must be paid back over an extended time period (more than one year from the balance sheet date).

Equity—represents the shareholders', partners', or owner's interest in the business. It is called "shareholders' equity" if the business is a corporation, "partners' equity" if the business is a partnership, or "owner's equity" if the business is owned by an individual. You can calculate equity by subtracting total liabilities from total assets. Of course, investors are always very concerned about how their equity is managed. This section of the balance sheet addresses those concerns.

The food and beverage department in a hotel plays an important role in the "numbers" as they show up on the balance sheet. Owner's equity is affected by the amount of profit or loss of the hotel which is reflected in the retained earnings section of the equity calculation on the balance sheet. However, in a restaurant operation there are few, if any, additional opportunities, other than profits from food and beverage sales, to affect the equity of the property.

Special Food and Beverage Operating Ratios

We have studied the income statement and the balance sheet in the above sections. These are very helpful financial tools which can assist you in making operating decisions. In addition to these statements, you can collect and utilize other financial information. When this is done in a consistent manner, the data (called operating ratios) can help identify potential problems and suggest corrective action if necessary.

Operating ratios look at the relationships between two factors that are judged to be important to the financial success of your food and beverage operation. For example, a food cost percentage (cost of food sales ÷ food sales) will help you keep track of food expenses. Similarly, each category of actual expenses expressed as a percentage of change from the operating budget tells you whether closer analysis and, possibly, corrective action is necessary. We will review just some of the many ratios that can be used.

Food, Beverage, and Labor Percentages

In most food and beverage operations, expenses incurred for the purchase of products (food and beverages) and for labor constitute the largest categories of costs. These costs (often called prime costs) must be closely monitored. The process of budgetary control—already noted in several sections—provides an excellent way to monitor these expenses. For example, if you know the amount of revenue which should be spent for food, beverages, and labor (from the operating budget), then these standard costs can be compared against the actual costs (as reported in the income statement).

Let's make sure that you understand how percentages are calculated (please refer to Figure 16.6). Note the following:

(a) **food sales** = $533,250

(b) **beverage sales** = $208,500

(c) **cost of sales: food** = $217,033

(d) **cost of sales: beverages** = $58,172

Food and Beverage Cost Percentages. These percentages can be calculated as follows:

$217,033 (cost of sales: food)	÷	$533,250 (food sales)	=	40.7% (food cost percent)
$58,172 (cost of sales: beverages)	÷	$208,500 (beverage sales)	=	27.9% (beverage cost percent)

Total Labor Cost Percentage. In Figure 16.6, the amount of labor costs applicable to the food and beverage operation are not separated. Therefore, to figure the total labor cost percentage, two calculations are necessary:

(a) $203,981   ÷ $741,750   =   27.5%
       (payroll costs)   (total food and   (payroll percent)
                          beverage sales)

(b) $35,604   ÷ $741,750   =   4.8%
       (benefits cost)   (total food and   (employee
                          beverage sales)   benefits
                                                  expense)

When you make these calculations, you can see that the total amount of food and beverage sales that must be used to pay for labor-related expenses equals 32.3% of sales (payroll expenses of 27.5% plus employee benefits of 4.8%).

Ratios dealing with the percentage of food and/or beverage sales for any category of expense in the income statement can, of course, be developed. Examples of other common percentage calculations are shown in this section.

Inventory Turnover

You may wish to calculate the number of times that your food and/or beverage inventory turns over during a fiscal period. The turnover rate for food is calculated: food costs for the month ÷ average inventory cost for the month. This calculation can be made monthly, annually, or on some other basis. Normally, it should be calculated monthly to help ensure that any problems are noted so that corrective action can be taken.

In order to calculate food costs for the month, a simple formula you can use is: beginning inventory + purchases - ending inventory = food costs for the month. Various types of adjustments to this calculation can be made, but are eliminated here to simplify the discussion. Average inventory can be calculated as follows: (inventory at the beginning of the month + the value of inventory at the end of the month) ÷ 2 = average inventory.

You can calculate the inventory turnover as follows: (a) assume beginning inventory of $5,000, (b) purchases of $20,000, and (c) ending inventory of $6,000.

Using the above information the inventory turnover is:

Food Costs

(a) $5,000   + $20,000   − $6,000   = $19,000
       (beginning   (purchases)   (ending   (food costs for
       inventory)   inventory)   the month)

Average Inventory Costs

(b) (5,000 + 6,000) ÷ 2 = $5,500
     (inventory: (inventory: (to calculate   (average
     beginning   end of   average)   inventory:
     of month)   month)   month)

Turnover Formula

(c) $19,000 ÷ $5,500 = 3.45
     (food cost: (average   (inventory
     month)   inventory: turnover)
                     month)

The food service operation must buy enough food products to completely stock its storeroom approximately 3.45 times during the month in order to have available all the food that is needed during the month.

It is important for you to know this information. If the turnover rate is tracked monthly, you can see if the turnover rate is increasing or decreasing. Reasons for changes, of course, must be understood. When inventory turnover rates *decrease* (a greater supply of products is kept in storage) the chances of increased theft, pilferage, or spoilage occur. Also, cash may be needlessly tied up in inventories which could be used to pay other bills. As the inventory turnover rate *increases* (a smaller quantity of products are kept in inventory), the likelihood of stockouts—with resulting customer dissatisfaction—increases. You can see, then, how inventory turnover information is used to make management decisions which will affect the profitability of the operation.

Seat Turnover   Seat turnover is the number of times that a given seat in a sit-down dining area is occupied during a meal period. When the seat turnover rate increases, more customers are being served during a meal period and more sales revenue is being generated.

Seat turnover is calculated by dividing the number of customers who are served in a meal period by the number of seats available. For example, if 300 guests are served during lunch in a dining room which seats 175 people, then the seat turnover rate is 1.71.

         300   ÷   175   =   1.71
       (guests)   (seats)   (seat turnover)

In other words, 1.71 guests are served at lunch for each chair that is available. Of course, you want high seat turnovers (assuming that quality service standards can be maintained). You should study the seat turnover rate, assess ways to increase it, and take corrective action when the turnover rate decreases.

Figure 16.10 Common Operating Ratios for Hotel Food and Beverage Programs

	% of Total Revenues	% of Dpt. Revenues	% of Dpt. Total Cost	% Change from Prior Period	% Change from Budget	Per Available Room	Per Occupied Room	Per Available Seats	Per Cover/Guest	Per Square Foot	Per Full-time Equiv. Employee	% of Total Salaries & Wages
Food												
Revenue	●			●	●	●	●	●	●	●	●	
Cost of Sales		●	●	●	●		●					
Salary, Wages & Burden		●	●	●	●		●	●				●
Other Expenses		●	●	●	●		●	●				
Departmental Profit		●		●	●			●	●	●	●	
Beverage												
Revenue	●			●	●	●	●	●	●	●	●	
Cost of Sales		●	●	●	●							
Salary, Wages & Burden		●	●	●	●			●				●
Other Expenses		●	●	●	●							
Departmental Profit		●		●	●			●		●	●	

Source: R.M. (Max) Gaunt and George R. Conrade, "How to Analyze Financial Statements," Lodging, February 1983, p. 47.

Average Check per Guest

The average check per guest is calculated by dividing the revenue which has been generated during a specific period by the number of guests that have been served. For example, if a restaurant generates $300 of revenue from the sale of food, and serves 95 guests, the check average is $3.16.

$300	÷	95	=	$3.16
(food sales)		(guests)		(average check per guest)

Normally, you want to increase the check average. This can be done by encouraging wine sales, dessert sales, after-dinner drinks, or higher cost entrees. You can monitor your operating performance by using guest check averages along with the other popular ratios discussed in this section.

Other Ratios

There is no specific rule about which ratios you should use to monitor your operation's performance. It depends on you and on your specific type of operation. Figure 16.10 illustrates some of the ratios which may interest you. While the listing is not comprehensive, it does give you an idea of the wide variety of relationships which you may want to study. The bottom line is that you must determine the factors for your own operation that can be used to monitor performance; then you can collect information to assess these factors in a meaningful way.

Responsibility for Accounting System Implementation

You have learned that you are ultimately responsible for attaining economic (and other) goals established for your food and beverage operation. Therefore, you should help design the accounting system to be used. The differences between your responsibilities (a line position) and those of the accountant (a staff/advisory position) must be completely understood. You have learned that it is usually unwise for a manager to automatically follow the advice of the accountant in establishing the accounting system or in interpreting financial information. You are responsible for telling the accountant what information is needed, and when it is needed, so that the accountant can use specialized skills to meet these requests.

Employees also play a role in the design and implementation of the accounting system. They may have many useful suggestions regarding ways to make data collection easier, to make the completion of required source documents less time consuming, and to correct problems which are observed through analysis of the accounting information. As in many other types of decision- making/problem-solving situations, you should consider ways to involve employees in the management tasks which affect their own performance.

Tip Reporting Presents New Accounting Concerns

In 1982, the U.S. Congress developed legislation designed to more accurately generate information about and collect income tax from tipped employees in the hospitality industry. The regulations affect "large" operations (generally those with more than the equivalent of ten full-time employees on a typical business day). The regulations provide an excellent example of the need to collect accounting and recordkeeping information which is required by tax authorities; at the same time, the data required by the regulations is useful to operations that did not previously generate the information.

The problem addressed by the new regulations (which were implemented on April 1, 1983) was that many tipped employees were not reporting tips received as part of the base upon which income taxes were to be assessed. Cash tips could not be identified, but charged tips included on credit card vouchers could normally be easily tracked and verified.

Reporting Tip Income   Managers with tipped employees must now determine whether reported tips equal at least 8% of the total sales generated by the tipped employees.[10] To the extent this percent is not reported, an allocation process must be undertaken to assess the additional tip income which is necessary to meet the minimum 8% requirement. Both the actual reported tip income and any additional tip income which has been allocated to the employee must be reported to the federal government and the employee on the W-2 forms used to report salary, wage, and other tax-related information. Operations with accounting information that is necessary for effective decision-making (per server income, charged income, and tips) usually have little difficulty in gaining access to information needed for compliance with the laws. However, operations lacking this basic information are required to revise procedures in order to generate the data. Likewise, procedures for handling service charges not treated as tips, but rather as wages under the laws, can be re-examined. Managers will now be able to track roles on a by-server basis (which might indicate whether any significant differences between servers are justified or if additional training might be necessary).

NOTES

1. Interested readers are referred to *Uniform System of Accounts and Expense Dictionary for Small Hotels and Motels*, rev. ed. (East Lansing, Mich.: Educational Institute of the American Hotel & Motel Association, 1981); *Uniform System of Accounts for Hotels*, 7th ed. (New York: The Hotel Association of New York City, Inc., 1976); and *Uniform System of Accounts for Restaurants*, 4th ed. (Chicago: National Restaurant Association, 1968). Standardized accounting procedures and forms have also been developed by groups representing club managers, the American Hospital Association, and American Health Care Association (nursing homes). Government-operated food service programs must generally comply with accounting standards used by the sponsoring government agency so financial information can be easily incorporated into existing accounting systems.

2. The next two sections are based upon Jack D. Ninemeier, *Beverage Management: Business Systems for Hotels, Restaurants and Clubs* (New York: Lebhar-Friedman, 1982), pp. 33-41.

3. Interested readers are referred to Ninemeier, *Beverage Management.*

4. Interested readers are referred to Clifford T. Fay, Jr., et al., *Basic Financial Accounting for the Hospitality Industry* (East Lansing, Mich.: The Educational Institute of the American Hotel & Motel Association, 1982).

5. Details of the bookkeeping process are reviewed in Fay, et al., *Basic Financial Accounting*, pp. 21-71.

6. *Restaurant Industry Operations Report* (Chicago: National Restaurant Association in cooperation with Laventhol & Horwath, 1981 for the United States).

7. Interested readers are referred to *Uniform System of Accounts for Hotels.*

8. For additional information on allocating overhead expenses see *Uniform System of Accounts for Hotels*, pp. 125-127.

9. For additional information on developing and using a balance sheet, interested readers are referred to Fay, Jr., et al., *Basic Financial Accounting*, pp. 79-88.

10. Readers desiring specific information are referred to *Tip Reporting: A Guide to Compliance* (Laventhol & Horwath, Certified Public Accountants, 1983).

17

Design, Layout, and Equipment Concerns

Management Challenges

As a result of studying this chapter you will:

1. understand the principle of product flow and how to incorporate it into the design of the facility layout.

2. recognize that sanitation, safety, and security concerns must be addressed and incorporated into the design of the facility layout.

3. recognize potential operating problems associated with noise, temperature, lighting, and related special problems and know how to reduce them.

4. understand the basic principles important in the design of kitchen, receiving, storage, serving, dining room, and cashier station areas.

5. be able to identify basic items of food service equipment and know when these equipment items can be useful.

6. understand the general factors which are important in selecting basic items of food service equipment.

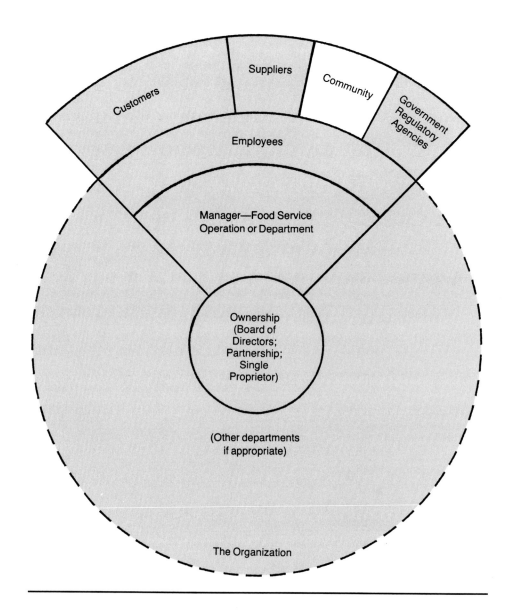

Customers

Suppliers

Community

Government Regulatory Agencies

Employees

Manager—Food Service Operation or Department

Ownership (Board of Directors; Partnership; Single Proprietor)

(Other departments if appropriate)

The Organization

Focus on the Food Service Publics

Chapter 17 deals with food service layout and equipment concerns. These topics are vitally important to the relationship between the food service manager and the employees. Employee attitudes are affected by the amount and type of work they do (which is influenced by layout, design, and equipment availability). Customers are also affected by these factors since work flow and labor efficiency are dictated in large measure by layout, design, and equipment concerns. Since these factors also influence the profitability of the operation, property ownership is naturally concerned. Design factors are also influenced by codes and other requirements of government regulatory agencies so the relationship between this external public and the facility is important. Space that is used for food service areas obviously cannot be used for other purposes; the relationship between other departments and the food service department must be emphasized. Suppliers deliver products and, while this is a minor concern, it is important that layout and design factors also be addressed as receiving and storage areas are planned.

Production staff—and often many other people—are needed to prepare food and beverage items for service. The way that the physical facility is designed and how the equipment is arranged have a definite impact on the efficiency and profitability of your food service operation. Consider just one category of expense: labor. If your food service facilities are poorly designed, much time can be wasted in walking between work stations in a kitchen and many motions can be wasted in preparing products. Also, guest dissatisfaction can occur because of dining facilities that contribute to the inefficiency of employee service.

The layout and design of your facility affects capital costs, too. If more space is designed into the facility than is needed, capital costs will increase needlessly. Likewise, operating costs for servicing the additional space (heating, ventilating, air conditioning, cleaning and maintenance, etc.) will be greater. You obviously would like the food service facility which is planned to be used for a long period of time. What if your menu needs change or new and different types of equipment are needed? Are there ways to design flexibility into the facility that is planned? Perhaps you have worked in a facility that is poorly designed. If so, you most likely noted some of the many problems this created. Perhaps you have also worked in a properly designed facility which utilized many of the basic design principles discussed in this chapter. You should understand and apply all principles of layout and design.

It is possible that experienced management staff may not have been involved when the facility in which they work was designed. You should solicit ideas from management staff; there may be personnel who have been involved with remodeling activities in the existing facility. Even simple rearrangements of the production equipment, dining room tables, etc., are based upon some very basic principles. Therefore, regardless of the management role that you have, or will play, in a food service operation, some knowledge about layout and design will be helpful to you.

The Design Team

Properly designed food service facilities do not just happen. Proper planning is necessary to ensure that the following goals are attained:

- A minimal investment is made for land, buildings, furniture, fixtures, and equipment. Leasing instead of purchasing is an option available to you.

- The completed facility appeals to both the guests and the employees.

- There is a maximum return on investment.

- There is an efficient flow of people, products, and equipment within the facility so that procedures for doing all tasks are as simple as possible.

- The facility provides safe working space for employees and public access space to guests. High standards of sanitation are maintained in all areas of the facility.

- The facility lends itself to employee work efficiency; this should cut down on the manpower needed to meet quality standards.

- Maintenance costs for the facility are low; since energy costs are a concern, buildings and equipment should be energy efficient.

- Design of the facility makes employee supervision and other management activities easy.

If it sounds like the accomplishment of these goals is a big job, you are right. Effective planning takes time and generally requires the specialized knowledge of at least several people as the process evolves. A basic outline of the planning process is presented in this chapter.[1]

Preliminary Considerations

To begin with, concepts and ideas for the facility must be developed. For example, is the project to be a new facility or a remodeling of an existing facility? Does it involve the exterior of a building or the interior only? Does it include the entire kitchen or just a specific work station in the kitchen? Factors such as the type of operation (commercial or institutional), its size and hours, the menu, and quality requirements of production, service, and atmosphere should be reviewed. By developing a realistic, thorough idea of exactly what the project involves, you will help ensure its successful completion. In many cases, a market analysis (a detailed study of potential customers and their wants and needs) is necessary. Likewise, a feasibility study will determine the cost effectiveness of the project. How much will the project cost? What will it generate in increased revenues or decreased costs? Will the project be worthwhile?

Of course, you, the manager, and the owner must also be members of the planning team. In many instances, an architect will be needed to work on the project planning team. Unless you are thoroughly familiar with the complex task of interior space design, a food service facility consultant may also be a requirement. After the planning team is in place, the concept must be "put on paper." Each activity and task that is performed in your food service operation must be identified so that space can be allocated and necessary equipment provided. In part, this involves the analysis of product flow which will be discussed in a later section of this chapter.

Determine Equipment and Space Needs

As you learned in Chapter 6, the menu is a primary factor in dictating equipment needs. Space requirements must also be considered. Generally, the food service operation is designed by first considering work stations (an area in which one employee works or where one menu item is made). These work stations are put together to form work sections (or production units) which are then organized into large work areas. For example, the work station for one bartender may be designed first. It is then matched with similar work stations (large equipment such as sinks and refrigerators often can be shared) to form a work section: the bar. Later, this bar area must be considered when the entire lounge and facility are designed. Figure 17.1 shows how this can be done. Two bartenders are required for this layout. One bartender works the service bar (he/she provides drinks to employees who then serve guests in the restaurant and/or lounge). The second bartender serves guests at the bar without the assistance of food and beverage servers. The primary work station is around the speedrail (10) which is used to hold bottles of the most frequently ordered liquor. Other necessary items (soda gun, ice, and glassware) are also conveniently located in this area. Sinks and refrigerators are installed in a convenient location and shared by each bartender. Finally, the design of the beverage production section must be compatible with the rest of the space in the facility.

Preliminary layout and equipment plans help allocate available space. Floor plans can show the general arrangement of equipment, work aisles, and the relationship of one spatial area to another. At this point, assemble some cost estimates and, if necessary, adjustments in preliminary plans can be made to allow for available funds.

When preliminary information has been reviewed, modified as necessary, and approved, final blueprints for the space can be drawn up and equipment specifications prepared. These are used to solicit price quotations and make decisions about hiring contractors/suppliers to work on the project. Construction and installation tasks follow, and should adhere to a schedule which meets the needs of all parties.

From this brief description of the planning process, you should realize that there are many steps and people involved. The commitment of capital funds is likely to be substantial; the amount of planning to help ensure that project goals are met without surprises also involves a substantial commitment of time from all concerned parties.

Figure 17.1 Layout of Public/Service Bar: Two Bartenders

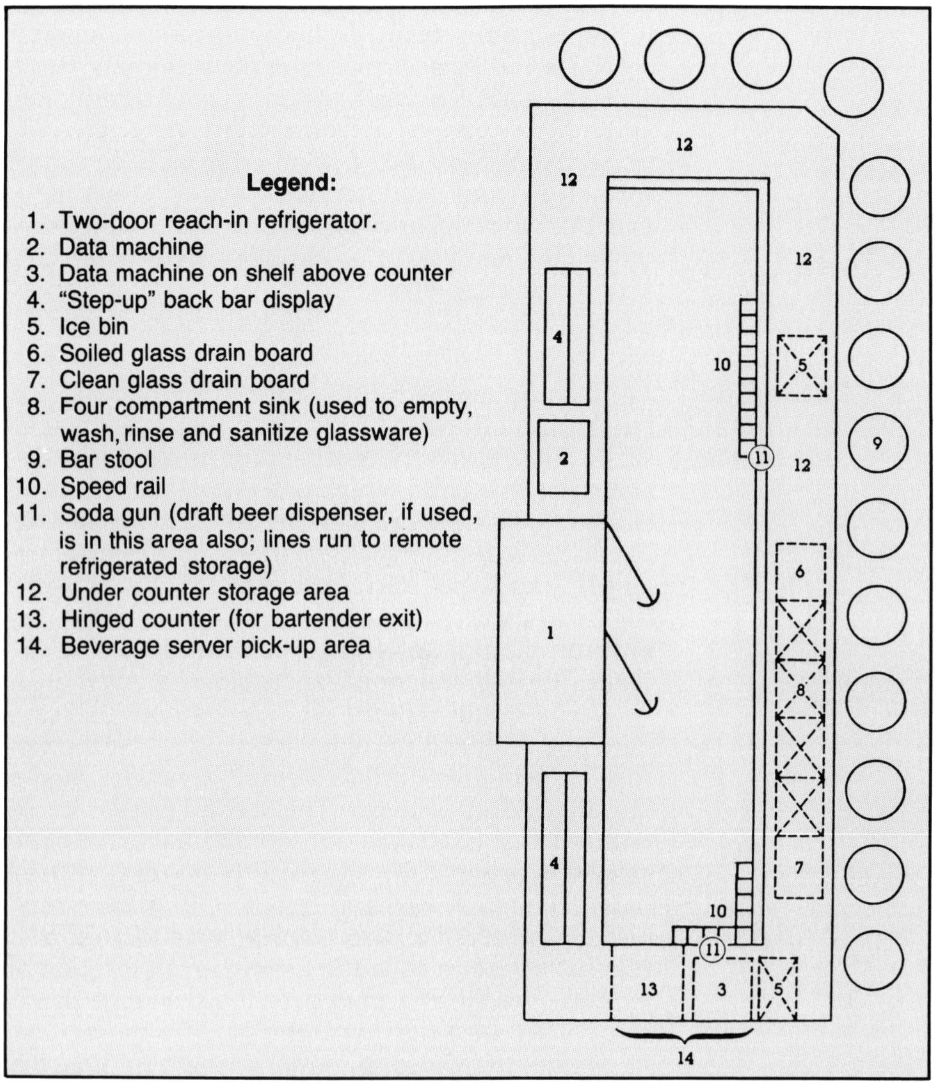

Legend:
1. Two-door reach-in refrigerator.
2. Data machine
3. Data machine on shelf above counter
4. "Step-up" back bar display
5. Ice bin
6. Soiled glass drain board
7. Clean glass drain board
8. Four compartment sink (used to empty, wash, rinse and sanitize glassware)
9. Bar stool
10. Speed rail
11. Soda gun (draft beer dispenser, if used, is in this area also; lines run to remote refrigerated storage)
12. Under counter storage area
13. Hinged counter (for bartender exit)
14. Beverage server pick-up area

Source: Jack D. Ninemeier, Beverage Management: Business Systems for Restaurants, Hotels, and Clubs *(New York: Lebhar-Friedman, 1982), p. 74.*

Product Flow Concerns

Food facilities should be designed so that the efficient flow of products and people through each sequence of activities is possible. For example, look at Figure 17.2. Note that incoming food products must be received and then placed into dry or refrigerated (including frozen) storage areas. Food products are then issued, as needed, from storage areas for use in baking, meat preparation, or vegetable preparation. As you can see in Figure 17.2, the baking area has little relationship to any other back of house areas except, perhaps, cooking (baked toppings and crusts are used in some entree items). With these exceptions, the flow of products

Figure 17.2 Work Flow Analysis In a Food Service Facility

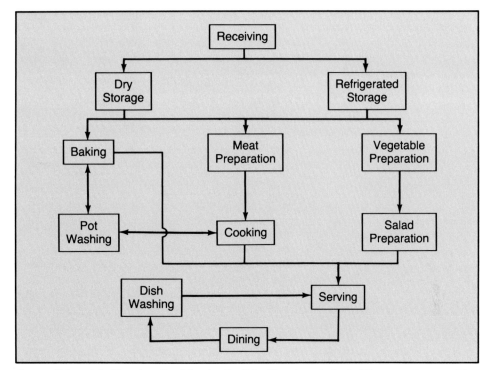

Source: Edward A. Kazarian, Food Service Facilities Planning, *2nd ed. (Westport, Conn.: AVI, 1983), p. 89.*

and people into and out of the bake shop really relates only to pot washing and serving areas. There are extensive relationships, however, between meat and vegetable preparation areas and between cooking and salad preparation areas. After preparation, products move from back of house production to front of house service personnel and are taken to the dining room. Soiled dishes are then removed to dishwashing areas and again cycled into serving areas.

Straight-Line Flow

While Figure 17.2 is simplified, it does suggest the type of functional relationships which must be considered as the flow of products and people is reviewed at the time of facility design. Wherever possible, the flow should be in a straight line—from back of house receiving through front of house dining areas—without "backtracking." This point is reviewed more extensively later in the chapter.

Figure 17.3 shows the relationship between various public areas through which guests and employees must travel. Notice that the entry and exit areas should be common ones (there is no need for separate areas) although designers may need to consider exits for fires and other emergencies. A reception area may be designed with close proximity to coat-check, telephone, or vending machine areas. Restrooms that service dining room and lounge areas are also a consideration as reception areas are planned. Guests desiring food service may need to go through a cashier station area in order to enter the dining room. When the meal is

Figure 17.3 Customer Traffic Flow Analysis in Public Areas

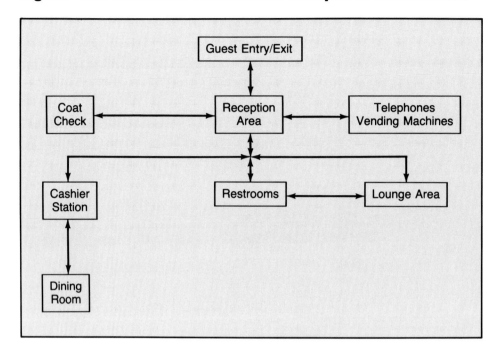

completed, the route is reversed; the guest travels from the dining room to the cashier's station and back to the reception area in order to exit.

Designing the Kitchen

The kitchen design team has a difficult job. Menus are likely to change during the life of the facility being planned. How can this flexibility be built into the design? You know that menus being planned must consider available equipment, space, and layout/design. A key to flexibility in menu planning is flexibility in layout/design. Today, many items of food service equipment can be placed on wheels and installed with quick disconnects which permit items to be more easily moved around. Use of multi-purpose equipment such as tilting braising pans and vertical cutter mixers is often a wiser choice than the purchase of limited use, specialty equipment items.

When the kitchen is being planned, you must consider the following: (1) flexibility, (2) costs for equipment and space, (3) labor needed to work in the kitchen, and (4) the menu that has been planned for the facility. The property's needs, resources, and special characteristics will greatly influence the facility being planned.

Kitchen Design Factors　　The menu is one of the most important determinants of kitchen needs. Space, people to work within it, equipment, and the ingredients themselves must be available in some form to prepare every item on the menu. You should also consider the amount and type of convenience foods used. As the extent of labor that is built into products increases, there is a reduced need for space, people, and equipment in the food service operation itself.

Menu Considerations. Let's consider a simple example: bread. Depending upon the needs of the operation, bread products can be prepared or provided in several ways: (a) baked and sliced—ready to serve, (b) baked only, (c) unbaked—frozen, preportioned, and ready to proof, (d) frozen dough only—must be portioned and proofed before baking. (The term "proof" refers to the process by which yeast bread products rise or become lighter because of carbon dioxide produced by the yeast.) Note that when properties use several bread products and have these options available, the impact of the purchase decision on layout and necessary equipment is obvious.

Quantity of Items. The quantity of items to be prepared must be considered. As more products are purchased, received, stored, and issued for production, as well as served, more space will be needed. Likewise, equipment needs with obvious space implications will become greater. As you have learned in Chapter 11, food quality is often enhanced when food is prepared as close as possible to the time of service. Therefore, "batch cooking" in which several items are made several times during a meal period—as opposed to all at once with the need for holding at the proper temperature—has not only quality, but also space, cost, and equipment implications.

For example, consider that batch cooking (cooking in small quantities) will reduce size and space requirements of production equipment; capital costs may be decreased. On the other hand, this practice may result in higher labor and therefore operating costs. Naturally, *quality* concerns should be of paramount importance.

Utility Concerns. We have already noted that equipment needed to prepare menu items and to properly serve guests is an important concern. You will see later in this chapter that there is a wide variety of equipment available to perform almost any storage, production, or service requirement. Utility concerns are closely aligned with equipment needs. Installation of equipment items can often be a cost which is as great or greater than the actual purchase of the equipment itself. It is time consuming and expensive to install equipment in areas that do not have convenient access to utilities (plumbing, electricity, gas, etc.). The availability and cost of utilities during the life of the equipment must be estimated, too.

Frequently, scarce funds for remodeling and new construction projects are a great restraint on the kitchen when it is designed. Preliminary planning must confirm that the desired results of the project can be achieved with the amount of funds available. If this is the case, you must learn to compromise and trade off advantages and disadvantages with alternate equipment items, space needs, and economic considerations.

Space Considerations. In new facilities, funds generally limit the amount of space which is available for the kitchen. Of course, when facilities are remodeled, basic kitchen space is already available. Usually, designers attempt to minimize back of house production space in order to provide additional areas in the front of the house for generating revenues. When space is limited, so is the number of employees, type and amount of equipment, and, perhaps, quantity of food which can be produced in the area. Space considerations are an important factor in kitchen design and analysis.

Sanitation and Safety. Sanitation and safety concerns must also be incorporated into kitchen design. These may be required by local and other codes, but you have a responsibility to meet these needs regardless of legal "minimums." Therefore, effective procedures for washing and sanitizing pots and pans and other cooking utensils, serviceware items (if disposables are not used), etc., are necessary. Sanitary facilities for storing food products and for holding prepared products until service are also important. When you consider that water, grease, and other items can make floors slippery, then wide work aisles in front of production equipment and effective lighting levels are necessary.

Food Service Characteristics. Characteristics required of a particular food service present a final example of factors which you need to consider when kitchens are designed. Examples are banquet food preparation where large quantities of food must be prepared and portioned in small amounts of time, work flow concerns when drive-in windows are installed, and preparing and serving family style versus gourmet food.

Work Station Designs

The process of designing a kitchen is complex and hinges upon many factors which subsequently affect how practical the facility will be for a specific food service operation. Now let's look at some principles that are helpful in designing kitchen areas.

You have already learned that kitchens and other areas in the food service facility are designed by first considering workload requirements and then designing work centers (stations) in which specific work tasks must be performed. There are many work flow and work simplification procedures which you should consider as these activities are undertaken. To aid in this discussion, let's see how the design of common work stations aids the work to be done.

L-Shaped Work Flow. The layout shown in Figure 17.4 is referred to as an "L-shape" and is often located along walls forming a corner. The work flow is diagrammed for a bake shop area that you might find in many institutional food service kitchens. Consider the task of making dinner rolls; the placement of the equipment makes this task easy for the worker. Water is necessary for many bakery recipes. Therefore, worker time can be saved if a sink (1) is located next to the mixer (2). When bread products are prepared, much hand work is necessary to knead, portion, and shape bread products so a bakery table (3) should be close to the mixer. Many dinner rolls can be quickly shaped by using a semi-automatic bun divider/rounder (4); this item should be located close to the table. When preportioned and shaped rolls come out of the divider, they must

Figure 17.4 L-Shaped Work Flow in Bake Shop Area

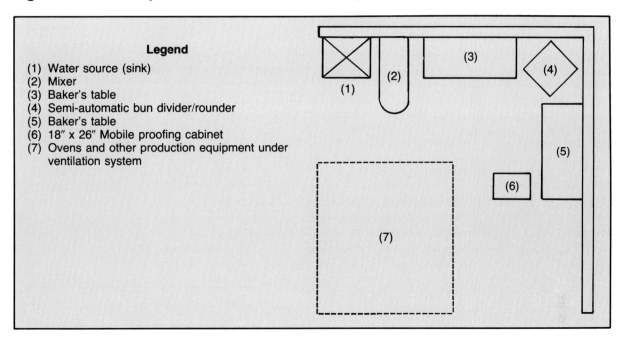

Legend

(1) Water source (sink)
(2) Mixer
(3) Baker's table
(4) Semi-automatic bun divider/rounder
(5) Baker's table
(6) 18″ x 26″ Mobile proofing cabinet
(7) Ovens and other production equipment under ventilation system

Figure 17.5 Straight-Line Work Flow in Pot/Pan Wash Area

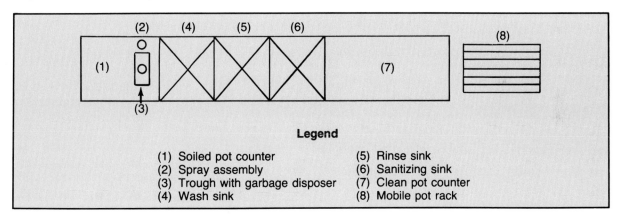

Legend

(1) Soiled pot counter
(2) Spray assembly
(3) Trough with garbage disposer
(4) Wash sink
(5) Rinse sink
(6) Sanitizing sink
(7) Clean pot counter
(8) Mobile pot rack

be put onto pans and a table (5) makes this task easier. After the rolls are panned, they must be proofed and transported to ovens for baking. A mobile proofing cabinet (6) helps with this task. Since bake shops frequently use ovens, they should be located close to the bakery area (7).

Straight-Line Work Flow. This is shown in Figure 17.5 as we consider how pots and pans may be washed. First, soiled pots must be brought to the area, so a soiled pot sink (1) is necessary. Soiled foods and other items on these pans can be scraped and sprayed into a garbage disposer trough (2 and 3) before being washed. Then, depending upon local sanitation codes, sinks for washing, rinsing, and sanitizing (4, 5, 6) are needed. After sanitizing, space is necessary for clean pots to air dry; a

Figure 17.6 U-Shaped Work Flow in Dishwashing Area

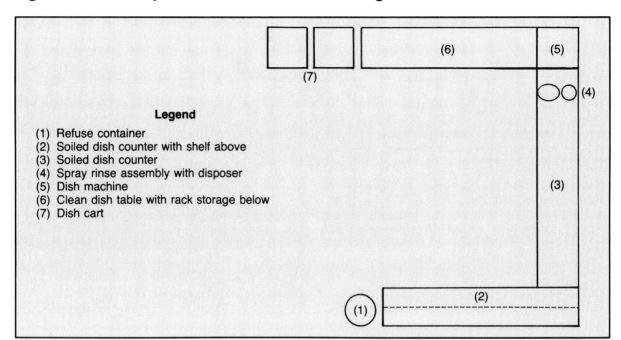

clean pot counter (7) is available for this purpose. Items must be stored after drying and a mobile pot rack (8) can be used. The mobile rack will be handy to transport pots and pans to work areas for their next use.

U-Shaped Work Flow. Figure 17.6 illustrates possible work flow in a U-shaped dishwashing area. The process begins at the refuse container (1) where service staff may bring back bus boxes and trays of soiled dishes. Shelves above the soiled dish counter (2) can be used for racks of glasses, cups, etc. The shelf below the soiled dish counter itself can be used to stack soiled dishes until they are washed. The soiled dish counter (3) is used to rack soiled dishes before prerinsing (4) and running through the dish machine (5). As with pots and pans, clean dishes must be air-dried and a clean dish table (6) is necessary for this task. After dishes are dry, they must be stacked and transported to the serving counter or food service stand; a dish cart (7) may be needed.

Parallel Work Flow. Figure 17.7 illustrates work flow in a frying station and it is set up to utilize the concept of parallel flow. The work counter with refrigerated storage below (1) can be used to store items for frying until they are ordered. After removal from the refrigerator, the items can be battered on the work counter and placed in the deep fryer (2). After frying, they can be taken to the counter (3) for plating and the employee can then pivot to the work counter/pickup station (5) and give the items to food servers or place them on dishes prepared by other cooks. In some operations, the fryer cook also works the grill and, if so, this item (4) should be located very close to or in the work station.

Figure 17.7 Parallel Work Flow In a Frying Station

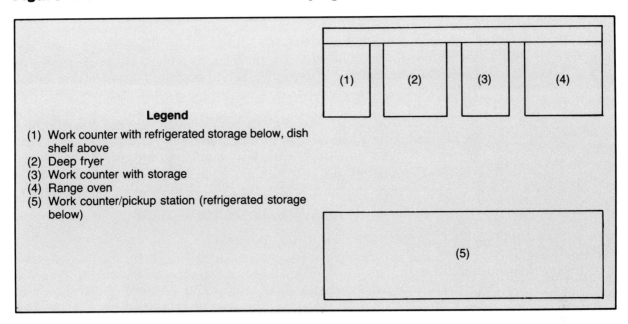

Legend

(1) Work counter with refrigerated storage below, dish shelf above
(2) Deep fryer
(3) Work counter with storage
(4) Range oven
(5) Work counter/pickup station (refrigerated storage below)

Notice that these examples are trying to use work flow to minimize the need for backtracking. Work simplification procedures, such as storing items at point of first use and having all equipment necessary for the task to be performed, are incorporated into the design of the work station.

Special Concerns in Kitchen Design

When you and the planning team develop the layout for the kitchen area, several special concerns should be addressed:

Physical Fatigue. Much physical work will be done in the kitchen area. Therefore, everything possible to reduce physical fatigue should be built into the facility design. Examples are reducing distances which employees must walk, adjusting heights of work areas so they are best suited to employees, and providing comfortable locker room, restroom, and employee dining facilities.

Noise. Not only does excessive noise make employees uncomfortable, but it can distract guests and customers as well. Noise can be minimized by using soundproofing materials and equipment that is not loud.

Lighting. Much detail work is done in kitchen preparation areas. Therefore, it is necessary to provide adequate lighting so that employees can work safely and without eyestrain. Inadequate lighting can contribute to physical fatigue so illumination requirements should be considered as front and back of house areas are designed.

Temperature. Kitchen areas can be hot. Cooking and cleaning equipment which generates heat, steam, and humidity often makes working conditions uncomfortable. Heating, ventilating, and air conditioning plans must deal with these problems.

Safety and Sanitation. These topics have been discussed, but are mentioned again because you and the planning team are both legally and morally responsible for designing safety and sanitation features into facilities that are developed.

By now you can see that there are many special considerations which must be addressed as production areas are designed. The same type of concern must be focused on layout of nonproduction areas in food service operations.

Design of Other Areas

Receiving and Storage Areas

Some attention must be given to facility needs for the proper receiving and storage of food and beverage products. Control of incoming products begins when they are received. If possible, receiving should take place in nonpublic areas (the back door is preferred to the front door). Depending upon the facility design and any union regulations of delivery personnel, the receiving area should be as close as possible to the receiving door. For control reasons, you do not want delivery personnel putting items in storage areas even if they want to; delivery personnel should be confined to one relatively small area in the back of the house.

The receiving area should be large enough to handle all items being received so that proper receiving practices can be practiced (see Chapter 12). There should be room for a receiving scale, dunnage racks (loose packing put around items for protection), and any other necessary equipment. Whenever possible, the receiving area should be close to the storage area; however, if a compromise must be made, it is much more important for storage areas to be closer to production areas. For example, consider a property which receives items on the ground level and has a kitchen on an upper floor. After items have been properly received and processed, it is much better for food and beverage receiving staff to bring them to storage areas near the kitchen than it is for them to place items in storage on the ground level. Employees would have to continually retrieve these items for use several floors above.

Storage areas include spaces required for dry, refrigerated, and frozen products. Some large properties may have separate refrigerated storage space for produce, meats, seafood, and dairy products. It is much more common, however, to have centralized walk-in refrigerated storage areas which house all items needing approximately 40-degree storage environments. When possible, the entrance to refrigerated units should be flush with the floor level because with stairs, it is no longer possible to use mobile carts and racks to wheel products into and out of storage areas.

Dry storage areas should be thought of as bank vaults holding money (which is required, of course, to purchase these items in the first place). Storage rooms should be designed with floor-to-ceiling walls and with ceilings that cannot be entered from an adjoining area. Some facilities incorporate a precious storage area into the storeroom. Often, perpetual inventory systems are used to track expensive items. Some large properties, especially institutions, plan ingredient rooms adjacent to or as part of dry storage areas. This way, items can be pre-weighed/measured before being issued so that chefs, bakers, and other specialized employees can work more quickly without being slowed down by these tasks.

We have noted that storage areas should be located as close as possible to production areas. This becomes less important if ample work station refrigeration is available. For example, items needing refrigeration might be issued only a few times a day to refrigerated storage areas in the work station itself. Therefore, fewer trips are necessary to replenish work stations.

Service Areas

After food is prepared, it must be readied for presentation to customers. In many food service operations, this activity brings service staff into contact with production staff. Some cafeterias and buffet operations present food directly to customers who then help themselves to desired items.

In either event, care must be taken to maintain the quality which has been "built into" the food items through procedures used during purchasing, receiving, storing, issuing, and production. Equipment needed to prepare items on an as-ordered basis must be conveniently located. Other equipment used to hold hot or cold foods prepared in advance also requires space. Pickup areas should be close to dish return areas and both should be close to the dining area. Cafeteria operations frequently have walls which separate serving areas from production areas. In many instances, hot and cold food pass-throughs are available to save employee steps when cafeteria lines need to be replenished.

Table service operations that use precheck registers should have income control equipment close to traffic aisles used by service employees. In large and busy operations, ample space is needed at the point of food pickup so that several orders can be prepared, plated, and picked up at one time. Storage for serviceware should, of course, also be located in serving areas.

Many table service operations utilize food server supply stations in dining areas. These stations are often screened from customers and can be used to store clean dishes needed for table service, soiled dishes awaiting transport to the dishwashing area, and may often store beverage service equipment and supplies needed for dining room service. Other items that might be located in food server supply stations are calculators, precheck registers, and cash drawers if service employees keep money until the end of the shift.

By now, you should realize the importance of thinking through exactly what activities need to be performed in an area before the design and layout are undertaken. While it is not possible to look ahead 15 years (if that or a longer period of time represents the "life" of the facility being planned), it is still important to estimate the general types of work activities which will be performed and to provide some flexibility in plans which are developed.

Dining Room Areas

You and the planning team must pay special attention to the design of dining room areas. Often, the customer's reactions to the food and its service will depend on the atmosphere of the dining areas and whether they add to or detract from the total dining experience. Cleanliness—and the ease with which dining areas can be kept that way—is extremely important in any food service operation. Also, the dining atmosphere becomes critically important from a marketing perspective in theme restaurants. The size of the dining area must be matched with the production capacity of the kitchen area. Recall the discussion earlier in this chapter about seat turnover and the impact of different menu items on preparation and service time. Traffic flow patterns by both customers and employees in dining areas are affected by the width of aisles, location of restrooms and other public areas, placement of the cashier stand, etc.

In many food service operations, dining room service employees must have access to public or service bar areas so beverages can be ordered and/or obtained for dining room customers. If proper thought has not been given to the task, service employees may have to go through the kitchen, the dishwashing area, or the lobby in order to obtain necessary drinks. Needless to say, this impedes traffic flow, wastes steps and time for employees, and contributes to lower quality levels of service for customers.

Some of today's modern cafeteria operations feature a "scramble system" in contrast to the more traditional "straight line" cafeteria operation. With the scramble system of dining room service, customers enter the cafeteria line at a point where they may pick up trays, serviceware, etc. Then they can go to any number of intermediate stations where different menu items are served. Customers do not need to wait in line and are able to move from station to station. Time can be saved and the element of customer choice which this provides often has positive marketing implications.

Cashier Station

As you learned in Chapter 11, there are two basic ways the customers can pay for meals. One way (server banking system) requires the food server to retain all money that is collected until the end of the shift. The second way (cashier banking system) uses a cashier, who often doubles as a host/hostess, and a cash register.

It is important that the cashier work station be effectively designed. The cashier station should be located in the customer traffic flow; customers should be required to pass by the cashier station as they leave the dining area. It is more likely that the cashier will notice them and the possibility of customers leaving the area without paying will be reduced. A convenient location is better for the customers, too; they will not have to go out of their way as they leave.

The cash register/data collection machine is, of course, the primary piece of equipment which must be located in this area. It is best to place this machine in a location where both the cashier and the customer can see pricing information rung up in the display window. Other items that should be located in this area include:

Telephone. When the cashier serves as receptionist, a telephone becomes important for taking reservations. Credit card companies require that charges in excess of specified amounts be preauthorized so a telephone is needed for this purpose, too.

Miscellaneous. Some food service operations have a variety of items for sale at the cashier's stand. For example, cigars and cigarettes, curios of all types, and recipe books may be sold. A place to house them and to protect them against theft becomes necessary.

Menus. Customers may wish to examine the menu before they decide to eat at your property. Offering take-home menus is another option.

Protected Storage. This is needed for used and unused customer checks when the cashier is responsible for them until processing by the manager.

Dining Room Sketch and Server Station Assignments. Space for these items must be available if the cashier is also the receptionist.

The process of meeting and greeting the customers, managing the sales income collection, and visiting with customers as they leave are all important activities that are carried out in the general cashier station area. For these reasons, it is important that much thought be given to its location and design. Often, however, any available corner is used and effective work procedures become more difficult.

Beverage Production/ Service Areas

The design of the beverage production (bar) area is just as important as the design of the food preparation and dining areas.[2] You must consider the facility from the customer's perspective and how it relates to the beverage area. Of course, you will also need to work within the limits of available funds when this area is designed. Food preparation areas are designed by first developing individual work stations and this same concept is important when beverage areas are designed.

There are two basic types of beverage production units. While there are some similarities in their design, there are also some differences. Figures 17.8 and 17.9 illustrate principles of design which are of special concern as these areas are planned. For example, perhaps the design should accommodate only one bartender during slow periods, but recognize that two or more bartenders may be necessary during busy times.

The bar is an area where work simplification should be carefully built into the design. The task of preparing a variety of drinks in a short time requires careful thought about the placement of all necessary equipment. A primary reason why bartenders are fast or slow is the way that the facility helps/hinders their work performance. Therefore, the bar

Figure 17.8 Service Bar: One Bartender

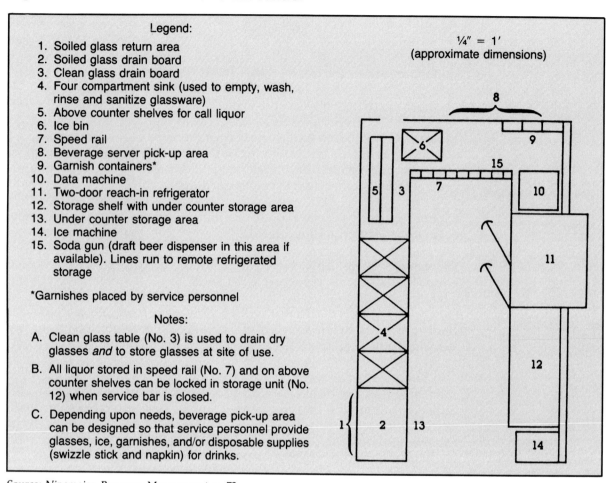

Legend:

1. Soiled glass return area
2. Soiled glass drain board
3. Clean glass drain board
4. Four compartment sink (used to empty, wash, rinse and sanitize glassware)
5. Above counter shelves for call liquor
6. Ice bin
7. Speed rail
8. Beverage server pick-up area
9. Garnish containers*
10. Data machine
11. Two-door reach-in refrigerator
12. Storage shelf with under counter storage area
13. Under counter storage area
14. Ice machine
15. Soda gun (draft beer dispenser in this area if available). Lines run to remote refrigerated storage

*Garnishes placed by service personnel

Notes:

A. Clean glass table (No. 3) is used to drain dry glasses *and* to store glasses at site of use.

B. All liquor stored in speed rail (No. 7) and on above counter shelves can be locked in storage unit (No. 12) when service bar is closed.

C. Depending upon needs, beverage pick-up area can be designed so that service personnel provide glasses, ice, garnishes, and/or disposable supplies (swizzle stick and napkin) for drinks.

¼" = 1'
(approximate dimensions)

Source: Ninemeier, Beverage Management *p. 72.*

must be designed for productive work. Examples of how this can be done include the following:

1. The bartender should be able to perform related activities in one place. For example, fruit garnishes can be cleaned, prepared, and stored in a specific area.

2. Provide ample space for producing drinks which have been ordered.

3. Consider the sequence of activities for each task the bartender must perform. For example, how is a drink made? A glass is selected, ice scooped into it, a beverage poured, and perhaps a mixer added. Finally, a garnish may be necessary; then the glass is given to the customer or server. How can the bar be designed to help the bartender perform, in sequence, each of these tasks?

Figure 17.9 Public Bar: Two Bartenders

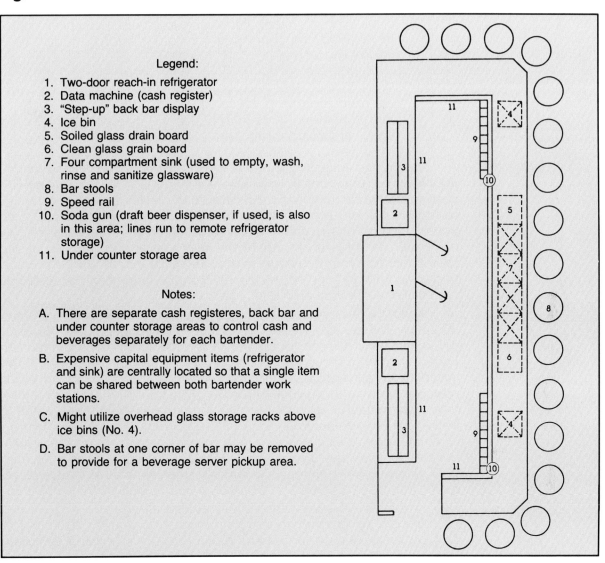

Legend:

1. Two-door reach-in refrigerator
2. Data machine (cash register)
3. "Step-up" back bar display
4. Ice bin
5. Soiled glass drain board
6. Clean glass grain board
7. Four compartment sink (used to empty, wash, rinse and sanitize glassware)
8. Bar stools
9. Speed rail
10. Soda gun (draft beer dispenser, if used, is also in this area; lines run to remote refrigerator storage)
11. Under counter storage area

Notes:

A. There are separate cash registeres, back bar and under counter storage areas to control cash and beverages separately for each bartender.

B. Expensive capital equipment items (refrigerator and sink) are centrally located so that a single item can be shared between both bartender work stations.

C. Might utilize overhead glass storage racks above ice bins (No. 4).

D. Bar stools at one corner of bar may be removed to provide for a beverage server pickup area.

Source: Ninemeier, Beverage Management, *p. 73.*

4. When possible, have individual work stations share expensive and/or space-consuming equipment for preparing garnishes, washing and storing glassware, storing refrigerated/frozen bar supplies and drinks, etc.

5. Provide sufficient lighting and work counters at proper heights. Countertops should be approximately 34 inches from floor level.

6. Consider product flow. Pass-throughs should accommodate products requiring entry into bar areas. Frequently, half-barrels or other sizes of draught beer are difficult to bring into bar areas for placement in behind-bar dispenser units.

7. Build control aspects into the bar design. When possible, provide separate cash registers or cash drawers. Establish an income control system. For example, should a precheck register be required? Separate space for storing bar inventories should also be considered.

8. Work space should accommodate employees. Beverage servers need room to place and pick up orders. Space is also required to store items that the servers may need such as napkins, bar picks, ashtrays, etc.

Lounge Area

The lounge area should reflect the atmosphere and related marketing objectives that your property wishes to project. Customers must be comfortable while they visit the facility so the selection and placement of tables, chairs, and other fixtures are important decisions. Usually, the physical length of the public bar is determined by the need for equipment space behind the bar, not by the need for a specific number of seats (or for standing room) in front of the bar. Many drinks will be prepared in the bar area and served to customers in the lounge and/or restaurant who will never see the preparation process.

When the lounge area is designed, recall that beverage personnel may have to interact with the restaurant cashier/receptionist (for example, when processing beverage transfers). Therefore, the location of the lounge relative to the cashier/receptionist area may be important. If food is served in the lounge, its location relative to the kitchen/food pickup areas is a concern. It is usually unwise for customers who want food service to be required to pass through lounge areas after they enter the building if they do not wish to purchase alcoholic beverages. Therefore, a general foyer, coat check, or public restrooms may by used to separate the lounge from the dining areas. Finally, you should consider traffic flow patterns. After taking a customer's order, how do beverage servers move from the customers to the bar or server station (which has precheck registers, cash drawers, service supplies, etc.)?

You can see from even this brief discussion that the design of bar and lounge areas is important and rather complex. The bar is an integral part of the entire food and beverage operation and generates a sizeable amount of revenue and profit. It is unwise to allocate space to the bar based upon what's left after food service needs are met.

The Equipment Selection Task

Food and beverage employees cannot effectively store, prepare, or serve products unless the proper equipment is available. Thanks to twentieth century technology, there is currently available a wide array of equipment that can help increase employee efficiency and, at the same time, improve the quality of products which are produced.

The equipment selection task is very important. Equipment is often expensive so you must make sure that your decisions are cost effective. Since there is a wide range of available equipment from which to choose, how can you decide which equipment item is really best? The decision that you make will affect your property for a long time (the useful life span of many items is more than 15 years).

Supervisors and their employees should be part of the team which makes equipment decisions. Employees who regularly use the equipment know how it works. Since they are the ones who use the equipment which is chosen, their ideas about equipment selection should be solicited.

Normally, we think of food service equipment as expensive "tools" which must be used as products are processed and served. It may be useful, however, to separate large, expensive equipment that usually lasts many years from small, low-cost equipment which is expendable. Examples of the former are ovens, refrigerators, and freezers while the latter includes cutting boards, knives, and other hand tools.

Important Factors in Equipment Selection Decisions

When you evaluate food service equipment for its usefulness to your property, consider several factors. These include:

Cost. The purchase price of the equipment is an important initial consideration. Staff members must cost justify equipment which is purchased. Interest (financing) charges often serve to increase the purchase price dramatically and even if equipment is leased, the price of the equipment will be factored into the lease agreement and rates which are developed.

The initial purchase price is not the only cost factor to assess. Operating costs (utility charges) can be substantial. With energy costs constantly increasing, this factor will have an even greater impact on your future purchase decisions. Also, installation expenses are often more than the actual equipment cost. For example, some equipment may need adequate ventilation, plumbing, or electrical hook-ups. If utilities are not available in the immediate vicinity of equipment placement, expenses to provide utility hook-ups can be significant. You should consider repair, depreciation, and insurance expenses, too; it is important that all relevant costs be identified and factored into the purchase decision.

Safety. Naturally, the equipment must be safe to use. Protruding, sharp edges and easy access to the working mechanisms of equipment are examples of safety violations. The Occupational Safety and Health Act (OSHA) has established minimum standards to help ensure that equipment is free of hazards. Even if, for some reason, food and beverage operations are not covered by OSHA laws, these standards provide meaningful safety information when equipment purchase decisions are made.

You should look for Underwriters Laboratories (UL) approval on electrical equipment and American Gas Association (AGA) approval on gas power equipment. You should also confirm that safety is "built into" equipment which is purchased; for example, safety catches on steamer doors, safety pilot lights on gas equipment, and overload protection on electrical equipment.

Sanitation. Equipment should be easy to clean and it should be designed so that sanitation practices are easy to follow. The National Sanitation

Foundation (NSF) develops and issues guidelines on sanitary aspects of equipment design and on the way that equipment is constructed.[3]

Only those materials that can withstand normal wear, penetration of vermin, corrosive action of food and beverages, cleaning compounds, etc., and that will not impart odor, color, or taste to food should be used. Surface materials used in food contact areas (equipment surfaces with which products normally come in contact) should be smooth, corrosion resistant, nontoxic, stable, and nonabsorbent. Exposed surfaces should be easily cleanable. Splash contact surfaces (surfaces which are subject to routine splashes or spills) and nonfood contact surfaces should also be smooth, easily cleanable, and corrosion resistant. Use nontoxic solder in all food contact areas; avoid lead-based paint.

In general, all food service equipment and related items should be cleanable and relatively easy to keep in a sanitary condition. Let's look at some of the materials used in food service equipment:

- **Wood**—while lightweight and economical, is difficult to keep clean because it is porous. It can easily absorb food odors and stains so its use should be restricted in food and beverage operations. Wood is frequently used for shelving in production and storage areas and, because of its durability and adaptability, it has many applications in front of house public areas.

- **Metal**—especially stainless steel, is commonly used for food preparation equipment and working surfaces with which food comes into frequent contact. It is possible to plate metals such as steel, copper, or brass with chromium, tin, or nickel coverings. These treatments are frequently used on many food service equipment items where a shiny finish is desired (toasters, equipment trim, etc.). Likewise, copper utensils are usually plated to make items corrosion resistant and steel plating is often used for lining in equipment. Iron and other metal materials are used for structural/framing purposes as well as for plumbing fixtures. Steel sheets can be treated, covered with zinc, and used to make galvanized metal for sinks, tables, and related service equipment. Over time, however, this metal is subject to wear; the steel can be exposed which will result in rust and corrosion.

There are other materials which are used in food service equipment. Glass of all types is frequently used in equipment doors. Plastic or rubber-based products are gaining popularity in food service equipment today. These latter materials are lightweight, nonporous, easy to clean, and resist cuts and odors. Compared to various types of metal-based materials, these compounds are often much less expensive.

Figure 17.10 lists some government and industry groups that are concerned about equipment safety and sanitation. The seals of approval of the UL, AGA, and NSF, indicating the acceptance of a piece of equipment by these organizations, were shown in Chapter 10, Figure 10.1.

Figure 17.10 Government and Industry Groups Concerned with Equipment Safety and Sanitation

Name of Group	Type	Special Concerns
1. Occupational Safety and Health Administration (OSHA)	Government	Equipment safety and related concerns
2. National Sanitation Foundation (NSF)	Private	Equipment sanitation
3. Underwriters Laboratories (UL)	Private	Electrical equipment safety
4. American Gas Association (AGA)	Private	Safety for gas-fueled equipment
5. Municipal and State Agencies	Government	Safety and sanitation
6. National Electric Manufacturers' Association (NEMA)	Industry	Electrical equipment safety
7. National Board of Fire	Industry	Equipment installation
8. American Society of Sanitary Engineers	Industry	Facility design

Design and Performance. Equipment must, of course, do what it is designed for. The design should be simple yet functional, provide value (price relative to quality), incorporate sanitation and safety standards, and help employees provide high quality products in the volume and time that is necessary. It should be easy to operate and, whenever possible, should be able to perform several functions. (For example, a mixer with the proper attachments can be used to slice, grind, or shred food products.) You should consider purchasing multi-purpose equipment items. Often, for very little additional cost, equipment can be purchased with optional features which are very worthwhile. Sometimes equipment may have built-in options or features that increase the purchase price, but will never be needed by the property. These types of performance concerns should be addressed as equipment selection decisions are made. Performance features might best be assessed by talking with properties that currently use equipment similar to that being considered. Some equipment is easier to operate than other equipment so the skills and abilities of employees who use the equipment must be considered. Also, evaluate the time that is necessary to clean equipment after it is used.

Maintenance. Most equipment requires careful, periodic maintenance in order to operate effectively. Can this be done by on-site staff or must skilled technicians be retained? How often and at what cost must equipment maintenance activities be performed? How long does maintenance take? Will there be a need to make menu or other adjustments during this time? As the above questions indicate, you must be concerned about maintenance issues. If the equipment being considered replaces items currently used, Figure 17.11 may be consulted for helpful information. Excessive repairs suggest that either the equipment is not suitable or that it was not properly used. In either case, equipment which is frequently "down" is of little use. Also, if an extensive amount of employee training

Figure 17.11 Preventive Maintenance and Repair Record

Service	Type Machine	Equipment Number
Location	Serial Number	Model Number
Make	Date Purchased	Purchase Cost

Preventative Maintenance Procedure	
Function	Interval

Special Instructions

Specifications	
Voltage	Drive
Amperage	Belts
Phase	Fuse
Pressure	Lubrication
Horsepower	Filter
RPM	Fluids

Spare Parts Required			
Part	Mfr. Part Number	Hotel Stock Number	Quantity

is necessary before equipment can be used, this fact should be compared with other equipment alternatives.

Size (Capacity) of Equipment. Food and beverage operations should have the proper type, size, capacity, and amount (number) of equipment items which are necessary. If insufficient capacities or quantities of equipment are available, efficiency will be impaired; for example, several batches of foods may need to be made instead of combining production quantities. Equipment can limit the variety of menu items which are offered. On the other hand, if too much equipment is available (capacity or number of items), both purchase price and operating costs will be excessive. Space needed to house the excessive equipment will also be wasted.

Construction. The National Sanitation Foundation has developed detailed construction specifications relating to many types of food service equipment.[4] This source can be consulted when equipment construction standards are being considered. High-quality construction concerns are often more adequately addressed when reputable manufacturers and/or suppliers provide equipment. Examples of construction standards frequently include the following:

- Avoid square corners; all angles should be rounded.

- Use raised edges wherever dripping or seepage can occur.

- Round off exposed edges to make cleaning easier.

- Openings which can harbor vermin should be closed.

- Tightly attach splashbacks (raised back of sinks) which are fitted to a wall to prevent the entrance of vermin.

- Avoid using bolts and screws on fixtures because they are hard to clean (fixtures should be welded).

- Do not use trim which is attached for appearance only.

- Be sure that all exposed gaskets can be cleaned properly.

- Depressed openings in doors are often better than handles.

- Use removable doors in bins to facilitate cleaning.

- Shelving should be removable and adjustable. Replace wall shelving with mobile shelving where practical.

While the list of construction standards can get lengthy, it will help ensure that the equipment being selected is right for your food and beverage operation. Properly constructed equipment is more expensive than its lower-quality counterparts. However, because of its extended life and other advantages, it is generally worth the additional investment. When you consider that a dish machine can easily cost as much as a high-priced luxury car, and even a simple pot or pan may cost $50 or more, the need to pay attention to design becomes much more evident.

Other Important Concerns. Normally, equipment should be made for commercial—not home—use. Food service employees are not always careful with how they use equipment. It must, therefore, be durable to withstand the hard use it will receive. If front of house equipment is being purchased, or if production equipment will be seen by customers, its appearance becomes important. Equipment should also be compatible with other items that are already available and with existing space. Attachments may be available for one brand or model of equipment so it makes sense to replace an old item with similar equipment to permit the use of these attachments. Likewise, a dish machine which is compatible with existing space and dish counters may be in order.

Generally, "stock" as opposed to "custom" equipment is recommended. Stock equipment is available in catalogs and can be ordered through dealers without modification to basic designs. Custom equipment is tailored to the operation and is much more expensive. In some operations, the quietness of equipment will be an important concern. Equipment mobility may be important, too.

You should now realize that there are a large number of factors which must be considered when equipment is purchased. While some are general and pertain to broad concerns that should be addressed every time equipment is purchased, other factors are specific to the property and the items being purchased. These latter factors will be discussed in the next section.

Food Service Equipment Items

Whenever any equipment item is being purchased, there are certain factors that are applicable to each major item. We will review some of these factors below. Also, included throughout the remainder of this chapter are photographs showing food service equipment items which are discussed.

Refrigerated Storage Equipment. Refrigerated storage equipment is used to hold foods at refrigerated temperatures (32°F-40°F) and at frozen temperatures (0°F-⁻10°F). There are basically two types of refrigerated equipment: walk-in units and reach-in units.

Walk-in units. These are essentially refrigerated rooms. Walk-ins range in size from approximately 4'x4' to 20'x20' (or even larger) in high volume food service operations. As with any food service equipment item, the interior surfaces of refrigerated walk-ins should be nonporous and easily cleanable. Walk-in units are usually lighted and, whenever possible, they should be installed flush with the floor so that mobile carts and other storage equipment can be easily rolled into and out of them.

For safety reasons, it should be possible to open doors from the inside even if the door is locked from the outside. A thermostat, perhaps with an accompanying noise or lighting alert device, can be used to monitor the internal temperature of the unit.

Walk-ins can be sectional (installed in sections after the building is constructed) or built-in. A separate refrigeration system should generally be used for walk-in refrigerator and freezer compartments. These units are either water- or air-cooled depending upon the specific needs. Locking panels should ensure an airtight, durable seal; normally the manufacturer will warrant refrigerated units for several years under normal usage. Insulation is usually foamed-in-place or made of a froth-type urethane. If prefabricated units are installed on concrete floors, insulated panels may also be necessary for flooring. A flooring load of at least 300 pounds per square foot is generally necessary to prevent floor distortion. Sheet plating or aluminum floor coverings should be used when there is continuous use of loaded transport equipment. Obviously, the compressor, condenser, and evaporator must be fitted to the size of the unit which is used.

Refrigerated walk-in units are used for central storage purposes. They can also be used to hold items awaiting production, items which are being processed, items that have already been produced, and leftovers. Walk-in freezers are used to hold frozen items awaiting production and, sometimes, frozen leftovers which will not be used in the immediate future.

Reach-in or roll-in units. Smaller refrigerated units are referred to as reach-ins or roll-ins. As the name implies, reach-in refrigerators and freezers have doors that swing open (such as a refrigerator in the home) or swing up (such as a chest-type freezer or milk cooler). These refrigerators and freezers may be used as central storage units in smaller facilities and are also used to store food products at point-of-use in production areas. Often, they are used in server or customer areas in the front of the house as well. Reach-in refrigerators may open on one side only or be the pass-through type. Reach-in units may have from one to three or more sections of full-length doors or two to six sections of half-size doors. It is also possible to buy under-counter units which are used to store small quantities of food items in preparation/service areas. A pass-through is generally located between a preparation area and a service area. For example, in a cafeteria operation, salads, sandwiches, refrigerated desserts, etc., can be prepared in the kitchen, placed in the pass-through by food preparation employees, and retrieved through the other side by employees in the service area. Units may have fixed shelves, slides for modular pans, or they can even be designed to accommodate roll-in carts.

As with walk-in refrigerators and freezers, the proper size of compressor, condenser, and evaporator is essential, and foamed-in-place or froth-type urethane insulation is also necessary. Both should have a seamless interior construction with self-closing doors (safety stops are a wise investment). Other wise investments are adjustable legs that make the equipment level with the floor, an automatic defroster-timer for the freezer, an exterior-mounted thermometer, and locking doors.

Range Equipment. A range can be used, along with various pots and pans, to do almost any type of cooking except roasting and baking.

Figure 17.12 A Bank of Three Separate Grills

Range equipment can be used to boil, stew, simmer, fry, braise, grill, and steam. Ranges have been very popular and widely used in commercial and institutional food service operations over the years. However, specialized equipment is becoming available which has reduced the dependence upon ranges in many operations. It is not uncommon, especially in older operations, to see banks of ranges installed in a straight-line working station in back of house food service pickup counters. Contrast this with one range top, a high-speed pressure steamer, a pressure fryer, and other equipment items which can do the job in reduced square footage.

There are two types of ranges: solid-top ranges and round-top ranges.Ranges may be operated by either gas or electricity. Solid-top ranges apply heat uniformly over the entire top section of the range. With round-top units, heat is applied to each unit which is adjusted separately. It is also possible to have combination range units.

Heavy-duty ranges can meet the requirements of continuous high production volume. Restaurant-type units are also available, but are of lighter construction and are not as durable. They are, however, quite acceptable for smaller operations and for limited use.

While most ranges come equipped with ovens underneath, there are models available which, in effect, are countertop models with shelves and/or storage cabinets below.

It is possible to buy special types of ranges such as a chop suey range and a range griddle. A griddle or a grill can also be purchased as a separate piece of equipment (see Figure 17.12), but it is then usually placed close to the range. Griddle-top units generally have a splashback to prevent spillage and a grease collection pan underneath. A griddle is used for frying or scrambling eggs, for grilling sandwiches, and for various types of sauteing, etc.

Carbon dioxide or nontoxic chemical fire extinguishers which are approved by applicable regulations should be available near the range. Employees should, of course, know both the location of and procedures to properly use this equipment. Often, ventilation systems (with ranges underneath) have fire extinguishing systems built into them. Grease fires are always possible when working with range equipment. You should stress safety concerns during equipment layout, employee training, and related program plans.

Ovens. An oven can be used to bake, cook, roast, heat, and oven-fry many kinds of food. There are several types of ovens:

Range ovens have been a traditional and versatile piece of production equipment in most food service operations. As noted above, many ranges have ovens located beneath them.

Deck ovens are decked (stacked) on top of each other to increase capacity without requiring additional floor space. These units are available in single or multiple decks and in combination with roasting or baking ovens. (A roasting oven has an interior cavity that is 12-15 inches high while baking decks are usually approximately 8 inches high.) Both types of units are available in a wide range of interior cavity lengths and widths.

When practical, the oven door should come equipped with a window in it to eliminate the need to open the door (and lose heat) when the product is being checked. An interior light, of course, is also helpful.

Convection ovens are heated by gas or electricity and have fans or blowers to constantly circulate the heat and air in the closed oven chamber. The moving air allows the heat to penetrate food products more quickly; this shortens the cooking time. It also permits the use of lower temperatures in the oven. There are several types of convection ovens. A single-stack convection oven comes in various sizes. The normal size can handle and properly cook food using a minimum of ten pans (12" x 20" x 2 1/2") on five racks. It can also accommodate nine sheet pans (26" x 18" x 1") using a minimum of nine racks.

A double-stack convection oven is really two single-stack convection ovens mounted on top of each other. Roll-in convection ovens allow a mobile rack containing pans of food to be wheeled directly into the oven. Convection ovens come with various types of doors. For example, a single door hinged at either the right or left side and, alternatively, double French doors hinged on each side of the oven can be used. Double Dutch doors hinged at the top and bottom and opening outward are another possibility.

A convection oven can be used to prepare many items which can be made in a conventional range or deck oven. Since convection ovens permit items to be prepared in a shorter time and at a lower temperature, food quality is often enhanced. Output is also increased and, because the oven itself is smaller than a conventional deck oven, more efficient use is made of available floor space.

Rotary ovens or revolving tray ovens use flat trays (shelves) which are suspended between two reels that rotate the trays. Food items which are to be roasted or baked are loaded onto the trays as they appear at the door opening. These ovens are designed to prevent the escape of hot air when the door is opened to load or unload food items.

Rotary ovens are frequently used in large, especially institutional food service operations. Commercial properties also use them when extensive baking operations are part of the food service program.

Microwave ovens cook food by converting microwave energy into heat energy within the food. Molecules absorb the energy, and the friction which is generated by the fast-moving food molecules produces heat. This movement occurs simultaneously throughout the food and greatly shortens the cooking time.

Microwave ovens lend themselves to heating small amounts of food quickly. They are frequently used to complement existing equipment since it is not possible to cook very large quantities of food in the microwave. Microwave ovens are very helpful in the fast thawing of frozen food items.

Microwave ovens are frequently placed on food production lines and food pickup stations where several portions of food can be cooked/ heated. They are also used in service station areas where items such as breakfast or dessert pastries may be heated.

We have already cited one disadvantage of using microwave ovens: bulk preparation of large amounts of food is not possible. Also, some items such as bread products are hard to prepare in microwave ovens. Unless a special attachment is provided, browning is not possible in a microwave oven.

Infrared (quartz) ovens may be used by large volume operations to heat, roast, and brown products; they are especially good to reconstitute frozen foods packaged in bulk. A quartz oven is very useful for broiling and is an excellent item to finish dishes that have been heated in a microwave oven since the quartz oven has the capacity for browning.

Recon ovens are used to reconstitute frozen, prepared entrees. They can also be used as a high-speed conventional oven. Recon ovens have many uses and come in various sizes to accommodate most needs.

Tilting Braising Pan. This is a flat-bottomed cooking item that can be used as a kettle, griddle, fry pan, steamer, grill, oven, or warmer/server. The bottom of an electric tilting braising pan is a heavy stainless steel plate which is heated by an electric heating element.

A gas tilting braising pan is heated by gas flame which can be provided by natural gas or manufactured gas.

The tilting braising pan can reduce the total cooking time of many

Figure 17.13 Bank of Steam Production Equipment in an Institutional Setting

Courtesy of St. Lawrence Hospital, Lansing, Michigan.

food products by as much as 25%. It is very flexible and can be used for a wide variety of food products. Since it tilts, both pouring and cleaning are easy.

Steam Cooking Equipment. This type of equipment (see Figure 17.13) is commonly used in many food service operations. There may be a self-contained boiler which produces steam for the equipment. It is a common practice to purchase steam equipment with a larger than necessary boiler so that additional steam-generated equipment can be run off the boiler. Steam equipment can also be purchased without a boiler and connected to a centralized steam source. With some steam-generated equipment (the steam kettle for example), live steam does not come in contact with the food being cooked. With other steam equipment (the compartment steamer for example), food is cooked with live steam.

A steam-jacketed kettle is a large cooking pot which can range in size from several quarts to 100 or more gallons. It is generally used to steam, boil, or simmer food items. Food is heated by steam which is in a jacket surrounding the walls of the kettle. Steam-jacketed kettles have a double wall. In some kettles, the double wall extends only approximately three-fourths of the way up the side. In other kettles the double wall extends up the entire side.

Kettles can be used to produce many types of foods including meats and poultry (which can be browned or steamed if a small amount of liquid is added and lids are available). Steam-jacketed kettles are also useful for preparing casseroles, eggs, soups, fresh or frozen vegetables, sauces, pie fillings, etc.

Some steam-jacketed kettles can be tilted. This makes it easy to remove food products and to draw off water needed to clean the kettle after use. Tilting kettles may have draw-off valves. They can be pedal-based, wall-mounted, or even attached to the legs. Non-tilting kettles, as the name implies, cannot be tilted. Food must be removed by ladling or by a draw-off valve (pedal-based, wall-mounted, or on legs) at the base of the kettle.

Steam-jacketed kettles reduce the amount of range space which is needed in the kitchen and the number of top-of-range cooking utensils. When large kettles are used, cooking can be done in one cooking vessel rather than in many. Also, since heat tends to be more even, problems with scorching are reduced.

A large amount of water is necessary to clean the kettles, too. It is a good idea to have a water source close to the kettle location because water is an ingredient in many of the soups, stews, and other items commonly prepared in kettles. A drain to remove water used in cleaning is a very helpful convenience.

As with any steam equipment, proper safety features are a must. These include pressure-reducing and safety valves.

Compartment Steamers. A compartment steamer is a heating vessel that cooks food with live steam. The steam comes in direct contact with the food, but does not penetrate it. A steamer works much like a pressure cooker which is used in many homes. It can be used to cook almost any food except items which need to be cooked with dry heat, deep fat fried, or sauteed. A low-pressure conventional steamer usually operates at approximately five pounds per square inch (psi) of steam pressure. The normal size compartment in a steamer will hold about six 12″ x 20″ x 2-1/2″ steam table pans. Low-pressure steamers are found in the kitchens of many large volume commercial and institutional food service operations. They can be used to prepare large volumes of food so they are excellent for cooking vegetables, macaroni, and eggs. Low-pressure steamers also thaw frozen products and perform many of the preparation tasks done by steam kettles.

A high-pressure steamer is a compartment steamer that operates at approximately 15 psi. It generally holds one or two 12″ x 20″ x 2-1/2″ pans and is designed to cook small quantities of food in a very short time period. High-pressure steamers and convection steamers are often placed on cooking lines in commercial properties. Food items which can be cooked in batches provide creative opportunities to produce portions of exceptionally high quality very quickly. These high-capacity steamers are used to prepare convenience foods such as frozen, preportioned items in pouches, fresh shellfish, and a large variety of other items which can be reconstituted on an as-needed basis. Room-pressure convection steamers are very useful for cooking seafood, vegetables, and other items in which nutrient retention is a high priority.

Broilers. There are two common types of broilers: overhead broilers and underfired broilers. They utilize radiant heat to rapidly cook foods and are fired by either gas or electricity.

Overhead broilers. These broilers have heating units which radiate heat down to foods which are placed on a shelf below. The shelf is usually adjustable so that food can be brought closer to or placed farther away from the heat source. This, of course, affects the boiling time. For example, a thick piece of meat may char on the outside before it is done on the inside (this is why the shelf might be placed farther away from the heat source). A thinner cut of meat may need to be placed closer to the heat source.

A small broiler unit, called a salamander or shelf broiler, can be mounted above the top of a range or above a spreader plate which is part of a back-shelf assembly. While the capacity of these units is small, they are very adequate in operations where broiling loads are not great. They are popularly used as finish broilers (for example, to melt cheese or brown bread crumb toppings) and as auxiliary broilers during slow periods.

Underfired (char) broilers. These broilers use a heat source which is placed under the food rather than on top. Ceramic or other refractory materials create a radiant "floor" above the burners. Food items to be char broiled are placed on a grate which is above this radiant floor. While cooking, the food juices drip directly on the hot bed and burn. This, of course, creates the typical charcoal flavor and appearance. A great deal of smoke and odor is generally emitted during the process; therefore, char broilers—like most other pieces of cooking equipment—should be used under an efficient ventilation system.

Char broilers with very small cooking surfaces are available for light use. It is also possible to buy larger units with different cooking sections to increase the grid area which is necessary when large volumes of products must be broiled.

These equipment items are usually most popular in commercial restaurant and hotel operations. They are placed on the actual cooking line where food such as meat can be broiled on an as-needed basis. In some operations with high volumes during peak hours, meat products may be initially broiled for a short time period to begin the cooking process. They are then removed and are finished being broiled as orders come in. While this procedure does hasten the broiling time after the order has been placed, some concern must focus on the sanitary handling of these food items after they are initially removed from the broiler. Unfortunately, in many operations, these prefinished items are held at room temperature in the broiler station. When this occurs, sanitary and food quality concerns become important.

Deep Fryers. These fryers can be fueled by electric or gas energy. Conventional fryers may hold 15 pounds or less of frying fat (these are table

Figure 17.14 Bank of Deep Fryers in an Institutional Setting

top model units). Large free-standing fryer models hold 130 pounds or more of frying fat. (A bank of deep fryers in an institutional setting is shown in Figure 17.14.) As a rule of thumb, fryers can handle one and a half to two times the weight of the fat in each batch of food which is being fried.

Pressure fryers utilize lids which are sealed. When the unit is in operation, pressure is built up within the kettle. This hastens frying time and is ideal for certain specialty items such as deep fried chicken.

Large volume operations may use a continuous-type deep fryer. These units have a screw conveyor that continuously moves products being processed through the fat. Items which require a longer frying time would be placed at the extreme end of a conveyor so that they remain in the fat over a longer distance; time in the fat will increase. They will then be cooked throughout when the frying process is complete.

Conventional and pressure fryers are often equipped with two frying baskets. This is useful to fry a large quantity at one time or, alternatively, one basket load can be frying while the other is being prepared for "dropping" into the basket. Newer models may be equipped with computerized controls that automatically lower frying baskets into the fat, time the product while it is frying, and then automatically raise the basket out of the frying pan.

Many fires in the kitchen originate at the deep fryer. For this reason, it must be well ventilated, with fire extinguishing equipment readily available, and personnel should be carefully trained in how the fryer is to be used. Since breading or other prepreparation activities are fre-

Figure 17.15 Cook's Line in a Restaurant

quently necessary for products being deep fried, work space close to the fryer unit must be available for these tasks. Likewise, space must be available to "land" products being removed from the unit. In too many operations, this work space is across the work aisle from the unit. The work area quickly becomes unsanitary and unsafe as breading/batter is dropped on the floor, baskets are loaded, or frying fat drips on the floor as products are removed.

A rapid recovery rate is necessary in fryers so that the temperature of the fat, which will drop when large quantities of cold food are placed in it, will rapidly regain proper frying temperature. If there is not rapid recovery, food products will absorb an excessive amount of grease and this will affect food quality. The task of properly cleaning deep fryers can be time consuming unless a siphon or effective manual filtering device is available. High-quality fat must be used to enhance food flavor and prevent rapid deterioration of the grease. Better quality products and higher smoke points (the temperature at which the fat disintegrates and smokes) are important concerns in selecting the frying fat products to be used.

Several of the production equipment items just discussed are shown in Figure 17.15.

Other Equipment

Mixers and Choppers. The equipment which has been discussed so far applies heat in the cooking of food. There are other preparation items which are used to process the food before the cooking process. A mixer is a mechanical device which is used to combine or blend food materials.

An electric motor drives a mixing arm. A shaft which holds special attachments can be attached to the mixing motor. Mixers are commonly used in preparation areas for making salad dressings, whipping potatoes, and blending casserole mixtures. In the baking area, a mixer is necessary to produce dough and batter. Attachments for mixers allow employees to cut, shred, grind, and chop food products for casserole dishes, salads, and other items.

Mixers are of two general types: bench models which have a capacity of 5 to 20 quarts and floor model mixers which have a capacity of 20 to 80 quarts or more. A floor model mixer has three standard attachments: (1) a beater which is used for general mixing and can be used to mash, cream, mix, and blend food products; (2) a whip that incorporates air into light mixtures and can be used to dry mix, whip cream, whip egg whites, mix light icing, etc.; and (3) a dough hook which is used to mix heavy doughs that require a folding and stretching action for best development.

The drive shaft of a mixer can be used to operate a wide array of food processing tools such as knife sharpeners, juice extractors, food slicers, etc. Three very popular units are cutters, choppers, and grinders. While these can be purchased as attachments to food mixers, they can also be purchased as individual equipment items if volume warrants it. Cutters and choppers cut vegetables and other products as the food products pass against/between rotating blades. Grinders are screw assembly units that push food items through grinding plates or blades. These attachments can significantly increase productivity of the kitchen staff when they are properly used. They must, however, be properly cared for and cleaned in order to maximize their usefulness. In many kitchen operations, mixer attachments are less than useful and sometimes even inoperative because of the lack of attention given to their use and maintenance. Standard recipes should specify which equipment/attachment should be used; do not give production staff the option of using hand tools or attachments.

As we have noted, each of the mixer attachments can be purchased as a separate piece of equipment. For example, you could purchase a table model vegetable cutter/slicer. Food products being processed such as celery, carrots, cabbage, etc., are pushed through the chute with the safety handle, come in contact with breading plates, knives, or other assembly and are quickly processed. A table model food chopper is another popular equipment item. Items to be chopped, such as onions, are placed in the bowl which revolves and pushes the products through revolving knives. The chopped products are removed when the bowl has circulated or, if a finer chop is desired, the bowl is allowed to pass through the knives several times before removing the product. You can purchase a vertical cutter mixer in a floor or bench model. It has a stationary bowl with horizontal blades or paddles that rotate at very high speeds. Its capacity is significantly greater than the traditional food cutter which is attached to a mixer or even to a table model floor cutter. Full size capacity is commonly 25 to 60 quarts.

Food Slicers. Food slicers can also be purchased as attachments for mixers or they may be purchased in individual table models. Units can be purchased which automatically move the carriage containing the food products back and forth across the blade. More commonly, though, manually operated machines are used. As is true with all food service equipment, but especially for the slicer, there is much danger involved if the item is not properly used. Manufacturer's instructions relating to cleaning and safe use should be consistently followed. You must, of course, train employees in the safe operation and cleaning of food service equipment items.

Dishwashing Machines. A dishwashing machine is a valuable and expensive food service equipment item that is found in many operations. While fast food operations use disposable serviceware items and have therefore eliminated the need for a dish machine, many other properties still provide the quality of service which requires washable serviceware.

Dish machines come in many types. The most basic is a rack-type machine in which dishes to be washed are racked. A door to the machine is opened for inserting the rack and, after closing, dishes are washed. Normally, there is an automatic cycle of washing and sanitizing to eliminate the need for operator control of these cycles. Larger rack-type machines are also available. With these models, dishes are racked and placed on a conveyor which pulls the rack through the machine. Larger, flight-type machines do not use racks. Rather, dishes are placed on a conveyor belt which moves the dishes through a machine. They are then picked from the conveyor belt at the other end.

Dishwashers may have automatic detergent dispensers and units to automatically supply drying agents. Most machines require a booster heater to bring the water temperature up to the required 180°F minimum temperature that is necessary for safe sanitizing of dishes. Newer units, however, may be equipped with low temperature, chemical sanitizing units which rely on chemicals instead of heat to sanitize the dishes.

The dish machine is clearly the single most expensive item of food service equipment in many operations. Besides spending money on the required soiled and clean dish counters, disposers, racks, dish carts, etc., you can easily invest thousands of dollars in a dishwashing area. Proper layout and design is important to ensure that employees can work efficiently in this area. Likewise, you must train employees so that they know how to properly operate and maintain equipment in order to protect the owner's investment.

There are several nationwide chemical supply companies which offer quality services to the hospitality industry. When products are purchased from these companies, it is common for them to supply attachments such as detergent and wetting agent dispensing equipment. Likewise, service personnel may visit the property to perform routine checking and preventive maintenance tasks. They may offer necessary parts at a discount. While the cost of these services is, of course, included in the product price charged to the operation, it can often be justified. These tasks are sometimes overlooked with expensive repair bills and excessive "down time" resulting.

Figure 17.16 Guide for Utensil Selection in Kitchen to Feed 100 People

Bake Shop Items	Quan.	Bake Shop Items	Quan.
Egg Beater	1	Pastry Bags	6
Measuring Spoons	1 set	Pastry Tiips	6
Oven/Freezer Mit	2 pr.	Food Storage Boxes	6
Pastry Brushes, flat & round	4	Ingredient Bins	3
Rolling Pin	1	Utility/Dish Pans	2
Whip, Piano 10″, 12″, 16″, 18″	4	Mixing Bowls, assorted sizes	12
Whip, French 14″	1	Scale, portion control	1
Cake Covers/Stands	2	Scale, bakery	1
Display Cases	1	**Utensils**	
Pie Markers	1	Storage Containers	12 ea.
Bread Pans	12	Insulated Coffee Tank, 3.5 gal.	1
Cake/Sheet Pans, assorted sizes	6-12	Multipurpose Rubber Matting (26″ x 50′)	1 roll
Jello Molds, Individual or Large	36/3	Safe-t-mats	3-6 ea.
Muffin Tins, 24 cup	6	Ice Cream Scoops, various sizes	6
Pie Tins	12	Juice Dispenser	1-2
Dredges	2	Juice Extractor	1
Funnels, several sizes	3	Boning Knives	2
Measures 1, 2, 4 qt.	3	Cleaver	1
Coffee Making Equipment	1-2	Paring Knives	6
Coffee Decanters	6-12	Pot Forks	2
Silver Compartment Storage Boxes	3	Slicers, assorted sizes	4-6
Sauce pans 1½, 2¾, 3¾, 5½, 7, 10 qts.	6	Spatulas	2
Sauce Pots 14, 26 qts.	2	Box Grater	1
Stock Pots 3, 6, 10 gal. or larger	3	Broiler Scraper	1
Double Boilers 8, 12 qts.	2	Carton Opener	1
Bake Pans, various sizes	6	Lobster Crackers	24
Roast Pans, various sizes	2	Parers & Corers	6
China Cups 9″	1	Poultry Shears	6
Colander	1	Clam/Oyster Knives	3
Strainer 6″, 8″, 10 ″, 12″	4	Sharpening Stones	1
Hot Food Service Pan 200 series full, ½, ⅓, ¼, ⅙	24	Storage Containers 2-22 qts.	10-12
Covers for Pans, assorted	12	Chopping Bowls	1
Skimmers 4½″, 6″	2	Cutting Boards	2
Fry Pans 8″, 10″, 12″, 14″	6	Dish Cloths	24
Butter Spreaders	1	Towels, linen	36
Egg Poacher	1	S/S Pails	1-2
Steak Weight	1	Liquid Grill Cleaner	1 gal.
Thermometers:		S/S cleaner	1 case
Deep Fat	1	Aluminum Foil (several sizes)	3 units
Oven	1	Grill Bricks	12
Pocket	1	Neoprene Gloves	6 pr.
Roast	1	Plastic Aprons	6
Basting Spoon (solid, perforated, slotted)	6	Plastic Bags for garbage	1 unit
Ladles, 1-24 oz., assorted	6	Scouring Pads/Sponges	12
Paddles 30-48	1	Floor Squeegee	1
Tongs, 6″, 9″, 12″	6	Mops/heads	6
Turner	2	Brooms	2
Can Opener, #1 or #2	1	Mop Wringer/Pail	1
Cheese Cutter	1	Pickup Brush/Pan	1
Egg Slicer	2	Storage Container, flour, sugar, etc.	3
Food Mill	1	Waste Receptacles (various sizes)	6-12
Tomato Tamer	1	Glass Washing Brush	1
Baker's Scrapers	2	Oven Brush/Scraper	1
Scoops	3	Urn Brush	1

Source: Carl Scriven and James Stevens, Food Equipment Facts: A Handbook for the Food Service Industry *(New York: Wiley, 1982), pp. 249-250.*

Inexpensive Food Service Equipment

This discussion of common items of food service equipment has focused on larger, more expensive items only. There are many other equipment items that are commonly found in food and beverage operations. A short list of examples would include coffee makers, toasters, warmers, peelers, scales, preparation tables, and pot and pan sinks. Likewise, there is an entire array of small equipment and hand tools such as knives, ladles, pots and pans, etc., which are required to prepare and serve food items needed by an operation.

Figure 17.16 will give you an idea of the type of small utensils needed and how many are needed of each. While it is just a guide—needs for each specific operation must be assessed based upon factors unique to the property—it does provide a useful starting point for making this assessment.

NOTES

1. For additional information about the planning process see Edward A. Kazarian, *Food Service Facilities Planning* (Westport, Conn.: AVI, 1975), pp. 16-126.

2. This discussion is based upon Jack D. Ninemeier, *Beverage Management: Business Systems for Hotels, Restaurants and Clubs* (New York: Lebhar Friedman, 1982), pp. 65-78.

3. National Sanitation Foundation, *Food Service Equipment Standards* (Ann Arbor, Mich., November, 1976).

4. National Sanitation Foundation, *Food Service Equipment Standards* (Ann Arbor, Mich., November, 1976).

The Educational Institute Board of Trustees

The Educational Institute of the American Hotel & Motel Association is fortunate to have both industry and academic leaders, as well as allied members, on its Board of Trustees. Individually and collectively, the following persons play leading roles in supporting the Institute and determining the direction of its programs.

Index